THE EDIBLE MAN

The EDIBLE MAN

ANNE KINGSTON

*Dave Nichol, President's Choice,
& the making of popular taste*

MACFARLANE WALTER & ROSS
TORONTO

Macfarlane Walter & Ross
37A Hazelton Avenue
Toronto, Canada M5R 2E3

Canadian Cataloguing in Publication Data

Kingston, Anne, 1957 –
    The edible man: Dave Nichol, President's Choice & the making of popular taste

Includes index
ISBN 0–92192–72–2

1. Nichol, Dave, 1940–   . 2. Grocery trade – Canada.
3. Food industry and trade – Canada.   4. Wine industry – Canada.
5. Loblaw Companies Limited – Biography.
6. Businessmen – Canada – Biography.   I. Title.

HD9325.C22K5   1994   381'.45664'0092   C94–932175–3

The publisher gratefully acknowledges the support of the Ontario Arts Council

Printed and bound in Canada

For my mother

CONTENTS

*It seemed to me that Babette and I, in the mass and variety of our
purchases, in the sheer plenitude those crowded bags suggested,
the weight and size and number, the familiar package designs and vivid
lettering, the giant sizes, the family bargain packs with Day-Glo sales
stickers, in the sense of replenishment we felt, the sense of well-being,
the security and contentment these products brought to some snug
home in our souls—it seemed we had achieved a fullness of being that
is not known to people who need less, expect less, who plan their lives
around lonely walks in the evening.*

DON DELILLO, WHITE NOISE

*What thoughts I have of you tonight, Walt Whitman, for I walked
down the sidestreets under the trees with a headache self-consciousness
looking at the full moon.*

*In my hungry fatigue, and shopping for images, I went into the
neon fruit supermarket, dreaming of your enumerations!*

*What peaches and what penumbras! Whole families shopping
at night! Aisles full of husbands! Wives in the avocados, babies in the
tomatoes!*

ALAN GINSBERG, "A SUPERMARKET IN CALIFORNIA"

Money creates taste

JENNY HOLTZER

CHAPTER ONE

THE ABDICATION

D ave Nichol stared into the darkness of the night sky. The Virgin Atlantic Airways jet was traveling between New York and London on June 30, 1993. He sat restlessly in B class, Virgin's equivalent of first class, his wife Terri beside him, his mind racing forward and then backward. There could be no retreat, he knew that. He had mapped it out, as best he could in the face of the unknowns and with the kind of strategic calculation that prefaced everything he did. Tomorrow, he and Terri would attend the twenty-first birthday party of his god-daughter, Alannah, the daughter of Galen and Hilary Weston. After that, he knew, he would sit down with Galen Weston and finish the conversation the two men had begun on the telephone a week earlier. This was it — the inevitable break from Galen, his closest friend of more than thirty years, and the valedictory to Loblaw.

Alannah's party was to be held at Fort Belvedere, an eighteenth-century Gothic Revival castle-like folly situated on six hundred acres deep in the green of the Great Park of Windsor Castle, west of London. The place was once a summer home to the British monarchy. It was at Belvedere, in 1936, that King Edward VIII had signed his abdication from the British throne, relinquishing the crown for his lover, Mrs. Wallace Simpson. More recently, the Westons summered there. Weston had leased the landmark from the Crown Estate in 1981 on invitation from the Royal family. The Westons were on friendly terms with the Royals. Prince Charles had been Weston's polo team-mate on the Maple Leafs, which played at the Guards Polo Club in Ascot, only a short drive away.

When he wasn't riding the ponies with the heir to the British throne, Weston, age fifty-two, presided over George Weston Ltd., an $11-billion (in annual sales) conglomerate founded by his grandfather in 1882. With interests in supermarkets, bakeries, salmon farms, sardine plants, dairies, candy factories, and saw, paper, and pulp mills, George Weston was the largest food retailing and manufacturing company in Canada. The family's interests spanned continents. Garry Weston, Galen's older brother, ran Associated British Foods PLC, the $8-billion European and Australian arm of the dynasty, which counted venerable British institutions such as the Fortnum & Mason department store and Twinings Tea among its holdings.

Dave Nichol had worked for Loblaw Companies, a pivotal prong of the Weston empire, for twenty-one of his fifty-three years. He had come to see his relationship with Loblaw as if it were a marriage — a tumultuous, often-on-the-brink-of-divorce marriage, but a marriage nevertheless. He had been there, right alongside Galen, in the early 1970s as part of the inner team that resurrected the supermarket chain from a moribund enterprise into a colossus. With annual sales of $9.4 billion, Loblaw Companies was by 1993 the country's largest supermarket chain and a dominant presence in food manufacturing.

One in every five supermarkets in the country was owned by Loblaw Companies, which was in turn 70% owned by George Weston Ltd. The stores were operated under different names across Canada and in the United States, a corporate acknowledgment of the regional fragmentation of the country. In the west, Loblaw ran The Real Canadian Superstore, OK Economy, and The Real Canadian Wholesale Club stores. In Ontario, it managed the Loblaws and Zehrs chains. It had no holdings in Quebec. In the Atlantic provinces, Loblaw holdings included the Real Atlantic Superstores and SuperValu. Franchised operations included valu-mart, Mr. Grocer, no frills, save-easy, Shop-Rite, Lucky Dollar, Tom-Boy Foods, Extra Foods, SuperValu, Your Independent Grocer, and Fortinos. The company's holdings in the United States — primarily in St. Louis and New Orleans — included National Tea, National Market, canal villere, the Real Superstore, and, the most strangely named, "That Stanley!"

Dave Nichol was the public face of the grocery chain. From the Loblaw platform, the manic Nichol had turned himself into a household name in Canada. As the mastermind behind thousands of No Name and President's Choice products sold at Loblaw stores, he was widely credited as the father of premium private-label brands, the term used to describe products manufactured under a store's own label. Through the President's Choice line, Nichol had democratized "gourmet" food, bringing extra virgin olive oil, "decadent" chocolate chip cookies, balsamic vinegar, environmentally friendly coffee filters, and decaffeinated Swiss water-processed coffee to the supermarket and to the Canadian middle class.

Nichol's unprecedented transformation from faceless executive to grocery superstar had been achieved under the aegis of Loblaw International Merchants, the division of Loblaw Companies of which he was president. Under Nichol's autocratic rule, LIM, as it was known around the company, had become the most prolific taste factory in North America; its staff of seventy oversaw the development, manufacture, and packaging of hundreds of products each year — everything from gourmet pet food to low-fat frozen entrées to exotic-sounding sauces such as Memories of Marrakech — all precisely tuned to mass-market desires. LIM also produced television commercials, infomercials, videos, and an advertising supplement known as the *Insider's Report*, which grew to reach over 10 million households in Canada and the United States. In all of these, Nichol's exuberant presence was front and center.

By 1993, President's Choice and No Name products were recording sales of over $1 billion a year. LIM's consulting work brought the division's annual revenues close to almost $2 billion. It was a success story that had spawned imitators around the world. Sam Walton, the down-home founder of Wal-Mart, the biggest retail chain in the United States, learned of Nichol's talents and hired Loblaw to consult on development of Wal-Mart's corporate brands, Sam's American Choice and Great American Value. "What is remarkable about David," his friend Stanley Marcus, founder of the Neiman Marcus department stores and a renowned taste arbiter in his own right, said of him, "is that he's a brilliant merchant *and* a brilliant communicator. Often you find one. Rarely do you find both."

LIM was a pure patronage operation: Galen Weston was its Lorenzo de Medici, bestowing creative autonomy in the order of $20 million annually on David Nichol, his food-obsessed Leonardo. In recent years, however, Nichol's loyalty to his patron had been fractured by something that appeared to him bigger than friendship. Bigger than Loblaw. Bigger even than Weston. Nichol had begun to see himself working on a larger canvas, on the international stage. Seduced by the idea of greatness, by his own omnipotence as a tastemaker, he had come to view himself as the leader of a revolution in the world's largest industry — food.

As he gazed into the night from his airplane seat, Nichol revisited the previous day's victory. He had stood before a roomful of Wall Street analysts at an Oppenheimer & Co. conference in New York, delivering his well-honed evangelical spiel on the collapse of brand loyalty among shoppers. There were many reasons for its demise, not least the fragmentation of mass media, which had dissipated the control that national brand manufacturers — the RJR Nabiscos, Kraft General Foods, Procter & Gambles, and Coca-Colas of the world — once had over consumers' buying decisions. "In two years, Americans will have access to over five hundred channels," Nichol told the crowd. "How will P&G get their message to the consumer then? Through a Crisco channel?"

The crowd listened intently as Nichol, his slightly nasal voice rising almost to a shout, explained the "brand tax," his term for the premiums that shoppers routinely paid to cover the tens of millions of dollars spent on product launches, promotions, and advertising by the national brands. But consumers were fed up with being gouged, Nichol told the group. And they were now willing to alter traditional buying habits in return for genuine quality and value. The lesson of the 1990s, Nichol said, was that people did not want to change their lifestyle. "They just want to pay less for it." That, Nichol told them, was where retailer-branded goods came in. By manufacturing goods themselves under the store banner, retailers could control the cost, the placement, the price — and the shopper.

Bringing national brand manufacturers to their knees had become almost a moral crusade with Nichol. He took delight in the fact that PC Cola outsold Coke in Loblaw supermarkets; that The Decadent Chocolate Chip Cookie had replaced Nabisco's Chips Ahoy! as the company's best-selling cookie; that his Memories of Szechwan Peanut Sauce and Dressing was more popular in some outlets than Heinz ketchup. At Loblaw, private-label penetration in its largest divisions had averaged more than 48% in 1992.

The food industry's revolution was happening not only on Loblaw shelves. In Europe, private-label sales had grown 74% in the past five years, almost twice the rate of total retail sales. In the United States, the penetration of private labels was expected to reach 40% by 1998. Retailers couldn't lose. National brands, frustrated at being squeezed out, would "wheel up to the back door with a tractor trailer full of money," Nichol observed, just to keep the business. "Wall Street," Nichol told the audience, "was oblivious to the revolution. It's time to come back from the Hamptons, guys." The New York audience had lapped it up.

Nichol had been giving variations on this speech for years but, by 1993, his prophecies appeared to be coming true. In the face of lower-priced private-label and generic product competition, the national brands that had dominated the North American consumer landscape for generations were showing unmistakable signs of decline. That spring, Philip Morris Cos. Inc., the conglomerate that owned General Foods, Kraft and Miller Beer, cut the price of Marlboro cigarettes, its most valuable brand, by 40 cents a pack in an attempt to halt the rapid market growth of generic cigarettes. The company's stock lost $13 million in value in one day, a day that would come to be referred to as "Marlboro Friday." Shares of Coca-Cola, Kellogg, Campbell Soup, Heinz, Gillette, Colgate-Palmolive, and Sara Lee also tumbled. In Canada, Coca-Cola, the world's most established brand name, was actually losing money. Procter & Gamble, which had introduced a defensive concept called everyday low pricing, laid off 13,000 people.

Nichol understood that shoppers' shifting loyalties reflected a deeper, darker malaise. He called this percolating consumer discontent "The Boston Tea Party — part two." Political dissent in the late twentieth century had metastasized from the government to the supermarket and the mall. Shoppers were no longer buoyed by the expectation of progress, by the prospect of getting ahead, and by the certitude that life would get better with every generation. Faithlessness was a trend. The public was united in the belief that nothing seemed to work anymore, that no one was protecting their interests. Incomes were down, unemployment was up. The once apolitical consumer — watching quality of life erode but unwilling to adjust expectations accordingly — was at the barricades, fighting back the only way she knew how. By shopping.

The media were all over the story. To his delight, Nichol frequently found himself quoted in the *Wall Street Journal*, the *New York Times* and *USA Today*. The British and European press had also begun to follow Nichol's star. In his Toronto office hung editorial cartoons reflecting the trust he had established with Canadians. One, from the *Ottawa Sun*, pictured a disgruntled Canadian talking to his TV set: "Why can't they just let Quebec be distinct, dump the Senate, lower the GST, end the recession and let Dave Nichol run the country?" *Toronto Life* published a piece called "The Only Man Who Can Save Canada," which parodied Nichol as "someone fresh, someone with taste, someone who can sell the country and in the process tell us what we are. Someone who delivers and never disappoints us. Someone who is everywhere. Someone we can trust...."

After seventeen years as a spokesman for Loblaw, Nichol had been transformed from supermarket executive into a hero to the middle class, himself a trusted brand name. He received fan mail from children. "Dear Mr. Nichol," one letter read. "Thank you for all the peanut butter. I think your chunky peanut butter is great. Love from Kirsten." A couple who had vacationed in Cuba wrote to tell him they couldn't have made it through their stay without their suitcase full of President's Choice dehydrated Too Good To Be True! soups.

During public appearances, he moved with the air and the entourage of a celebrity. As the airplane droned on across the Atlantic, he recalled the adoration shown only a few weeks earlier at Ribfest '93, a three-day barbecue trade show in Toronto's cavernous SkyDome. The structure sweated concrete heat under the June sun. Sweet, acrid mesquite and hickory smoke hung low in the air, mingling with the pungent odor of sizzling pork back ribs basted with barbecue sauce. The twang of country guitar was punctuated by porcine squeals of the entrants in the upcoming pig races and hog-calling events. Champion barbecuers from across North America gathered to compete for $15,000 in prizes for the Best Spareribs, the Best Baby Backs, the Best Sauce, the Best Whole Hog. The *mise en scène* resembled a casting call for an episode of "Roseanne": a sea of slogan-emblazoned T-shirts, baseball hats, and beer bellies drooping over belt buckles.

It had been Nichol's idea that Loblaw sponsor the event — to raise "barbecue awareness." In turn, "barbecue awareness" would translate into demand for President's Choice Gourmet Barbecue Sauce, President's Choice Memories of Kobe Frozen Beef Burgers, and President's Choice wire mesh barbecue baskets. Nichol understood that the average supermarket shopper craved a more profound understanding of the grilling process. Two summers earlier, he had sold 55,000 copies of his sixty-minute barbecue video.

Dressed in a Ribfest '93 T-shirt, white cotton slacks, and Stetson and shadowed by one of his employees video-taping a commercial, he moved through the crowd like a juggernaut, discussing the metaphysics of grilling, sniffing, tasting, offering praise, advice, and thank yous to those who shyly approached him to say how much they liked President's Choice products. People who had seen him only on television commercials were surprised by his bulky six-foot, three-inch frame. Television seemed to contain him, make him look short and dumpy, like the stereotypical grocery executive. In the flesh, Nichol was commanding. "He walks just like John Wayne," one woman whispered as he passed. As he had made his way to the stage to announce the President's Choice barbecue awards, a group of teenage girls called out to him. "Dave, Dave, we love you." He waved and forced a smile.

With his round face set off by wire-rimmed aviator-style glasses and thin lips, the middle-aged Nichol was an unlikely heart-throb. His thick, dark, gray-streaked hair was so neatly coiffed that it suggested a toupee. He once received a letter that praised his "smooth, folksy, Arthur Godfrey style" on TV and then attacked "that black squirrel on your head. You obviously went to the hair club for bad rugs," the writer chastised.

To the Ribfest crowd of 27,000, he was Dave, one of them, some-one attuned to their inner needs, their fears, their anxieties, their secret pleasures. Nichol understood this power. "If anything," he said, "what I have done is associate myself with the common man." But if the common man felt a profound rapport with Nichol, it was entirely unreciprocated. The corn-fed, middle-manager demeanor that came across on television, the almost Olympian scope of his ordinariness, was deceiving.

Indeed, Nichol had devoted his own life to transcending the com-mon and the ordinary, to cultivating a higher life form governed by arti-fice, taste, and style. He had bonded himself to the élite taste network of international food cognoscenti — critics, restaurateurs, chefs, writers, editors, designers, retailers. He had once branded those out of touch with his higher plane of taste awareness as the "unwashed masses," UMs for short. In fact, he abhorred the common and nursed an almost pathological fear of the witless, the ugly, and the mundane.

In the course of two decades, Nichol had created a self-referential universe, obsessively focused on food and style. He had objectified his life to the point where he spoke of himself in the third person. "Dave Nichol hasn't figured out how to do it," he would say, in answer to questions. When he was asked about the seminal moments in his life, he did not speak of his marriage or family, but rather of meals he had eaten. He came to refer to President's Choice products as "his children." Food was his religion. Each meal was taken like Communion. If he could select his last meal on earth, he once said, it would include "a fab-ulous set of ribs slathered with my PC Gourmet Barbecue Sauce."

Nichol spent the better part of his life in restaurants, hotels, and stores around the world — on Weston's tab — looking for products to appropriate. He was a regular at Fauchon in Paris, although he consid-ered it "too precious." He preferred Peck in Milan, Dallmayr and Kafer in Munich, Boqueria in Barcelona. He considered Tokyo's Tsukiji fish market "the ultimate food marketing experience in the world." Whatev-er he consumed had to be the ultimate — the best beef, the best cheese, the best mustard, the best wine. It was a great though hidden irony that the man who gained fame eschewing brand names professionally should devote his private life to consuming products bearing the world's most exclusive labels.

He delighted in the offbeat. For a brief while, his most treasured possession was a pig roaster he had found at the Anuga food fair in Frankfurt. The stainless steel utensil measured 1.5 meters long and stood almost five feet high — perfect for a whole suckling pig. He had the manufacturer convert it to North American electrical standards and ship it over. For a month it was his favorite object; then, the quintessential consumer, he moved on to something else.

The Virgin Atlantic steward removed the remnants of dinner. Pedestrian, Nichol thought; the wine, undistinguished. Nichol had been curious about Virgin, a fleet of planes transformed by Virgin Records' founder, Richard Branson, into a major-league competitor with on-board manicurists and seat-back video monitors. He had heard much about the British airline's style but, so far, the experience had fallen short of his expectations. Happiness was an equation to Nichol: it equaled the sum of expectation divided by reality. The airline had promised that a limousine would pick him up at The Carlyle hotel, but the car was little more than a glorified taxicab. Now the meal, thoroughly forgettable. But then, so much of the world was. No, this wasn't how he'd do it if he were running things.

He had been thinking about leaving Loblaw and discussing it with Terri and a select few friends for almost two years. He saw it as an essential step, one that would require him to move outside the Weston cocoon and fly on the strength of his own name, bolstered by a group of like-minded entrepreneurs with epic plans. The private-label story had gained momentum, in good part due to the promotional work of his close friends, Gerry Pencer, head of Cott Corporation, the world's largest producer of private-label soda pop, and Don Watt, the man who had redesigned the North American supermarket. Both Pencer and Watt had established their names at Loblaw and then teamed up to move on to bigger things. That very month, *Fortune* had published a story on the private-label revolution, featuring a large photo of Pencer and Watt.

There were other push factors as well. The situation at Loblaw had become untenable. The creation of President's Choice had been a testament to Nichol's indomitable will, but he was tiring of the fight. Increasingly, Nichol felt constrained by his boss, Loblaw Companies' hard-driving president, Richard Currie. A showdown was inevitable. In the end, it all came down to money. Although Nichol was well-paid, earning more than $1 million a year in salary and bonuses, he knew his income was minuscule compared to what he could take in as a global taste and product consultant.

The timing for leaving was opportune. In addition to his Canadian renown, he had established a modest profile among U.S. retailers, where President's Choice products were available in more than 1,000 supermarkets. In November, Australia's Choice, a line of products the team at LIM had helped develop for Coles Myer, Australia's largest retailer, was scheduled to be launched.

Even Galen Weston, living within his removed, rarefied universe, had heard rumors about Nichol's impending departure. Subterranean conflict had existed at Loblaw for years, but he had expected everything to remain civil. Civility was elemental to Weston, who seemed to lead a life straight out of a Ralph Lauren ad. There were the ponies, the blue-blood pals, and the tastefully appointed homes — one in the Forest Hill section of Toronto, where his business concerns were centered, the summer retreat at Fort Belvedere, and an ocean-front house that was part of the exclusive development complex he was underwriting near Vero Beach, Florida, called Windsor, a name that capitalized nicely on his royal connections.

And there was the wife — the blonde, lithe Hilary, a former fashion model in Dublin, where the couple met. Hilary and Galen Weston were seen as a fabulous couple, both tall, elegant, aristocratic, golden. A fixture on best-dressed lists, Hilary was known to be more imperious and less immune to the allure of publicity than her husband; she proudly displayed her Toronto home in the pages of the American decorating magazine *HG* in 1992 and had more recently been the subject of a fashion shoot in the Virgin Islands for the British society magazine *Tatler*. Hilary Weston held the position of deputy chairman of Holt Renfrew, a

12-store high-end clothing chain that Galen bought for $43 million in 1986, reportedly because his wife was bored and wanted something to do. Hilary counted among her hobbies a fondness for well-tailored greenery and had co-authored a glossy coffee-table book of Canadian gardens, inspired by her visits to Sissinghurst, the former estate of Vita Sackville-West.

"Elegance is restraint," Diana Vreeland, the late taste arbiter and former editor of *Vogue*, once said, and Galen Weston was walking proof of the axiom. In manner, he was unfailingly polite and good-natured, possessed of immense charm, the rare kind that made the object of his attention feel charming. He appeared equally in his element navigating Princess Diana across a dance floor or discussing the latest agricultural techniques for growing grain in China. The Weston enigma — one that fascinated those who moved in his circles — was how one of the wealthiest men in the country could be so damned decent. He took a personal interest whenever he bumped into one of his 62,000 employees, much as Prince Charles did on walk-abouts with his subjects. One long-time Loblaw executive still remembers the outpouring of kindness and support shown by both Galen and Hilary Weston after the death of his wife.

His public persona notwithstanding, Weston cultivates a genteel, perfect, almost robotic distance. His seeming flawlessness can be unsettling; it is almost as if he had been genetically engineered. He guards his family's privacy zealously and seldom grants interviews unless they are directly associated with business or involved with one of the charities he supports — the Royal Agricultural Winter Fair, the United World Colleges International, or the W. Garfield Weston Foundation, which was set up by his father. Privacy also means security. In 1983, the IRA had mounted a botched kidnapping attempt at Roundwood Park, his 245-acre Irish estate. Officials, tipped off by an informer, lay in wait for the terrorists, while Weston played polo in England. A decade later, he still travels under aliases. Weston's vast wealth, estimated at $2 billion, and his ties to the Royal family make him an ever-vulnerable target.

Weston's life was virtually programmed from the moment of his birth on November 28, 1940. He was the last of nine children and the third son of food and retailing magnate W. Garfield Weston and his wife, Lela. The Weston family shuttled between Britain, Canada, and the United States, depending on what assets Garfield was acquiring that year. Before he reached university, Galen had attended seventeen schools. It was assumed that the Weston boys — Grainger, Garry, and Galen — would one day inherit the family business; their upbringings were structured accordingly, and from an early age they were exposed to the workings and the problems of the family business. They attended day, not boarding, schools. Boarding schools, Garfield Weston believed, were anachronistic and would not expose his sons to the day-to-day workings of the real world. Such enlightened thinking did not extend to the raising of his six daughters, who were prepped principally for suitable marriages.

Dave Nichol and Galen Weston met in 1958, when they were both freshman business students at the University of Western Ontario in London. Nichol spotted the tall, whippet-slim seventeen-year-old Weston across the dining room of Huron College and was immediately drawn to his aristocratic bearing. "I was mesmerized," he recalled years later. "But then, I've always been a sucker for style." The two boys quickly became friends and, later, room-mates.

At first glance, they seemed to have little in common, the well-bred heir to a food dynasty and the brash, outspoken son of a small-town train station agent. David Alexander Nichol was born on February 9, 1940, in Chatham, Ontario, the first baby delivered in the newly built wing of the Chatham General Hospital. In the small southern Ontario outpost, this event constituted news, and the *Chatham Daily News* promptly dispatched a photographer. The image of the one-day-old Nichol with a full head of dark hair was featured in the next edition. The new arrival was the youngest of four children, a late and unexpected addition to the lives of his parents, Gladys and John. The family lived above a tire store. On the morning of Nichol's birth, his father returned from the hospital to find his three older children gathered at the top of the stairs. John Nichol looked up at them, beaming with joy. "That guy is sure to put all you kids to shame," he said.

John Nichol was a large, dark-haired man, born into a poor family. His wife, Gladys McGuigan, came from more affluent circumstances, having been raised on a prosperous farm in Cedar Springs, Ontario. The couple met at a church function (Gladys was impressed by John's silk shirt) and married in 1925. Having taught himself Morse code at seventeen, John Nichol found work as a station agent for the Chesapeake and Ohio railroad. Theirs was a religious, hard-working family. As in the Weston family, industry and sobriety were highly valued. Gladys was involved in the Church of Christian Science and saw to it that her children attended Sunday school and were steeped in Bible stories. The dominant force in the family, Gladys harbored high expectations for her children. All were expected to attend university, and there were frequent warnings that if they failed to earn at least B averages, they would end up peeling tomatoes at the nearby Libby's ketchup factory. Young David found that excelling at school was a way to win favor in Mother's eyes.

John Nichol's position required him to frequently uproot his family to different stops along the southern Ontario spur line; Dave Nichol grew up in towns called Ridgetown, Blenheim, Walkerville, all stations on the way to someplace else. The constant dislocation affected the young boy. Nichol remembered returning from a winter in Florida where his father was recuperating from an illness to discover that everyone else in his grade three class had learned to read. The experience forced him to be flexible and resilient; it also taught him not to form close attachments.

The father was devoted to his family, but emotionally and physically withdrawn. Nichol remembers walking by his father's room, watching him read, alone in his imagination. He was a dreamer, a man who liked to memorize and recite long passages from the Bible, Shakespeare, Robert Service, Keats, Wordsworth, and Longfellow. Often, he sat up late at night, typing poems, which he placed carefully in a scrapbook. He collected second-hand books — they were all he could afford — and hid them under his bed, much to his wife's irritation. It frustrated him that his intellect had been denied the advantages of education.

There was never open friction between Gladys and John Nichol, just the growing, silent drift of different characters sharing the same space. She was dismissive of his family, who was less successful than her own. Later in life, Dave Nichol would ally himself with his maternal ancestors, boasting that they brought the first peach tree from Kentucky to Ontario. From his father, Dave Nichol inherited his large physique and a love of language. But it was his mother who spurred his ambition. "If it had been up to my father, I wouldn't have got out," he says. "I was raised with the maternal point of view. I was raised to believe that women are stronger than the rest of us." That strength seemed to frighten him a little though, and, even years later, he was never as comfortable in the company of women as he was among men.

The difference between his parents was reflected in their attitudes toward food. To his father, food was sustenance; eating your share and no more was virtuous. His mother, on the other hand, equated cooking with love. She valued abundance. The quality of her mother's cooking had persuaded otherwise transient farmhands to stay on the farm. Gladys Nichol used her own memorable apple pie and roast beef to lure respectable boarders to the rooming house she ran in Chatham during the 1930s. Food for her had a strong gravitational pull. It represented a means of control. Even as a child, the young Nichol seems to have had an uncommon interest in the subject. When he was ten, he wrote a letter to his sister Joanne, thanking her for a birthday gift; the letter was almost entirely devoted to describing his birthday dinner.

By all accounts, Nichol's childhood and teenage years were charmed. "I was Isaac to my parents," he said, in reference to the biblical story of Abraham and Sarah. His next closest sibling, John, a star athlete who would go on to become a Baptist preacher, was already ten years old when Dave was born. This gap in age resulted in him being raised like an only child.

A well-mannered son, Nichol never seems to have given his parents grounds for worry. There were no bouts of rebellion, delinquency, or truancy. Nichol applied himself to his studies. When another boy was given first-place honors in the graduating class at Walkerville Collegiate, Nichol, suspecting there was an error, wrote to the principal requesting that the grades be recalculated. This was done, and it was discovered that Nichol in fact placed first. Nichol didn't want public recognition, just the records corrected. Not even the other boy was told.

"It was a rare moment of consideration for others," his sister Joanne said later.

Even as a boy, Nichol had a disdain for frivolity and for people who lacked direction. He was disappointed in a girlfriend who missed exams because she had spent too much time in the sun. His summers were spent in the fields picking tobacco or tomatoes. When he was sixteen, he was awarded a bronze medal in swimming. This allowed him to work as the waterfront director at affluent Christian Science summer camps in Michigan and Colorado.

Despite the obvious class differences, Nichol and Weston were in many respects very much alike. Both were the adored youngest child in abstemious households that valued hard work. Both shared peripatetic childhoods and were familiar with the new-kid syndrome, the sense of otherness that came from not belonging to a group. At Western, both existed outside the mainstream of private-school boys, removing themselves from the raucous fraternity culture of the university. "We were both loners," Weston says. "We chose to be outsiders." And each saw in the other what they had been raised to admire. In Weston, Nichol saw success, culture, and innate style. In Nichol, Weston saw industry and innate confidence. "Whether it was a girl or soul music, he was laser-like in his intensity," Weston says of Nichol. "Nothing distracted him."

At school breaks, Nichol often took Weston home to stay with the family. One summer, between second and third years, Weston was sent by his father to work at Deutscher Supermarket Handels-GmbH, a German chain in which the family held an interest. He took Nichol and another schoolmate, Jim Hannah, with him. It was Nichol's first glimpse at the inner workings of a supermarket. He was put in charge of bottle returns, not for a minute thinking the summer would be a foreshadowing of his life's work.

Galen and Hilary Weston were known for throwing a good bash, and Alannah's coming-of-age party at Fort Belvedere was one of their best. The theme of the black-tie event was Alice in Wonderland, a tribute to the blonde, blue-eyed Alannah. The five hundred guests, including Prince Charles and Australian supermodel Elle Macpherson, mingled in the ballroom, decorated in a woodland glade decor. Hilary wore a black and white sheath from Chanel couture; Alannah, a green jacket and bouffant skirt from Catherine Walker. The event was rumored to have cost the Westons close to $500,000 — small change. The day after the party, Dave and Terri Nichol left for France to, as Nichol put it, "eat our way through the Dordogne Valley."

On their return trip, they stayed a few days with the Westons at Belvedere. Here, although he was oblivious to the historical precedent, Nichol delivered his own abdication speech. The two men — a study in physical contrasts — sat across from each other in the solarium the Westons had added to the property. Weston knew what Nichol was about to say. Still, the assured finality of Nichol's news appeared to surprise him. "It's like a marriage," Nichol later said. "Even if you know it's in trouble, you're always shocked when it's finally over."

Nichol told Weston that he wanted to continue helping him with the President's Choice brand. His products were his children, he said, and he could never entirely desert them. But he could see he was constrained by circumstances. He wanted the flexibility to work with whom he wanted on whatever projects he wanted. Within the current corporate structure, he knew, that would be impossible.

Weston, a straightforward man, did not contain his disappointment. He had harbored the illusion that he would walk into the supermarket sunset with Dave Nichol and Richard Currie, his two loyal aides. But Weston also understood Nichol's grandiose ambition, his insatiable need for the next glory, bigger than the last. The Nichol ego was legendary in the industry. His aggressive, occasionally abusive personality was both his weakness and his strength. It had made him many enemies, within the Weston family of companies and beyond. The success of President's Choice had been achieved only by fighting opposition at every turn. Within the Weston executive suite, he was regarded with a mixture of awe and contempt. "Who else could have overturned such a stodgy, old-fashioned, repressed industry?" one Weston executive said. "You had to be a prick."

Still, Weston believed that Nichol was malleable and could be persuaded to stay. He asked his old friend to reconsider his decision,

promising more money and more autonomy. Nichol agreed to reconsider. His mother, Gladys — at ninety still taking an avid interest in her
son's career — told him that nothing was more important than his
friendship with Galen. Don't rupture that, she warned him. Privately,
though, his mind was made up.

He knew he was repeating himself. Besides, Loblaw was no longer
where the action was. He wanted to break new ground and he had only
ten productive years left to achieve immortality. The revolution needed
him. At Loblaw, he had watched many others capitalize on the private-
label bandwagon, including his new best friend, Gerry Pencer, who was
riding high on the soaring value of his private-label cola empire, Cott
Corp. Now, Pencer had invited him to join Cott's global express. Finally, it would be Dave Nichol's turn to enjoy the wealth that had been
denied him at Loblaw.

He observed the situation from a distance. Obsessed about keeping control, he began writing the last chapter of the Loblaw saga in his
mind. "It ends with the tenth anniversary of the *Insider's Report*," he
said. "It ends with a 48% penetration of private label within Loblaw. It
ends with me sitting on a beach in Bali, asking if it's exportable or not.
It ends with me wondering if the expression 'Canadian hero' is really an
oxymoron? And is there a hit man from Coca-Cola lurking behind the
tree waiting for me with a sniper rifle?"

In fact, Nichol had no idea how the next few months, never mind the
next decade, would unfold. Loblaw had been a fantastic, though sometimes frustrating, adventure, a mad, exhilarating romp. It had allowed him
to change the eating habits of an entire nation. And it had taught him a
valuable lesson: money created taste, and taste could make money.

Nichol could see that the retailing landscape was changing radically. Power was shifting. Could he continue to be seen as a private-label
visionary, the architect of a revolution in the food retailing and manufacturing industries? Could he turn Dave Nichol into a trusted brand
name throughout North America and Europe? Could he put his imprimatur on anything from cola to Cabernet? Or would he perish without
the support of the taste factory he had created or the clout of the Weston conglomerate? Had his insatiable hunger turned into insatiable

greed? At heart, Dave Nichol nursed deep-rooted fears of risk and change. And here he was, about to make the biggest change in his life, one that could risk it all.

CHAPTER TWO

"IT'S GONNA BE MARVELLOUS"

I t all began, appropriately, with the illusion of choice. Galen Weston had been called to his father's office above Fortnum & Mason, the Queen's grocer, on Regent Street in the spring of 1971. The elder Weston had decided it was time that Galen took a stronger hand in running the family dynasty. George Weston Ltd. was a household name across Canada, the producer of staples and treats that included Clover Leaf tuna, Hostess Chocolate Cream Delights, E.B. Eddy matches, Neilson's Crispy Crunch chocolate bars, White Swan toilet tissue, and the complete line of Weston bakery products, including that ubiquitous middle-class staple, Wonder Bread. With sales of $1.4 billion in 1970, George Weston Ltd. was the largest food company in Canada and the third largest in the world.

Like other stories involving the accumulation of serious money, the Weston story had attained the status of myth: how in 1876 Garfield's father, George, then twelve, had logged ten-hour days, six days a week as a baker's apprentice; how, while still a teenager, he had graduated to breadman, delivering bread and cakes in a horse-drawn carriage to Toronto housewives; how by 1882, he had saved enough money to buy two bread routes; how he had introduced the Homemade Loaf, selling it for pennies in hopes of breaking housewives of the bread-baking habit; and how by the turn of the century, his Homemade Loaf was available in more than five hundred stores.

In 1897, Weston opened the Model Bakery, making use of the latest in automation and assembly-line technology. In 1911, the business merged with four other Toronto bakers in a venture called Canada Bread, which later became Corporate Foods, a subsidiary of Canadian Pacific. As part of that deal, the partners agreed not to compete with Canada Bread for ten years following the merger. But Weston was eager to get back into business for himself. According to *Bread Men*, Charles Davies's history of the Weston empire, by the time George Weston severed his ties with the company in 1920, he had already been operating a factory for a year, a shocking detail, given Weston's strict Methodist morality.

When Weston died in 1924, the business fell to his eldest son, Willard Garfield, a charismatic, persuasive personality. Garfield Weston immediately set out on a $150-million acquisition binge that would expand the company's reach to the United States, the United Kingdom, Australia, and New Zealand. He spent the better part of his life acquiring assets that built George Weston into an international conglomerate with holdings in fisheries, forest products, bakeries, and candy. The reach of the operation was underscored in 1935, when Weston moved his family to England — to Whittington, a two-hundred-acre estate on the Thames. He was named a British Member of Parliament in the 1939 election, standing unopposed in Macclesfield, a working-class Midlands riding.

Like his father, Garfield Weston championed industry, sobriety, and philanthropy. He made sizeable donations, often anonymously, to medical research, art galleries, museums, and the Salvation Army. His personal spending habits were often contradictory. At the Weston summer cottage on an island in Muskoka, the family routinely used stale coffee left over from the previous summer. Yet Weston thought nothing of airlifting wieners from one of his German supermarkets for barbecues at his English estate.

Although the empire seemed to be humming along, by 1970 Garfield Weston saw serious fault lines forming. He had summoned Galen to discuss one of its more problematic provinces — Loblaw Companies, an ailing chain of 1,800 supermarkets in North America. When Weston purchased his initial stake in Loblaw Groceterias in 1947, it was a flourishing operation. The chain, founded in 1919 by J. Milton Cork and Theodore Pringle Loblaw, then operated 113 stores in Ontario and posted annual sales of $50 million. Loblaw was only one supermarket Weston acquired. The late 1940s had been a boom time for supermarkets in North America. What was lost in their impersonality, shoppers believed, was amply repaid in savings and convenience.

In 1956, Weston gained voting control of Loblaw Groceterias and created the holding company, Loblaw Companies Ltd., to operate Weston supermarket interests across the continent. By the end of the decade, its holdings included the O.K. Economy Stores Ltd. in Saskatoon; National Grocers Co. Ltd. in central Canada; Kelly Douglas & Co. of Vancouver; Atlantic Wholesalers of Sackville, New Brunswick; and National Tea in the American midwest.

By the mid-sixties, however, Loblaw had lost its dominant position in the Ontario market, where more than half its 454 Canadian supermarkets were located. The new front runner was Dominion Stores Ltd., also founded in 1919, which had 210 stores in Ontario. It also faced competition from A&P and Steinbergs Ltd., which ran Miracle Mart stores in Ontario. There were problems within as well. Loblaws' stores had become shabby. The mix of products sold failed to reflect changing tastes and shifting demographics. Staff were poorly trained. Many stores were inner-city; no one at head office had taken sufficient note of the exodus to the suburbs. A series of price wars instigated in the early 1970s further eroded Loblaw's position and underlined its reputation as the "high-cost" chain. On George Weston Ltd. books, Loblaw had become a depreciating asset, burdened by more than $200 million in debt.

The troubles at Loblaw, Garfield Weston knew, were symptomatic of larger, deeply rooted problems within Weston's North American operations. The company's entrenched management had become conservative and complacent. Food-processing operations were a mess, mismanaged, and often duplicated. Occasionally, divisions sued one another, not knowing they belonged to the same parent. The company was facing charges of corporate concentration by the federal government. Indeed, the business had become so convoluted that financial analysts who followed it were dubbed Westonologists.

Galen Weston knew intuitively that the assignment his father was about to give him was more an assumed responsibility than a choice.

Within the family, duty was a valued virtue. The Weston sons, Grainger, Garry, and Galen, engaged in activities designed to teach a rich man's sons how ordinary people live. From an early age, the boys worked in the family business. As a teenager, Galen packed Christmas hampers at Fortnum & Mason. The summer before he entered university, he washed photo pans in the advertising department of Loblaw Groceterias.

Weston left university in 1961 one course short of a bachelor's degree to go to Dublin, where he purchased a grocery store with an inheritance from his grandmother. He was guided in this venture by his older brother Garry, who had a hand in operating Associated British Foods, the family's U.K. operations. Dublin was then a retailing wasteland. From his one store, Galen built Power, Ireland's first supermarket chain. He also bought the Brown, Thomas & Co. department store, service and supply companies, and various real estate assets.

Early on, Weston displayed the sort of cutthroat competitive instincts needed to succeed in the industry. He would send employees over to Quinnsworth, a competitor he eventually bought out, to purchase the complete supply of low-priced specials being sold at a loss to lure shoppers into the store. Gradually, his father exposed him to more of the family business. In 1968, he was named to the boards of Associated British Foods and of George Weston Ltd., where he first learned of the problems at Loblaw.

In 1971, Garfield Weston asked Galen to examine whether Loblaw should be closed or sold or salvaged. Both father and son knew that the Loblaw discussion was a pretext. The real subject was Galen's readiness to take over George Weston Ltd.'s North American operations. Galen seemed to be the logical heir. Grainger, the eldest son, had shown little inclination to carry the Weston mantle and had dissociated himself from the family's business concerns. (He later started the Frenchman's Cove resort in Jamaica and ran a cookie company in Texas.) Garry, a stolid, cautious personality, was doing a competent job managing the British arm of the business, but he lacked Galen's charm and ambition. Untangling the Loblaw knot would be Galen's opportunity to prove his management acumen.

After taking the summer and fall of 1971 to consider the Loblaw situation, Weston was ready for what he later referred to as his "corporate baptism." He packed up his wife, Hilary, six-month-old Alannah, and her nanny and moved to Toronto in February 1972. He became chief executive officer of Loblaw Companies that spring. Uneasy about inheriting his father's advisers, Galen brought in consultants from Fine Fair chain in England to oversee operation of the stores. They told him that the equity had vanished from the Loblaw name, that he should shut down the worst locations and rename the rest.

One of his first calls was to Dave Nichol.

After university, Nichol had gone to work as a salesman for Federal Mogul Bower Bearings in Saskatchewan. He traveled from garage to garage across the prairies, selling industrial bearings and seals to automotive and industrial wholesalers. It was work he disliked, but it taught him how to close a deal.

Weston and Nichol had remained close after university. Nichol was Weston's best man at his 1966 wedding in England at Henley-on-Thames. The event had an 1890s' Klondike theme, with the participants dressed accordingly. Nichol and Weston wore double-breasted suits with string ties and wide-brimmed hats. The revelrous affair ended with a ride down the river in a vintage steamboat. Weston returned the favor the next year when Nichol married Dianne Mollenaux, an attractive woman from a well-to-do family. They were wed in Vancouver in 1967. "The two of them have enough brains for four people," a guest at their wedding whispered to Nichol's sister, Joanne. On their honeymoon, the Nichols traveled around the world, a gift from her family.

The life of a traveling salesman, however, did not fit Nichol's ambitions. When an aunt died, leaving the family ownership of a parking lot in central Los Angeles, Nichol used his share of the profits — almost $10,000 — to finance his attendance at law school at the University of British Columbia. To supplement his income, he set up a business selling cram notes to other students. He graduated second out of two hundred, fully expecting to be given a clerkship to the Supreme Court of Canada. He was passed over in favor of a student with better connections, an event that shook him. "It was then that I realized the world was not fair," he said. Deciding to attend Harvard Business School, he applied twice, to be both times rejected. He was accepted in the Master's program at Harvard Law School and moved to Boston, intending to become a law professor. After graduation, Nichol attended a recruitment seminar staged by management consultants McKinsey & Co. and was offered a job. He spent three years at McKinsey, suffering all the while from an acute inferiority complex. Everyone there, he believed, was brighter than he was. To compensate, he would work all night preparing for eight a.m. presentations. It was a discipline that taught him the importance of research, of always being prepared, and of always having a plan.

When Weston asked Nichol to work on the Loblaw turnaround, Nichol readily agreed. Soon after, Nichol introduced Weston to Richard Currie, a fellow McKinseyite who was on site at George Weston's Toronto headquarters, designing a sugar refinery for its food-processing operations. Nichol and Currie had got to know each other while reorganizing the purchasing department of H.J. Heinz when Nichol was at a vulnerable point. Shortly before, Dianne had walked out on him. By then she was a psychologist. But the marriage couldn't withstand the pressures of two demanding careers and two strong-willed people. "They were too much alike," says Nichol's sister Joanne. "That was the problem." He was devastated. Currie listened sympathetically. He suggested Nichol relax, play a few rounds of golf. "That's when I hit bottom," Nichol recalled. "Then I began to fight."

Currie, hired at Loblaw in 1972, was a short, plump, amiable-looking man, a facade that masked a shrewd mind and a quest for power. Born in Saint John, New Brunswick, in 1937, Currie studied chemical engineering at the Technical University of Nova Scotia and business at the University of Western Ontario. After working for the Atlantic Sugar Co., he obtained an MBA from Harvard in 1970, then joined McKinsey & Co., specializing in strategic planning and profit improvement in the food manufacturing and distribution industries. He was well-suited to the work. Currie possesses a taciturn nature and was given to drawing flow charts in the air with his hands when discussing a business problem.

Dick Currie is a methodical thinker — able to walk out of a room in mid-sentence and return two minutes later on the next word. In his spare time, he reads military history. He was a keen student of Winston Churchill and took it as the highest compliment when friends described him as Churchillian, which they often did; however, those who emerged as losers from a confrontation with him preferred the term Machiavellian. Currie also has a more sentimental side, not often seen by his colleagues. He likes music of the fifties and had a soft spot for Elvis Presley, old-fashioned Broadway musicals, and schmaltzy movies.

Weston, Nichol, and Currie arrived at a grocery chain in shambles. There wasn't a profit and loss statement to be found, an unforgivable lapse to anyone trained in McKinsey methodology. McKinsey's hard-line profit-driven corporate culture would come to play an influential role in the way Loblaw was managed. Founded in 1930, it had grown into a powerful and prestigious consulting firm of international renown, teaching other companies how to become more efficient. Insiders called it The Firm. Elitist by design, McKinsey was filled with the best and the brightest — Baker scholars from Harvard Business School, Rhodes scholars, even nuclear physicists. It placed a premium on analytic ability, on being "bright." Pure, intellectual Darwinism ruled. "We...hire people who are one, very smart; two, insecure, and thus driven by their insecurity; and three, competitive," a former managing director told *Fortune*. The goal was always to increase profits.

Applying those principles to the mundane, retrograde supermarket industry was bound to have startling effects. The business, as Galen Weston once allowed, "did not tend to attract intellectuals." That was not only an epic understatement; it failed to capture the often thuggish ethos of the business. In fact, anyone who spent any time in the industry knew that it was secretive and cutthroat. Net profits, traditionally, were razor's edge, ranging from 0.5% to 2% of total sales. To make money, it was necessary to know what shoppers wanted and to stock shelves in a way that made them buy the products that provided the greatest profit.

Weston quickly deduced that Currie's strength was corporate strategy. Nichol, he knew, had the aggressive personality needed to shake up a complacent management. Weston named Currie director of profit development; Nichol became director of corporate development. The two came to call themselves "the change agents." Early on, Nichol and Currie made a bid to reassure Weston that his efforts would not be in vain. They presented Weston with a photograph of themselves, smiling. Under the photo was the caption "...it's gonna be marvellous."

Appropriately, given the state of the business, Loblaw's headquarters were located in a decrepit, four-story 140,000-square-foot Toronto warehouse situated beneath a busy waterfront expressway. For a time, the three men shared an office, carpeted in a hideous lime green shag. They worked eleven-hour days, six days a week. Currie handled the core business issues: paying down debt, restructuring operations, selling or closing unprofitable operations. He applied battlefield tactics. Dominion, the leader with approximately 25% of the market, was The Enemy. But it, too — despite excellent urban locations — was burdened by complacent management and questionable buying practices.

Currie reasoned that if he could maintain sales per store at the profitable outlets while closing unprofitable ones, Loblaw could keep up with its payables while turning its inventory into the cash needed to remodel its operations. The strategy was intended to mislead the competition. Dominion, intent on maintaining its market share, believed that Loblaw was getting weaker with each closure. In fact, it was acquiring a source of cash. For the moment, Currie was not concerned about market share. His military reading had taught him that no general won every battle. The final victory, he knew, often went to the general who first conducted an orderly retreat. That allowed forces to conserve strength and maintain flexibility.

Together, Currie and Weston closed 1,200 stores in Canada and the United States, including many members of its National Tea chain; they kept ownership of the real estate. Twelve divisions or companies were closed outright. In three years, Currie consolidated all retail and wholesale operations and centralized the finance, real estate, and procurement divisions.

Nichol, responsible for operating the stores, slowly rebuilt management. He was put in charge of recruitment, although Weston had the final say on key hires. Nichol tore through the Canadian supermarket business looking for ambitious young men. He knocked on so many doors that he was threatened with harassment suits. One of his early recruits was another McKinsey alumnus, Serge Darkazanli, who worked in head office in business development. Acerbic and quick-witted, the Syrian-born Darkazanli held an MBA from McGill University in Montreal. He later went west to head Westfair Food, the company's western operations.

Other key Nichol recruits included Doug Lunau, a somewhat abrasive man who was taken from Dominion to head up purchasing; Warren Tutton, a slim elegant fellow brought in from M. Loeb in Ottawa to run in-house advertising; and David Stewart, an Oxford graduate with U.K. retailing experience, was hired to handle merchandising. When prospective hires turned him down, Nichol was unmoved. "It's just a matter of time before you work for me," he'd say.

Over time, Nichol honed his corporate persona: that of a driven perfectionist who could be rude and dismissive not only to those who failed to meet his standards, but to those who did. The Loblaw staff he inherited was demoralized. Many of them had adopted a defeatist mentality. Nichol applied shock treatment. He practised motivation through sarcasm. Anyone regarded as a traditional thinker was out. "If this is the conventional wisdom, let's not do it," he'd say. Swinging confidently through the art department, cocksure of his taste, he'd tell art director Russ Rudd: "I don't like this, don't like this, like this." Like his other enthusiasms, his interest in people would wax and wane. "It was a high to think that he respected what you had to say," says a former Loblaw employee. "But nothing was more chilling than having him freeze you out after he lost interest."

Nichol's critics — a growing battalion — griped that the Weston clout was going to Nichol's head. He'd call meetings for eight a.m. then show up at eleven. He did not hesitate to reprimand presenters in front of their colleagues. "This is trash," he'd bark. "Do it over." But bravado was a mask. Deep down, Nichol was terrified, more so than when he had been selling ball bearings on the Prairies or presenting slide shows at McKinsey. He knew the company had to change to survive, but he had no idea of what form that change should take. He didn't know what he was doing. He knew only two things for certain. The first was that he needed a strategy. The second was that no one could ever find out how scared he really was.

The most visible sign of Loblaw's deterioration was the stores themselves. Just how pathetic things had become was evident at the 28,000-square-foot store at the southeast corner of Bayview and Moore avenues, a middle-class enclave in midtown Toronto. Weeds grew between the cracks in the parking lot. The lines on the parking spaces had been painted so closely together to conserve space that customers couldn't open their car doors if the lot was full. The store looked like an abandoned warehouse. The only nod to aesthetics was a Loblaw logo that ran vertically down the side, each letter a different color. Inside was supermarket hell. A 1940s time-warp prevailed. Metal casings, unhinged from display cases, snagged women's stockings as they walked by. Overhead lighting was dingy. Display was an afterthought. Employees' uniforms were stained and tattered. Weekly sales were $35,000. Not surprisingly, the store was losing money.

In search of a new look, Galen Weston held discussions with many of the big names in retail design — people such as Lippencott & Margolis. Eventually, however, the contract went to Don Watt, a thirty-six-year-old graphic designer with no track record in store design. Born in Regina in 1936, Watt had studied industrial design at the Ontario College of Art and later took a design course in the engineering school of the University of Toronto. His first ambition, to be a navy pilot, was sidetracked by color-blindness. After graduation, he joined the A.V. Roe aircraft company and worked on the ergonomics of the cockpit for the Avro Arrow fighter jet that was later scuttled by the Diefenbaker government.

Watt kicked around in a number of design jobs — Bugs Bunny animation director for Warner Brothers in Los Angeles, an illustrator of children's books, and various positions in advertising agencies — before he hooked up with copywriter Paul Break and creative director Howard Pain to form the design firm Break, Pain & Watt in the fall of 1969. The trio merged advertising and marketing, co-ordinating copywriting with design and advertising. Watt and Weston met in the late spring of 1972. According to Watt, he approached Weston after Dominion rejected a proposed store redesign.

Watt was an impressive figure — intelligent, articulate, and hearty in a Kennedyesque style. He told Weston his firm would redesign a store for $30,000. The established firms were asking several million. How much more damage could he do, Weston thought. He gave Watt creative autonomy and one condition: "Just get rid of that Loblaws sign."

Pain and Watt went to work in the fall of 1972. Their lack of expertise in supermarkets was their greatest strength. The industry was deeply conservative; style was almost non-existent. Closing the store to refurbish it was out of the question, so the work was done at night, over ten weeks. They repaved the parking lot and repainted the parking lines. In a bold move, they painted the storefront chocolate brown. These were the 1970s, and brown was the apotheosis of cool. For the logo, they created a stylized L in orange and red, and a simple Loblaw sign in Helvetica type. Watt's color-blindness made him partial to a brownish yellow ocher, which was vibrant to his eye. He insisted that the store's ceilings be painted ocher yellow.

Budget constraints forced them to be inventive. For example, without money to widen aisles, they removed the top shelf to give the illusion of space. Large, colorful photographs of fruit, vegetables, and fresh baking were positioned overhead to guide shoppers. Signage was bold but simple. Bright yellow signs indicated price reductions. Watt raised banners with bold red and orange type. Floating bins with rubberized corners replaced antiquated metal cases. Cracked mirrors were covered with wood boards, which created a rustic effect and was cheaper than removing the mirrors.

But repositioning Loblaw, Weston and the others knew, required more than cosmetic changes; it had to be perceived to be different from the competition. Dominion's slogan was "Mainly because of the meat," a motto that became increasingly passé with changing tastes in food. Nichol and Currie traveled with Weston to study successful North American supermarket chains. They noted the proliferation of produce at Californian retailers such as Trader Joe's, Lucky's, Alpha Beta, and Acme. They were inspired by Gelson's Markets, a Los Angeles chain that offered what seemed astounding variety and state-of-the-art spray systems that kept produce glistening. Later, Loblaw employees were sent to Gelson's to learn how to stack vegetables and fruit.

Copying the Americans, Loblaw removed fruit from plastic packaging and introduced exotic items previously unknown to Canadians, including kiwi and pear apples. It sunk money into refrigeration and put warm-colored filters on high-intensity lights to make the food look appetizing. It put produce at the front of the store, so it was the first thing shoppers saw. The convention had been to keep it at the back, near loading docks.

These changes weren't exactly radical, but they seemed so within the staid universe of food retailing. Watt did encounter opposition from some of the old school consultants Weston had brought in from England. They wanted to change the L. They wanted to hang curtains in the store. When Watt told them this idea was suicide, they fired him. Weston persuaded him to come back and urged him to call Nichol if he had problems. "He's a very bright fellow," Weston told Watt. "He knows nothing about food, but if you have a problem, he'll fix it." When Watt hit his first snag, he went immediately down to Loblaw headquarters, where he met Dave Nichol. Nichol ran interference. "You have no taste," he told Watt's critics. "You know where to take money at the end of the day; he has taste." Watt and Nichol bonded with the shared vision of becoming the one Canadian supermarket chain with style and class.

Two weeks after its reopening in the summer of 1973, sales at the refurbished Bayview-Moore store had jumped from $39,000 a week to $165,000. Weston said there were some things he didn't like but refused to tamper with the mix. After all, sales had climbed more than 60% within a few months of the redesign. With the Bayview store as a model, ten others were chosen as priority sites for redesign.

Having done the store, Watt turned to the products, repackaging thirty-five Loblaw house brands, including peas, beans, and carrots. The new packaging was classic Watt: graphic simplicity, boldly colored photographs of the product inside, clear color, strong type. Inspired by

Scandinavian design, it won Galen Weston the 1974 National Design Council Chairman's Award for Design Management.

The redesigns were part of the larger strategy to improve profit margins. An established way to do this was to add an in-store bakery or a deli, which charged higher mark-ups. Here, the team's inexperience was not an asset. What they needed was someone who knew the food business inside out. Watt suggested Brian Davidson, whom he had met while redesigning the apartment of Sam Shopsowitz, Toronto's deli king. Weston met Davidson at Shopsy's main delicatessen along with Currie and Nichol and offered him a job; Davidson accepted.

Davidson was a Rabelaisian figure, a three hundred-pound elf with a love for food and a nose for the deal. Born Brian Yitzhak Davidson — Yitz to his many friends — in 1933, he was the youngest of seven children of Polish immigrant parents. The family name was Davidman, but a Canada Customs clerk had written down "Davidson" and the name stuck. Brian started work at the age of eight in a local bakery. At thirteen, he took a job at Shopsy's deli on Spadina Avenue, peeling wieners for shipping. He nearly lost the job when it was discovered he was packing wieners that had gone bad. When it came to light that Davidson, like Watt, was color-blind and could not separate a moldy green wiener from the rest, he became a driver-salesman, a position far better suited to his skills.

So compelling were Davidson's selling talents that they won him his future wife, Thelma. He showed up at her door on a blind date. She was seventeen and taken aback by the large man in a hat and suit. He seemed so old, she recalled. "But he was a good salesman," she says. Davidson worked for Shopsy's for twenty-three years and knew everyone in the trade. When the delicatessen was sold to the Unilever conglomerate, he went into the restaurant business, setting up Ponderosa and Frank Vetere's, two now-defunct chains.

At first glance, Davidson seemed ill-fitted to the new Loblaw style. He was rotund, street smart, and Jewish; the company's executive offices were dominated by slick MBAs, in the WASP tradition. But what Davidson lacked in schooling or polish, he compensated for in zeal and deal-making savvy. He was a ten-ideas-a-minute kind of guy. One of the first and most valuable connections he made was to Siegfried Wauro, an ebullient character known as Ziggy.

Wauro had trained as a master butcher in Stuttgart, Germany, and immigrated to Canada in 1954 at the age of nineteen. He had worked for a kosher butcher and a few supermarket chains, but wanted to be in business for himself. In 1957, with his wife, Marie, Wauro set up Tip Top Meats in Toronto's west end. When Yorkdale, then the world's largest enclosed shopping mall, was built, he opened the first of what became a series of Ziggy's fast-food shops. Wauro's exposure to mall culture taught him about the growing demand for convenience — for sliced meats, fresh-baked pies, prepared salads, and entrées that could be heated up at home. In 1973, shortly after he joined Loblaw, Davidson called and arranged for Wauro to meet Nichol, Weston, and Currie for breakfast at a downtown hotel. Selling his business to a big, rich outfit like Weston was his dream. It was a dream soon realized. Galen Weston bought Wauro's five stores and signed him to a five-year contract to set up in-store delis, to be known as Ziggy's Fantastic Foods. The first opened in April of that year, in Hamilton. Within a few years, there were two hundred Ziggy's in operation.

Wauro operated the delis as independent businesses, with a higher set of profit margins than applied elsewhere in the supermarket. Ziggy's was the service-gourmet section of the store; the area was styled in a Sound of Music Teutonic theme, with women behind the counter attired in red and white dirndls. In addition to selling cold cuts and salads, it packaged fruit pies and stocked then-exotic cheeses such as Brie and Camembert. The meat was presliced for quicker service. Ziggy's outlets were located either right inside the front door or by the exit. Location was crucial, Wauro knew. "You have to be seen as first in or last out," he explained. "That way, you offer the perception of convenience." Wauro ran the operation until 1978, when he moved to Arizona.

In 1974, Galen Weston was named chairman and managing director of George Weston Ltd. That year, he earmarked $40 million for Loblaw to develop its line of private-label products. The Toronto advertising agency Vickers & Benson was hired to change the company's image. The agency applied the same psychology it had used in Liberal party political campaigns. V&B president Terry O'Malley had learned from those campaigns to "never talk the other guy's issue." Loblaw's major competitor, Dominion, had convinced shoppers that the main purpose of the supermarket was to provide meat. V&B chose instead to focus on prices. They came up with the slogan, "The price is right," and presented it to Loblaw executives. The consultants from England fretted. "Jesus Christ," one said, "the price better be right." The amended line became: "More than the price is right...but by gosh the price is right."

Vickers & Benson also scripted a television campaign to dovetail with the refurbishing of the stores. Gabor Apor, a sophisticated Hungarian emigré who later became a successful molder of political images, directed the first commercials, using testimonials from shoppers. William Shatner, Captain Kirk on "Star Trek," was signed as the company spokesman. Shatner was in his post-"Star Trek," pre-"T.J. Hooker" phase and willing to shill for supermarkets. V&B thought his wholesome sex appeal would attract female interest. The ads were contrived to exude energy, with Shatner always in motion. "We needed to convince people that even if the stores were physically the same, attitudinally the company had changed," O'Malley explained. After the first commercials aired in 1974, sales jumped 10%. Dominion responded to the campaign by talking prices, just as Loblaw had hoped.

At Loblaw offices, the turnaround frayed everyone's nerves. Screaming matches were common. Davidson screamed at Ziggy, Ziggy at Nichol, Nichol at Davidson. Currie wasn't a screamer. As ideas were bandied about, Watt sat, sketching them out. Davidson was treated as a reference center. He knew everyone, set up relationships, found the lowest-cost producers, and dreamt up in-store promotions. He bought the Canadian rights to sell Weight Watchers frozen entrees and Häagen-Dazs, shrewd moves that covered both ends of the spectrum. He was constantly walking into meetings with new foods discovered in his travels. "Try this," he'd say, shoving a sausage in someone's face.

Despite the redesigns, the TV ads, and Ziggy's, Loblaw continued to lose money, piling up losses that reached a crescendo of $83.6 million by 1977. George Weston Ltd. absorbed the shortfall, posting its first corporate loss — $15 million — in 1976. Weston's deep pockets made optimism possible. Between 1968 and 1974, Garfield Weston pumped more than $165 million into Loblaw Companies. Shareholders were unhappy; to avoid them, Galen Weston changed the venue of the 1974 annual meeting from Toronto's Royal York Hotel to a remote suburban warehouse. But busloads of shareholders arrived, more than 12,000. Garfield Weston was in the audience. "If you don't want your shares," he told the crowd, "sell them to me." No one did.

Although the new Loblaw managers regarded themselves as entrepreneurs who funded expansion only by retained earnings or new debt, Garfield Weston's support provided the luxury of long-term planning. There were no bankers breathing down their necks. Loblaw was the corporate equivalent of a Rockefeller or a Getty heir, comfortable in the knowledge that the money was there if it were really needed.

Even while piling up losses, Loblaw executives embarked on adventures that read like the Hardy Boys let loose with a Michelin guide. One year, after attending the Anuga food fair in Germany, a group that included Wauro, Currie, Davidson, Nichol, and suppliers Michael Firestone and Peter Gibline, traveled by barge up the Rhône toward Carcassonne, France, the alleged birthplace of cassoulet, hell-bent on finding out if it really was the best in the world. The verdict was mixed. Afterwards, they piled into two Mercedeses and embarked on a three-day, three-star restaurant binge.

The pretence of boys' club collegiality failed to mask the fact that a power struggle was beginning to unfold. In the summer of 1975, Loblaw Companies moved into the newly constructed Weston Centre, an octagonal, twenty-floor gray steel structure located in midtown Toronto. Senior management did not arrive until the fall, when the nineteenth and twentieth floors were completed, a two-story aerie that housed both George Weston and Loblaw executives. Designed by architect Leslie Rebanks, the space won design awards. The look was a weird hybrid of Star Trek-Canadiana. The ninteenth-floor receptionist sat perched in a white plastic module that resembled a 1960s version of a flying saucer. Taupe suede banquettes lined the gray walls, adorned with Running Fences, the series by Bulgarian artist Christo. A thirty-foot totem pole from British Columbia jutted up beside the stainless

steel spiral staircase to the twentieth floor. Beside it stood a flagpole flying a yellow flag adorned with the Weston family crest. Glass bowls in
the waiting area contained Hallowe'en-sized samples of Weston products — Pep chocolate mints, Jersey Milk and Caramilk chocolate bars.

In 1976, Weston appointed Currie president of Loblaw Companies Ltd; Nichol became president of Loblaws Supermarkets Ltd., an
operation that ran 132 Loblaws supermarkets in Ontario. The appointments were logical. Currie was the corporate strategist, a conceptual
thinker, and a shrewd manager. Nichol was the consummate marketing
man, with insight into the modern consumer psyche. Even so, Nichol
resented being passed over for the top job.

The corporate power nexus was reflected in office placement
within the Weston Tower. Galen Weston and Currie remained on the
top floor, which could be reached only by private elevator banks. Davidson remained on the eighteenth; Nichol moved down to the ninth floor,
taking over a conference room.

Although Nichol's corporate stature was diminished, his public
profile was about to rise. When it came time to renegotiate Shatner's
contract in 1977, Vickers & Benson held a conference at Niagara-on-
the-Lake. Those present, including former V&B chairman Bill Bremner,
president O'Malley, Gabor Apor, Nichol, and Watt, realized that Shatner was effective in commercials because he differentiated Loblaws from
the other supermarkets. But did they really need him? Perhaps Nichol
could be used as company spokesman. Chicken magnate Frank Perdue
had done it in the United States with his "It takes a tough man to make
a tender chicken" television spot. In the years that followed, everyone
would claim credit for the idea of putting Nichol on television. In fact,
it was Bill Bremner who first suggested that Nichol replace Shatner.
Nichol, of course, agreed.

In the first commercial aired in 1977, Shatner introduced Nichol.
"I want you to hear directly from the president," he told the camera. In
his navy blazer and gray flannels, Nichol was hardly a natural on camera. But his stiff Ivy League demeanor only added to his credibility. He
explained Loblaws' "Save" aisles and promised to lower the shopper's
food bill. "If you were the president, would you go on television to tell

people the prices are competitive, if they weren't?" he asked. When the agency asked focus groups to critique the spots, they discovered that Nichol was only slightly less appealing than Shatner. He scored particularly high on the credibility measure. "His greatest strength is that he never became a natural," Apor said. "People trusted him. They knew he was there to tell them something." Nichol wrote his own thirty-second spots and gave them to Warren Tutton, who oversaw in-house advertising, to polish.

Some thought the exposure and recognition were going to his head. "I'm not David Nichol anymore," he told the *Financial Post* in 1978. "I'm a walking Loblaw logo." His nickname within the industry became Mr. Ego. "The joke," recalls Gabor Apor, "was now that you've put him on television, how are you going to get him off?"

Nichol fixated about ways to bring shoppers into the stores. At one point, he had a supermarket aisle duplicated in his office. He became preoccupied with the metaphysical concept of The Shelf. The traditional methodology of selling Coke, Tide, and Maxwell House coffee below cost to lure customers didn't make sense to him. Why should H.J. Heinz occupy 70% of the facings — the industry term for the number of product fronts the shoppers could see on the shelf — in the ketchup category when it did not generate 70% of a store's profit in the ketchup category. It quickly dawned on him that the supermarket was organized to benefit the manufacturer, not the retailer.

Coffee became a particular obsession. It occupied as much as seventy-five feet of shelf space, yet it was a supermarket dead zone. Many retailers were content to sell Maxwell House or Chock-Full-O-Nuts at cost, simply to bring in shoppers. But if you could sell coffee at a profit, Nichol mused, it could become one of the store's major money-earning categories.

Some of Nichol's schemes to bring customers into the store backfired. Trying to beat Dominion at its own game, he decided to advertise porterhouse steaks — his favorite cut — at $2.99 a pound; the going price was then $4.99. These were the days before meat parts were shipped in boxes; when Loblaw ordered T-bones, it got the remaining carcass. Customers would line up for the product, but the meat department was working overtime, cutting frantically. "It took weeks to get rid of the remaining meat," recalls Bill Clubine, a long-time Loblaw meat buyer. On another occasion, Nichol offered a blade steak special at 99 cents a pound. "We probably killed every cow between Toronto and Moose Jaw," he boasted. "Customers were assaulting one another to get to the meat section."

Later, Nichol took his red 280 SL Mercedes on the road to ask store managers for advice. They explained that fantastic prices were not the answer. Instead, they suggested, maintain good, consistent value; that would inspire loyalty in a way that killer promotions or fantastic prices could not. The fact-finding mission was instructive. "Everyone has something important to tell you," Nichol says. "I don't care whether it's the janitor or the chairman of Marks & Spencer."

Nichol also began weekly meetings, at which heads of the deli, meat, produce, and bakery departments offered opinions and reported on sales, customer responses to advertisements and complaints. Nichol actively solicited their ideas — a novelty at Loblaws. Previous Weston managers had imposed change at the store level without consultation. In his discussions with store managers, Nichol learned that store opera- tions were marred by poor communication. So, in 1978, Nichol built his own in-house advertising department, at a cost of more than $1 million, complete with a studio to shoot commercials and videos. He outfitted supermarkets with televisions and produced weekly show-and-tell videos explaining how to stack fruit and vegetables. By 1979, Loblaw had taken control of all of its advertising.

Control was important to Nichol. Ultimate control, he believed, would come from putting more of their own products on the shelf. "If you own the theater and you're writing the play, you ought to be able to choose the star," he liked to say. By manufacturing its own products, Loblaw could take bigger margins, as much as 5% versus an average of 1.5 to 2%. These were not, of course, the sort of ruminations that would ever win a Nobel prize. But in the conservative supermarket industry, such thoughts were iconoclastic, even profound. Taking on the big brands was consid- ered heresy. "Who ever has been able to outrace the great Campbell or the great Kraft or the great Kellogg or the great Coca-Cola?" wrote Dominion store executive Robert F. Chisholm in *The Darlings*, his 1970 book about the supermarket business.

The concept of retailer house brands was more common in Europe. There, Galen Weston's model had been Marks & Spencer, the British chain founded in 1894 and famed for selling underwear to the Royals. Its popular house-brand label was St. Michael. Weston had acted as an agent for the chain when he was in Ireland and got to know Lord Marcus Sieff, its chairman. Weston's idea was to give Loblaw the identity of a brand in shopper's minds, one that offered unique products or services they could not get anywhere else. In 1976, Weston, Watt, Currie and Nichol made the grand tour of European private labels. They visited Casino and Le Carrefour stores in France. Carrefour had gained retailing fame for being the first supermarket with no-name products. Its *Produit Libre* line, which translated into "brand free," was perceived to offer the same quality as national brands at lower prices. They also visited the Aldi chain in Germany, Migros in Switzerland, and Marks & Spencer, Tesco, and J. Sainsbury in England. (In the United States, Chicago's Jewel Tea was the first chain to launch a generic line — in 1978. These were products with price tags 15% lower on food and 20 to 50% lower on beauty and health items such as toothpaste and toilet paper.)

The Loblaw contingent was only one of many North American supermarket groups making the pilgrimage. The lesson most of them returned with was to put black and white packaging on standard-grade items produced by large manufacturers — often the ends of runs — and sell them for less than the national brands. They were guided solely by cost. The results, however, were often inconsistent and a disappointment to shoppers. "The A&P curse," is how Watt and Nichol dismissively referred to it. Nichol drew a different lesson from the European trip. He saw an opportunity to offer quality on par with the national brands.

To compete with the big name brands, it was necessary to source the products as cheaply as possible. Davidson taught Loblaw executives that procurement represented as much as 80% of the cost of goods sold (the rest was operating expenses), so the smartest way to raise profit margins was to buy goods as cheaply as possible. And a company with the buying clout of Loblaw should take advantage of it. Buying at

Loblaw was carried out under its centralized procurement arms, Inter-save Canada and Intersave U.S.A., which Currie had created in 1975 as part of the restructuring.

In the United States, Intersave's operations were limited by the Robinson-Patman Act, which prohibited volume discounts unless the price reduction could be justified in operations such as packaging or transporta-tion. The goal was to curb the advantage of mass purchases, based on the buyer's size and bargaining power, and to foster competition. In Canada, there were no such limitations. Food retailers commonly joined in buying groups to trigger volume rebates from manufacturers and suppliers. Inter-save capitalized on the buying clout of Weston and charged a fee of 3% to manufacturers. As the head of Intersave, Davidson negotiated contracts with national manufacturers; sourced corporate brands; bought produce, meat, and seafood; and was the liaison between Loblaw Companies and the national marketing boards. Over time, his staff grew to forty-five people.

Nichol's first attempt at a generic line, in the mid-1970s, failed. With Don Watt, he had conceived the idea of a line called Exceptional Value. These were things like large containers of detergent, peanut but-ter, paper towels, and other products, their prices based on special deals engineered by Intersave. The concept sounded great on paper but did not conform to conventional shopping patterns. People went to super-markets with a list and a budget; it was confusing to have to buy some-thing unexpectedly. And most of the stores were still urban. Lugging the food to high-rises posed a real problem.

They took another run at a low-price line the following year with No Name. It was based on a six-point strategy: product selection, qual-ity testing, packaging, advertising, display, and guarantees. Nichol enforced strict quality guidelines. The products used "fancy" rather than "standard" grades of fruits and vegetables. Seventy technicians at Weston's Diversified Lab worked at quality control; professional taste-test panels judged each product. Consensus had to be reached before a product was launched.

Toward the end of the development phase, Nichol learned that arch rival Dominion was also bringing out a line of generics. He was determined to be there first. Early in March 1978, Loblaw got its hands on press proofs of Dominion's advertising campaign. That was on a Thursday. The next day, No Name was given the green light. A week later, sixteen No Name products were launched at 135 stores in Ontario. All were major categories in the supermarket, and staples in the Canadian home: bleach, fabric softener, liquid detergent, baby shampoo, apple and tomato juice, raspberry and strawberry jam, white vinegar, powdered skim milk, ground coffee, tea bags, garbage bags, powdered detergent, toilet paper, and serviettes.

Lower prices were the lure. A twenty-four-ounce jar of No Name raspberry jam cost 95 cents; the same size jar of Kraft Pure Raspberry Jam retailed at $1.87. A forty-eight-ounce tin of No Name tomato juice sold for 55 cents; the same size of Heinz tomato juice was priced at 87 cents. There were some complaints about quality, but generally consumers welcomed the innovation. And, as acceptance grew, prices rose. Dominion followed shortly after with its own generic line of thirty products.

What distinguished No Name in part was its bold, stylish look. Other generic lines were packaged in rudimentary white and black. Watt had been using yellow signage in the store to indicate price reductions. The yellow and black No Name package made sense for practical reasons. Yellow, the most visible color, was also the most irritating to the eye. That color combination had the greatest legibility, followed by green on white, red on white, blue on white, and black on white. Watt selected an uncluttered Helvetica type that was easy to read. The letters, in bold black, were tightly compacted and butted together instead of spaced conventionally. The design shouted from the shelf.

The No Name launch was accompanied by a massive television and billboard campaign — price comparisons, testimonials, sincere straight-in-the-eye messages. Nichol went to television to tell shoppers how much money they could save. He presented two supermarket carts, one filled with No Name products, one with equivalent national brands. The No Name cart was $50 less. He also promised to replace No Name products with the national brand if customers were not satisfied. What Watt and Nichol had not anticipated was what they called the "Mercedes-Benz phenomenon" — the most enthusiastic No Name purchasers were upper middle-class urbanites. Less affluent shoppers, people who depended on taxicabs to travel to and from the grocery store and perhaps were less confident in their taste levels, stuck with national brands.

In August 1978, Rhonda Maxwell, a twenty-eight-year-old Toronto housewife who had started a coupon-clipping club and written a book *Supershopping and You*, wrote to Nichol commending No Name products but complaining about Loblaw's inability to keep them in stock. A few months later, Nichol invited her to lunch. When she declined, explaining that she had children and would need a babysitter, Loblaw dispatched an office secretary to look after the children. At lunch, Nichol proposed that Maxwell become involved in the store ads. She agreed, subject to having script approval. She was then featured in a series of radio, television, and print ads. In the thirty-second TV commercials, Maxwell walked through the store, explaining how to get value from managers' specials, coupons, and No Name products. But according to Maxwell, Nichol did not enjoy sharing the spotlight. Within a few years, Maxwell was gone, joining Global Television as a consumer advocate.

Among those who attended Nichol's initial lunch with Maxwell was his girlfriend and soon-to-be-wife, a Loblaw secretary named Terri Gravenor. When they met in 1975, he was the president of the supermarket chain and she was a receptionist in the executive suite — blonde, petite, and very pretty. Like Nichol, she had a failed first marriage behind her. Unlike Nichol, she had children, a daughter, Leigh, then six, and a son, Michael, still a toddler. Although she had set her sights on Nichol, he believed himself to be the pursuer. For months, Nichol dogged her with the same intensity he brought to his work. Every Friday, he would ask her out for that weekend. Every Friday, she said no. Finally, he asked her out on a Wednesday; she said yes.

On their first date, he took her to Noodles, a once-fashionable, now-defunct, Italian restaurant in downtown Toronto. He ordered. She didn't have a clue what the pesto and carpaccio on her plate was. Her own kitchen cupboard contained Kraft Dinner. Inevitably, food became a central theme in their courtship. Nichol played the *bec fin*, introducing her to the gastronomical world. They took cooking classes together. They attended Robert Mondavi's cooking school in the Napa Valley. In time, Terri became a skilled cook and an accomplished baker. "One of the best pastry chefs in the world," Nichol would say of her, when he was feeling generous. To illustrate how far she had come, he would playfully deride a dessert concoction she had made for him when they were dating — frozen blueberries and Cool Whip.

They moved in together, although their romance was kept quiet within Loblaw. Nichol's mother objected to the arrangement. Terri was not entirely happy either. She felt frozen out by his family. One day in November 1978, Nichol came home and surprised her with plane tickets to Hawaii. He had planned everything. They were married at the Mauna Kea resort on the island of Hawaii.

Afterwards, Terri left Loblaw to become the Wife, the behind-the-scenes helpmate, and public necessity. The Wife who planned dinner parties, instructed gardeners, attended to details. The Wife who was free to travel and at her husband's side when he won awards or gave speeches. The Wife who, in aid of President's Choice, worked in the kitchen of Toronto's Picolit Restaurant, flew to New York for food styling courses, and apprenticed in France for several weeks at Troisgros.

His wife, Nichol often acknowledged, also played an active role in product development. When his own people couldn't get a recipe to his liking, Nichol would take it home for Terri to fiddle with. She accepted the fact that people either loved or hated her husband. An unflaggingly loyal ambassador, she was invaluable in other ways as well, sharing his enthusiasms, calling people he had upset to smooth things over, and providing support when he fell, as he frequently did, into black moods.

A kind, soft-spoken woman with an enthusiastic presence, Terri Nichol projects a steely survivor's edge that makes her at once empathetic and wary. She watches carefully and pays attention. With her children away at boarding schools, she had been free to accompany Nichol on his travels, becoming a trusted second opinion. Over the years, she had acquired a more polished, sophisticated demeanor. Her hair was blonder, her skin more tan, her body more aerobicized. She dressed to please her husband, who liked to see women in white or black — preferably, in impeccably tailored black suits with a short skirt and pearls, the Catherine-Deneuve-in-*Belle-du-Jour* look. She also learned to deal with his mercurial, domineering temperament, his penchant for cruel teasing, his tendency to dismiss. People who socialized with the couple noted her ability to handle him. "He would dominate the conversation if he had his way," says one prominent Toronto chef. "But she knows how to talk about what she wants to talk about. I've seen her shut him down." In fact, friends and colleagues agree that Terri had managed to neutralize Dave Nichol's acidity. She always calls him David — never Dave. "Terri brought balance into his life," says Russ Rudd, Loblaw's in-house art director. "She has mellowed him."

The same year that the Nichols married, 1978, Garfield Weston died — at age eighty. Nichol had been fond of him, closer to him perhaps than he had been with his own father. Weston had once given him a Patek Phillipe watch with a leather strap, which he liked to show off proudly and rarely took off.

That year, Loblaw announced its first dividend payout in several years. It was on its way to challenging Dominion's supremacy. The next year, Loblaw Companies actually turned a profit — $43 million on sales of $5.4 billion. The success of No Name in 1978 created the impetus for No Frills stores — yellow and black painted outlets that devoted 60 to 70% of their stock to the No Name line. Smaller unprofitable stores were repackaged on this model, based on the German Aldi chain, which sold only house-brand products. Merchandise was kept in cartons to keep labor costs down. The stores also sold bulk food — a new wrinkle for Canadian shoppers who liked everything hermetically sealed. No Frills was overseen by David Stewart, Loblaw's vice-president of merchandising, and by John Lederer and Michael Bregman.

Lederer and Bregman both fit the brash-but-bright young man profile Nichol liked so much. Bregman, who would later found upscale fast-food outlets Michel's Baguettes, mmmmmuffins, and Second Cup, had been recruited by Nichol from Harvard Business School. Lederer, who would move his way up the Loblaw ladder to become an executive vice-president of Loblaw Supermarkets and National Grocers, was discovered by Nichol in a sporting goods store in 1975, while studying economics at university. Nichol, who had never skied before, was buying skiing equipment. "Turn me into an Olympic skier," he told Lederer.

He was so impressed with the young man that he invited him to interview for a summer job. When Lederer showed up several weeks later, Nichol had his leg in a cast. He had broken it on the first run.

Nichol became convinced that the No Frills approach had applications well beyond the world of supermarkets. "If a Canadian politician ever packages no-frills government and then communicates its value to the Canadian consumer," he said in an address to the Advertising and Sales Club of Toronto in 1978, "he or she will be overwhelmed by the vast untapped electorate that they'll find waiting for them."

In the spring of 1982, Nichol and Davidson set up an international arm of Intersave called International Trade. The idea, again, was to eliminate intermediary brokers; Loblaw buyers would purchase directly from offshore suppliers. Davidson spent two months in China obtaining an exclusive distribution contract from the Chinese government to import mandarin oranges. In return, Loblaw agreed to provide technical advice, packaging, and markets. Davidson also designed a complex deal to import products from Yugoslavia through airplane manufacturer McDonnell Douglas.

One of the International division's first recruits was Andy Wallace, a young man who had worked with Davidson and Doug Lunau as a broker of No Name products to the Caribbean. Wallace's family had longstanding ties to Loblaw. His great-grandfather was J. Milton Cork, one of the founders of Loblaw Groceterias. His grandfather had been president of Loblaw before Garfield Weston acquired the company. Soon, Wallace was closing deals for olive oils from Italy, jams from France, balsamic vinegar from Italy. He and Nichol often traveled together to international food shows.

Every year, Nichol and a few Intersave buyers traveled to the Sial and Anuga food shows in Europe and the ISM candy and cookie show in Cologne. They secured rights for a lingonberry sauce from Denmark, Boda glassware from Sweden, matzoh and jaffa oranges from Israel. Some products did not move, among them a lemon-cheese butter from England and a twenty-five-year-old sherry vinegar from Spain. By 1988, the division was importing more than $30 million worth of goods and was the largest offshore importer in Canada.

Direct access to imported products gave Loblaw a unique edge over its competition. It also helped lay the foundation on which the upscale President's Choice line would be built. The idea for a premium house brand — or No Name gourmet, as Nichol and Watt referred to it — was born in 1983. It was the result of the success of the President's Blend coffee in the stores. President's Blend had been created as a promotional item to be given out to suppliers. Nichol had insisted that the mix be modeled after the coffee served at the Three Smalls Rooms in the Windsor Arms Hotel, then regarded as one of Toronto's best restaurants. He thought that most coffee sold in supermarkets was without taste, mud-like. "Maxwell House and General Foods produced rubbish," he says. On Nichol's orders, President's Blend contained the more aromatic Arabica coffee bean, rather than the somewhat bitter Robusta bean found in most instant coffees.

The coffee was a huge success and a confirmation to Nichol that the tastes of the average consumer were changing. As the economy strengthened, consumers wanted to trade up to better products. Increasingly, shoppers were eager to know the difference between Robusta and Arabica beans. Moreover, they were willing to pay a premium for what they believed to be a superior product.

And it was not only coffee. To a more affluent middle class, food itself became a measure of status. Suddenly, MBAs were literate in the declensions of lettuces. Gourmet, a term once reserved for disciples of Julia Child, became a common adjective. The term "foodie" was coined by the British magazine *Harpers & Queen* in 1982 to describe people who elevated food to the realm of art, on a par with painting or drama.

Nichol set about mastering foodism with the same diligence he had applied to his academic studies. He became a three-star restaurant junkie, cultivating influential maître d's and owners. He pushed his way into the kitchen of the Four Seasons in New York to inquire about recipes. He read, took cooking classes, learned who was who. His travel itineraries were plotted around restaurants. "If that restaurant isn't open on Thursday night, I won't go to Belgium," he'd tell his secretary. When Michael Bregman married in 1978, Nichol gave him two first-class plane tickets to Paris, complete with a map marking the three-star restaurants he and his wife should eat at and an itemized list of the dishes they should order.

With some justification, he came to regard himself as the gourmet of the group. He had worked his way through Julia Child's *Mastering the Art of French Cooking* in the sixties and had prepared soufflé aux blancs d'oeufs, farce aux rognons, sauté de veau marengo, and poulet en gelée a l'estragon. He had come a long way since the meal that Galen Weston remembers him preparing in 1973, a rendition of steak in a wine-mushroom sauce. "Not exactly gourmet," Weston recalled.

Nichol worked at his image. In 1978, the *Financial Post Magazine* published a picture of Nichol in his kitchen wearing a Ziggy's Fantastic Foods apron. "Food is my passion," he exclaimed. The article included Nichol's recipe for zucchini spaghetti with pesto, borrowed from the Four Seasons in New York.

Others had to share his passion. He sent his secretary, Anne Marie Halliday, to study at the Bonnie Stern cooking school in Toronto; the office frequently received calls asking about recipes, and he wanted her to be knowledgeable. He presented her with subscriptions to food magazines and gave her a Cuisinart and professional cooking knives for Christmas. When she traveled with her husband, Nichol would suggest restaurants and demand that she bring him the bill. She also looked for foods he might like to feature. It was Halliday, for example, who discovered Cox's orange pippin apples in England.

Nichol was obsessed with finding "the best." He became frustrated when his impeccable standards were not met. He demanded that fresh flowers be placed in marble planters in his office and had temper tantrums if they were not arranged to his taste. In the mid-1970s, Nichol and Gabor Apor of Vickers & Benson flew to Milan. Apor was unable to get first-class seats, a situation he knew would upset Nichol. As a compromise, Apor wrangled the front seats in the economy section so Nichol would not have to look at the back of someone's head. Recalling an article that discussed how *New York Times* food writer Craig Claiborne liked to travel, Apor packed a picnic basket with pâtés and cheeses so Nichol wouldn't have to partake of mediocre fare during the flight.

Cost was of no consequence to Nichol when it came to pursuing the finest. He and Terri would frequently take weekend jaunts to California or New York. Often, he'd show up for the regular Monday morning staff meeting with new products. One day, he tossed a bag at Paul Futtrup, the director of Loblaw bakeries in Ontario. "See if you can make this," he said. The bag contained something called "crunch" buns he had tasted at a hotel in Santa Barbara. Futtrup tried repeatedly but could not reproduce the texture. Nichol suggested that he call the hotel to talk to the chef. He did; still no crunch. Nichol then told him to fly the chef up. And so the chef came, a Mexican who spoke no English. For three days, Futtrup learned how to make the buns. They were perfect. But freshness was part of their perfection, and freshness did not last on the shelf. The cost of indulging such explorations was enormous, but Nichol did not care.

During one trip to California, Nichol came across *Insider's Report*, a 7 1/2-by-10-inch flyer, styled like a comic book and printed on newsprint. The *Report* was published by Trader Joe's, a small chain of Los Angeles-area grocery stores started in 1966 by California businessman Joe Coulombe. Catering to well-traveled, educated shoppers, Trader Joe's offered wine and liquor at discounts, Camembert laced with basil, Vienna roast coffee beans, copper cookware, pistachios in bulk, and photo finishing. Coulombe designed his *Insider's Report* in the format of popular consumer reports, but tempered with cartoons and jokes. The title was a double entendre, alluding to both the stock market and the stomach. But it also appealed to the post-Nixon sensibility that another reality existed beneath the surface.

Aimed at food sophisticates, the *Report* did not mention cigarettes or Coca-Cola. Instead, it flogged walnut oil from California for salads, yeast and garlic wafers for dogs, barrel-fermented Chardonnay for $2.99 a bottle, yogurt candy peanut clusters, synthetic Vitamin E capsules, Kiss My Face Olive Oil soap, salsa from Mexico for 49 cents a tin, whole-wheat tortillas, and eaux de vie fruit brandies from Europe for $9.99.

Nichol and Terri met Coulombe at the faculty club of the California Institute of Technology in Pasadena in the spring of 1983. They immediately struck a deal. Nichol bought the *Insider's Report* name and format for $25,000 (U.S.). Coulombe continued to issue his report but changed its name to *The Fearless Flyer*. Nichol published his first issue — *Dave Nichol's Insider's Report* — in November 1983. He wrote the copy. The cover featured Nichol in a business suit holding his French bulldog, Georgie Girl, in a Santa Claus hat, her ears sticking out. Nichol proclaimed on page one that he had "searched the world for unique values that will make your holiday season more exciting and save you money."

The sixteen-page flyer was unlike anything that had ever come out of a Canadian supermarket. What people expected from supermarkets were promotions with discount coupons for national brands, not information about food. By its second issue, Loblaw was besieged by people asking when the next installment would be ready.

Nichol broadened the scope to appeal to the mass market but did not tamper with Coulombe's format. The pages were dense with copy blocks, filled with recipes, explanations, special promotions, and cartoons. Nichol liked to call it *Consumer Reports* crossed with *Mad* magazine. Regardless, the publication established his role as food savant. A mythology was created about Nichol himself — small-town farm boy turned food connoisseur, emissary of the common man in an endless search to procure the best for the mass market. In the pages of the *Report*, Nichol shared with readers his life of consumption: the expensive hotels and restaurants he had visited, the memorable meals he had eaten, the food luminaries he had met. It was access to a privileged circuit otherwise inaccessible to most of his readers.

Included in the first edition was a coupon deal that Davidson had secured for Häagen-Dazs ice cream. If shoppers bought four cartons, they got another one free. "I am personally addicted to Häagen-Dazs Strawberry," Nichol wrote, "and I once had lunch with Reuben Matters, the man who founded Häagen-Dazs." (Either Nichol's memory was faulty or the typesetters were; the ice cream's founder was Reuben Mattus.) "He explained to me the secret of their strawberry ice cream was that they select all of their strawberries from one grower in Washington State."

Elsewhere in that issue, Nichol described his first encounter with St. André cheese "as a religious experience. It was at the Troisgros Brothers Restaurant in Roanne, France (without doubt the greatest

restaurant in the world). They wheeled up two tables of cheese. I chose
several small ash-covered rounds of Chevre and the waiter suggested a
'Soupcon of St. André.' I tasted it. It was love at 'first bite.'"

The *Report* offered all-butter croissants and a recipe for a Bellini,
a peach nectar and champagne concoction from the famed Harry's Bar
in Venice, made with Yoga brand peach nectar. It promoted a soap
inspired by a lemon glycerine soap Nichol had tried at the Berkeley Hotel
in London; Big Eye Tuna, from California ("the best I've ever tasted");
and Art Keller's cheesecake from Buffalo ("the best I've ever tasted").

Buoyed by the success of the *Insider's Report*, Nichol appeared to
be riding high. Behind the scenes, however, internecine conflict ruled.
Nichol's increasing visibility irritated some senior executives. It was
rumored that an advertising campaign had been leaked to Dominion to
embarrass him. And despite all the hoop-la, the performance of stores in
the highly competitive Ontario market had been flat, even slipping
slightly. Nichol and Currie were engaged in a kind of sibling rivalry.
Nichol resented the fact that Galen Weston had given Currie more
power; Currie knew that Weston's bond with Nichol was closer.

All through the fall of 1984, there was talk of change within the
Weston Tower. The announcement was made on December 6: Dave
Nichol was out as president of Loblaw Supermarkets, replaced by David
Stewart, his vice-president of merchandising. Nichol became president
of Loblaw International Merchants, a newly formed division that would
develop corporate brands and publish the *Insider's Report.*

It was Currie, not Weston, who broke the news to Nichol who
was furious and hurt, though it was not his style to complain. He knew
he was being sidelined. Terri played the ever-supportive role, telling him
that the change would allow them to travel more. It would permit him
to concentrate on what he did best. He was not a pure numbers man,
and that was what was required to supervise the expanding grocery
chain. Nichol, too, was able to rationalize the move. He would be more
a tastemaker, less a businessman.

Yet there was the unescapable fact that repositioning had
removed his bottom-line responsibility, which within the Loblaw culture symbolized corporate castration. It also put Nichol outside the

executive loop and was seen within the industry as a shift that would reduce his power. "A kick upstairs," was how one industry analyst described it. Nichol was taken off television. Currie told associates, "Sometimes you have to cut people's legs off at the knees, just to show them who is boss." Within the company, there was speculation that Galen Weston had really wanted to get rid of his old college buddy, but could not. Nichol was too entrenched as the public face of the chain. He got on people's nerves, perhaps, but they had come to trust him.

Creating Loblaw International Merchants was just one prong of Currie's strategy of diversifying geographically, creating larger store formats, and cultivating shopper loyalty. Nichol's role would be to win that loyalty, to bring shoppers into the store. Tucked away on the ninth floor, Currie reasoned, Nichol would occupy himself with packaging fancy jams and knock-offs of Kraft Dinner. Currie himself would turn to more important issues, such as controlling costs and his new pet project — monster supercombo formats in Canada and the United States. These stores, which often exceeded 100,000 square feet, were four times the size of an average supermarket and cost about $10 million to run annually, double the cost of conventional stores. One-third of their merchandise was devoted to higher-margin non-food items.

What Currie did not know — and never could have predicted — was that his attempt to rein in Dave Nichol that December was doomed to failure. Instead of shuffling him to obscurity, Currie had given Nichol the stage to reinvent the supermarket itself and, in the process, to become a household name. Years later, when Currie was asked by a colleague whether he had any regrets, he replied, "There's only one thing I would do differently. December 1984."

CHAPTER THREE

LOST IN THE SUPERMARKET

T he entire history of civilization is written on the shelves of the supermarket. It can be often difficult to read, amid the harsh fluorescent lighting, the stacks of hermetically sealed packaging, and the odorless, stagnant, temperature-controlled air. There, in those garish, joyless surroundings, the careful observer can still catch sight of primitive lessons passed on through time. There, one can appreciate the necessity that found the meat inside a walnut's shell; the imagination that thought to harness oil from the olive; and the inspiration that produced the miracle of bread. There are also reminders of other core ethics of Western society, a primary one being the fact that it is acceptable to take the life of another animal in order to sustain one's own. The supermarket is also a showcase of more recent technological marvels that duplicate the formation of ice crystals and create unpronounceable chemicals that serve as life support for artificial food.

Although the supermarket is hardly a conventional setting for tragic or comic opera, the scale of human emotion that echoes through its aisles on any given day — hope and fear, joy and sadness, hunger and satisfaction — is worthy of the Broadway stage. It was while shopping in the supermarket, the *New York Times* reported in 1992, that a woman named Peggy Morrison first began to comprehend the loss of her husband, who went missing in action in Viet Nam. Seeing a couple standing hand and hand, deciding what type of cereal to buy, Mrs. Morrison was unable to proceed. She unloaded her cart, item by item, ran to her car, and fell on the steering wheel, weeping. There are also the many poignant stories of East European immigrants, newly arrived in America, who make their first pilgrimage to their local supermarket and stand mesmerized at the cornucopia they behold. Completely confounded by choices they had never before been forced to make, they are utterly unable to choose — and often leave without making a single purchase.

For most people, though, the supermarket is not wondrous. It is commonplace, an uncontemplated obligation. The Food Marketing Institute, the Washington-based industry group that keeps track of industry statistics, defines a supermarket as a food store with annual sales of more than $2 million. By this definition, in 1994 there were 34,400 supermarkets in the United States and 7,034 in Canada. The Institute and similar agencies serve as quasi-historians of supermarket culture, offering insight into the significant, yet often ignored, role the supermarket plays in modern life. They report, for instance, that more than half the food eaten in North American homes is bought at the supermarket; that close to 97% of Canadian households shopped in supermarkets an average of two times a week; that of the $185 billion Canadians spent in retail stores in 1993, just over 26% or $48.5 billion is spent on food; that shoppers in the United States spent $359 billion (U.S.) on food bought in supermarkets in 1993.

The supermarket was inevitable, the result of concentrated urbanization, the automobile, refrigeration, vacuum-packing, and other technological breakthroughs. An impersonal link in the food chain, the supermarket is an anonymous, clinical place, where food is processed, packaged, shrink-wrapped, stickered, and shelved — alienated from its natural sources. It is the natural habitat of non-dairy creamers, Kool-Aid, Cheez Whiz, and Tang. It is a business that calls lettuce not wrapped in plastic "naked."

Supermarket culture creates artificial and unrealistic expectations. Not only does food seem to be limitless in supply, it also appears unnaturally flawless. Tomatoes are shipped green and gassed with carbon dioxide during transport, which renders them red but tasteless. Oranges are injected with dye to appear more orange. Fruit and vegetables are waxed for display. Chickens are deboned, shrimp peeled and deveined, fish beheaded. Nature has been all but banned; the supermarket of the latter part of the twentieth century is a high-profit harbor for carcinogenic fruit sprays, sulfites, nitrites, and other chemicals that make modern eating a minefield.

Supermarket shoppers have become inured to the artificial and the ersatz. The top five sales categories in Canadian supermarkets in 1993 were flavored soft drinks ($1.6 billion), snack foods ($743 million), cigarettes ($727 million), ready-to-eat cereals ($625 million), and packaged cookies ($395 million). Predictably, there was a correlation between the biggest spenders in media advertising and the top sellers in the supermarkets. The largest media categories in 1993, as defined by A.C. Nielsen Marketing Research, were ready-to-eat cereals, flavored soft drinks, chocolate bars, cold remedies, and gum.

The fastest-growing supermarket categories in 1993 were razors, Mexican sauce, pre-moistened towelettes, flat water, and frozen breakfast entrées. In 1993, the five most popular products based on dollar sales were Kraft Thins Singles cheese slices, Maxwell House Jar instant coffee, Kraft Cheez Whiz, Nestlé's Carnation evaporated milk, and Kellogg's corn flakes.

The antiseptic atmosphere of most big grocery stores is so pervasive that urban North Americans are amazed by food sold in its more natural forms. North American tourists to London stand with their mouths agape when they first encounter Harrod's famous Food Hall with its hanging unplucked game; imported fruit and nuts in traveling crates; fish, not in battered frozen fish sticks, but with their heads on; and blood oranges from Spain. Tourists visiting open-air markets in villages in France return with tales of open containers of fresh oysters and mussels, cheeses wrapped in grape leaves, freshly killed and plucked chickens.

The history of the supermarket both mirrored and advanced the evolution of modern consumer society. Its precursor was the cash-and-carry grocery store, started by food-trading companies that won discounts by buying in large quantities. The Great Atlantic and Pacific Tea Company, more familiarly known as A&P, led the way in 1859 in New York City. By 1890, there were ninety-five A&Ps strung out from Boston to Milwaukee, selling staples such as coffee, tea, bread, and canned goods under the Quaker Maid brand name at a fraction of the price of the big national brands.

Self-serve was introduced in 1916 in Memphis, Tennessee, by Clarence Saunders at a store called Piggly Wiggly. Shoppers entered through a turnstile, walked with a wicker basket through the aisles stocked with 605 items, and paid at the cashier. The concept of self-serve set the foundation for the fundamental consumer tenets of choice and convenience. It also created the need for food packaging. Biscuits, sugar, flour, and pickles, which had been sold in open barrels or bins, now needed to be packaged, and the package had to display information about price, size, and ingredients, information that previously had been provided by clerks. Hence, self-serve radically transformed the dynamic between shopper and store owner. With a standardized package, the shopper could no longer haggle for a better price. The trust formerly placed in the shopkeeper was transferred to the manufacturer and the package.

The first supermarket to establish the contemporary format was opened in Jamaica, Long Island, in 1930 by Michael Cullen, a former employee of A&P and Kroger Grocery. King Kullen stores eliminated decorative frills, sold national brands at lower markups, added meat and dairy departments, provided free parking, and advertised itself as the World's Greatest Price Wrecker. Cullen opened twenty supermarkets, ranging in size from 5,000 to 10,000 square feet, each carrying 1,100 items. Small grocery chains tried to get newspapers to refuse King Kullen advertising, but failed.

In the 1930s, when supermarkets were in their infancy, most operators were independents. Increasingly, however, size triumphed. Chains, which could buy in quantity and eliminate middlemen, undercut smaller competitors. The independent grocer became an anachronism as the leading chains dictated merchandise, display, prices, and employee and consumer policies.

The industry is not known for innovation. In fact, major developments in North American supermarkets over the next sixty years can be counted on one hand. In 1968, Jack Hooley opened Power Alley, the first discount warehouse store in the Minneapolis suburb of Fridley. Power Alley's aisles were lined two stories high with cartons of products. Hooley dispensed with all decor and most service, except in the meat department. In return for lower prices, customers were expected to make compromises and to bag their own groceries.

The supermarket industry in Canada gained momentum following World War I. Canadians had become used to buying groceries from the T. Eaton Company retail chain. The Loblaw Groceterias and Dominion chains were founded in 1919. In 1927, A&P entered the Canadian market in Montreal. The chain opened stores in Toronto in 1929.

There have been creative iconoclasts in the business, but they were rare. U.S. store owner Stew Leonard gained celebrity for the fun, rustic, Disneyland-like atmosphere at Stew Leonard stores in Norwalk and Danbury, Connecticut, which are still thriving. Shoppers followed a path that snaked past the in-store bakery, fish shop, vegetable stands, and deli counters. Country music blasted over speakers, while mechanical chickens, cows, and fruit entertained. Another innovator was Joe Coulombe, from whom Nichol bought the idea for the *Insider's Report*.

The fact that profit margins are the lowest of any industry demands that the supermarket business be cutthroat and competitive. Net margins after tax average between 0.5% and 2%, with the higher percentages going to independent operators who have lower sales and revenues. Such slim margins dictate that supermarket operators concentrate on costs, more than product, to operate efficiently. A strike or increased wage demands from unionized workers can decimate profits. Supermarket owners also demand that every cost be carefully calculated. This is a business in which nothing is arbitrary.

Supermarkets are divided and subdivided into zones known as categories, each with its own manager and profit expectations. One manager is in charge of grocery items, segmented into dry goods, canned goods, frozen food, and so on. Another will cover dairy, another meat, another baked goods, another produce, another the deli section.

On average, a supermarket expects to earn an average gross profit (that is, profit before taxes and administrative and sales costs) of 30% on the total products it sells. This profitability, referred to simply as "margin," varies from section to section. Money made is quantified in pennies and dollars per cubic foot of shelf space. Certain aspects of the supermarket defy business logic. For example, it is the only business in the world where prices drop when demand rises. At Thanksgiving and Christmas, stores compete to see who can sell turkeys at the greatest loss. Products sold this way are known as loss leaders. It is assumed that the profits lost on the loss leader, which draws customers into the store, are made up in other categories.

Staples such as milk, butter, eggs, and sugar that serve to routinely bring people into the store are sold at lower margins, from 10 to 15%, although Canadian supermarkets generally receive handsome allowances from dairies to stock their products. The highest markups in the store are on "non-food" or "general merchandise" items, things such as cigarettes, cleaning products, shampoo, and garbage bags. Margins on these items frequently exceed 30%. Canned goods and frozen foods, popular super-market staples, also provide high margins, as do items such as paper tow-els and olives. The idea is to have a minimum of strategic, necessary items sold at low prices to lure traffic — the industry term for shoppers — and maximum high prices on everything else to increase profit. To this end, retailers depend on what they call "impressionable" items, products that the shoppers have grown to like and trust. Products deemed to be "impressionable" included Campbell's soup, Kellogg's corn flakes, Coca-Cola, and Scott's paper towels. Store owners know that if they put these items on special, they will provide great drawing power.

The supermarket owner is essentially a landlord who rents out shelf space to the highest bidder. Typically, manufacturers pay many different types of "allowances" to get their products on the shelf, to get shoppers to notice them and embark on the steps to brand loyalty: prod-uct awareness, acceptance, preference, and finally fidelity to that prod-uct. The price a manufacturer pays to get a product on the shelf is known as a "listing allowance." The more facings a product has, the more a manufacturer pays the store. There are no standard listing fees; it is up to each store manager. "You get as much as you can," says one long-time grocery executive, pretty much summing up the governing principle of the business. In addition to listing fees, a company launch-ing a new product can also be asked to pay a "slotting fee," which guar-antees space in a retailer's warehouses. Companies with their own distribution network and direct sales force can avoid this cost.

Supermarkets set the selling price of all products and each manager has authority over how shelves are stocked. Small independent manufacturers can avoid listing fees if their product is in demand. Retailers also tend not to charge listing allowances to suppliers of the store's own private-label products. But stores that sell private-label products, for instance, might choose to list only the number two brand in the category if the number two manufacturer is willing to pay more to keep the number one brand off the shelves.

Other money paid by suppliers that exceeds basic listing costs is known euphemistically as "over and aboves." Supermarket lore abounds with tales of suppliers offering under-the-table incentives in the form of cash, season tickets for baseball and hockey, even Caribbean cruises, to get store owners to stock products and "delist" the competition.

The dynamic of the supermarket is not complex. Clout rules. The most powerful supermarkets can demand and receive more money for shelf space; the more powerful manufacturers can afford to pay the most for preferred positions and promotions. It is a system that perpetuates the status quo.

If an item does not move, or "turn," in keeping with a category manager's expectations, it is delisted. One turn means that an item is purchased, restocked, and reshelved once. Turn expectations vary, depending on the category. Fresh produce is expected to turn weekly, more perishable produce such as lettuce are expected to turn daily. The total inventory of a supermarket is expected to turn thirty times, on average, annually.

Because such small margins do not allow stores to compete by radically lowering prices, most supermarkets compete through marketing. Suppliers are expected to share, if not subsidize, marketing costs through what is known as "promotional allowances." Promotions take different forms — placing the product in coveted end-of-aisle displays, a special in-store display on the shelf, sale stickers to announce a reduced price, or media advertising. Items featured as special products can multiply sales rates by eight times.

It became common industry practice for grocers to put aside

excess product bought at discount from the supplier, then sell it at regular prices when the supplier's promotion ended and pocket the difference. Not all the money paid by manufacturers and the like was accounted for. According to *The Economist* magazine, as much as one-third of promotional money paid to retailers went not to pay for flyers but into someone's pocket.

Since bargain prices are a major draw to consumers, retailers often lean on suppliers for discounts. Big manufacturers often pay what is known as "sliding-scale volume allowances" on high-volume items on which the costs are reduced after established sales levels have been achieved.

Prices are carefully calculated. It was once industry convention to end prices in a nine, the thinking being that the shopper would perceive $3.99 to be much cheaper than $4.00. Then the magic number switched to eight, then to five. The practice of multi-pricing — offering goods at two for 29 cents or four for 99 cents, for example — induces people to stockpile. Prices for staples such as milk, eggs, and meat are generally known to consumers and do not vary much. Store owners have more latitude to manipulate the prices of goods shoppers do not buy as often — spices, olives, and mustards; these can be altered by as much as a dime without shoppers noticing. In the industry, this is known as "chain-store wizardry."

Most supermarket owners have followed certain rules of design, as if supermarket shopping were a tribal ritual. The entrance is crucial, as it sets the tone. A shrewd grocer knows his customer and the demographics of the surrounding neighborhood and manipulates displays accordingly. No matter where the store is located, however, high-margin goods — candy, plants, and produce — are usually placed close to the front door. The supermarket shopper is one of the most closely observed species alive, and studies have shown that nearly three-quarters of shoppers cruise the perimeter before they probe the aisles. This is the first pass, taken while the budget is still intact and before fatigue sets in. Most stores stock popular and higher-margin products (produce, meat, baked goods, deli items, dairy, frozen foods) along this perimeter. The task for the store owner is to expose shoppers to as many items per pass as possible, without wearing them out. Dairy items are often placed at the back, forcing people through the store. The coveted end display areas are often used for specials and to sell off surplus inventories.

The ideal position for a product on a shelf or display counter is eye level. One study indicated that the same four items sold 63% more during a two-week period after being raised from waist to eye level, 78% more when raised from floor to eye level. The exception is food that appealed to children, such as sugar-drenched cereals. Then the canny manager would lower the product to within a child's plane of vision. Products stocked at aisle ends, known as gondolas, also have an advantage, since shoppers clearly notice the display when negotiating the turn with their buggy.

As the supermarket evolved, items were organized to encourage the purchase of related goods in different categories. Salad dressing is placed with lettuce, for example, straws are located by soft drinks and juices, pacifiers next to baby food, pizza cutters with the frozen pizzas. Impulse items such as candy, cigarettes, magazines are placed by checkouts, in part to tempt shoppers while they stand in line, in part to deter shoplifters.

Historically, the supermarket has been a woman's domain, an extension of the traditional role within the family. According to the Food Marketing Institute, in 1993 women still took responsibility as the primary shopper. For women who remained at home, the supermarket, with its hygienically packaged goods, reinforced the isolation of their lives, as they moved from home to car to supermarket.

After World War II, food was increasingly designed to appeal to women who had less space and time for cooking. In 1946, Gold Medal flour introduced the revolutionary one-bowl cake, along with the superfluous requirement to add an egg; this gratified the cook's residual impulse to be involved. Women, motivational researcher Ernst Dichter had demonstrated, wanted to feel as if they were actively participating in the baking process. With technological advances such as canning, refrigeration, and frozen foods (made possible by a patented process for quick freezing perfected by Clarence Birdseye in 1923), cooking became assembly rather than creation.

In the 1940s, convenience foods began to flood the market. In

1946, French's instant potatoes and General Food's Minute Rice were introduced. The following year, Minute Maid frozen juice concentrate debuted in supermarket freezers. The arrival of television, in the mid-1940s, had a profound influence on marketing and food consumption. Bing Crosby flogged Minute Maid orange juice, the "Jackie Gleason Show" was sponsored by Nescafé, and the "Ed Sullivan Show" was interrupted by recipes from Kraft. In 1954, Swanson introduced its first TV dinner—turkey and corn bread dressing, peas and whipped sweet potatoes. The first cartons even simulated the design of television sets. By the end of the decade, TV dinners made up an astonishing 10% of the food sold in supermarkets. Television also helped create the children's market. In 1965, Spaghetti-Os, the first food aimed at children, was introduced.

More than any other retail outlet, the supermarket came to be seen as a showcase of the American way of life. Queen Elizabeth requested a tour of one during a visit to the United States in 1957. Two years later, then Soviet premier Nikita Krushchev also asked to see the monument to American prosperity and free market ideology. "Beyond their impact on consumers," said *Life* magazine in 1958, "supermarkets are having even more far-reaching effects. As their bright display and mass-selling fill old demands at lower prices, they also create new demands, thereby creating new agriculture, new industry — and new living standards." The supermarket came to be the great equalizer, a place visited by the rich and poor, the young and old, the fat and thin, the blue collar and white collar.

Well-stocked supermarkets represent the fruit of a developed, industrialized society. Most urban North Americans unquestioningly frequent stores that offer tens of thousands of products, a seemingly limitless number of choices. It was considered normal that shoppers should be able to select from a hundred kinds of cereal, twenty-two types of deodorant (differentiated for women, men, and teenagers), twenty-five kinds of coffee, nineteen flavors of ice cream, an eighty-foot wall of pet food, fourteen flavors of yogurt, eleven types of Bick's pickles, and sixteen kinds of diapers.

Such displays perpetuate the belief that resources are limitless. They are also predicated on the assumption that everything is constantly subject to improvement, that "new and improved" is a virtue. Choices have escalated over the decades. Supermarkets in the 1940s offered 2,000 to 3,000 items; by the 1990s, shoppers confronted 25,000 products in the average supermarket and well over 30,000 items in the larger format stores, which averaged between 60,000 and 100,000 square feet in floor space.

The sheer number of products fosters the false illusion among shoppers that they are being presented with greater choice and thus greater freedom. Yet there is little breadth in these decisions. The shopper in 1994 might decide between several different formulas of Crest toothpaste (regular, mint, gel, tartar-fighting, and so on) in a dozen varieties of sizes and containers. But one had to ask whether the basic product was significantly better than the single formula in three sizes offered to the shopper in 1955. Did selecting from unscented, unscented with bleach, ultra, superconcentrated, or liquid detergent reduce the drudgery of clothes washing? Probably not, yet such choices offered the illusion of control and the assertion of individuality.

Unlimited choice — the hallmark of civilized democracy in the late 1950s — became a narcotic. Bombarded by advertisements and a confusing array of choices, the synapses of shoppers had shut down. According to the U.S Association of National Advertisers, Americans in the late 1980s were watching an average of 5,600 commercial messages a week. *Progressive Grocer* reported that 42% of shoppers took five seconds or less to make a choice. Most buying decisions were made on the spot, based on pricing and the visceral pull of the package. Loyalty to brand names had eroded.

By the 1980s, it became possible to decipher intimate details about someone's life by peering into his or her shopping cart. One could discern whether he or she had allergies or was lactose intolerant; was worried about cholesterol, fat, and fiber; or was anxious about tartar build-up on his or her teeth. At the checkout counter, one could determine marital and social status, economic circumstances, family composition, body image, ethnic background, sleeping patterns, health concerns, nutritional knowledge, taste preferences, television viewing habits — even political leanings.

Shoppers paid dearly for the luxury of choice. According to the Food Marketing Institute, almost 20,000 new products were launched in North America in 1991. Of this number, nearly 80% eventually failed. Inevitably, the costs of research and development, focus groups, packaging, and store listings are passed on to shoppers. Moreover, 90% of all new products aren't new at all; they are simply line extensions of existing brands. Six percent are category extensions, the term used when a product such as Arm and Hammer baking soda expands into a new area such as Arm and Hammer rug and carpet cleaner or Arm and Hammer toothpaste. Similarly, Procter & Gamble's Attends are simply diapers repackaged for incontinent adults. Distinctions between products have become absurdly subtle. The Aero and Mirage chocolate bar are both made by Nestlé. The only difference is that the bubbles in the Aero bar are slightly larger.

Some social commentators argue that the impact of unlimited choice has gone well beyond the supermarket. Writing in the *New Republic*, Stephen Waldman noted: "The compulsion to take inventory of one's wants and continually upgrade to a better deal can help explain everything from the rise of the pathological channel switcher who can never watch one TV show straight through to staggering divorce rates and employer-employee disloyalty." The consequence of too much choice was elevated to the status of psychosis by Kenneth Gergen in *The Saturated Self*. Gergen coined the term "multiphrenia" to describe the manic condition of a population trying to take advantage of the sea of choices while besieged with the notion that anything can be appropriated, anything can be improved.

The increasing concentration of the food-processing industry meant that shoppers were selecting products made by the same sources but marketed under different corporate banners. Today, the food industry is dominated by seven mega-companies — Cargill, Unilever, Nestlé, Philip Morris/Kraft/General Foods, RJR Nabisco, Procter & Gamble, and ConAgra. In 1993, these companies accounted for $276 billion of the $421 billion sales of major food producers in the United States, Canada, and Britain.

The concentration, clout, and distribution patterns of the food industry in North America had a more insidious social consequence, one that was made bleakly apparent during the 1980s with the emergence of food banks to feed the hungry. In 1984, Loblaw Companies leased out rent-free the 140,000-square-foot Lakeshore Boulevard warehouse that had served as its executive offices before it moved uptown to the Weston Centre. Its tenant was a new enterprise, The Daily Bread, Toronto's first food bank. Such acts of generosity by the food retailing and manufacturing industries would become increasingly commonplace as the number of hungry increased in Canada over the next decade. When the Daily Bread food bank opened its doors in 1984, it served 500 people a month. By 1994, it was feeding over 200,000 people a month.

The alliance between the food industry and social agencies feeding the hungry was a direct if uneasy one. Wastage in the food industry due to poor distribution channels was profound. Close to 20% of food produced was estimated to go to waste, which in turn drove food prices up. In Canada, about 70% of food bank donations — about 13 million kilograms a year — were given by food manufacturers and distributors. Such charitable donations were usually of items that would be shunned by supermarket shoppers conditioned to reject anything but a flawless product. The hungry ate the leftovers from the supermarket — food that came from dented cans or bashed-in boxes, fruit and produce that was bruised, and products close to their expiry date.

The supermarket industry had been structured to reinforce and perpetuate the dominance of the trusted national and international brands — Procter & Gamble, Nabisco, Kraft, and General Foods. In the vortex of the supermarket, brand names served as a beacon. They signified a product's origin, like the brand given livestock by their owners or the thumbprint the first potters gave to their wares. The word itself derives from an Old Norse word, *brandr*, which means to burn. In modern times, the brand name of manufactured goods has assumed a larger, symbolic meaning. It is a talisman, a pact between producers and consumers. Producers implicitly vow that the product will taste or perform in a consistent way. Shoppers accept that promise with their purchase.

The proliferation of brand-name manufacturers began in the late nineteenth century, with the advent of trains, railways, and steamships.

Geography dictated the ascendancy of goods produced by centrally located companies, such as Procter & Gamble in Cincinnati and Kraft's cheese processing business in Chicago. Shoppers' brand preferences have wavered little over the past sixty years. The same brands that were ranked number one in 1925 — Nabisco biscuits, Kellogg cereal, Del Monte canned fruit, Crisco shortening, Ivory soap, Coca-Cola, Campbell's soup, Colgate toothpaste, Gillette, Goodyear, Gold Medal flour — remained best sellers sixty years later.

In a world reeling from the pace of change, such familiarity was reassuring. The obsequious Uncle Ben, the avuncular Quaker Oats man, the virile yet asexual Mr. Clean, the ebullient Chef Boy-ar-dee, the efficient Betty Crocker, the flexed bicep of Arm and Hammer, the red and white Campbell's soup cans that have been around since 1889 — all of these became heralded icons. What Andy Warhol saw in the Campbell's soup can was not product but image — a seminal symbol of the role of consumer packaging in mass culture.

Through careful management, promotion, packaging, and use, the brand acquired an identity that transcended the product itself. One of the first of such mythologies was Betty Crocker, invented by the Washburn Crosby Co., a forerunner of General Mills, in 1921. To sell flour to women, it seemed logical to link the product to womanhood and domesticity. The name "Betty" sounded friendly, perky; Crocker honored the location of the company's flour mill in Minneapolis. In time, Betty Crocker came to represent the Platonic ideal of the homemaker, the perfect cake baker. The Betty Crocker Cooking School of the Air broadcast during the golden years of radio — from 1924 to 1948. Her picture was first used in 1936 in Gold Medal flour advertising. Since then, her image has been revised six times to stay abreast of fashion. The mythical housewife was voted the second most popular woman in the United States in a 1946 poll, right behind Eleanor Roosevelt. In her latest incarnation, she is dressed for success in a business suit, mirroring the larger social myth of the working woman who has it all. The figure of Aunt Jemima, introduced in 1890, marked the first use of a black image in advertising. She, too, has evolved over the years, from plantation slave to light-skinned African-American housewife.

Although early brand mythology emphasized the notion of product quality, it later implied qualities that could be transmitted to the consumer. As if by osmosis, the owner absorbed the mythical qualities of the brand. Calvin Klein did not sell white T-shirts and jeans, but sinewy, glistening bodies ripe for erotica. BMW delivered a carefully crafted, precision machine; the ambitious young careerists who flocked to buy the car assumed that this imagery would define their success as well. Watches became particularly suitable for brand imagery. Not only could a wrist express success, adorned by a Cartier or Rolex, but expensive watches declared an advanced need to keep track of time, a commodity in increasingly short supply.

While brands were marketed to appeal to the individualist, the underlying message was deeply conformist. In an award-winning 1984 ad campaign by New York agency Fallon McElligott, *Rolling Stone* magazine tried to convince advertisers that its readers cared about brand names and were malleable, susceptible to suasion. An illustration showed the word "Perception" above a bag of bulk granola on one side. On the other was the word "Reality," above a box of Post Grape Nut Flakes. The accompanying text challenged the assumption that *Rolling Stone* readers were non-conformist. "For a new generation of *Rolling Stone* readers, breakfast comes from places like the A&P instead of the bulk bin at Alfalfa's Co-op," the copy read. "Last year, *Rolling Stone* readers crunched through more than 38 million servings of ready-made breakfast cereal. And the total bill at checkouts exceeded $18 billion. If you're looking for healthy appetites, you're invited to breakfast, lunch and dinner in the pages of the *Rolling Stone.*" The message was one the people at Post and advertising agencies wanted to hear. The magazine's readers wanted their food — and by extension their other needs — to be provided in a controlled form by an established, brand-named source.

The cumulative power of the brand — encompassing the sum of the package, name awareness, perceived quality, and consumer loyalty — came to be known as brand equity. By the 1980s, brand equity was seen as such an integral part of a consumer-product company's worth that it was assigned a value and included on the balance sheet under "goodwill." The idea that a retailer could profit by creating its own brand equity, by producing products under its own label, had been pre-sent in the marketplace for decades, but no one had bothered to exploit it. European supermarkets had long provided food and general mer-chandise under their store brands, as had North American retailers, but never had this been conceived as a possible threat to the national brand manufacturers. Nor had any retailer seized on private labels as a way to achieve a competitive advantage. Never had anyone possessed the hubris to disrupt the long-entrenched supermarket culture. And then, in 1984, Dave Nichol was named president of Loblaw International Merchants.

CHAPTER FOUR

THE MAKING OF THE PRESIDENT

O nly one aspect of Dave Nichol's corporate life was unchanged by Loblaw's 1984 reorganization: his physical setting. He remained in his large, airy office on the ninth floor of the Weston Centre, with its wall of windows overlooking northwest Toronto. Each morning, he drove six blocks from his house, rode the elevator from the underground parking garage, walked nine steps from the elevator bank, across the beige marble reception area and through a mirrored door, embedded in a mirrored wall upon which were stenciled in orange the names Loblaw International Merchants and ADX, which stood for "advertising excellence." The mirrored door led to the anteroom of his office, where Anne Doremus, his new secretary, and her assistant, Heather Hohol, sat. His long-time secretary Anne-Marie Halliday had been promoted by David Stewart. The easygoing, eminently competent Doremus, a native of Chicoutimi, Quebec, was familiar with the inner machinations of Loblaw, having worked for Brian Davidson for years. She also possessed the temperament needed to deal with Nichol. "I was once married to an actor," she explains in her lilting French-Canadian accent, "so I understand ego and theatricality."

Stripped of his former identity, Nichol was forced to redefine his role within Loblaw. As president of Loblaw Supermarkets, thousands of people had reported to him; when he walked into stores, staff snapped to attention. Now, that power was gone. As president of Loblaw International Merchants, he was subject to greater supervision. He had no control over buying decisions; that was Intersave's domain, under Brian Davidson and Doug Lunau. In fact, his entire budget was extracted from the 3% service fee that Intersave billed its corporate-brand suppliers. Now, too, he was vulnerable to retaliation from people within Loblaw he had slighted or abused. "A lot of people tore a strip off him," one former Intersave employee remembered. "It was pay-back time." As Nichol was to discover, the Weston Tower could be a cruel and vengeful place.

In the beginning, his staff was small, consisting of Doremus and Hohol; art director Russ Rudd (with his own five-person department); Boris Polakow; Jim White; and Larry Griffin (with twelve employees). Rudd, a solidly built man with a head of thick, silver hair, had joined Loblaw straight out of the Ontario College of Art in 1956. He had directed advertising and the packaging of house brands since the early 1970s. Polakow — known as Bo — coordinated the distribution of products featured in the *Insider's Report*. After the first *Reports* were published, store managers complained about late product deliveries. Coordinating shipments from around the world required militaristic planning. Polakow, a serious young man, seemed suited to the task. He understood the dynamics of the grocery business with a proverbial sixth sense. Born in Toronto in 1951, he had worked part-time as a buggy boy at a Loblaws store in North Toronto while still in high school. He soon was promoted to dairy, where he learned how to rotate products to avoid spoiling. After graduating from Ryerson Polytechnic Institute in business administration, he joined Loblaw full-time. He had worked on store redesign and with the No Frills stores in the early 1980s, and then had been assigned to Nichol.

Larry Griffin, in his early thirties, was a calm, organized man with dark hair and cool blue eyes. Griffin was responsible for quality assurance, or QA, as it was known around Loblaw. With a degree in chemistry from Concordia University in Montreal, Griffin had joined Loblaw in 1982. When LIM was created, QA was folded into its structure to ensure that technical production and packaging specifications were met. QA was the processed-food police. The unit monitored the gauge of plastic wrap, the chunkiness of tomatoes in pasta sauce, the viscosity of ketchup, the consistency of colorings and flavorings, the weight of cookie packages and mineral water bottles, and the accuracy of ingredient lists. It also compared house lines with the leading national brands and suggested new product opportunities.

QA monitored food in various ways. Staff routinely visited suppliers' factories to check quality-control measures and production volumes and tested random samples from warehouses and store shelves. In some cases, when products were being shipped in batches across North America, they demanded samples from every production run. Food items were checked ten to fifteen times a year; general merchandise products, such as sponges, were scrutinized less often. QA also fielded complaints from customers. In time they would compile a list of regular complaints, including those from customers who were chronic complainers and those from customers who were seeking damages for allegedly finding foreign material in the food; the latter — things such as glass, hair, or metal — were known in the industry as "extraneous matter."

Jim White assumed two roles — chief *Insider's Report* writer and Nichol's right hand. Born in 1946, White was a native New Yorker who had moved to Toronto with his family as a teenager. He studied journalism at Northwestern University in Chicago and returned to Toronto, eventually landing an on-air job in television news. After a few years, he grew frustrated with the medium (it didn't help that he was forced to wear a toupee). He took off to Africa, where he spent several years as a photojournalist. He met the famed anthropologist Louis Leakey and Ethiopian emperor Haile Selassie, before he returned to Canada. In 1972, he joined the Canadian International Development Agency, where he worked on films in support of relief efforts. In 1979, White traded famine for feast and found a job writing for the *Toronto Star*'s food section. He soon was promoted to editor of the section and, in his spare time, wrote several cookbooks.

White amassed almost instant credibility as a foodie. Nichol was originally taken with White's food knowledge and theatrical flair. The two men had met at food-related events over the years, and in late 1983 Nichol approached him to write the *Insider's Report*. White wanted the job. He arrived for a lunch appointment with Nichol with a dossier absurdly wrapped with a bicycle chain and heavy metal lock. He threw it on a glass table in front of Nichol. "Here are the hundred hooks," he said, referring to a previous discussion they had had about how to hook shoppers. White then named his price, a sum considerably more than he was earning as a journalist. The job was his.

Relentlessly upbeat and possessing a gift for one-liners, White infused the *Insider's Report* with a manic energy. Like Nichol, White kept track of seminal food moments in his life. He remembered the best sandwich he had ever eaten — bacon, lettuce, and tomato with Hellmann's mayonnaise on olive bread — on July 4, 1971, in Ethiopia, made by Mary Leakey, Louis's wife. He insisted that the white clam pizza at Pepe's in New Haven, Connecticut, was North America's best. And he reveled in the food circuit and all the name-dropping that went with it.

White's infectious enthusiasm helped to dispel Nichol's black moods. For months after the launch of LIM, Nichol was in deep denial. He had believed that he could continue to run a corporate label program *and* manage the stores. He was miffed that Currie and Davidson had conceived the name, Loblaw International Merchants, without consulting him. He sat in meetings chaired by Currie drafting text for the *Insider's Report*, ignoring the proceedings. "It took me about a year to pull out of the slump," he later admitted. Frequently he cited an inspirational dictum from Mary Baker Eddy, founder of the First Church of Christ Scientist: "Stand porter to the door of your thoughts."

When LIM was founded, the corporate brand program made up less than 20% of the merchandise sold in Loblaw Companies' supermarkets and was worth several hundreds of millions of dollars (close to $500 million according to one Intersave executive) in annual sales. The President's Choice name was introduced in 1984, evolving from President's Blend coffee. Over the years, many people claimed to have suggested the name, including designer Don Watt and Jim White. In what was to become a pattern of behavior, it was Nichol who ultimately took credit for the idea. There was an irony to the name, given Nichol's demotion. In the years to come, it created the public perception that Nichol was, in fact, Loblaw's president, a misconception Dick Currie never complained about, but which others believed rankled him privately.

The *Insider's Report*'s publication dates created an internal clock

— Easter, summer, Thanksgiving, Christmas — against which to measure and advance product development. Nichol never deviated from the formula of the first edition; no matter how many people had a hand in the publication, his was the dominant authorial voice; he was the final arbiter of taste. Nichol never let the facts get in the way of a good marketing hook. It didn't matter whether the inspiration for a product had been uncovered by some eager Loblaw lackey at a strip mall in north Toronto, the *Insider's Report* version had Nichol stalking it down in some exotic or fashionable locale. At Loblaw, history was relative.

In time, the *Insider's Report* format grew bolder, moving to four-color printing, using more capitals and exclamation points, yellow highlighting, and cartoons supplied by in-house artist Jim Philips. The writing was a cross between that of the respected food historian Waverly Root and the effusive pitches of a carnival barker. A plug for vine-ripened tomatoes in November 1984 was titled: "Hooray!!!! The Arrival of Vine-Ripened Tomatoes!!!!" The text read: "Another common complaint that I hear relates to Tennis Ball Tomatoes—you know, the standard California Issue that, in our opinion, has no texture, no taste, no attraction. But why should they? They are a tomato-breeder's delight; they are bred for their ability to be picked green, for their hardiness to travel (hardiness? They have skins that would make an armadillo jealous)." The blurb went on to explain that, on one of his European junkets, Nichol had found a supplier of vine-ripened tomatoes which were grown in the Canary Islands, Spain, and the Middle East, who agreed to export directly to Loblaw.

White could find a story in the most mundane facts. His mock-erudite tone reflected his own interest in food trivia — the history of the potato chip; why apple cider was brown; where the first hamburger was made in the United States (at Louis Lunch in New Haven, Connecticut); that the Latin for snow pea was *Pisum sativum macrocarpon*; that 260 million glasses of Coke were drunk every day; that the name Ivory soap was conceived by Harley Procter, son of the co-founder of Procter & Gamble, while sitting in church when the 45th psalm was read: "All thy garments smell of myrrh, and aloes, and cassia, out of the ivory palaces, whereby they have made thee glad"; and that most of the white vinegar made in Canada was derived from spirits synthesized from petroleum derivatives. In the 1980s, possession of such trivial information came to be construed as knowledge.

The *Insider's Report* was published three to four times a year, at a cost of about $400,000 per issue. Sixteen-page versions featuring between one hundred and two hundred special promotions or new products were produced in June and November. The June edition was filled with barbecue and gardening specials; the November *Report* was geared to the upcoming holiday season. Four-page versions were produced at Easter and Thanksgiving. The *Report* was customized for regional markets in the United States as well. Delivered with Saturday newspapers across the country, it reached more than 10 million Canadian and U.S. homes and drew shoppers into Loblaw Companies' supermarkets like pilgrims to Mecca. Traffic in stores increased by as much as 10% on the Saturdays it was published. Customers would ask when the next *Report* was due. Surveys revealed that 59.1% of Ontario residents spent twenty-eight minutes, on average, reading the copy-dense *Report*, more time than was spent reading most newspapers.

The *Report* spurred people to try new products at introductory low prices. Of course, when they returned to buy the product a second time, the price would be higher. Shoppers were drawn by the glamour of extra virgin olive oil, escargots in seasoned butter from France, Peugeot pepper mills, Alaska King Crab legs, mixed peppercorns, canned lychees in syrup, Pinney's Scottish smoked salmon, chèvre, and President's Choice Spring Green Bath and Shower Gelee, which sold for less than half the price of Vitabath. The *Report*'s readers had no inkling of the corporate conflicts or the cost-profit analysis that attended the development of these products. They simply perceived Nichol as a helpful emissary, supplying a personal connection that had been lacking in the supermarket. He seemed accessible, attentive to the concerns of readers. "After the launch of our No Name Pot Pies last Christmas," he wrote in one *Report*, "I received a letter complaining that the beef pie was not meaty enough, nor did it contain enough vegetables....I tasted samples from different production lots and I had to agree that Mrs. Thompson was right!! As a result, we set right out to reformulate the pies."

Nichol believed that the success of the *Insider's Report* hinged on the fact that it gave people something to talk about. If the attention was created under false pretense, so be it. In what could only be described as the marketing of marketing, White put an ad in *Toronto Life* magazine asking for "mint condition" copies of the first *Insider's Report*. It was a complete ruse. "We wanted to give it a mystique, make it something people would talk about", White recalls. This "something-to-talk-about" theory was given a measure of academic credence by sociologist Richard Sennett. In *The Fall of Public Man*, Sennett warned that North Americans had lost the art of impersonal civility, without which urban life could be nasty and brutish. People no longer spoke to strangers, not even about the weather; the rift between those who lived in climate-controlled condos and those who spent their winters sleeping on street grates was growing wider. But the *Insider's Report* also played to a darker fear — the social and political insecurity that increasingly found its focus in food. It exploited uncertainty about the safety of drinking water and mass-manufactured food. It preyed on the middle class's anxiety about getting ahead. Nichol came to be perceived as the defender of middle-class values, fighting the tyranny of national-brand dominance, protecting consumers in the face of intrusive and ineffective governments.

In fact, the *Report*'s subtext was quasi-revolutionary: the current economic and political orders were fundamentally flawed. The establishment, it hinted — of which the national brands were painted as part — was not working in the consumer's best interest. Tucked between recipes for crème brulée from Le Cirque and specials on Brie cheese were blunt reminders of the declining standard of living and the need for shoppers to protect themselves. In September 1984, Nichol addressed the subject of over-taxation: "Congratulations. If you are an average Canadian, you have just completed working 8 months to pay for your share of federal and provincial income taxes....Canada's take, as a share of GNP, ranks it the third highest in the world." That same year, Nichol again raised the empowerment issue. "By now," he wrote, "even antique flower children realize that if we're going to straighten out our economy, it's not the politicians who are going to do it, but entrepreneurs acting in their own enlightened self-interest." On another occasion, he ventured into the volatile old-age security issue. "Recently, I was reading *Esquire* magazine's Dubious Awards Issue and ran across this headline: 'HANGMAN IN ONTARIO LEFT ON THE GOVERNMENT PAYROLL FOR 9 YEARS AFTER CAPITAL PUNISHMENT OUTLAWED IN 1976.' The reason the Ontario government gave was that it was an administrative oversight! AN ADMIN-ISTRATIVE OVERSITE! Would you expect people who do this to take care of you in your old age? OF COURSE NOT!! Obviously, you're going to have to take care of yourself. START SAVING NOW!!"

But Nichol's social sermonettes also contained an explicit corporate message: that buying No Name and President's Choice offered deliverance. In one issue, he addressed the time-compression anxiety experienced by many careerists during the 1980s. "Most of us spend 5 YEARS of our lives waiting in lines, according to a recent time study. It's estimated that we also spend 1 YEAR SEARCHING FOR MISPLACED OBJECTS, 4 YEARS DOING HOUSEWORK AND UP TO 2 YEARS TRYING TO RETURN TELE-PHONE CALLS!! THE INSIDER'S REPORT TO THE RESCUE! Here's a way to put a 3-STAR QUALITY MEAL ON YOUR TABLE IN ONLY 10 MINUTES — AND YOU DON'T EVEN NEED A MICROWAVE TO DO IT!"

On another occasion, Nichol captured readers with his economic Cassandra act and then delivered his President's Choice pitch. "LOOK-OUT," screamed the headline, "Insider's Report has proof positive that the economy is going to collapse! To predict economic collapse, Jim Rogers, a Yale graduate who teaches at Columbia's Business School, SIMPLY MEASURED THE % OF GRADUATING YALIES WHO INTEND TO WORK ON WALL STREET!...50% OF YALE'S 1986 GRADUATING CLASS INTEND TO TAKE JOBS ON WALL STREET (OR WITH FINANCIAL INSTITUTIONS)!!! What can you do to minimize the effect of this devastating, soon-to-material-ize economic hardship? Buy gourmet cheeses at slashed prices."

To careerists concerned about pleasing their bosses, he offered a recipe for President's Choice Frenched Rib Roast. "Probably the most frenzied, stress-provoking meal of the year is the one you cook for your boss (or your spouse's boss!)!" he wrote. "IT DOESN'T HAVE TO BE!! RELAX!! Just follow our step-by-step No Nonsense Guide To Impressing the Boss." Playing pop psychologist, Nichol also confronted the phenomenon of yuppies who thought "nothing of spending $1 on a single chocolate truffle or buying exotic vinegars instead of everyday white, distilled vinegar. HOWEVER, AFFORDABLE LUXURIES ARE, ESSENTIALLY, NOTHING MORE THAN CONSOLATION PRIZES FOR YUPPIES WHO, BECAUSE OF OVERALL ECONOMIC CONDITIONS, CAN'T AFFORD MORE, SO LEAVE THEM ALONE!!!" By the end of the decade, even Loblaw recognized that food had become a social passport. In a November 1989 blurb headlined, "You are what you serve," Nichol quoted food historian Margaret Visser: "If what you serve is mediocre and boring, your guests will spread the word that YOU'RE mediocre and boring!"

On occasion, Nichol and White went too far. In a bizarre incident in September 1984, before the startup of LIM, Loblaw was threatened with a lawsuit for copy that promoted what White called the "first annual Marshall McLuhan bulk candy festival." The mock ad quoted Tom Wolfe's book, *The Pump House Gang*, which had quoted McLuhan: "Of, course, packages will be obsolete in a few years. People will want tactile experiences. They'll want to feel the product they're getting. Goods will be sold in bins. People will go right to bins to pick things up and feel them rather than accepting a package." The McLuhan family was not pleased about the revered mass-media theorist being lumped in with jelly beans. McLuhan's widow threatened to sue. The matter was quietly settled out of court, the Weston way. The experience was enough to propel Loblaw lawyer John McCullough to compile a list of celebrities or their estates that had successfully sued retailers for using their names. The list, later given to the *Insider's Report* writers, included Jack Webb, Bela Lugosi, Carole Lombard, Ansel Adams, Marvin Gaye, Buddy Holly, Edgar Bergen, Elvis Presley, Ozzie Nelson, Glenn Miller, The Three Stooges, Coco Chanel, Cass Elliot, L. Ron Hubbard, Jimmy Durante, Piet Mondrian, Dian Fosse, Liberace, Cary Grant, and Marilyn Monroe.

The McLuhan affair was not the only time that the *Report* prompted unusual outrage. The RCMP once called Loblaw in response to a *Report*'s ad for President's Choice pantyhose. White had written a headline, "Attention all bank robbers," with a cartoon of a holdup man with pantyhose pulled over his head as a disguise. The tongue-in-cheek copy suggested that thieves who used President's Choice pantyhose could be assured their disguise wouldn't run while in flight. "You're encouraging crime," an RCMP staff officer berated an unsuspecting *Report* writer.

Other readers expressed indignation over a *Report*'s advertise-ment for No Name Low-Ash cat food, which said: "Cats are like Bap-tists — they raise hell — but you can't catch them at it!" "I know I'm going to hear from my brother on this one — John the Baptist," Nichol wrote in the copy. "My brother's name is really John — he's a great guy who also happens to be a southern Baptist minister in Daytona Beach, Florida. What has this got to do with cat food? ABSOLUTELY NOTHING!! However, I had to find some way to work John in because he constant-ly complains that in my Insider's Reports, I always talk about my sisters, Marilyn and Joanne, my mother and even my French bulldogs — yet Brother John is always conspicuous by his absence...." Nichol later wrote a formal apology to his Baptist followers. The furor again made it clear that the *Report* was more than a supermarket flyer; for its read-ers, it had editorial credibility.

White used his contacts to assemble a team of writers and product developers with a background in magazines and catering. They included Chris Grikscheit and Christine Mullen, a married couple who had run a Toronto catering outfit; they were quickly dubbed the Mullens, because Grikscheit was too difficult to pronounce; Ladka Sweeney, an old friend of White's who ran Toronto's Abbey Catering; writers Frances Litwin from the Montreal *Gazette* and John Hofsess, a former film reviewer at *Maclean's*. Nichol wanted to hire Carol White, a food editor at *Canadi-an Living* and wife of Jim, but Jim White didn't want his first hire to be his wife. Carol White finally joined Loblaw in 1986; by then, the team included six product developers and six editorial people.

The group's inspiration came from magazines, medical journals, and television. Nichol devoured the popular press — everything from *Wom-en's Wear Daily* to the *New England Journal of Medicine* to *Vogue* and *Bon Appétit*. The endorsement of the taste establishment — food critics, restaurateurs, celebrities — was sought to give President's Choice products cachet and credibility. Thus, the reference to *Women's Wear Daily*'s annu-al listing of HOT & COLD in 1988. "Peach nectar (with or without cham-pagne) is really HOT!" Thus, the allusions to "one of the finest hotels I've ever stayed at — the Mansion on Turtle Creek, in Dallas, Texas," which was not only on the top ten hotels list of "Lifestyles of the Rich and Famous," but served the same guinea fowl — Ontario Pintelle — that was served at New York's swank Lutece. Another copy block promoted President's Choice English muffins by quoting a study from the Massachusetts Institute of Technology: "Researchers at MIT are convinced sweet and starchy foods may reduce one's level of stress and increase one's mental performance."

The *Report* was equally shameless in milking Nichol's pastoral roots. "I had the good fortune of being born into a generation when most grandmothers still owned farms," he wrote in a promo for frozen corn. "My grandmother McGuigan had a farm at Cedar Springs, Ontario (I know it sounds fictional but that's the real name). I spent every summer there. I remember setting up a stand in front of the farm house where I sold our freshly picked Peaches 'N' Cream Corn (if you don't know this sweet variety, you're missing out on one of gastronomy's greatest pleasures). I suppose my lifelong devotion to food was born at my grandmother's table because her cooking was exemplary. It had to be; after all, in those days good food was the key to attracting and keeping the best hired hands." Nichol's frequent invocation of his humble beginnings as a "station agent's son" came to irritate his mother. It implied that he had been raised in poverty, whereas, as she reminded him, she had worked hard so that her family would get ahead. "You grew up in a nice house with nice things," she would remind him.

But Nichol continued to exploit his past, exaggerated or otherwise. In another issue, he was the subject of this shamelessly sentimental plug for beef pies: "When I was in grade 3, I attended a one-room schoolhouse on the outskirts of Ridgetown, Ontario. I can still remember trudging home from school in the dark during one of those infamous Ridgetown ice storms where the fierce, freezing rain turned the trees into exotic ice sculptures and caused huge branches to come crashing down. Just when I began to think that I couldn't go on, I caught the first glimpse of our porch light glowing on the snowbanks. My mother took one look at me, wrapped me in a blanket and put me in a rocking chair by the fireplace. Marker, the 'almost' St. Bernard we inherited when Grandmother McGuigan sold her farm at Cedar Springs, lay beside me, hypnotized by the dancing flames. And there, in front of the fireplace, my mother served me supper — a rich ground beef pie with not too many vegetables and an unforgettable crust of mashed potatoes mixed with tangy Cheddar cheese."

The editorial mix was regularly leavened with jottings from Nichol's extensive travels, to New Zealand, where he purchased the entire crop of Cox's orange pippin apple concentrate; to San Francisco, where he lunched at the famous Zuni café, ordering "what turned out to be a Lucullan epiphany — goat's milk cheese pizza topped with California dried tomatoes"; to Kyoto, Japan, where he stayed at what *Esquire* billed the world's best hotel, the Tawaraya Inn; to India, where he stayed "at the fabulous Rambagh Palace Hotel in Jaipur (once home to the famous polo-playing Maharaja of Jaipur). There, we discovered shrimp grilled with a sweet and sour curry sauce that I was certain was made with divine intervention"; to Lisse, near Amsterdam, "where I went to see the greatest show of flowering bulbs in the world at the famous Keukenhof Gardens."

In addition to introductory low prices, the *Report* tempted shoppers with recipes: his wife Terri's recipe for brownies; his sister Marilyn's recipe for grilled vegetables; and a recipe for sausages that Nichol had tasted at the Empress Hotel at his mother's eighty-eighth birthday party. After tasting the cheesecake delivered by room service at New York's Carlyle Hotel, he formulated a similar desert. He admitted to interrogating Mr. Bovo, then maître d' of the Grill Room at London's posh Connaught Hotel about peas — "they had so much more flavor than the ones we get in North America." He engaged in restaurant espionage, penetrating Le Cirque in New York for crème brulée, Toronto's Winston's for its house pâté, Chanticleer restaurant in Santa Barbara for hot spinach salad, and the Jaegerhof Hotel in the Bavarian Alps for pork roast.

Hyperbole aside, the *Report* offered information lacking in most supermarket advertising. Traditional flyers said nothing about product, only price. The *Report* harkened back to another era, when merchants were founts of product knowledge. But it had an eighties' spin, allowing readers to dip in and out at whim, as if they were surfing through TV channels. To many shoppers who had never heard of Vidalia onions or

oyster mushrooms or who felt intimidated by a mango, it opened hith-
erto unknown worlds. To an increasingly food-aware public, the *Report*
put a gourmet gloss on reality — on everything from coffee to dog food
to popcorn to wild birdseed.

As the staff prepared each new edition of the *Report*, Nichol
would berate them, attempting to ignite a fire. "There's nothing here
that's interesting," he'd gripe, reading the "story" lineup. In fact,
Nichol's tantrums were legendary. In December 1987, the Globe and
Mail's *Report on Business* magazine named Nichol one of the worst
bosses in Canada, citing his unbridled arrogance. Once, asked to give a
twenty-minute speech, he spent nearly an hour at the podium. He often
walked out of meetings if he was bored. And he could be cruel. He told
one *Insider's Report* writer she was stupid, causing her to cry. It wasn't
the first, or the last, time Nichol drew tears with his vitriol. "We could-
n't win," one staff member recalled. "If we made a suggestion, Mr.
Nichol would turn to us and say, 'That would be fine if it were your
Insider's Report. But it's my *Insider's Report*.' But if you said nothing,
he'd yell, 'Am I the only one with any ideas around here.'" Another
staffer said simply, "He was mean for three years." Nichol, one writer
remembered, "made changes in everyone's copy right up to press time."

Working for Nichol could not only be thankless; it sometimes
involved marginal physical peril. At meetings, he would often lean back
in his chair and nonchalantly clip his fingernails in a display of bore-
dom. The people sitting around his glass-topped desk would wince
inwardly as the tips went whizzing across the table. It required discipline
not to move, one former employee recalled. As a gag, staff joked privately about putting on motorcycle helmets and goggles when the clip-
pers appeared. No one ever did.

Staff could also be put at peril outside the office when it served
Nichol's personal needs, according to LIM legend. Once, he decided to
serve prosciutto, the Italian cured ham, as the first course at a dinner
party. This posed a problem, for, as connoisseurs in meat matters know,
the finest, most authentic prosciutto comes from San Daniele in northern Italy. Because it is uncooked, however, the genuine article is not
allowed past Canada Customs for fear of importing nasty bacteria.

Smuggling is the only way to get it into the country.

Nichol refused to settle for a cheap domestic version. He asked a buyer in Intersave who had plans to spend the weekend in the United States with his wife and child to make a special pickup at New York's Four Seasons restaurant. Nichol insisted the minion take his wife to dinner at the restaurant and had his office call ahead to put the meal on his tab. After dinner, the young man approached maître d' Julian Nicholani, with whom Nichol was friends, with his request. Nicholani disappeared into the kitchen, reappearing with a ten-pound package wrapped in layers of waxed paper and foil — hundreds of dollars worth of ham. For the trip home, the employee stashed the side of pig into the diaper bag in his one-year-old's stroller. Aware that customs agents like few things less than dealing with a howling baby, he gently kicked the stroller containing his sleeping child as he approached the customs booth in Toronto. The toddler squalled on cue. The agent waved them through. Nichol got his prosciutto.

At the outset, the *Report* was used to advertise the brand-name deals and special orders secured by Intersave — glassware from Portugal, Lean Cuisine frozen dinners, Toblerone chocolate bars, Scotch-guard, Kodak film, Luvs disposable diapers, Heinz ketchup, 3M video cassettes. But from the beginning, the "tyranny" of "high-priced" national brands was a central theme. Under a headline asking, "What does one 30-second commercial on the CBS evening news cost?" Nichol promoted President's Choice Calcium Carbonate Tablets by noting that on the "CBS Evening News," sponsors paid up to $70,000 (U.S.) for a thirty-second spot. "I was struck by the fact that the program had so many ads for calcium-related products," Nichol wrote. "Small wonder name-brand health and beauty aids cost so much." The President's Choice version sold at half the price of the national brand.

Nichol liked to proclaim that "advertising was one of the greatest wastes in modern society," hardly an original or damning observation in light of the fact that since the earliest days of mass market advertising, waste was seen as one of its prime virtues. Glenna Matthews in *Just a Housewife: The Rise and Fall of Domesticity in America* quotes an associate editor of the magazine *Advertising and Selling* in 1919: "I want advertising copy to arouse me, to create in me a desire to possess the thing that's advertised." In *Selling Mrs. Consumer*, a book aimed at the advertising industry, Christine Fredericks, the household editor for the *Ladies' Home Journal*, set forth the best means of inducing housewives to spend as much as possible. Fredericks coined the term "creative waste" to describe the goal to which the advertising agency should urge women. An accelerating rate of obsolescence for products was to the good, she advised. Often, the advertisements bullied housewives into believing that these new products would better meet their families' emotional needs.

The emergence of a national market in the late nineteenth century and developments in packaging in the early twentieth century created the need for advertising to heighten consumer demand. Brand names such as Jell-O, Kleenex, and Frigidaire entered the vocabulary. Television, introduced in 1946, would have a profound influence on the way food was marketed and consumed. Bing Crosby shilled for Minute Maid orange juice, Jackie Gleason was sponsored by Nestlé's Nescafé coffee, the Ed Sullivan show was punctuated by recipes from Kraft Foods.

But the power of the mass media would become weakened and fragmented with the advent of remote control which permitted viewers to elude commercials, and the arrival of cable networks which challenged the dominance of the big networks. It was no longer a given that the family would be gathered around the Ed Sullivan show on a Sunday night. Studies showed that more than one-third of the time viewers would leave the room when commercials began. The money spent by large consumer conglomerates on media advertising seemed increasingly spent in vain.

Nichol rebelled against the vacuous slogans used by advertisers that told consumers nothing about the product. "What does 'It's the real thing' mean?" he'd ask derisively. The use of celebrity endorsers such as Bill Cosby and Michael Jackson also aroused his wrath and he would often point out that the million-dollar contracts demanded by these stars would be built into the product's price. In comparison, Nichol's commercials were Shaker-like in their simplicity. They were produced in-house at a cost of $10,000 per thirty-second spot, a far cry from the industry average of $150,000. The production values were plain. He would write the wordy scripts, and would often film a half dozen in a row, A graphic image of the promoted product floated over his left shoulder.

Nichol had an innate understanding of the financial foundation of merchandising — and, on the basis of numbers, of what would win and lose. This, in part, distinguished him from White, who often got carried away with enthusiasm for his own ideas. "Jim was always dreaming up line extensions," one Intersave executive recalled. "If we had a hit with pasta and cheese and mushrooms, he'd want to do pasta and cheese and mushrooms and bacon."

White could become so enthusiastic about how something tasted or what its appeal could be that he did not consider the basic economics of the business, the primacy of The Deal. At meetings attended by Nichol and Intersave buyers, White might suggest that Loblaw import five cases of a product — an uneconomical amount. "Leave it alone, Jim," Nichol would say.

White deflected the criticism with good humor. "I guess the drugs haven't kicked in yet," White would joke to colleagues. Indeed, Nichol's manic mood swings became an integral part of his control over the staff. They kept everyone on edge, always uncertain about exactly what state he would be in at any given moment. In time, and as he built a staff he trusted, he became less frenetic.

As LIM's empire-within-an-empire grew, so did its physical needs. The Tower was under constant renovation. Nichol called in Don Watt to consult on the expansion. Black leather and chrome chairs were purchased; they were so expensive they were referred to as a form of currency. The inside joke was "I need to go to Texas. It's going to cost about a chair." In 1986, Nichol spent $150,000 to turn an office into a conference room, which came to be known as the War Room. It featured eight TV screens and an elaborate projection system that displayed computer-generated information about products sold at Loblaws stores.

The computer program responsible for the data was named Pierre (after Pierre Chaumette, a minor figure in the French Revolution). Pierre was the brainchild of Ray Goodman, a flamboyant vice-president of information services who had been hired away from McKinsey & Co. in 1983. Soon after arriving at Loblaw, Goodman created a system that tracked product sales at ten Loblaws supermarkets. He called it Poindexter because, like the character in Felix the Cat, it always had the answer. Pierre, the second generation, provided access to product information in every Loblaws store, using the universal product codes scanned at checkout. Pierre was unlike anything then being used in the supermarket industry. Conventional thinking regarded scanning simply as a way to boost productivity or efficiency — to speed customers through checkout. But Goodman recognized that scanning could create a vital merchandising tool. Using Pierre, Nichol and others could analyze information by chain, by store, by category. It revealed entire pricing structures, complete with gross and net profit margins and the product's penetration of its category. Loblaw executives, category managers, and Intersave buyers could electronically enter any store in the country and learn precisely how many items had been sold that day and at what price.

Goodman sent out a memo that heralded the computerization of supermarket data as a historical event: "The overthrow of oppressive manual systems, and insensitive or nonexistent computer solutions is no less historic, no less noble, and NO LESS RELIANT ON THE ACTIVITIES OF THE ORDINARY." Napoleonic references were always well-received in the Tower.

Nichol was Pierre's primary user and beneficiary. He came to call it his Rosetta stone. He would face the screen like Leonard Bernstein before his Philharmonic. Each product was shown with a colored band behind it. Yellow bands indicated No Name and President's Choice items; green bands indicated products at or above average depending on the category being assessed, be it sales, profit margins, or volumes; red bands indicated products lagging behind. If Nichol wanted to survey peanut butter, he would call up the department (grocery); the sub-department (dry); the category (peanut butter); and then the sub-category (smooth). In ten seconds, he could learn that No Name peanut butter claimed 31% of the category and a 37% profit margin, compared with Kraft, which had 59% of the category, but a margin of only 14.5%. Often, he would formulate a theory about a category or product before he used Pierre. The technology would then be used as a reality check.

At the outset, the most attention in product development was paid to high-volume categories — cookies, coffee, detergent, processed cheese products, dog food, cereal, and soft drinks. Sold at lower prices yet higher margins, the corporate brands were designed to go head to head with the national brands. Thus, No Name Salad Dressing was introduced in 1984 at $1.99 versus $3.35 for Kraft's Miracle Whip. No Name Macaroni and Cheese Dinner followed. Billed as more popular in taste tests than Kraft Dinner, it sold for 55 cents a package, 24 cents less than Kraft. No Name Popcorn went up against Orville Redenbacher; No Name Luxury Dog Food undermined sales of the leading brand, Dr. Ballard's; and No Name Process Cheese Spread was introduced to rival Cheez Whiz, at nearly one dollar less per jar. And so it went: the Chocolate Chip Cookie for the Connoisseur versus Chips Ahoy!; President's Choice Instant Chocolate Drink versus Nestlé's Quik; President's Choice Toasted O's versus Cheerios; President's Choice Superior Laundry Detergent versus Tide; President's Choice Orange Pekoe Tea versus Twinings (ironically a Weston-owned brand); President's Choice Superior Green Dishwashing Liquid versus Procter & Gamble's Palmolive; President's Choice Pearl White Dish Liquid versus Ivory; No Name Real Mayonnaise versus Hellmann's; the Lucullan Delights versus Oreo; President's Choice Corn Flakes versus Kellogg's.

The central strategy was to sell national brands at cost and use private labels, No Name and President's Choice, with their higher gross margins, to generate profits. The creation of both economy and premium house brands gave shoppers added choice, while still tying them to the highly profitable store brand. They could select the high-end Cookie for the Connoisseur or the low-end No Name version at a lower price. This tactic allowed Loblaw to use a merchandising technique called bracketing. Corporate brands were displayed on both sides of the national brand — President's Choice products to the left, lower-priced No Names to the right. To limit the effects of national-brand price wars on gross profits, they also invented a concept called shielding. If a national brand competing with President's Choice went on sale at a competitor's store, Loblaw reduced the price of both the national brand and the President's Choice item, but advertised the price-reduced national brand to bring customers into the store.

Inevitably, Nichol's national-brand bashing — and the creation of quality substitutes — provoked an outcry from the big brands. Every time he added a President's Choice item to the roster, an existing brand risked losing its prominent position on supermarket shelves or being pushed off entirely. Many manufacturers protested, demanding that Loblaw cease and desist. Cadbury Schweppes, for example, was outraged when Loblaw stopped buying its Extra Spicy Mott's Clamato Juice only months after launching the house-brand version, a spicy clam and tomato cocktail mix. But short of paying more for its shelf space, there was little Cadbury could do; Loblaw's control of the shelves gave it the freedom to place, price, and delist products in competition with its own brands.

In the early years, product development was ad hoc, an adventure. White and Nichol used the kitchens of a Toronto caterer every other lunch hour to test recipes. White was a relentless idea machine, producing many ideas for which Nichol later took credit. Nichol nevertheless respected White's palate, which would come to have a significant influence in the evolution of the President's Choice brand. One of White's obsessions was with preservatives and additives. "Eat the national brands," he said, "and you wake up with garbage breath." He insisted that President's Choice products be as free as possible of unnecessary chemicals. "I want to make the supermarket a safe place to shop," he said repeatedly. Nichol had little personal interest in high-fiber cereal or low-fat yogurt, items that White lobbied to produce; Nichol was strictly a triple creme cheese man. But he saw the growing market for "healthier" foods and acquiesced.

The first product White recommended after arriving at Loblaw was an all-natural frankfurter made at Kwinter's, a small Toronto company. The problem was the price. Made from the remains of meat processing, hot dogs routinely sold in supermarkets for about 99 cents a pound, 69 cents on special. Kwinter's hot dogs were billed as all beef, with no binders or fillers. They retailed for $2.99, the price of steak. That price, said Intersave's Brian Davidson, defied everything he had learned in the deli business. "Nobody's gonna pay that much for hot dogs," Davidson yelled at Nichol. Later, it occurred to Davidson that Z&W, a joint-venture meat company he had set up for Loblaw, could make the wieners at lower cost. Jack Kwinter, owner of Kwinter's, agreed, and a deal was struck for the recipe. The product, billed as "The best hot dog in Canada" and "the Kwinter-sential hot dog," was introduced in the summer of 1984 at $2.99 a pound. It offered proof that yuppies would pay steak prices for quality wieners: within eighteen months, the Kwinter creation had garnered 20% of Loblaw's hot dog sales.

Searching for products he could cross-market with the wiener, Nichol came up with No Name Stoneground Prepared Mustard with Horseradish. Mustard was a high-volume, high-margin item. Then he decided he wanted a cheese bun. He went off to visit Toronto baker Alphons Dimpflmeier, whose breads had been favorably reviewed in *Bon Appétit*. Dimpflmeier later made a variety of breads for Loblaw's corporate label program, including President's Choice 80% Whole Wheat Stoneground Raisin Bread. The cheese bun, however, was produced by Weston Bakeries, as a Montreal Forum-style hot dog bun.

There were many failures, products that appeared and then disappeared overnight. Some, such as truffle oil — imported from Italy and sold at $9.99 a small bottle — were too rarefied for the average supermarket shopper. The truffle oil was put on Ziggy's counters where it sat, untouched. Even less esoteric oils — a sesame oil, a walnut oil — also failed, as did Passionata nectar from France and a microwavable chili found at a cookout in Texas. Although it was a relatively simple procedure to delist unsuccessful house brands, Nichol occasionally protested when divisions wanted to eliminate a President's Choice item. "My orphan geniuses," he called these products.

As the list of products increased, a subclass emerged at LIM: the suppliers. These were manufacturers — often tiny companies — that produced No Name and President's Choice products. If LIM was the mouth behind Loblaw's corporate brands, the Intersave division on the eighteenth floor was the muscle. The fact that Loblaw was the largest chain in the country allowed Intersave to negotiate volume deals at reduced prices: size equaled clout. It routinely made record sales orders — everything from Toblerone chocolate bars to Lean Cuisine entrées. In effect, division president Doug Lunau once declared, "Intersave *is* President's Choice."

Intersave scoped the globe looking for deals. Its buying clout became legendary. Often Intersave buyers became crucial players in the formation of the *Insider's Report* lineup.

At one *Insider's Report* planning meeting in 1993, for example, Angelo Lamanna, an Intersave fish buyer, was summoned to answer Nichol's questions about shrimp. Lamanna knew his shellfish. He was about to leave on a buying trip to China, Thailand, Singapore, Indonesia, and India.

"We're looking at under tens — blue tigers from Indonesia," Lamanna reported. In shrimp talk, under tens meant fewer than ten shrimp per pound. Nichol's mind raced ahead. "This is exciting stuff," he said. "Blue tigers. What a great name. Quarter pounders; that will sell. There's romance there. You'll need a rotisserie to cook one. That would make a great cartoon." He plotted the sell. "I'll go on TV. I'll tell people there's only 10,000. I'll say that we cleaned out supply, that we beat the Japanese to it....Go down and tie up the volumes," he instructed Lamanna.

"The world supply of shrimp is high," Lamanna explained. "That's why we're seeing good prices. A lot of middlemen, importers, have been eliminated. People are buying direct. Japan is the single largest force dictating prices in the seafood industry."

"China is trying so hard to get into the market, they'll do anything," Nichol said. "And with 25-cents-a-day labor, we can do this. With the support of major chains, it would be scary how much power you'd get to exercise." Lamanna turned to leave. "Stay at the Oberi Hotel in Bangkok," Nichol said. "Fantastic."

Most of Nichol's meetings were held in the LIM conference room. On its ten-foot-long white laminate wall, he used a red marker pen to list product categories — killers, muggers, thugs, esoteric but intriguing, and fillers. Killers were items people would respond to without prompting. "Sirloin at 99 cents a pound is a killer," Nichol explained. "A mugger is an item that won't appeal to a broad audience. The trick with the mugger is to get people to try it once." Thugs were new items or concepts, such as Too Good To Be True! and The Decadent line. Esoteric but intriguing might include an ice-cream maker, Lamburghini sausage meatballs, President's Choice iced coffee and tea.

Many suppliers assumed that securing a deal with Loblaw to produce private-label goods would be lucrative. That, they later discovered, was a sweet dream. Often, an initial deal would be struck at a price that offered the manufacturer attractive profits. If the product was a success, Intersave would negotiate a lower price, occasionally so low that the supplier was not making a profit. By then, though, he was indentured, having either retooled his production line to Loblaw specifications or having sacrificed other potential business.

Intersave's power gained a mythic dimension with the story of Harry Van, a maker of Belgian-style waffles. Van had achieved a measure of fame in 1962, when his waffles were immortalized in a scene in an Elvis Presley film, *It Happened at the World's Fair*. Early in 1987, he began to produce frozen Belgian waffles in Niagara Falls, Ontario, for President's Choice. They were featured in the June 1987 *Insider's Report* — only $1.99 for six. That fall, Lunau called him in and asked for a lower price. "It was a problem," Lunau remembers. Van couldn't easily cut his price because he had ordered three years' supply of packaging. Shortly after the meeting, Van suddenly died of an apparent heart attack. "His business was weak," Lunau said years later. "He must have had other pressures." But inside the Tower and out, it became a popular, cautionary tale that Doug Lunau had killed a supplier.

Dealing with Dave Nichol could be equally gruelling. His standard routine was to keep people waiting — anywhere from fifteen minutes to more than an hour. Nichol decided within sixty seconds whether he liked someone and considered him or her worth his time. If he did, he could spend an hour cross-examining, absorbing information, a process he called "vacuuming their minds." In 1987, a German company that made Gummi candies arranged a private-label distribution agreement to package them for Loblaw. A meeting was set up between Nichol; Andy Wallace, who handled international buying; Herbert Marderer, president of Trolli, the manufacturer; and Michael Hulwich, a food broker. When Marderer and Hulwich arrived for their appointment, they were told Nichol was too busy to see them. They returned ninety minutes later and were instructed to wait in the board room. Twenty minutes later, Nichol finally strolled in. He began firing questions at Wallace, as if no one else were in the room. "How much did these people do last year? What's their gross margin?" Wallace did not have all the answers with him. "What the hell are you doing here without information?" Nichol shouted, walking toward the door. "I want you to cut the buying price by 20%. Then I'll put it in *Insider's Report*. Maybe we can do fifty truckloads." Marderer, accustomed to European civility in business dealings, was shocked.

Trolli's Gummi Bears became part of the Teddy's Choice line for children, introduced in March 1987. Nichol would claim the motif had presented itself to him a few years earlier when he went into a fancy toy store and saw teddy bears for $56. He figured the markup was at least 100%. He traveled to South Korea, found a teddy bear for $19.99 and, in November 1986, introduced his own collectible teddy bear family with a papa bear (Teddy), a mama bear (Terri) and a baby bear (TJ). The Teddy's Choice product line, adorned with a photo of a plush golden teddy bear, included almost thirty items, among them Swedish bear , cookies, diapers, baby oil, an infant feeding set, Teddy stationery, baby lotion and bubble bath, multiple vitamins, four varieties of cold cereal, a photo album, alphabet cookies, and a metal truck and car set.

Creating a separate children's line was consistent with the prevalent view that children had become independent consumers. Not only did children purchase products made specifically for them; they pressured their parents to buy foods they wanted — such as Spaghetti-Os and Teenage Mutant Ninja Turtles cereal. One academic study, by James McNeal of Texas A&M University, found that children influenced family spending in sixty-two product categories. The weight of their influence varied depending on the product — from 4% for cars to 80% for fruit snacks. In the supermarket, children had a say 75% of the time in which frozen novelties were purchased, 60% in the choice of canned pasta, 50% in hot cereals, and 40% in packaged cookies and frozen pizza.

Nichol's heart, however, was never in Teddy's Choice. The line bore little relevance to his own life. He had never had a child of his own, never changed a diaper, and he disliked candy. One ongoing source of frustration was that Teddy products had to be natural — no additives or artificial ingredients — to sell to vigilant parents. But if it took that approach, which would be costly, Loblaw would not be able to compete on price. Another source of frustration was that the major baby food manufacturers, Heinz and Gerber, had a hammerlock on the category. Teddy never had a chance. By the early 1990s, the line was in limbo, a weak link in the President's Choice chain. It created no winners — and Nichol liked winners. Eventually, it was decided that new products aimed at children would be launched under the President's Choice label.

A few times, Nichol met his match. One story he never tells involves a deal that never happened with Texas sausage king Jimmy Dean. Nichol summoned Dean to his office in 1985 after tasting Dean's sausages. He coveted them for the President's Choice line. Before he went into meat processing, Dean had been a singer who had gained a modicum of fame in the 1960s for a song called "Big Bad John." That sort of off-the-wall detail appealed to Nichol. He and Brian Davidson started talking about producing the Jimmy Dean sausage at Z&W meats. They contacted Dean and invited him to Canada for a meeting. Dean strode into Nichol's white shag-carpeted office, where Nichol, Davidson, and Jim White were waiting. A big burly man, taller than Nichol, he flashed a diamond-studded ring, shaped like the map of Texas. It was rare for Nichol to be in the company of a man of larger stature; around LIM, there was speculation that he only hired men considerably shorter than himself so he could tower over them. Dean took a chair at the conference table and, much to everyone's surprise, leaned back and put his cowboy boots up on the glass-topped table.

Nichol began with the standard interrogation he gave other suppliers. What part of the animal did Dean use? How much fat did his sausages contain? Where did he get the recipe? What spices did he use? Dean answered, but with each question he became progressively more irritated. Finally, Nichol asked him where his factory was located. "Noneya," Dean replied. "Noneya, Texas?" Nichol asked. "Noneya fuckin' business," Dean responded. It was the first time White and Davidson ever saw Dave Nichol at a loss for words.

CHAPTER FIVE

THE TASTE FACTORY

N oon tastings became a formal ritual at LIM in early 1988 with the construction of the LIM test kitchen — a sleek, airy, white room adjacent to Nichol's office that was built at a cost of $600,000. A wall of glass provided a sweeping southern exposure of the city, stretching to Lake Ontario on the horizon. The room was bisected by a gently curving twenty-foot black Formica counter, which unfailingly at twelve p.m. was lined with white dishes, plates, and bowls containing prospective President's Choice and No Name products awaiting the arrival of Dave Nichol.

The kitchen was well-ventilated and offered no odiferous hints as to the panoply of products on display. Product developers set up the offerings and waited. As a rule, hot dishes were laid out first in line, spicy foods and desserts at the end. The smorgasbord, which changed daily, looked like the set-up for a Pepto Bismol commercial. Weird, discordant combinations were the norm. One day, for instance, scallops baked in lemon sauce sat next to bruschetta, which lay next to onion rings, positioned to the left of three versions of a pork-vegetable stir-fry in peanut sauce beside a steak sauce next to processed turkey patties proximate to mayonnaise next to whipped salad dressing sitting next to soda crackers on a plate followed by two bowls of fruit-flavored children's cereal next to processed cheese spread next to chocolate-covered peanut butter cups next to lemon cookies beside key lime pie, all of it washed down with diet cola.

In tie and shirtsleeves, Dave Nichol would work his way down the counter with a steely intensity — sniffing, licking, sipping, swallowing, appraising, critiquing. Nichol generally disregarded the established order, homing in on whatever captured his attention first. After one gulp, he made his proclamation. There was nothing scientific about the process — no sips of water to cleanse the palate between spicy salsa and sweet biscuit, no focus group data to comb through, no statistical analysis to perform, only the judgment of his seemingly golden palate.

This approach was unheard of in the world of processed food. Formal guidelines by which the sensory characteristics of food could be measured in an objective, scientific manner did exist and were commonly used in the food industry. The Sensory Evaluation Division of the Institute of Food Technologists defined sensory evaluation in 1975 as "the scientific discipline used to evoke, measure, analyze and interpret those reactions to characteristics of foods and materials as perceived through the senses of sight, smell, taste, touch and hearing." Certain benchmarks were accepted. Indeed, as early as 1949, Arthur D. Little Co. in Cambridge, Massachusetts, came up with a method to describe a flavor profile of a product in qualitative and quantitative terms. In the mid-1960s, General Foods created a system for assessing a food's texture; it included not only geometrical and mechanical properties, but moisture and fat content.

In Canada, the federal Department of Agriculture issued a handbook containing methods for the sensory analysis of food. First published in 1967, it was aimed at controlling all testing methods to overcome errors caused by psychological factors. Error, in this instance, did not mean mistake, but rather the extraneous influences that affected taste, such as the physical and mental condition of the tasters or the influence of the testing environment. The book outlined the proper physical setting in which to taste food, complete with room temperature (22 degrees Celsius) and humidity (44 to 45%), acceptable lighting (no dim or colored lighting; sodium lighting to help mask color differences in food), correct temperatures for different foods to be tasted at, and regulations (no smoking, perfume, or cosmetics allowed). The guide included a raft of questionnaires, which tasters were to use to rate such factors as sweetness, hardness, chewiness, and juiciness, as well as complete statistical procedures and tests that could be used to interpret the data. Implicit in such methods was the notion that food could and would be tested both within the laboratory by trained experts and without, by consumer panels, to assess consumer acceptance.

Within LIM, none of this scientific mumbo jumbo mattered. Product development revolved around one subjective reality: whether Dave liked it. If he did, it became a President's Choice product. If he found fault, the item was returned to the manufacturer for modifications. At the noon tastings Nichol would usually taste at least one item for the first time — a formulation of an item he had discovered in his travels or a product one of the developers had found at a trade show. If he approved, development commenced. Imitations of successful brand name products were judged against the best-selling brand in that category. Thus, President's Choice macaroni and cheese was measured against Kraft Dinner; the President's Choice Taco Kit competed with the version from Pet Inc.'s Old El Paso; President's Choice Orange Juice was rated against Coca-Cola Food's Minute Maid brand; and President's Choice Mayonnaise was tested beside Hellmann's. Frequently, the lineup featured a manufacturer vying to take over the production of a President's Choice product at a lower cost. On these occasions, Nichol judged the new offering against the existing product. With time, there would be an increasing number of unique products created within LIM — things such as Memories of Asiago Cheese Sauce, which were assessed on their own merits. There were frequently line extensions — a new flavor added to a product already on the shelves.

Product development was put on a more systematic footing with the 1987 recruitment of Paul Uys (pronounced "ace"), from Woolworth's in Capetown, South Africa. Woolworth's was an affiliate of the U.K. chain Marks & Spencer, home of the St. Michael label. Galen Weston had become familiar with the Marks & Spencer operation when he ran Weston food stores in Dublin. From the outset of his Loblaw rescue, Weston wanted St. Michael to be used as the model for the development of the store's corporate label products. Nichol too became a St. Michael zealot. He would visit the main Marks & Spencer store near Marble

Arch in London and spend hours cruising the aisles, looking for products to copy. "I worship at the shrine of St. Michael" became one of his oft-repeated catch phrases. In pre-boycott days, Loblaw canned fruit in South Africa. In 1983, on a trip to South Africa, Nichol met Uys. When he heard that Woolworth's staff were migrating to Australia, Nichol placed an advertisement in the Johannesburg *Sunday Times* and sent a headhunter over to recruit. Uys took over the product development side of Jim White's job, leaving White to write the *Insider's Report* full-time.

Uys was a short, good-natured, brown-haired man whose sweat-stained shirts bore witness to the fact that he was juggling fifty products through development at any time. By his own admission, he knew less about food fashions than White and the others. What Uys did understand was food development and production schedules. At Woolworth's, he had been trained in the Marks & Spencer methodology of producing food to specifications: to set up a flavor profile, to organize pre-production, to handle the transformation of a recipe from kitchen to factory, to ensure consistent standards. Uys recruited people with Marks & Spencer training. One, Maria Charvat, was a colleague at Woolworth's. Jean Palmier and Margaret Jeffery were hired from Marks & Spencer in Britain. Jim White, the Mullenses, and Ladka Sweeney were also present at the early tastings. Later, Mary-Pat Hearn from Marks & Spencer in Canada was recruited in 1991.

The M&S approach was to hire people with culinary training or an education in domestic science, rather than in food science. Working for a retailer offered a closer view of shoppers' needs and the acceptance of products in the stores. Selectors, as they were known at Marks & Spencer, were responsible for presenting ideas inspired by the products of other manufacturers that they came across in trade shows or stores. At Loblaw, the product developers found they had greater autonomy in what they could present, but soon came to the sobering understanding that all the credit for the idea would ultimately go to Nichol.

The product developers screened all the food presented to Nichol. Almost 80% of the products viewed by the product developers never made it to the noon tasting. Those that did were carefully tailored to meet Nichol's taste idiosyncrasies — the likes and dislikes he developed at his mother's table during the 1940s and later during the culinary education he acquired after joining Loblaw. Predictably, Nichol's taste preferences reflected his age, cultural background, and socioeconomic standing. In the nutritionally correct late 1980s and early 1990s, many of his tastes could be seen as anachronistic. He was a big fan of red meat and dairy products. He devoured butter, potatoes, and cheeses with frightening gusto. Nichol is a man whose idea of gustatory nirvana is a main course of suckling pig with crackling followed by a dessert course of super-rich bread and butter pudding, slathered with double thick Devon cream. He approached red meat with a nearly spiritual gratitude, his knife eagerly piercing the flesh in anticipation of the juicy co-mingling of blood and fat, as if it were a celebration of the primal reunion of body and soul.

Nichol did not have much interest in candy, unless it was top-notch dark Belgian chocolate, so confectionery was never a priority in the corporate brand lineup, despite its high profit margins. Nichol liked the tartness of lemon, so there were always a number of lemon products under development. His eyes would go hard and flinty when he discussed the fact that no major lemon cookie had been produced in the United States. "I really believe," he would say with gravity, "that the lemon hasn't been fully exploited yet." Because he was partial to highly acidic foods, there was a preponderance of tomato-based products in the President's Choice line. The secret to great cuisine in Nichol's view was achieving a fine balance between high acidity and high sugar, between sweet and sour. "Bring on the battery acid," the developers would mutter to themselves. His acid intake, combined with workplace stress in the early 1980s, contributed to the development of an ulcer, for which he constantly took medication — first Tums by the carton and then the prescription drug Losec. He liked ginger, but not green pepper. He enjoyed tamarind, a tropical fruit used in preservatives and steak sauces, but did not appreciate Indian, Mexican, or Greek flavorings, perhaps a reflection of the fact that there are few three-star Indian, Mexican, or Greek restaurants.

While Nichol went through his paces, the product developers hovered watchfully, like schoolchildren about to have their science projects judged. Each came to be responsible for specific categories — one for meats and drinks; another for cookies, candies, and colas; another for snacks, condiments, sauces, ice cream, and so-called "ethnic" foods; another for the Too Good To Be True! nutritional line; another for bakery products; another for entrées and frozen foods. As Nichol swallowed, a silence filled the room, like the pause before an orchestra conductor signals the music to begin. Then came the verdict, swiftly. One glance at the sample and one mouthful was all he needed to know whether an item was too sweet, not sweet enough, too sour, too thick, too thin, too fishy, too salty, not salty enough, too bland, or needed another type of sauce or coating.

On the rare occasions Nichol did ask for a second opinion, product developers would sip or chew silently, then discreetly deposit the masticated food in a napkin. Nichol became irritated when people ate noisily. "You sound like the unwashed masses," he would grumble. People who worked for him were quickly made aware of his aesthetic quirks. He did not, for example, like to see women with frizzy permed hair or wearing bright colors.

Because his taste is exacting, Nichol dislikes dining anywhere but in his home or in a restaurant where he can be assured that the culinary skill and presentation meet his standards. On those rare occasions when he deigns to eat at friends' homes, he does not hesitate to offer criticism. One evening, Gerry Pencer, the chairman of Cott Corporation, invited Dave and Terri Nichol to dinner. Nancy Pencer prepared her barley soup, a recipe that always won raves. After one sip, Nichol announced that the soup needed a few shavings of Parmesan cheese. The cheese was duly summoned, then grated over the soup. A masterstroke, the diners affirmed, just what the dish lacked.

Given the respect accorded Nichol's tasting prowess, it would not be unreasonable to assume that the Smithsonian will one day seek posthumous rights to and mount for display his taste buds. That is where taste begins, in a cluster of cells in the epithelium of the tongue; they act as sensors for everything we consume. The science of how taste works is ever evolving. The notion that there are four basic taste sensations — sweetness, acidity, salt, and bitterness — stems from German philosopher Hans Henning. Henning likened taste to a tetrahedron, a pyramid-like structure with four corners. Each corner represented a basic taste, he said; every other flavor had its spot between the tastes that combine to create it. Thus it was believed that each sensation was experienced by different parts of the tongue: sweetness at the front, acidity on the upper sides, saltiness at the lateral edges, and bitterness at the back. More philosophic inquiry than quantitative science, Henning's hypothesis nonetheless stuck in the popular imagination. Researchers are continuing to discover that taste buds are more sophisticated and that the healthy mouth can differentiate more than 100 distinctive tastes, ranging from nicotine to honey to horseradish, throughout the mouth and tongue.

Overall, taste is more of a physical sensation than a chemical one. It's a composite perception involving consistency, texture, temperature, visual appeal, and smell. In fact, about 90% of what we interpret as taste or flavor is really aroma determined by sensory tissues on the inner surface of our nasal passages covering an area about the size of a postage stamp. When we chew and swallow, molecules from food or drink travel through the mouth into the upper nasal cavity by means of saliva. The sense of smell is the only sense that directly reaches the cerebrum — the thinking part of the brain — and the olfactory bulb. This contact is the reason smell can influence our limbic system, which controls our emotions, moods, and memories. That is why a specific odor, of a certain flower or food, for example, can trigger instantaneous memories.

From an evolutionary standpoint, taste is a survival mechanism. A highly bitter taste can alert us to poisons and also to fruits and vegetables that are not yet ready to be consumed. The fact that studies have shown that women have greater olfactory sensitivity than men is believed to be a predisposition tied to their role of bearing and raising children — a conclusion borne out by the finding that women are most sensitive to the nuances of aroma and flavor during ovulation, or when they are the most fertile. Universally, humans respond favorably to sweetness — a primordial legacy, since our first nourishment, mother's milk, is sweet. What makes a person prefer one taste to another is still something of a mystery. Why a child who hasn't been exposed to the conventional influences that condition our tastes prefers the taste of avocado to banana can't yet be explained scientifically.

It is more likely that Nichol's hypersensitive tastes were the result of forces outside the understanding of science. Taste is the most complex of the four senses in that it relies on intellect as much as physiology. As British academic E.G. Richards noted in a 1987 address to the Oxford Symposium, "The experiences encountered whilst eating and drinking are mediated by the nerve endings in the mouth and nose and modulated by our knowledge, our beliefs, our predilections and what the morsel looked and felt like before we popped it in our maw."

Nichol's focused concentration and sharp memory helped enable him to discern and differentiate tastes as well as recall them. With confidence he could proclaim that a piece of key lime pie under development was not as tart or as dense as one he had tasted two weeks previously. Equally important to his taste judgment was his cultivation of and exposure to the unofficial "taste network": the critics, chefs, writers, designers, retailers, editors, first-class restaurateurs and hoteliers who dictated what constituted "good taste" in the material sense. When Dave Nichol homed in on a plate of food, the experience was modulated by decades of dining at the world's most celebrated restaurants — Les Frères Troisgros in Raonne, Taillevent and Restaurant Jamin in Paris, Bernardin and Four Seasons in New York, The Grill Room in London's Connaught Hotel, the Gallua Restaurant in Olbia, Sardinia, Michael's in Santa Monica, California, Harry's Bar in Venice — places most supermarket shoppers only read about, if that.

As British architect Stephen Bayley argues in *Taste: The Secret Meaning of Things*: "Taste is not as much about what things look like [as] the ideas that give rise to them." Nichol is living proof of this axiom. He is highly influenced by the "idea" behind the food he eats — its cultural heritage, the reputation and virtuosity of the chef who prepared it, the quality and service of the restaurant in which he ate it, even the status of the magazine that recommended the recipe or restaurant. He scours *Vogue, Gourmet, Bon Appétit, Taste, Food & Wine*, and *Condé Nast Traveler* magazines for tips. Nichol's compulsive quest for "the best" within the highly self-referential and self-promotional taste network gave him credibility as the food prophet who would mediate between this rarefied stratum and the supermarket shopper. President's Choice Memories of Sardinia Pasta Sauce promised an approximation of famed cooking instructor Marcella Hazan's famed pasta sauce. President's Choice Memories of Kobe Marinade Sauce offered reference to $150-a-pound Kobe beef from Japanese beer-fed cattle — a delicacy not available in Canada.

Nichol's idea of what constituted good taste could be inflexible. Here Uys and his people would sometimes intervene. If they agreed a product was wonderful, Nichol considered it, even if he wasn't entirely enthusiastic. He balked at the idea of salsa at first, as well as the idea for what came to be known as Ribettes, a rib-shaped pork steakette. He thought both were too downscale for the line, food vulgarities in the same category as Hamburger Helper, aerosol cheese, and Cool Whip. When both the salsa and Ribettes proved to be popular, it served as a reminder that his judgment was not, as he liked to believe, infallible.

The notion that food could have inherent status — that it could fall into "good" or "bad" taste categories — first took root in France after the Revolution. Food, or more accurately, dining, became an expression of social competition. Proletarian or peasant values were rejected; bourgeois values were celebrated. "Tell me what you eat, and I shall tell you what you are," declared famed gastronome Jean-Anthelme Brillat-Savarin in his 1825 classic, *La Physiologie du Goût* (The Physiology of Taste).

The restaurant itself, as Brillat-Savarin observed, was created for the middle classes, which nurtured aspirations to eat like Louis XIV. Tellingly, it was only after the Revolution that dining-room furniture for the middle class began to be manufactured. As cooks vacated the households of decapitated aristocrats, the number of restaurants in Paris rose from fewer than one hundred in 1789 to more than five hundred in 1804. In 1803, the first restaurant guide, the *Almanach des Gourmands*, was published. In time, restaurants — public feeding places where people could afford to consume food at a cost many times that of its ingredients — became one of the most visible symbols of a society's general wealth.

The rise of restaurants conferred increasing influence — and status — on chefs. François Pierre de la Varenne, who wrote what is believed to be the first recorded cookbook in 1651, turned what was considered craft into gastronomy, defining patterns of behavior, ideas about manners, and assumptions about the cultural role of food. Antonin Careme, who cooked for Napoleon and the Rothschilds, dominated nineteenth-century cuisine. Careme, founder of *la grande cuisine*, fashioned spun sugar and molded lard into fake palm trees, military trophies, and ornamental plinths. In the early twentieth century, the renowned Georges Auguste Escoffier established the class system of the kitchen at London's Savoy Hotel, where he put French peasant dishes such as Provençal potato and artichoke on the menu and turned them into haute cuisine for the English upper classes.

By the 1980s, the restaurant chef had been elevated to celebrity, starting with Paul Bocuse, a founder of nouvelle cuisine. North America had its share of celebrated innovators — people such as Alice Waters of Berkeley's Chez Panisse, who espoused the virtues of the freshest, indigenous ingredients, and Wolfgang Puck of Los Angeles' Spago whose pan-cultural offerings were embraced by Hollywood. With celebrity came marketability — in the form of cookbooks and commercial contracts. Bocuse signed a raft of endorsements, from wine to tourism, in France. Puck produced a line of frozen pizzas sold in supermarkets.

Although good taste is implied to be an absolute value, a natural gift one is born with, like perfect pitch, it is more analogous to the ability to sing opera, requiring not only innate ability but considerable training. As the history of fashion teaches, good taste is not an objective value. It is culturally ingrained, a set of learned and specific preferences that reflect prevailing social, cultural, and economic values. In food, particularly, taste is largely acquired, determined by conditioning as much as nutritional value or sensory responses. Food tastes, like fashion in home decor or clothing, are also not fixed and have fluctuated throughout history — the popularity of dryness or sweetness shifting with swings between austerity and excess, authenticity and artifice.

The very existence of taste as a concept — whether it be in food, clothing, or home furnishings — underlies class assertion and differentiation. In industrial societies, most expressions of taste and fashion are influenced by organizations that have a stake in their acceptance. Designers, manufacturers, retailers, magazines each have a financial interest in promoting the virtue of "taste." Of course, it is simplistic to assume that accepted mass market taste is the product of institutions that set standards in their own self-interest. Cultural and social interests also play a role. The legendary French designer Coco Chanel was embraced as a taste arbiter not only because she was part of the French fashion establishment, but also because her endorsement of a mannish uniform for woman corresponded to changes in the social and economic role of women following World War I.

The quest for "good" taste is a pump that keeps the mass market primed, constantly striving to imitate the values of the class above. Mass market taste, by definition, tends to reinforce political, cultural, and social conformity.

Food tastes can be even more complex. The food we eat offers both a mirror and a window to cultural values. No society will eat all the foods available to it. The average North American might recoil at the thought of whale blubber for dessert but thinks nothing of downing a pint of Häagen-Dazs or other so-called "gourmet" ice creams with an animal fat content of 15 to 20%. The natives of Brunei prize rotten eggs. Chinese eat chickens' feet and lambs' eyeballs.

The affinity one nation feels for the food of another often reflects the relationship between the two. Men do not eat the food of their enemies or that of nations held in disrepute. The popularity of sushi in North America would have been unthinkable forty years ago, for example. But Japan's emergence as a global business power caused the affluent North American business class to cultivate Japanese cuisine — and mimic Japanese-inspired systems of management in the workplace. Similarly, *Bon Appétit* devoted one feature story in 1992 to the Russian staple kasha, something unthinkable in a mainstream American publication before the collapse of Communism. Likewise, Mexican food achieved mass market acceptability only after that nation was seen to be a legitimate economic force.

Fashion in food, like all material fashions, is inextricably linked to commerce. In *Good to Eat: Riddles of Food and Culture*, anthropologist Marvin Harris argues that food preferences and aversions have little to do with how things actually taste, but rather arise out of the balance of practical costs and benefits. Harris points out that it is socially unacceptable in North America to eat dog because of the emotional bond between pet and owner. But, from a practical point of view, dogs are an inefficient form of protein because they are carnivorous. Conversely, the fact that beef and milk are central to the North American diet cannot be viewed in isolation from the existence of the multi-billion-dollar meat and dairy industries and their considerable advertising and lobbying clout.

The basic economic tenet of supply and demand has always influenced what is considered good taste. "Esthetic norms and pecuniary norms are highly correlated in this society," wrote sociologist James A. Davis in 1958. "For it is remarkable how, despite constant change in taste, a material object considered to be in good taste at a given moment is also hideously expensive." Thus, scarce items such as Périgord truffles, beluga caviar, and foie gras became elevated as food for the refined palate. Ironically, as technology assumed a greater role in food production, the high-fat, meat-intensive "rich" diet favored by the affluent when calories were seen to be in short supply was eventually replaced in status by organic, preservative-free fare. Food that was fresh, authentic, and free from adulteration became increasingly difficult to procure in urban centers and thus became synonymous with refined taste. Ingesting fresh goat's milk cheese or organic greens was the mark of a refined palate, while scarfing down processed cheese slices and iceberg lettuce branded the eater as irredeemably *déclassé*.

The rise of the tourism industry, fueled by the automobile, broadened demand for taste arbitration. Tourists venturing into foreign terrain needed guidance, both physical and gustatory. Where nobility had once required tasters to detect poisons, now the upper middle classes required professional tasters to discern the value of food and to help alleviate social insecurity that came from being uninformed. Food writers Curnonsky (the pen name of the French food critic Maurice Edmond Sailland) was at the forefront with his influential series *La France gastronomique*, beginning in 1921. Five years later, Michelin, the tire manufacturer, eager to encourage motor travel, established guides that quickly became the bible of restaurant rating systems.

In North America, traveling salesman Duncan Hines made a name by publishing *Adventures in Good Eating*, a chronicle of his travels. The first issue was published in 1936. By 1938, Hines was a full-time gourmet, crisscrossing the country. A cookbook, newspaper column, and magazine articles followed. Hotels and restaurants put out signs with his recommendation. His collected chronicles were published in forty-six editions until discontinued in 1963. In the 1950s, selected manufacturers, including Procter & Gamble, began putting his name on their products and Hines was immortalized on the front of cake mixes.

With television and post-war affluence, "good taste" underwent a process of democratization. Now, what once were exclusively tastes of the wealthy became accessible to a much broader audience. *Gourmet*, the magazine founded in 1941, originally catered to an audience comprising mostly upper-income men. California native Julia Child took the concept of "gourmet" mainstream in the 1960s as she demystified classic French cuisine for the North American audience with her 1961 bestseller, *Mastering the Art of French Cooking*. Written with Louisette Bertholle and Simone Beck, the book was a step-by-step guide with instructions of unparalleled length and depth, including a thirty-four-page explanation of equipment, terms, ingredients, measures, temperatures, cutting techniques, and wines. Child taught an eager public how to chop shallots just as they did it at Le Cordon Bleu, Paris's premier *école de cuisine*. In the preface, she pointed out that the book "could well be titled 'French Cooking from the American Supermarket'." Middle-class North America raced out to stock its kitchens with soufflé pans and charlotte dishes. Child herself became a celebrity as the host of "The French Chef," a public television program that ran for more than a decade. Coq au vin and boeuf stroganoff became a staple of frozen TV dinners.

After Child, the kitchen increasingly became the domain of social competition and class differentiation. Nichol, like many other young social aspirants in the 1960s, fell under her influence. He worked his way through *Mastering the Art of French Cooking* while selling industrial bearings and seals in Saskatoon. He prepared soufflé aux blancs d'oeufs, farce aux rognons, sauté de veau Marengo, poulet en gelée à l'estragon, and chocolate soufflé. "She taught me how simple it was to take something as basic as cooking and make it extraordinary," he would say years later. While studying law at Harvard, Nichol began tracking the restaurant scene in France. He read about chef Paul Bocuse in *Holiday* magazine. In 1969, after graduation, he visited Restaurant Troisgros where to this day he vividly remembers dining on foie gras, sorrel-sauced escalope of salmon, crayfish in beurre blanc, Charolais beef with marrow in Fleurie wine sauce, and Dauphinois potatoes followed by chèvre and St. André cheese. This meal he would later refer to as "my first culinary epiphany." He pushed his way back into the kitchen to watch the Troisgros brothers Jean and Pierre prepare the salmon. Troisgros would also come to influence his tastes in wine. He once asked Jean Troisgros what his favorite wine was. "Musigny from the Comte de Vogue's old vines," Troisgros told him. It quickly became Nichol's favorite. Likewise, his aversions were influenced by the imagery. He held beer in disdain, for instance, in part because the stereotypical image of the beer drinker was loud, brutish, unrefined.

Paradoxically, during taste testings at LIM, Nichol judged industrially produced food by the standards of a taste network that viewed anything created by mass production as suspect. Industrialization — and the concurrent rise of domestic economy — was held responsible for the erosion in the taste of food during the twentieth century. During the late nineteenth century, the quality of cuisine deteriorated as chemical leavenings came into greater use. Cheap sugar made its appearance and factory-ground flour replaced stoneground. Jell-O, the ultimate ersatz food, was introduced in 1897 and swept the continent.

By the end of the last century, cooking had lost touch with many of the fragrances, tastes, and textures of the past. This was evident in the cookbooks of Fannie Farmer, the patron saint of the American kitchen. Succeeding editions of her *Boston Cooking School Cook Book*, first published in 1896, saw ever-increasing amounts of sugar in bread and salad dressings, and the substitution of sugary lemon gelatin full of artificial flavoring and coloring for traditional aspic mixtures. Food critic Karen Hess contends that by the turn of the century, most cookbook writers had become "handmaidens of industry, wittingly or no." With the arrival of chemical leavening, cooks could substitute pearl ash, soda, cream of tartar, and baking powder for such natural leavenings as beaten eggs. Women who had routinely ground coffee beans were taught to buy tasteless canned, vacuum-packed, and already ground coffee. Advertising copywriters told women that food in cans, first produced commercially in the 1870s, was superior to anything they could prepare on their own.

In *Just a Housewife*, Glenna Matthews's study of the rise and fall of domesticity in North America, the impact of nineteenth-century industrialization on taste is seen to fall into two distinct stages: "The first stage produced more abundance and more time for the housewife, without any noticeable de-skilling of the cooking process. In fact, the cuisine of the average household improved inasmuch as the housewife could devote more time to it as well as having access to more ingredients than she had in the eighteenth century. But as the century wore on — scholars identify the Gilded Age as the watershed — industrialization began to have the opposite effect, and a de-skilling process began, along with the concomitant deterioration of the cuisine. This process would accelerate in the 20th century." From the outset, President's Choice was positioned as an alternative to the mediocrity of most processed food.

Nichol's responses during the noon tasting went well beyond how the product tasted in the mouth. He grilled his staff on ingredients, packaging, pricing, calorie count, and how reformulation would alter the overall effect. For example, a vanilla-flavored yogurt reformulated into a low-fat product would "read" differently because of the higher relative acidity. The "finish" was another important concept. A finish was too short if it did not linger in the mouth. Yet too sharp a flavor in a cookie, for example, could be dangerous. A subtle sugar undertone was important. Otherwise, people would eat only one. Nichol sought intensity of flavor, to capture the authentic. Lemon was sharp, peanut butter peanutty, coffee rich and deep. Jim White would talk about the absence of the "flavor hit" in most mass-produced food. "The reason so many people in North America are overweight," he would say, "is that they never get a flavor hit. You can eat a box of Chips Ahoy! and never taste chocolate. You can drink fifty cups of coffee without tasting coffee beans. You think you're eating blueberries in a muffin, but you're just eating coloring. So people keep eating and eating, in search of the flavor hit."

As he sampled, Nichol also paid close attention to presentation, color, texture. "Add more tomatoes to the bruschetta," he would bark. Food had to look fresh and natural, not processed. "Mouthfeel" — the texture of a product — was also crucial. A slimy or mealy texture was to be avoided. At the first forkful of a dry soybean patty, he would grimace. "Nobody is going to want to eat this," he would tell Uys.

During tasting, Nichol would look for ways to market the item in a fashionable, desirable context. He saw the banality of most people's lives. He wanted to imbue his product with "romance." Plain, ordinary frozen onion rings had no romance, he knew. "Maui" onion rings miraculously did. The brand establishment had made lame gestures in this direction with products such as Tahiti Treat and Eskimo Pies but Nichol embraced the concept with relentless and sometimes bizarre passion. After a trip to Japan, for instance, Nichol wanted a meat sauce that could be marketed using the association of expensive Japanese Kobe beef. After the recipe was put through a few trial runs, it was found that if the sauce was left on the meat longer than a few minutes, it would overpower the taste of the meat. The idea for Memories of Kobe The 2-Minute Miracle Tamari Garlic Marinade was born.

Then there would be the logistics of convenience — how a product poured or spread. Convenience was a cardinal concept at LIM, in keeping with changes in eating patterns. The point of view that North American eating habits are undergoing a transformation is advanced by author Raymond Sokolov in *Why We Eat What We Eat*. Changes in American diet are not spurred by external influences such as migration or food scarcity or abundance, he argues, but rather internal forces such as health concerns or time and money constraints. This, too, did not escape Nichol.

President's Choice was targeted at people with little time to cook but who valued food. Thus, garlic, ginger, and shallots were minced and individually packed in oil, Zipper Back Shrimp were sold deveined and marinated. An instant stir-fry was miraculously possible with Shanghai Stir-Fry Frozen Oriental Vegetable Mix. Hamburgers and boneless skinless chicken breasts were marinated, ready to go straight from freezer to barbecue or oven. Sauces were designed to provide a flavorful topping instantly. It was mass-produced, instant "gourmet" food, a brilliant contradiction.

Versatility was underscored. A sauce, for example, would be tested as a marinade, a salad dressing, or a basting sauce, accompanying fish, fowl, and meat. Some dishes showcased President's Choice products in a recipe that could be featured in *Insider's Report*. Creating recipes that employed President's Choice products was one ploy used to enhance acceptance; it not only taught shoppers how to use the new item — it forced them to buy other President's Choice products for the recipe. In 1991, Alison Jarvest, a trained chef who had worked at some of Toronto's best restaurants, was hired to prepare recipes. Often she would be asked to recreate dishes Terri had taken from a cooking class or a magazine and had served Nichol for dinner.

Most items in the noon lineup were snubbed by Nichol, failing what he referred to as "the audition." Of the thousands of President's Choice products produced while he was at Loblaw, he tasted millions of wannabe formulations. On the rare times a product met Nichol's approval, the tension in the kitchen would break. His praise for an item he believed would be a winner tended to the hyperbolic. "This is fantastic," he would roar. "Just fantastic." Occasionally, after he ingested something that gave him pleasure, a look of rapture would flicker across his face. "I can hear angels singing," he would say. Or he would look ceilingward and utter his highest accolade: "It's a religious experience." And, for a moment as fleeting as a swallow, he could delude himself into thinking that it actually was.

At LIM, the time frame between the approval of a new-product concept and its debut on store shelves averaged three months — a pittance compared with the years it would take the brands to launch a product. Inevitably, the number of reformulations required to bring a product into the President's Choice stable varied. Some — Memories of Dijon Raisin Mustard Sauce and President's Choice English Breakfast Tea — took less than two weeks for Nichol's approval. A minority took months, sometimes years. President's Choice Macaroni and Cheese Dinner went through twenty-one revisions before the flavor and consistency of the powdered cheese coating were deemed to be acceptable.

The cost of developing and launching a new President's Choice product could be as low as $20,000 — dramatically less than the average $50 million spent by such national brands as Procter & Gamble, RJR Nabisco and Kraft/General Foods for a North America-wide rollout. The reasons for the discrepancy were simple. Manufacturers absorbed the development costs of a potential President's Choice product, no matter how long the process, in hope of landing the right to produce it. And once produced, they also contributed to in-store advertising campaigns for the product. Moreover, since Loblaw owned and controlled the shelf on which products were displayed, there were no slotting fees. Slotting fees charged by supermarkets for an untried product could run as high as $200,000; sometimes there would be delisting fees, as well. If a No Name or President's Choice product failed to make its required turns, it was quietly removed. Finally, most food conglomerates operated with bulky bureaucratic structures. Their product development was usually initiated by bloated marketing departments, which relied on costly market surveys and focus groups, along with extensive in-store testing and home surveys, to ensure that the product would appeal to a broad audience. Development schedules of five years were not unusual.

Nichol's amiable, common-man public persona gave many people the impression that he was eager to entertain new product ideas from the public. Nichol even occasionally appealed for people to come forward with their products. And, when cornered by a Loblaw shopper wanting to talk about a product or a request for a new one, he would usually listen politely and intently. As a rule, though, anyone making a pitch had to go through Uys. Uys, who was deluged with such calls daily, soon discovered that most recipes — whether they be for marmalades or beef stews or some baked dessert — were pathetically ordinary. "A lot of people saw Loblaw as the pot at the end of the rainbow," Uys said. Most were disappointed.

Many petitioners wanted Loblaw to sign confidentiality agreements before they would reveal their ideas, something LIM refused to do. One American manufacturer who claimed the ability to produce fat-free potato chips that tasted just like the fat-laden ones was so afraid his technology would be appropriated that he wanted Mary-Pat Hearn, the product developer in charge of snack food, to wait in a hotel room near his factory while the chip samples were shuttled back and forth by courier. In the end, she persuaded him to ship the chips to LIM, which decided the product wasn't up to President's Choice standards. Like so many other suggestions, it disappeared into the ether.

Then there were the infrequent stories of tiny businesses that actually scored big hits for the President's Choice line. Such is the tale of the
Chocolate Crackle Man. For half a dozen years, Cort Kortschot, the
founder of Research Applications Inc. in Cambridge, Ontario, had been
working on technology that would inject vein-like strands of hard chocolate into ice cream. Kortschot, who had worked in product development
at Nestlé, Salada, and Corporate Foods, before striking out on his own,
worked with a small dairy for a year and a half before shopping the idea
around at the major dairies Ault and Beatrice. Everyone thought the idea
was interesting but nobody wanted to commit to further development. In
the fall of 1990, Larry Griffin in QA heard of the technology and
approached Kortschot who gave him a sample. Griffin brought the ice
cream to Nichol, who saw its market appeal immediately. "Dave Nichol
saw that it could be a blockbuster," Kortschot says. "It was a product
everyone knew yet he could hype it." Kortschot struck an exclusivity
agreement with Loblaw for one year (which was extended another year)
and installed equipment at his cost at Ault Dairy in Toronto which
would produce the product. Nichol had long wanted to make an ice
cream based on the best-selling The Decadent Chocolate Chip Cookie —
but the biscuit had always turned soggy in the ice cream.

Kortschot's ice-cream technology required some modifications.
The first challenge was to make the injected chocolate melt in the mouth
at the same time as the ice cream did. In most chocolate chip ice creams,
the chips stayed hard in the mouth after the ice cream melted. Ensuring
simultaneous mouth-melt required restructuring the cocoa butter and
recalculating the length of metal tubing through which the chocolate
traveled before injection into the ice-cream base.

Once the meltdown problem was solved, the flavor issue had to be
addressed. The chocolate would "eat" differently, to use the language of
product development, depending on the vanilla flavor used in the ice
cream. Eleven vanillas were tested before the one with the most discernible vanilla bean flavor was chosen. Then came production trials, to
ensure that the chocolate ribbons could be evenly distributed throughout, so that every spoonful yielded both ice cream and crackle. Various
widths of chocolate crackle were tried. It took more than a year of work

in the lab to pin down the specifications. Even then, it took forty-eight hours of continuous ice-cream production before a product that they considered saleable could begin to be packaged. The Decadent Chocolate Fudge Crackle Ice Cream was launched in November 1991 — "The most exciting President's Choice dessert product we've ever launched," Nichol proclaimed in the Christmas *Report*. When Nichol liked a product concept, he often couldn't let go of it. The ice cream was the beginning of the Crackle line, which included President's Choice "Beyond Decadence" Dutch Chocolate Fudge Crackle Ice Cream and President's Choice Peanut Butter Decadence Chocolate Fudge Crackle Ice Cream.

Nichol was not always so patient. He gave up on a variation of the potato chip made with yams, for instance, after eight months of test runs. At other times, product development was delayed until Nichol came around. In the middle of the G.R.E.E.N. marketing campaign in 1989, Uys approached him to suggest a cream cheese produced in Winnipeg. Nichol ignored the suggestion. Uys made a second pitch a year later and found Nichol more receptive. Memories of Winnipeg cream cheese was launched several months later. Uys would use his knack for subtle persuasion to great advantage over the years.

The product taste test was subject to only one override: profit. No matter how delicious a product might be, it would never enter the President's Choice lineup if it could not be procured or manufactured at a price that would guarantee a predetermined profit margin. In this regard, Nichol's taste wasn't given absolute reign. Business interests also had to be appeased. Before an item would be featured in the *Report*, it would be presented at a roundup of close to fifty divisional buyers. These events, staged at a downtown hotel before the publication of each issue, gave Loblaw Companies' buyers from across Canada a chance to taste the new product and place their orders. If there was no interest, the product would be pulled from the lineup. At Loblaw, Dave Nichol notwithstanding, the ultimate taste arbiter was money.

THE ULTIMATE RETAIL WEAPON

Seven minutes and six seconds. That's how long it took to transform the raw commodities of cocoa, coconut, sugar, salt, baking soda, flour, and butter — pumped up with dextrose, soya bean lecithin, niacin, reduced iron, thiamine mononitrate and riboflavin, dried whole egg, whey powder, sodium metabisulfite plus artificial and natural flavor — into a "premium" chocolate chip cookie. Seven minutes and six seconds. That's precisely how long it took one Decadent cookie to begin and end its assembly-line journey through the 240-foot-long, 39-inch-wide oven at Colonial Cookies in Kitchener, Ontario.

Between Nichol and The Decadent, there was a kind of harmonic convergence. The cookie became one of his favorite "children," admired and nurtured not only for itself but for its strategic value. It was his first blockbuster and, as such, provided his first glimpse of the awesome potential of premium private-label goods. Between 1988, when The Decadent was introduced, and 1994, Loblaw sold 47 million packages, or approximately 1.175 billion butter-based, chocolate-studded biscuits. Its success not only bolstered Nichol's confidence, it offered him and others at Loblaw evidence that President's Choice could compete in the big leagues, head to head with Nabisco, the original cookie monster. And what could be done with cookies, they believed, could be done with other products as well.

Olive oils, fancy mustards, President's Choice Macaroni and Cheese Dinners — these were but *amuse-gueules* before The Decadent.

The cookie's popularity gave Nichol a reason to push his way back into public consciousness on television commercials. In these, he boasted that The Decadent was the best-selling cookie in Ontario, and later that it had become the best-selling cookie in Canada. Both claims, predictably, were hotly contested by the people at Christie Brown & Co. in Toronto, the Canadian arm of Nabisco Biscuit Co., which controlled 40% of the Canadian cookie market. No matter. The cookie conferred leverage, with which Loblaw could exact greater payments from suppliers and bolster the profile of the entire corporate brand program. It was, Nichol said, the "ultimate retail weapon."

The evolution of The Decadent chocolate chip cookie had its Darwinian underside — a litany of discarded failures. The origin of the Loblaw species was the No Name chocolate chip cookie, introduced in 1978. But as a food form, the cookie itself dated back to the beginning of the eighteenth century. The word was derived from the Dutch *koejke*, a diminutive of the term for a small raised cake. The idea of putting chocolate chips into the cookie format was a more recent innovation. According to baking legend,, the chocolate chip cookie was invented in 1930 when Ruth Wakefield, proprietress of the Toll House Inn at Whitman, Massachusetts, added pieces from a bar of semi-sweet chocolate to shortbread cookie dough. Wakefield was so pleased with the result that she notified the chocolate's maker, Nestlé Foods Corp., which then printed the recipe for Toll House Cookies on its semi-sweet bars of chocolate. Nine years later, Nestlé introduced teardrop-shaped pieces of chocolate as chocolate chips.

In time, the chocolate chip cookie became a staple of the North American mother's cookie repertoire, acquiring an almost mythic dimension. Perhaps not coincidentally, the packaged cookie was becoming a domestic fixture just as the full-time housewife was ceasing to be one. In 1961, close to 24% of women with at least one child under sixteen worked outside the home. By 1992, that number was 71%. In effect, the packaged cookie became the working mother's new-era proxy for domesticity. In fact, Nabisco's Chips Ahoy! cookies were introduced in 1963, the same year Betty Friedan's ground-breaking feminist treatise

The Feminine Mystique was published.

By the mid-1970s, the relative scarcity of the homemade chocolate chip cookie had imbued it with gourmet status. Cookie boutiques with names such as David's and Mrs. Fields popped up on the urban landscape, producing expensive, freshly baked versions and hooking passersby with the powerful, increasingly uncommon aroma of home baking. Class lines emerged in the takeout dessert business: on one side, the blue collars who frequented Mister Donut; on the other, white-collared yuppies, willing to pay a premium to the corporate Mrs. Fields for chunks of dark or white milk chocolate buried in a sugar-charged lump of fresh-baked dough.

When Jim White presented Nichol with a list of "100 hooks," or products that would lure shoppers, before he was hired at Loblaw, a first-rate chocolate chip cookie was at the top of the list. In 1984, Nichol capitalized on the growing gourmet status of the chocolate chip cookie by introducing the unambiguously named Chocolate Chip Cookie for the Connoisseur. The cookie was designed to do battle with Nabisco's Chips Ahoy!, the number one chocolate chip cookie on the market. This was an ambitious venture, to put it mildly. The Nabisco Biscuit Co., a unit of RJR Nabisco Holdings Corp., was the Goliath of biscuit makers in North America. In 1990, it recorded cookie sales in the United States of $1.1 billion and controlled one-third of the market.

Nabisco's stranglehold on the cookie dated back more than a century. The company had been formed in 1889 as the National Biscuit Co. In those days, it was known as the Biscuit Trust, since it was the product of a merger that ended competition between eastern and western bakers. Under its founding chairman, Adolphus Green, Nabisco introduced many cookies that still dominate the supermarket landscape, including the Fig Newton, invented by a Boston baker and named for a Boston suburb; the Saltine; Animal Crackers; and the Mallomar. Green also invented the Uneeda biscuit — an octagonal soda cracker sold in a package rather than the traditional barrel — and distributed the first mass-produced shortbread, Lorna Doone. The Oreo, based on a British product called Hydrox, was introduced in 1913.

Green created a direct sales force to distribute Nabisco products nationally, a practice continued to this day. This structure eliminated middlemen and allowed Nabisco to build nearly impenetrable beachheads in every major city across the country. With the company's cost-effective mass production techniques and powerful distribution channels, rival manufacturers had little chance to compete. When Green died in 1917, the innovative spirit that characterized his leadership dissipated. With the exception of the Ritz cracker, introduced to resounding success during the Depression, new product development slowed. Instead, the company built assets through acquisitions, adding new products such as Shredded Wheat cereal and Milkbone dog biscuits.

During the 1960s, Nabisco expanded into foreign markets. It also diversified senselessly, acquiring the manufacturers of frozen food, Geritol, toys, carpeting, and shower curtains. When these endeavors failed to take off, increasing pressure was placed on its cookie and cracker division to produce profits. By the early 1980s, the company had grown soft. It continued to add assets — Peak Frean and Dad's Cookies — but failed to refurbish its own bakeries. High operating costs translated into higher prices on the shelves.

In 1983, Nabisco was swept into war. The *cause de guerre* was the new, soft chocolate chip cookie, formulated to mimic the genuine home-baked article. Its primary competitor, Procter & Gamble, launched the Duncan Hines soft cookie. Nabisco retaliated by adding chips to Chips Ahoy! — an attempt to shore up the hard cookie market — and by unveiling its own soft cookie, Almost Home. But the war had little to do with which taste consumers might prefer. The real battlefield was the supermarket, as the combatants, using coupons and markdowns, vied for greater shelf space. In the end, Nabisco's muscle triumphed. Its competition lacked either the mass production know-how or the systems to handle national distribution. Ironically, the market for soft chocolate chip cookies itself softened: no manufacturer could produce a soft cookie that stayed soft and fresh.

In preparation for his first chocolate chip cookie salvo, Nichol sampled practically every chocolate chip cookie available in Canada. After exhaustive tasting, he decided not to imitate Chips Ahoy! but, surprisingly, rival Dominion Stores' house brand, Anniversary, which had pecans added to the batter. It was made by Colonial Cookie, the same company that had produced the No Name chocolate chip cookie.

Colonial was founded in 1967 by Phil Taylor, a former cookie salesmen for Dare Cookies, another small Kitchener operation. At Dare, Taylor had seen how difficult it was for small manufacturers to secure shelf space in supermarkets. He saw a potential export market in the United States and began producing house brands for supermarkets. In 1971, Colonial began producing private-label cookies for Dominion. The cookie was exactly the same as the one packaged under Colonial's own label, but Taylor was able to sell it at a lower price because the costs associated with marketing a house brand were lower. Later, Colonial added A&P and Steinbergs to its private-label client list.

By 1975, Colonial was so successful in its niche that Beatrice Foods Inc., then a part of Beatrice Cos. Inc., the Chicago-based dairy and baked goods giant, took notice and acquired it. Beatrice, whose Canadian assets were acquired by Toronto-based Onex Corp. in 1987 and then sold to Merrill Lynch Capital Partners in 1991, was one of the largest producers of fluid milk in Canada. It also manufactured dairy products and baked goods under the Good Humor, Reddi Wip, Heritage Farms, and Crescent brand names.

The task of creating the Chocolate Chip Cookie for the Connoisseur was assigned to veteran Colonial baker Joe Buchmann. Buchmann, who had been making cookies for thirty-three years, learned the trade in Germany, before immigrating to Canada, where he worked for a time as a baker for Weston Bakeries. Producing a cookie acceptable to Nichol took a year of trial and error. Buchmann suggested adding coconut for texture, which would help distinguish the product from Chips Ahoy! The Chocolate Chip Cookie for the Connoisseur was introduced at $1.99 a bag, compared to $2.39 for Chips Ahoy!

The selling strategy for the Chocolate Chip Cookie for the Connoisseur played to the status reference of its name. "We live in an age that is obsessed with chocolate chip cookies," Jim White wrote in the November 1984 *Insider's Report*. "Everywhere you turn, all you see are chocolate chip cookies: Big Tins, Little Tins, Brown Paper Bags, Hot-out-of-the-oven. Their baked aroma spills into suburban malls, their crunchy chewy-crumbly egos feed ours: You are what chocolate chip cookie you eat." But it also explicitly took a shot at Nabisco, pointing out that consumer taste tests organized by Loblaw rated it better than Chips Ahoy! four to one.

Nichol became consumed with improving it. He consulted Buchmann, who suggested replacing the pecans with more chocolate chips. This idea appealed to Nichol. The chocolate chip contents of most packaged cookies was between 13 and 20%. Chips Ahoy! cookies contained just under 19%; flour was its primary ingredient. In November 1985, President's Choice Extra chocolate chip cookies were introduced, boasting a chip proportion of 32%. Soon after, the Cookie for the Connoisseur was repackaged as "The Classic."

Given that Loblaw was owned by George Weston Ltd., a formidable force in the bakery industry, and that Weston was a rival of Colonial's parent, Beatrice Foods, it might seem odd to award the cookie contract to Colonial. George Weston's bakery division, Interbake, had been asked to deliver a prototype cookie, but Nichol declared it inferior in taste to the Colonial product.

Generally, Galen Weston did not object to Loblaw International Merchants sourcing suppliers for No Name and President's Choice outside of the Weston fold. His only firm policy was that products from the Weston-owned Neilson Dairy be sold in Loblaw-operated supermarkets. Beyond that, he did not interfere. This attitude marked a radical departure from his father's corporate strategy, which was for Weston to control every aspect of the process, from resources, to production, to packaging, to wholesale and retail distribution. Under Garfield Weston, a Weston cookie was baked in a Weston bakery, wrapped with Weston-produced paper, and distributed through Weston-owned supermarkets.

His son, however, took pride in the fact that he encouraged competition between Weston companies and the wider world. Beneath this laissez-faire attitude, however, lay another reality: Intersave and LIM could exert extraordinary pressure on suppliers; both came to be known in the industry for squeezing margins; in some cases suppliers, lured by the prospect of high volumes, ended up manufacturing No Name and President's Choice products at a loss. And Nichol was far more comfortable working with — or cattle-prodding — companies outside the Weston empire. "You don't abuse your relatives," one Loblaw insider explained. "Dave can be as ruthless as he likes with a non-Weston company. He wouldn't be able to deal with a Weston company the same way."

Executives at Weston Foods, the food manufacturing arm of George Weston, were for the most part happy that LIM was using other manufacturers. "One of the reasons Nichol was so successful was that he screwed manufacturers against the wall," commented one executive. "We saved a lot of money, not doing PC." Once or twice, however, Weston Foods rivals took advantage of the Loblaw-Weston connection to undermine the company. On one occasion, a bid went out for a President's Choice sorbet. Weston's competitor Ault Foods, then owned by Labatt, knew that Weston's Neilson division would ultimately be awarded the contract to produce the product. So it placed a bid that was below cost. Neilson was forced to underbid Ault and ultimately lost money on the product.

As progressive — and profitable — as this open-competition policy might have appeared, a troubling precedent was being overlooked: the fact that in cookies and other products, companies operated by Weston Foods were not achieving the quality demanded by Loblaw's corporate label program. Eventually, the use of outside suppliers for certain lucrative President's Choice products would become a source of frustration within Weston Foods.

But that was later. No protest was lodged when, in 1984, Jim White turned to Manning Biscuits, a small Toronto company, to produce an Oreo knock-off. Getting a piece of the Oreo market was alluring. With more than 300 billion sold, the little round black and white creme sandwich was the world's most popular cookie. The Oreo was the standard against which all creme cookie sandwiches were measured. "It's an edible, eponymous experience," White explained. Like Kleenex or Band-Aids, Oreo had become a generic term. It had very high, very defined flavors — the predominant one supplied by lard.

White wanted a harder biscuit than the Oreo, with more pronounced cocoa. He wanted the insides to be thinner but creamier in taste, and with a lower fat content. LIM product developers resigned themselves to the fact that they could not duplicate the Oreo flavor —

they could only hint at it. It took three years to formulate a satisfactory Oreo knock-off. It was launched in the summer of 1987, under the name Lucullan Delights.

Nichol had been wanting to call a product "Lucullan" ever since reading a restaurant review by New York magazine food critic Gael Greene in which she described a meal as a Lucullan Epiphany. Lucullus, a first century B.C. Roman senator and general, developed a sybaritic fondness for lavish banquets. Naturally, Nichol identified with Lucullus. He had to be dissuaded from calling the cookie Lucullan Epiphany; nobody, he was repeatedly told, would get it.

Lucullan Delights hit the shelves at $1.79 a bag versus $3.19 for Oreos. Despite the price break, it was anything but an instant hit. It might have had a "brighter" flavor, as Jim White bragged in the June 1987 *Insider's Report*, and "a cleaner, less sugary tasting finish" than the Oreo, but most shoppers failed to get the Lucullan reference — despite the fact that every package carried a definition.

Hoping to save the cookie, Loblaw eventually asked Manning Biscuits to make subtle changes in the cookie's formulation. In the summer of 1992, it was re-launched under a new, catchier name: Eat the Middle First. The new packaging design reinforced the childlike theme; the name was written in brightly colored letters as if a child had used crayons. And the bag contained a tongue-in-cheek warning: "These cookies are likely to bring back fond childhood memories." The gambit proved successful. Loblaw moved twice as many units of Eat the Middle First in its first two months as it had of Lucullan Delights in the preceding year. Even so, it did not dislodge the Oreo from its top position in Loblaw stores.

The initial failure of the Lucullan put pressure on the President's Choice Extra chocolate chip cookie to pick up the slack in the cookie category. Fearing that Nabisco might try to imitate the Extra, Nichol told Phil Taylor at Colonial that he wanted to make the definitive chocolate chip cookie. He wanted to blow conventional cookie-chip ratios out of the water. He wanted a cookie with 40% chocolate chips, something that had never been tried commercially.

White suggested other modifications. He urged Nichol to use

NICHOL AS NO NAME PITCHMAN IN 1978, WITH UNFAILING PROPS
GEORGIE GIRL AND NO NAME-DIAPERED TODDLER
(ALL PHOTOS COURTESY DAVE NICHOL UNLESS OTHERWISE CREDITED)

STYLE AND SOCIAL SUPERSTARS: HILARY AND GALEN WESTON
(COURTESY OF *THE GLOBE & MAIL*)

DAVE NICHOL AND HIS MOTHER, GLADYS, INSPECT ONE OF
HIS EARLY CULINARY EXPERIMENTS

THREE-STAR TOURISTS: TERRI AND DAVE NICHOL
WITH FAMED CHEF MICHEL TROISGROS IN THE
TROISGROS KITCHEN IN ROANNE, FRANCE

DON AND PATTY WATT, THE INNOVATIVE DESIGN TEAM BEHIND
THE PACKAGING OF LOBLAW STORES AND PRODUCTS

BRIAN DAVIDSON, LOBLAW'S BRILLIANT BEHIND-THE-SCENES DEAL MAKER,
WITH HIS WIFE THELMA. BEHIND THEM IS NICHOL'S PIG ROASTER,
HIS FAVORITE POSSESSION FOR A TIME

ZEIGFRIED WAURO, AKA "ZIGGY," MASTER BUTCHER AND
MASTERMIND BEHIND THE IN-STORE ZIGGY'S DELI CHAIN

BLACK, WHITE, YELLOW AND READ ALL OVER: THE *INSIDER'S REPORT* FORMATTED FOR VARIOUS NORTH AMERICAN MARKETS

GROCETERIA GOURMETMANIA: THE FIRST WAVE OF PRESIDENT'S CHOICE PRODUCTS

FOOD AND WINE ZEALOT JIM WHITE, EARLY *INSIDER'S REPORT*
WRITER AND PROLIFIC PRODUCT DEVELOPER
(PHOTO CREDIT: MICHAEL FOLLIOTT)

PAUL UYS, WHO WAS RECRUITED FROM SOUTH AFRICA IN 1988
TO HEAD AN EXPANDING PRODUCT DEVELOPMENT TEAM
(COURTESY OF PAUL UYS)

ingredients that were as natural as possible: higher quality semi-sweet chocolate chips, pure vanilla, 100% butter. Butter was a radical move for packaged baked goods in the 1980s. Seeking to prune costs, most large manufacturers had gradually engineered natural ingredients out of food, replacing them with cheaper, artificial flavors and preservatives that would ensure longer shelf life and were easier to handle. Even margarine, once a standard ingredient in commercially baked cookies, was being replaced with hydrogenated palm oil.

Butter was a topic tinged with almost a moral ambiguity. On the one hand, it still carried gourmet associations as the basis for nineteenth-century classic French cuisine. On the other, it was a semi-solid fat brimming with cholesterol and widely linked to hardening of the arteries. Butter posed other public relations problems — not least Nichol's own endorsement of margarine over butter in cookies in the June 1984 *Insider's Report*. There, Nichol had praised Famous Amos's (made with margarine) cookies and quoted Pierre Franey, the *New York Times* food writer, who had voted the Famous Amos cookie number one in a *People* magazine poll. Playing the contrarian, White argued that butter was less unhealthy than some of the saturated fats used as butter substitutes in processed food. Both Nichol and Ed Barr, a salesman for Colonial, questioned the inclusion of butter, noting that shelf life would be limited to three months. "Guys, it's never going to stay on the shelf long enough to go stale," White replied. Finally, they relented. Nichol, after all, was a butter fanatic. Adding butter to the recipe added a new hurdle. It had to be handled carefully to get the right consistency. A year into development, Buchmann discovered that butter from Quebec worked better. "It must be the way they churn it," he explained.

Buchmann's biggest challenge, however, was not butter. It was chocolate meltdown. Owing to the heat, the production line belt became awash in sweet, brown liquid. Colonial fitted the equipment with water jackets to keep it cool and kept the chips frozen at -40 Fahrenheit degrees until just before use. With the technology in place, Buchmann upped the chip count to experiment. He created a cookie with 45% chocolate chips, then 50%. These samples were rejected; the chocolate taste was overpowering. He went back to 40%.

Every two weeks, Phil Taylor, Ed Barr, a Colonial food broker, and, occasionally, Buchmann would make the ninety-minute trip from Kitchener to Toronto with cookie samples. Every two weeks, their offerings were rejected: too much sugar, not enough butter, the wrong shade, the wrong crispness. "It's very expensive to work with Dave," Taylor says. "But he knows what he wants, which in some ways makes it easier." It took six months and twenty-two different samples for Colonial to produce a satisfactory prototype.

Unlike most packaged cookies, The Decadent managed to avoid a cardboard aroma. Dry and crumbly, it had a distinctive coconut finish — the lingering aftertaste — and a dark bake — bakery talk for the shading. And unlike the brown waxy chips found in most other manufactured chocolate chip cookie products, the chocolate in The Decadent tasted dark and rich — and real. It delivered a serious chocolate hit.

Long before the cookie's recipe had been finalized, Nichol had decided on its name. He and White discussed calling the product The Quintessence, but The Decadent won out. It did not matter to Nichol that a cookie in the United Kingdom was already selling under that name. It had to be The Decadent. Among foodies, who measured morality in terms of what they ingested, the word itself had come to signify a forbidden pleasure. To a fitness-obsessed population, indulging in fattening food was a form of sin, a temporary lapse into moral depravity. Penance was paid at the Nautilus machine. The name Decadent was designed to capture attention. That it did, although not all of it was positive. Enraged shoppers wrote to Nichol to say they would not allow their children to shop in the store. "There is enough immorality in this world," one writer fumed, "without you [sic] glorifying decadence." When he received letters from people who believed "decadent" meant to decay or erode, he politely wrote back to explain that Decadent could also refer to self-indulgence. This was Protestant decadence, light-years away from the debauchery displayed in scenes from Petronius's *Satyricon*.

The Decadent chocolate chip cookie was introduced in the spring of 1988. "In my opinion, they're the best food product we've ever created," Nichol declared in his characteristic over-the-top style in *Insider's Report*. Its launch also marked the beginning of Nichol's Decadent food phase.

That fall, he introduced The Decadent pizza and The Decadent cheesecake. The Decadent deep-dish apple pie and Decadent ice cream followed. In 1992, he followed up with The Decadent #2, a knock-off of Nabisco's Mallomar, which failed to meet sales expectations and was delisted.

Very quickly, The Decadent Chocolate Chip Cookie became the best-selling President's Choice product, measured in dollar sales. It also boasted a gross profit margin of 46.1% compared with 33.5% for Chips Ahoy! Within a year, according to Loblaw's numbers, it was the best-selling cookie in Ontario, even though it was found in only 23% of the province's supermarkets. This was deemed major news, worthy of wide promotion. So after his five-year enforced hiatus from television, Nichol was allowed back, to tell Canadians about his cookie.

Currie had taken Nichol off television between 1985 and 1989. "He had nothing to say," Currie later explained. In early 1988, David Stewart, then president of Loblaw Supermarkets, oversaw a series of TV pitches for President's Choice products. Stewart also changed the look of Loblaws stores — replacing the No Name yellow with a gray he considered to look more "aristocratic." Weston was unhappy with the cost of the ad campaign and its results, Nichol was called back into duty.

In the aftermath of The Decadent's creation, the LIM clan faced the ever-present, always thorny problem of credit. In June 1988, four PC products — The Decadent, The Best Butterscotch Crunch Cookie, Leaner than Lean Sausages and Seafood Crepe in Mornay Sauce — were awarded Food Oscars by the Association des Detaillants en Alimentation du Québec. A letter of congratulation was sent to David Stewart, who asked Jim White to respond. White obliged, declaring for the record how proud he was to have "initiated the creation" of The Decadent. White clearly saw the issue as a matter of fact. He was oblivious to the fallout that ensued.

Shown a copy of White's letter, Nichol penned a note in red ink: "For the record, The Decadent was born when Scott [Lindsay, an Intersave executive] told me that Christie's was trying to duplicate the President's Choice CCC [Chocolate Chip Cookie for the Connoisseur] for Safeway." The Decadent was his, Nichol maintained, and his alone. Nichol tended to take a proprietary attitude toward attribution: if a member of his staff came up with an idea, it was no different than if he himself had come up with it. "He could have really made the people who worked with him feel terrific by giving them credit in the *Insider's*," said one former LIM staffer. "Instead, he wanted to take the credit himself." Nichol often referred to The Decadent as the first product to bear the President's Choice label. In fact, Russian-style sweet mustards and a passion fruit sorbet had borne the label earlier. But because it was the first product that Nichol had a hand in manufacturing, he remembered it as the first.

With The Decadent's success, Nichol gleaned the full potential of the President's Choice line. Its high sales ranking and volumes gave LIM leverage to demand a schedule of volume rebates from manufacturers on other PC products. In addition to the 3% sourcing fee paid to Intersave, suppliers of PC products faced what was known as an escalated buying scale; the more product that sold, the higher the percentage rebate paid back to Loblaw.

By 1993, Colonial was baking 3.6 million Decadent cookies a day, on top of producing nine other kinds of President's Choice cookies. The sales volume of the cookie gave president Phil Taylor the clout to appeal to the Dairy Commission in July 1992 for a discount on butter. Colonial, like other bakeries, was paying $5.60 a kilogram for butter, which was more expensive than buying it in the supermarket. The Dairy Commission, recognizing that use of butter would continue to decline unless it offered commercial bakers relief, agreed to a commercial rebate of $2 a kilogram.

Inevitably, The Decadent's success was closely tracked at Christie Brown & Co. in Toronto, which produced cookies under the Mr. Christie, Peak Frean, and Dad's labels. In 1991, Nichol boasted that The Decadent was the best-selling cookie in the country, as measured in dollar volume sales, even though it was sold in only 17% of the nation's food stores. Chips Ahoy!, he noted, was available in 98% of the stores. Christie Brown officials scoffed at Nichol's claim. "Chips Ahoy! is at least three times bigger than The Decadent," claimed Doug Miller, Christie Brown's vice-president of marketing. "And it's enjoying fantastic growth." Consumers, if they bothered to care, had to take Miller at his word, because Christie did not disclose revenues by cookie.

Market share was a sensitive topic in the food business. Executive compensation at RJR Nabisco and other firms was based on it. A fraction of a point decline could send tremors through the executive suite. During the 1980s, Christie Brown aggressively enhanced its chocolate chip cookie franchise. In 1984, it introduced Chewy Chips Ahoy!; in 1987, striped Chips Ahoy!; in 1989, Chunky Chips Ahoy!; in 1990, Rainbow Chips Ahoy!; and, most significantly, in 1993, Chunks Ahoy!, now its flagship brand. The latter was made with butter and coconut and contained almost 40% chocolate chips.

Despite this substantial investment, total cookie sales began to slip in the early 1990s, a victim of the cookie's stigmatization as a fat-laden, nutritionally empty, unhealthy product. According to the U.S.-based *Snack Food* magazine, the $7.3 billion snack and cracker category volume fell 1% in 1991, after growing 3 to 4% in previous years. Nabisco's supermarket volumes dropped by more than 3%. Another manufacturer, Keebler, plummeted 4.6%, according to Nielsen Marketing Research. Dollar volume sales slipped as well, for both Oreo and Chips Ahoy! (by 16%), in part because of price cutting.

What was particularly worrisome to Nabisco was the advance of private-label cookies; sales of these products grew 8% between 1990 and 1992. The decline in brand name market share was perceived as a backlash to the aggressive price increases Nabisco had instituted after going private in its 1989 takeover. At Nabisco, it was clear something had to be done. The Decadent, a major Loblaw export, was beginning to outsell Chips Ahoy! in major American chains, an alarming trend. What Nabisco needed was a new and better cookie. It decided to use Canada — The Decadent's birthplace — as its test market.

Late in 1990, Christie Brown & Co. began formulating a chocolate chunk cookie. The process was handled with a secrecy that would have satisfied the CIA. The idea for a chocolate chunk-based product came from shopping center polls. People explicitly wanted more chocolate than was available in Chips Ahoy! And they wanted generous chunks, not frugal, machine-dispensed chips.

Made with butter and 30% more chocolate (now its primary ingredient), the new cookie evolved through ten recipes and took eighteen months to perfect. (Nabisco also reformulated Chips Ahoy! with 25% more chocolate chips, but insisted that The Decadent had in no way inspired the reformulation.) Chunks Ahoy! was unveiled on January 11, 1993, with the sort of promotion worthy of a Spielberg epic. There were cryptic teaser ads on television, transit shelter posters, and extensive in-store sampling campaigns. On July 5, 1993, Nabisco recalled Chips Ahoy! Selections and began selling a reformulated Chunky Chips Ahoy! in the United States. Predictably, Loblaw chose to deal with the new cookie by not dealing with it. It refused to list it on its shelves.

The Decadent, however, continued to gain ground. In a major October 1993 spread, the U.S. magazine *Consumer Reports* ranked The Decadent first among twenty-five packaged cookies. The article praised it as having "light, crisp, browned, slight coconut flavors; lots of fairly soft chocolatey chips." Rated second was Pepperidge Farm's American Collection Nantucket. Number three was Sam's American Choice, the Wal-Mart house brand. Chips Ahoy! Selections came fourth. At Nabisco's headquarters in East Hanover, New Jersey, officials were irate, claiming that *Consumer Reports* had not evaluated the reformulated Chunks Ahoy!

The birth of The Decadent also marked a new emphasis on packaging. Until then, President's Choice packaging had been white, with red and blue lettering, a concept created by The Watt Group. Nichol and Russ Rudd, LIM's art director, conceived the idea for The Decadent package during a three-minute conversation. "What are we going to do with this, Russ?" Nichol had asked. They considered going with an early Canadiana motif — fuzzy shots of eggs, butter, a MixMaster — but decided it would be passé, too 1960s. Nichol wanted something powerful, immediate. "Let's just do a blanket of chips with a cookie in front," he suggested. "There was no great philosophy involved," Rudd recalls.

The search began for the ideal photogenic cookie to use on the package. Rudd lacked the technology that would have allowed him to artificially enhance the image, so he did it the old-fashioned way. He ordered six cases of cookies from Colonial and laid out hundreds of biscuits side by side on the conference table. With his assistants, he pruned the selection to a dozen, then two, and photographed them both. The image with the best contours and lighting was chosen and then enlarged.

The technique of using a photographic image of a package's contents was known as photosymbolism. The idea was to mythologize the contents. As Don Watt had learned at Nestlé in the 1960s, the front of a jar of instant coffee might carry a photograph of a steaming mug of coffee, sitting on a hill of coffee beans — suggesting its fresh-brewed flavor. The Decadent package showcased a romanticized chocolate chip cookie, twice the size of the actual two-and-a-half-inch-wide cookie. (When the government complained that the photograph was misleading, a small disclaimer was added to the bag: "Cookie enlarged to show texture.") The uber-cookie hovered over a rich, velvety bed of enlarged, glossy chocolate chips. Above the ingredient list on the sides was the message: "Made with fresh creamery butter and the maximum number of chocolate chips that we could cram in." The package was not only a departure from the standard conservative imagery used by most national brands; it had glamour. And the blanket backdrop concept — peanuts for Peanuts First, raspberries for Raspberry Temptations — quickly became the design prototype for all President's Choice cookie packages.

In the years to come, Nichol would admit he didn't know what had the greater appeal to shoppers — the cookie itself or its wrapper. Nichol was attuned to the value of the package, both literally and conceptually. His preoccupation with the surface of things had been longstanding. As time passed at LIM, Nichol's life became increasingly consumer referential and objectified. He was always aware of the image he was projecting, a byproduct of being on constant public display. In this, he was assisted by Don Watt, the talented designer who had been responsible for the Loblaws stores' renovation and No Name packaging. Watt had a hand in teaching Nichol the elements of style and good taste. More significantly, Watt was a major force in helping Nichol shape his most ambitious packaging project: his own life.

CHAPTER SEVEN

THE PACKAGE

T he word most commonly used to define Don Watt is genius. People who know him use it casually, the way they might say of someone else, "He's a nice guy." It was Watt who made Loblaw house brand packaging — both for No Name and President's Choice — something people talked about. From the outset Watt and Nichol worked to imbue private-label products with real style, with up-market cachet. They rejected the typical house brands packaging format that featured a photograph against a dark background. Instead, for President's Choice, Watt chose to use blue, red, and black sans serif type against a glossy white background, which allowed the President's Choice trademark and the product name to dominate the package. The President's Choice logo itself was Nichol's handwriting, representing his personal endorsement. The effect was simple yet bold. A stroke of genius, everyone said again.

On the subject of President's Choice packaging, however, Watt was not completely deserving of the accolades heaped on him. The person responsible for most of the innovative, award-winning packaging over the years was LIM art director Russ Rudd. Rudd's department arranged photography, hired food stylists, selected typefaces and colors, and presented Nichol with suggestions and prototypes from which to choose. Rudd was often called on to turn a package around — from concept to finished product — in less than a month. Over the years, his department produced thousands of No Name and President's Choice packages. Only rarely did Rudd, a gentle, diplomatic man, express frustration that Don Watt garnered the glory for work associated with Loblaw, including the acclaimed The Decadent package, which was in fact created by Nichol and Rudd.

That Watt had no hand in creating much of the design for which he was given credit became irrelevant. Watt, after all, was a genius: he had been there in the beginning with his Loblaw store redesigns and No Name success. Just because he *had not* done the later work did not mean he *couldn't* have. Watt was more than a masterful conceptualist with a talent for typography; he was a master salesman, gifted in the art of persuasion to the point where his utterances became automatic truths, unmotivated by personal interest. He spoke in a soothing, mellifluous baritone and exuded the intelligence of a first-class mind.

Watt was a devout believer in The Package. To be a success in the mass market, he knew, you had to distinguish yourself, package yourself, a lesson driven home by Andy Warhol in the 1960s. Perception is reality, Watt liked to affirm. He adeptly applied this thinking to his own life. Shortly after he went into partnership with copy writer Paul Break and designer Howard Pain in 1969, he persuaded the two men to buy Mercedes-Benzes. It was good for the image, he convinced them. Years later, when Honda launched a new model sporting the same shade of gray as Watt's Turbo Porsche, he rejected the commonness of it and had his own car repainted black. The Porsche took six different coats before he was satisfied with its effect.

Watt's interest in cars bordered on obsession. At one point, his collection boasted thirteen vehicles, including a 1953 Triumph two-seater and a 1954 Ford model A Roadster. He was given his first Rolls-Royce, a Silver Shadow II with a cream yellow body and dark brown top, as payment for a job in the late 1970s. At Loblaw, they quickly dubbed it the No Name car, on account of its color scheme. Later, Watt and Nichol talked about creating a car under the President's Choice brand. "We'd put the Big Three out of business," Watt claimed. Watt also collected antique guns. "If you can't drive or shoot it, why own it?" he liked to say. Those who knew Watt understood his interest in cars and guns as an extension of his quest for mastery, to be in control.

In the early 1970s, during the store redesign phase, Watt devoted so much time to the Loblaw account that it became a point of friction with his partners, Break and Pain. In 1975, the partnership dissolved. Watt formed The Watt Group, taking the Loblaw business with him. Though other clients were more important financially — Loblaw never constituted more than 25% of his business and later fell to less than 5% — he actively cultivated the account. The total retail packaging approach he was using at Loblaw, he recognized, could be sold to other clients. He approached retailers with a consumer packaging sensibility, offering a full range of services — store layout, packaging, promotional materials, and display. The store itself became the package.

The Watt look bordered on the formulaic: strong typography, bold photography, strong color, clean lines, and prominent signage. One of Watt's strengths was his ability to translate design concepts into the language of retail business: margins, sales per square foot, leverage, market share. "Don is a businessman," says Bill Fields, president of Wal-Mart, a Watt client. "He's a real practical guy. He's not like most designers who you can't even talk to." Watt refused to submit the firm's work in design contests, arguing that the relevant measures of the success of commercial design were sales and profits.

"What Don did first," says his former partner Paul Break, "and this required a Copernican-like leap of the mind, was to ask, 'I did the work for Loblaws — why can't I sell the concept to someone else?'" Many thought Watt would never get away with it, that other retailers would balk. "A major design set-up can cost between $500,000 and $2 million," Break said. "But Don would resell his work, at a cost of $40,000 to $50,000." He also knew how to extend his own work. For example, at National Tea, a Loblaw-owned chain in the United States, he created a stylized "N" logo that involved little more than turning Loblaw's "L" logo on its side.

With time and celebrity, Watt's fees increased. The Watt Group churned out imagery for Canadian retailers as diverse as Swiss Chalet, Cadet Cleaners, Michel's Baguettes, Majestic Sound Warehouse, Consumers Distributing, Speedy Muffler, and Famous Players cinemas. Watt also helped redesign labels for Kraft cheese slices, Lipton soup, Salada tea, Nescafé coffee, and Seagram's liquor. He designed a logo and the sets for CTV television. His approach was to objectify the package, to "package the package," as he put it. "Thank God there's so little taste in the world," he said. "It made what we had to do so much easier."

Watt's humility only added to his charm. His promotional style was so subtle it sometimes bordered on the subliminal. His slide show to potential clients occasionally included an image of a Benetton store-front, a Limited Express store, even the Canadian flag — none of which Watt had designed. When asked about them, he explained that they were designs he admired. If people got the wrong impression, well, that wasn't his fault. "Don would have the world believe that he was the first person to put a photograph on a can," said Richard Huczek, who worked for him during the 1980s as an architectural planner.

Don Watt's dominant personality also masked another reality — the existence of another Watt inside The Watt Group. The second, less visible, Watt was his talented wife, Patty. A blunt-spoken, unpretentious woman, Patty Turnball was born in England and had studied graphic design at London's St. Martin's Academy. She met Watt in 1962 when they both worked at a small Toronto ad agency. He was married with three children. She had just left the hip and adventurous London and was horrified by the primitivism of the North American design scene, the crudeness of package design, in particular.

In the mid-sixties, Watt broke away to form his own company, Centrum Designs. He took half the agency's staff, including Patty, with him. Patty, whom colleagues praise as a brilliant draftsman and as talent-ed a designer as her husband, became fascinated by the power of photo-graphic imagery. Instant painting, she called it. It was Patty who created the large photographic images of fruits and vegetables used in the redesigned Loblaws stores. It was her idea to use Dave Nichol's hand-writing for the President's Choice trademark and to abbreviate the logo to the PC wordmark.

In the fall of 1973, with the first store redesign in full swing, Don and Patty were involved in a serious car accident in England. In critical condition, Patty had to undergo reconstructive facial surgery. She lost sight in one eye. During her convalescence, she became pregnant with their daughter, Sarah. When Sarah was born in 1974, Dave Nichol was named godfather. Don and Patty were married in 1975 in Nichol's Avoca Avenue apartment.

The Watts' professional dynamic was modeled on the good-cop, bad-cop school of management. He was smooth; she was tempestuous. Patty ran the studio and aggressively managed a team of designers. Don acted as mediator, conceptualist — the big thinker. But he too could be difficult and demanding. Although he referred to Patty as "my secret weapon," he ran the meetings, dominated conversation, and cultivated the business. For the most part, colleagues commented, she was kept outside the loop. Like Nichol, Watt was a perfectionist who did not accept no for an answer.

Watt's agreement with Loblaw prohibited his working for Weston's or for Loblaws' direct competition in North America. But there was still Europe, and the success of the Loblaw redesign brought him contracts for hypermarkets with GB Co. in Belgium and Carrefour in France. Hypermarkets, or hypermarchés, were mammoth discount centers that contained restaurants, stores, and services such as photofinishing, banking, and video rentals. These "malls without walls" often exceeded 220,000 square feet. In the late seventies, Watt also contributed to the initial design concept of Home Depot Inc., the Atlantabased chain of building supply stores, one of the first retailers to embrace a bargain-basement aesthetic. The display played up, rather than disguised, the warehouse setting, the theory being that industrial surroundings and stenciled signage implied that products were cheaper.

At the time, the notion that mass-market merchants could compete through design was novel, if not heretical. But the proof could be read where it counted, on the bottom line. New projects continued to pour in to The Watt Group. The firm redesigned Ralph's Grocery stores in California, reformatted D'Agostino's grocery chain in New York City, and conceived the format of Super K-Mart stores and supermarkets for the Australian retailer, Coles Myer Ltd. Watt worked fourteen-hour days. Occasionally, staff would arrive in the morning to find him asleep under his drafting table.

By the mid-eighties, The Watt Group was so busy it was having difficulty delivering on time. Part of the problem stemmed from the fact Watt was constantly traveling to seek new business, yet refused to delegate control at home. Staff turnover was high. Senior designers became frustrated with the sweatshop atmosphere and the knowledge that their professional options were limited. Yet from the outside, the business had never looked better.

In 1984, Watt moved the company into a newly constructed corporate showplace, at the edge of an industrial strip. Fittingly, given Watt's car obsession, it offered an excellent view of Toronto's Don Valley Parkway, a busy commuter route. The structure, a joint effort between Watt and architect Barton Myers, was constructed on a $1.8-million budget. It was crucial to Watt that it project a precise image. He attended to every detail during planning and construction.

The 24,000 square foot building, like most of Watt's work, is arresting — a tetrahedron-shaped structure covered in deep blue metal siding, ribbed with red horizontal bands. Its only external identification — an ironic in-joke for a firm in the business of selling corporate identity — is its bright yellow street number, 300. The interior resembles a Bauhaus-inspired factory, punctuated with bright primary colors and oversized foliage. The wide open space featured exposed ducts and white metal catwalks linking offices on the second floor. A glass hydraulic elevator slid up and down one wall. The bold Industrial Chic design mirrored Watt's own aesthetic. It also avoided a risk that clients might think him profligate. Yet he spared no expense to achieve a frugal, minimalist effect. And he believed the open-plan layout would encourage a democratic workplace, even though it was understood that The Watt Group had only one boss: Don Watt. He vetoed a plan that would have allowed some offices to look down on others. No office had walls — not even his own. The company's approach was spelled out in brightly colored capital letters on a two-story-high wall: strategy, image, product, package, retail, total design.

Just as Nichol wanted to shatter the belief that quality food was the exclusive preserve of the élite, so Watt wanted to break the perception that good design could be found only at the upper end of the market. He wanted to banish design snobbery. "I have been consciously offended by the way people downgrade for the disadvantaged," he says. "The lower middle class shouldn't be expected to shop in a crappy store. If you want to offend me, do poor products for poor people." His hero was Gottlieb Duttweiler, founder of the Swiss store, Migros, who broke up the retailing cartels in the early 1920s and offered lower-priced goods.

Yet Watt's personal life seemed at odds with his philosophy of democratic design, steeped as it was in the trappings of the horsey aristocracy. There was the Rolls, the country house, and the horses. At one point Watt owned seven, which he kept at his historic farmhouse outside of Toronto which he and Patty painstakingly refurbished. Through Hilary Weston, he became involved in planning Toronto's Royal Agricultural Winter Fair, of which Galen Weston was president. To the horror of the staunchly conservative planning committee, he suggested sponsorship and signage around the jump ring, to increase revenues. The Watts encouraged their daughter Sarah to enter the horse trial circuit. Patty sold her Porsche for $25,000 to buy Sarah her first horse. Sarah became a champion jumper and a contender for Canada's Olympic team.

As talented as he was at recruiting clients, Watt's managerial skills were less imposing, and the business was never as profitable as appearances might have indicated. Soon after building the new headquarters, Watt sold the real estate for $3.4 million and took a ten-year lease. His rental costs were higher than the mortgage. Yet even when the recession began to pinch revenues, Watt was careful to keep up appearances. He spent $30,000 to repaint his Rolls-Royce, yet refused to fire any of his eighty employees. Perception is reality.

Following the success of No Name, Watt remained close to Nichol, both as a friend and adviser. He consulted on specific Loblaw projects, such as the G.R.E.E.N. line in 1989 and the revamping of No Name packaging in 1992. The two men shared the same birthday, February 9, although Watt was four years older. Nichol spoke of Watt as if they were brothers, separated at birth. "We're both intuitive, creative, apolitical, not interested in the numbers," he said. "We know what the other is going to say before he says it."

Although Watt did not play a day-to-day role in the development of President's Choice packaging, his design philosophy had a profound influence on Nichol. Packaging not only protected and identified contents, Watt understood, it gratified more subtle, psychological needs. Amorphous contents could be imparted by shape. An unopened package or unviolated seal offered assurance that it was new and that it had not been tampered with. More significantly, packaging gave Nichol the opportunity to again defy the conventional, conservative marketing approaches of most national brand manufacturers.

Typically, the food industry approached package design cautiously. It set up focus groups and hired psychologists to assess the nuances of consumer response before committing to a format. From these surveys emerged a prevailing orthodoxy about the imagery and colors used to package food. Complementary red and green were believed to be the best marketing colors. Red represented full-bodied flavor, heat, and warmth; it was seen to be stimulating, which was essential to moving product off the shelves. The correct hue was crucial, however; darker reds, which could suggest dried blood, tended to repel.

The color green was also potentially problematic. Although green could convey freshness, as in mint-flavored candy or mentholated cigarettes, it was also the color of decay and mold, and was therefore never used to wrap bread. Bread and other baked goods were traditionally packaged in browns, yellows or oranges, colors of the sun and harvest, of bounty. Blue, believed to induce nausea when used for food packaging, was often applied to frozen food containers to convey coldness. Combined with white, blue took on an antiseptic connotation and was widely used for detergents, bleaches, and female hygiene products.

The airy associations of clear blue and white also created the impression of lightness and low-fat. Decades ago, a Swedish milk company study found that brown, red, and orange colors were associated with fat; thereafter, the company packaged its lower-fat milks in blue containers. Today, most North American dairies follow the unwritten rule, using varying shades of blue for skim, 1%, and 2% milk-fat milks, and warmer hues for cheese and whipping cream, which has a higher fat content.

Nichol had little time for the findings of focus groups. In a supermarket containing more than 15,000 products, the package, he knew, had to suggest — quickly — a distinctive advantage and exert a visceral pull. By the 1990s, more than 80% of buying decisions were made inside the store, up from 60% a decade earlier and 33% in the late 1940s. "A package only has a nanosecond to speak to a person," he says. "It has only a second to say, 'I'm going to fill your needs. I'm going to make you a person of sophistication, or make you thin, or I'm going to stop your dog from being a gas factory or make you the world's greatest barbecuer.'"

In theory, according to clause 5(1) of Canada's Food and Drugs Act and Regulations, no person could "label, package, treat, process, sell or advertise food" in a manner that was false, misleading, deceptive, or "likely to create an erroneous impression regarding its character, value, quantity, composition, merit or safety." Reality was often something else.

A package, in short, was a kind of promise, and Nichol insisted that it deliver. When customers complained that the No Name foil-wrap box fell apart with use, Nichol concluded that the manufacturer had tried to save money by passing the package through glue once, not twice, as was necessary. He phoned the supplier to chew him out. When other shoppers noted that the ratio of pecans to cheesecake in the President's Choice Pecan Cheesecake did not correspond to the photograph of the dessert on the package, Nichol ordered the recipe reformulated to match the image.

With time, Nichol took pleasure in breaking some of the tacit rules of food packaging. President's Choice packaging became bolder, more distinctive, relying less on color and typography and more on photography. A food stylist was hired to ensure that photographs on package covers resembled layouts from *Bon Appétit* or *Gourmet* magazines. These were vastly more seductive than the cliché images that characterized most food packaging: a plate of dry cookies beside a glass of milk; four breaded fish sticks set forlornly on a white plate next to a lemon wedge.

Still, Nichol knew when to draw the line. Once, Russ Rudd approached him with a choice of package photographs for a President's Choice black ceramic serving platter. Included in the selection were photographs of the platter with a complete poached red snapper on the plate. "That's not real food," Nichol protested, knowing instinctively that the average shopper would see a dead fish, not an elegant entrée, on the plate. Instead, he used a photograph of a lemon tart, adorned with violets. It later won an international packaging award.

Inside LIM, product names and descriptions were considered an essential part of the package. The right name invoked nuance, hit a nerve. A No Name seafood sauce was renamed the more evocative Tangy Seafood Sauce. A biscuit mix was dubbed Uncommonly Light Biscuit Mix. Nichol, who abhorred the prosaic, turned an ordinary beef pie into a "Deep Dish" beef pie with an accompanying text that read: "A deep dish home-style pie made with 25% sirloin steak and 6 vegetables in a red wine sauce." Plain white tortilla chips came to be known as Great Whites, with a cartoon shark emblazoned on the bag.

Packaging, Nichol believed, should tell a story. Product names were selected to hype either an explicit or implicit product quality — hence Twice the Fruits jams; Just Peanuts peanut butter; Raisins First and Butter First cookies; Zipper Back Shrimp (because they were deveined by splitting the shell, making them easier to peel); Magic Soil gardening earth; Free and Clear low-calorie, non-caffeine cola; Too Good To Be True! "I Can't Believe There's No Meat" vegetarian pasta; and the G.R.E.E.N. product line.

Often, as with The Decadent and Lucullan Delights cookies, he had the name before he had the product. And occasionally, his names met resistance. Suicide Blues, a blue corn chip, was taken off the market after some shoppers protested that the name was in bad taste. He was forced to withdraw The World's Best Perogies after more literal-minded customers complained that the promise fell short of truth. "You look like a fool," he conceded, "if you say you have the world's best coffee and a Canadian Consumer Association report names your coffee the worst of the bunch."

The inspiration for President's Choice packaging came from everywhere, from fashion layouts, theater programs, Nichol's travels, and, most notably, other packages. Living in a self-contained consumer universe, Nichol mixed genres and often referred to other products or advertising. Lamburghini frozen meatballs, for example, alluded to the Italian sports car. His imitation Ritz crackers were called Tuxedo, inspired by the apparel worn in Ritz cracker commercials. He considered calling the product Savoy, after the posh London hotel, but decided the reference would be too upscale for most shoppers. Real Chocolate Peanut Butter Melts were placed in an orange bag — to suggest the popular Reese's Peanut Butter Cup wrapper. The orange label of Memories of Champagne sparkling grape juice was designed to evoke the label on the French Champagne, Veuve Cliquot.

The quintessential Nichol packaging story involved Memories of Kobe, the two-minute, tamarind garlic marinade created by Loblaw product developer Mary-Pat Hearn. For the product's label, Russ Rudd studied stock photographs and found a Kabuki actor wearing fierce white, red, and black skin paint with a shock of black hair. It had everything Nichol wanted: power, romance, intrigue. Moreover, using such a bizarre image was something the national brands would never do. He delighted in the perversity of it. He would use the image over and over. The package catered to an unsophisticated audience. It instructed buyers on the proper pronunciation of Kobe (Ko-bay or Ko-bee) and located Kobe on a map of Japan, adding that it was "renowned for their Famous Japanese black beef." Never mind that the entire product was made in Canada and that its only connection to the legendary cow was its name.

Every Thursday morning, Nichol presided over a packaging meeting. These were noisy brainstorming sessions that covered every facet — format, imagery, color, typeface, product names, economics, and legal requirements. The meeting usually included art director Rudd; Paul Uys, head of product development; Tom Stephens, who oversaw U.S. sales (U.S. packaging guidelines often required changes in the Canadian design); and Larry Griffin from Quality Assurance, to offer guidance on government regulations. An in-house lawyer fielded questions on copyright. Someone from Intersave discussed economics. Others sat in to discuss the logistics of production. Nichol often called on their expertise, but his mercurial judgment always ruled.

One morning in 1993, for example, the group began by discussing President's Choice All-Butter Coffee Cake. The product had been on the market for five years. A new size had been proposed, because the cake tended to jiggle in the box. "It says here the ingredient list has been upgraded," Nichol noted, reading an agenda for the meeting. "What's the story? Have we loaded them full of BHD [a meaningless acronym made up by Nichol] or something so they'll last into the next century?"

"Apparently, there's vegetable oil shortening in the product, so we can't say all butter," Paul Uys told him.

Nichol reached for the package to read the list of ingredients. "Who made the decision to change the ingredients?" he asked.

"Good question," said Uys. "Apparently, it's been like that for three years."

Nichol grew angry. "Brilliant. This is just brilliant," he barked. "Okay, let's get the supplier in, the bakery department in, and find out what the hell is going on. That's ridiculous. Pull that product. You can't sell that product."

The problem now fell into Larry Griffin's jurisdiction. It was up to QA to ensure that suppliers did not alter the product without approval. After the meeting, Griffin discovered that butter had not in fact been replaced by vegetable oil in the coffee cake, as was originally thought, but that vegetable oil had been listed as one of the ingredients in the filling.

The next item on the agenda was President's Choice Too Good To Be True! 2-Minute 174 Calorie Miracle 6-Bean Soup. The government had requested a name change.

"Larry, tell us about our government," Nichol said.

"They're trying to protect consumers from thinking that it's soup."

"What is it, by the way?"

"It's soup," Griffin said, drawing laughs around the table. "The problem is that it isn't in a standardized size for soup as required under the—"

"The British North America Act, isn't it?" Nichol quipped sarcastically.

"They've stopped us at the border," said Uys.

Nichol rolled his eyes. "What? Are guys with Uzis surrounding the truck? And they want us to oversticker the word 'soup'? Okay, this is what we're going to do. We're going to change the name to Magic. We're going to call it Six-Bean Magic. Okay? Just to totally confuse the government."

Griffin objected. "The problem with that is that if we say Magic, we'll have to come up with a another sticker that says what Magic is. The word 'stew' is already approved. Perhaps we can use that as an interim measure."

"Okay, why don't we say something like 'a burst of flavor with only 174 calories,'" Nichol suggested. Government regulations drove him crazy. "Let's tell them it reduces cholesterol," he joked. "Let's tell them it increases fertility."

"Then you wouldn't have Uzis around the truck," Uys quipped. "You'd have Howitzers."

"Why don't we write 'Six-bean Magic', then 'Stew' underneath," Griffin suggested.

"Let's do that," Nichol said. "Next, what's this about a request for redesign of the Memories of Napoli Basil Pasta Sauce, the Sun-Dried Tomato Pasta Sauce, and the Memories of Sardinia Marinara Pasta Sauce?" All of these products were packaged in glass jars with similar labels; only the words, the color of type, and the lid distinguished them.

"It's a recommendation from a National Groceries/Intersave review session," someone explained. "They say the labeling is confusing. For example, on Sardinia, they don't think it's recognizable as containing cheese. They think that if we revise the labels, they might sell better."

"In terms of copy, it would be good to play up the cheese issue," Nichol agreed. Every product needed its own hook.

Rudd handed him a box of couscous called Memories of Marrakech. The package featured a striking photograph of a (presumably) Muslim woman; her dark almond-shaped eyes peered through a royal blue veil. Nichol had found the photograph in a fashion magazine and wanted to use it on a package. Rudd purchased the image to use on the Memories of Ancient Damascus Pomegranate Sauce bottle. Nichol liked it so much, he wanted to use it again on the couscous box.

"This is one of the most fantastic packages we've ever done," Nichol said. "Outstanding. Can you see a national brand ever doing a package like that? It's beyond the realm. Can you see P&G [Procter & Gamble] doing a product like that?"

Next, a prototype for a box of Clear Choice dishwasher machine powder. Rudd's design featured a photograph of a shining plate standing on its side with a wine glass, also sparkling, in front of it. The background was black. Getting the plate to reflect light properly had been grueling. Rudd had a glass plate custom-made and then lacquered with ten coats of enamel in an auto body shop, but distortions appeared. Finally, he generated the image on his $100,000 state-of-the-art Macintosh Quadra 950 computer. It allowed him to manipulate images to a level of perfection that photographs could not achieve.

Generally, Nichol was a big fan of black packaging, particularly on luxury items. Chanel products' packaging was his favorite. "Instant sophistication," he said. "It tells the world you've got great taste." The association of darker colors with wealth and prestige was not a modern phenomenon. It actually dated back to before the Industrial Revolution, when only the clergy and the affluent could afford the expense of dark dyes. For the dishwasher detergent, however, Nichol rejected the black background. "I want to see that on a white background," he said. "Black doesn't work. It's negative from an emotional point of view. Dirty dishes is essentially what that says to me."

The group was ready to address a more serious issue. Rudd presented Nichol with artwork for new labels on a product called "25% Sirloin Pasta Sauce." The product had been launched in the spring of 1993, despite substandard printing on its label. The photograph of ground beef in the background had been blurred, making the meat look like a mound of worms. Everyone acknowledged the problem, but the package had to be approved, despite its imperfections, to meet the *Insider's Report* deadline.

Now, Rudd had created variations on the original theme. The photograph of the ground meat on the new label was a deeper red and it had lost the wormy effect. He had changed the typography and label format as well. "I don't know if this is the answer," Nichol said. "But this is the one to go with. Do you think that solves the problem?"

"It's far superior to what we have," he was assured.

"Yeah, but the one we have...we blew it," said Nichol, shaking his head.

Loblaw's idea was to emphasize the high ratio of sirloin in the sauce compared to competing brands. But using photosymbolism to depict meat had always been fraught with problems. Most North American supermarket shoppers were squeamish about direct references to the origins of meat in packaged goods, preferring not to associate dinner with living creatures. Lamb, for instance, was never sold with pictures of sheep on the package. Consumers ate beef or pork, not cow or pig. Cattle imagery worked best in a symbolic context, such as on dairy products to connote freshness or in products that could not legally be called dairy, such as "cheese product" slices.

Then Paul Uys asked the question on everyone's mind. "Do you actually think it's a good idea to show raw meat?"

"Everybody who looks at it comments on the raw beef," said Dori Burchat, an artist in Rudd's department. "And it's usually negative."

"That's my concern," Uys replied.

"What about black marble with thin lines of white?" Nichol suggested for the background. He liked marble.

"We can do that on the machine," Burchat said.

"We're asking people to pay a dollar more than the national brand," he pointed out. "So this label has to say this is a very special product. Now, 25% sirloin says very special, but from an image view it has to say very special....You don't see a black Aberdeen Angus cow on the front with a red 25% sirloin stretched along its back?"

Rudd shook his head. "Meat doesn't come from an animal. It comes from a box or a can," he told Nichol. "You taught me that."

"Remember the Texas longhorn sausage," said Uys. A few years earlier, Rudd had put an illustration of a longhorn steer on a package of sausages. The product failed to sell and was delisted.

"What about adopting a more glamorous approach?" someone suggested. "Like we do with the béarnaise sauce." PC Béarnaise Sauce had a stamped gold foil label.

"I'm not sure spaghetti sauce with gold-stamped lettering is going to work," Rudd says. "It's too feminine and sophisticated."

Nichol turned to Rudd. "There isn't a way you could give it, let's say, the elegance of a Chanel package?"

"Maybe we could do the background in gold foil," Rudd conceded.

Uys was still concerned about the photograph. "I'm not squeamish, but I think the red meat turns some people off."

But Rudd held firm. "The sort of package we use to sell French chocolate bars isn't going to work to sell beef," he said.

"Let's take another shot at it," Nichol said. In the end, however, the entire discussion proved academic. The product was pulled before Rudd's team could work its magic. To no one's surprise, it had failed to meet sales expectations.

Don Watt also played a significant role in creating the setting for Nichol's personal life. With Richard Huczek, Watt organized the renovation and redesign of Nichol's midtown Toronto apartment in 1978. The theme was Californian moderne — mirrors, marble, leather furniture, and fur throws here and there. Nichol was so pleased with the effect that when he and Terri moved into a large house on the edge of the Forest Hill district in 1982, he asked Watt and Huczek to oversee the grandiose changes he had in mind.

As ever, Nichol was exacting. It took nine months of trial and error to install the light box that illuminated a glass-etched scene that ran along the dining-room wall. The wood cabinetry used in the restaurant-worthy kitchen was ripped out when Nichol decided he wanted steel cupboards and marble instead. A buyer at Intersave told him that Pakistani marble was as good as Italian, but less expensive. Nichol had a shipment arranged. When it arrived, he discovered it came in one large block and had to be cut — at great expense. The marble lined the anteroom to the couple's compact, efficient kitchen. Done in travertine and mirror, the room boasted heavy-duty commercial equipment — including a professional pizza oven — and a walk-in refrigerator that contained a cooling section for champagne and wines. White wire mesh bins and shelves held fruit, vegetables, oils, vinegars, condiments, and a vast array of President's Choice products. Cartons from around the world — including a large wooden trunk from Fortnum & Mason —

sat on the floor. Nichol didn't shop, he shipped.

The most epic plan, however, was for a massive addition off the kitchen that would be an amalgam of artifacts and memories from Nichol's favorite destinations. Its creation typified Nichol's modus operandi: seek, observe, appropriate, package, and name. The original idea for a luxurious, tropical space occurred to Nichol during a mini-epiphany at Michael's Restaurant in Santa Monica. Michael's was opened in April 1979 by Michael McCarty, then a twenty-five-year-old Cordon Bleu graduate. The food was a hybrid of modern French and the Californian food aesthetic pioneered in the early 1970s at Chez Panisse in Berkeley. The front room was filled with the work of great modernist painters — Jasper Johns, Frank Stella, Sam Francis, Cy Twombly, David Hockney, to name a few. But the artwork people showed up for was served on McCarty's oversized white plates. Patrons dined on spaghettini with lobster and American caviar in Chardonnay sour cream sauce; wild mushroom salad with pine nuts, herbs, greens, and walnut oil; and saddle of lamb with cabernet-cassis sauce, fresh thyme, and tiny vegetables. The restaurant's wine list of more than three hundred bottles was updated daily and presented on a computer printout.

This was democratic haute cuisine: artfully informal, yet expensive — fancy food the stockbrokers, film producers, and orthodontists who flocked to the restaurant could understand. So could Dave and Terri Nichol. The couple ate there first in 1979, after reading a rave review in *Gourmet*. They returned often over the years, usually sitting on the patio, which was enveloped in the scent of hibiscus and bougainvillea. The linen-covered tables were protected by white canvas umbrellas. When the Nichols landscaped their backyard in 1982, they ordered the same style of umbrella from McCarty's supplier, the Santa Barbara Umbrella Co. Then, sitting on Michael's patio one day, Nichol looked up from his Villeroy & Boch plate, the glimmer of a concept in his eye. One umbrella just wasn't enough, he realized. He wanted to enjoy the order and tastefulness that Michael's exuded all year long. In 1986, long before the word "cocoon" became a Madison Avenue verb, architect Andrew Volgyesi was retained to create a Californian-Hawaiian-style luxe space under a huge glass bubble.

When Galen Weston heard about these plans, he told Nichol he was crazy. Weston's own taste ran to the more restrained and traditional. He had an aversion to flash. In his Toronto house, four long blocks north of Nichol's, visitors were greeted in the limestone-tiled entry hall with a marble fireplace topped by a gilt baroque mirror. Two serpentine-backed parcel-gilt eighteenth-century chairs stood against walls painted to resemble limestone. The faux effect continued in the living room, where the coral and ocher walls had been meticulously stenciled by hand with no repeating pattern, lest anyone confuse it with wallpaper. The pattern was chosen to echo the fifteenth-century Afghan embroidery tossed over a side table. In the library, off the wood-paneled dining room, the books were all catalogued, with stickers on their spines — art books, first editions, even the Robert Ludlum and Frederick Forsythe novels.

Weston advised Nichol to take it slowly. "One is always wanting to put an arm around Dave and say, 'Don't go too far,'" he remarked. "'You've got a great house. You don't have the kind of money to blow on a glass room that goes all the way to the back wall.'" Weston recommended Nichol do it in stages. "I said, 'Take it out thirty feet. Then take it out another thirty feet the next year. But don't put yourself in debt. The company is still in the red. Share options may not come through. Tax rules could change. Don't be foolhardy.'" Weston knew Nichol wouldn't listen. "He's always gone for the bundle," he says, "whatever it was."

Nichol shrewdly enlisted the help of a local alderman to assuage the concerns and potential opposition of neighbors. He invited some of them in for a glass of wine, over which he outlined his plans and assured them the project would be completed in three months.

The construction took a year and more than $1 million to complete. When the skylight was constructed, he wanted it lined with mirror to resemble Windows on the World, the restaurant atop the World Trade Center that overlooked the Manhattan skyline. After the mirror was installed, he called Huczek in a fit. "I looked up last night, Richard, and all I saw was the face of a guy living in the apartment building next door looking in." The mirror was removed.

When it was finished in the summer of 1987, Nichol named his creation. The Dome, he called it. The Dome was Xanadu north, a room bigger than a regulation tennis court, enclosed under a thirty-foot-high glass bubble. The floor was sandstone. Dense designer tropical foliage — bamboo and yucca trees, bird of paradises, white azaleas, orchids, philanthopis — filled the space on the advice of Jimmy Graham, who handled gardening merchandise for Loblaw. Its dramatic centerpiece was a twenty-foot Muskoka rock waterfall that turned on and off with the flick of a switch, a Zen decorator touch. The waterfall was not unlike one that had captivated Nichol in the lobby of the Dakota restaurant in Dallas, Texas. "If I had to nominate a restaurant for 'Most Unusual Architecture,'" he wrote in the *Insider's Report* in 1987, "it would be the Dakota in downtown Dallas. It's not the marble (although there's plenty of that), but the fact that the restaurant is built in an open pit below street level and its guests are surrounded by a CASCADING WATERFALL!!"

The Dome's furniture was custom-ordered from Nienkämper, a Toronto furniture manufacturer. A crescent-shaped chamois banquette that sat twelve was positioned on one wall, circling a thick white slab marble table with an open fireplace with brass appointments. Adornments included Navajo blanket throws and a kilim-covered ottoman. To one side, an iron magazine rack contains the latest issues of dozens of magazines — *Gourmet*, Australian *Vogue*, *Condé Nast Traveler*, *Food & Wine*, *Fortune*, *Bon Appétit*. A Mitsubishi big-screen television was nestled in greenery beside a compact-disc machine and video-cassette recorder. Off in the corner, a white metal spiral staircase leads to Nichol's second-floor home office, which overlooks the scene below. Across the room sat a glass-topped marble dining table covered by the Michael's-inspired white canvas umbrella and surrounded by eight sand-colored leather sling-back chairs.

This hermetic, high-concept Shangri-La would become his habitat, a sanctuary he could control. The Dome would come to play a central role in the Nichols' life. Under its glass bubble, they could take refuge from the lapses of taste and imperfections of the outside world. There, he and Terri entertained the culinary superstars they met in their travels — star chef Jacques Pepin who once cooked for French prime minister Charles DeGaulle; Michel Troisgros; Julian Nicolini from New York's

Four Seasons restaurant; Gordon Seagal from Crate & Barrel; Joe Coulombe from Trader Joe's. Special occasions were catered by the Toronto chef of the moment. The space served as the official site for male climacterics in the upper echelons of Loblaw — the fiftieth birthday parties of president Richard Currie, Galen Weston, and Nichol himself.

But while The Dome provided the Nichols with privacy, neighbors found that it encroached on theirs. Complaints were filed during the lengthy renovation about the noise. Protests were also registered with Nichol about the clunky satellite dish on the roof. Some particularly irate neighbors even filed a lawsuit; it was settled quietly out of court.

Nichol strove to isolate himself further from the madding crowd. To this end, he arranged with the superintendent of the four-story apartment on the west side of the house to plant five pyramidal English oak trees, at a cost of $5,000 each, on the apartment's property — to obscure The Dome. This particular variety of oak was chosen because it did not completely shed its leaves in the fall, and the cover would afford greater privacy throughout the winter. In the late fall, however, the leaves on the trees, which were suffering from transplant shock, began to drift down. Shortly after, residents of the apartment's fourth floor witnessed a strange sight: workmen wiring fabric leaves, printed a mottled green and brown pattern, onto the branches. Eventually, the trees were restored to health and the cloth facsimiles fell to the ground. Nichol had maple trees planted in between the oaks to ensure maximum leaf coverage. For Dave Nichol, there was nothing, not even nature, that could not be improved with packaging. And as the President's Choice line ventured into new territories, ethnicity and dog food, environmentalism and beer, nutrition and soft drinks, The Package became the overriding principle. Echoing McLuhan's "medium is the message," the product was The Package.

CHAPTER EIGHT

WHITE BREAD REBELLION

T he supermarket was conspicuously late in responding to the impact of ethnic diversity on North American taste. Interest in foreign cuisine had begun to percolate with the publication in 1961 of Julia Child's seminal *Mastering the Art of French Cooking* and her subsequent television shows. But it took decades for this shifting sensibility to trickle down to the supermarket. It was common for supermarkets to cater to the ethnic composition of their surrounding neighborhoods, but the broader, cosmopolitan makeup of most cities was not reflected on the shelves. When supermarkets did offer ethnic food (which, except in Quebec, was classified as anything not traceable to the British Isles), it was ghettoized in its own small section, with products that included chow mein noodles, pasta, soy sauce, and bottled spaghetti sauces.

Outside the supermarket, however, acceptance of ethnic cuisine was taking root, fueled by the post-war exodus of Europeans and Asians to Canada and by the influx of immigrants to the United States that followed the Immigration Reform Act of 1965. (The new law scrapped the quota system and opened the floodgates to immigrants from China, Thailand, Viet Nam, Korea, Italy, Mexico, and the Caribbean.) The most significant catalyst, however, was the appearance of the Boeing 747 wide-bodied jetliner, which went into service on the north Atlantic route in 1971. The plane, which carried almost five hundred people, made overseas travel affordable for the first time and opened North

Americans' culinary horizons. Connoisseurship of authentic exotic cuisines became a mark of sophistication. Specialty stores and restaurants sprouted up. The best-selling Time-Life Foods of the World series of books allowed people to prepare "ethnic" foods at home. By the 1980s, food conglomerates had jumped onto the bandwagon with what were known as "ethnic flavor-profiles" — Thai chicken, Indian curries, Italian sauces — that were not only perceived to be more flavorful, but were generally more salutary (read lower calories and lower fat) than traditional North American dishes. Usually these offerings were dissipated versions of the real thing; to cater to cautious supermarket shoppers, they had been modified, sanitized, and homogenized.

Dave Nichol understood both the deep-rooted phobias that could be elicited by the foods of other cultures, as well as the status they could convey. He instinctively knew how to package unfamiliar food, be it pita and nan breads, French cheeses, basmati rice, balsamic vinegar, extra virgin olive oil, croissants, salsa, spicy Thai marinades, or spicy Jamaican soups. To this end, he summoned the skills of a large and diverse cast of characters — Sam the Pita Man, Fabio the Olive Oil Broker, Arnold the Peanut Sauce Maker, José the Food Broker, Arpi the Restaurateur, Lew the Scion to a Southern Ontario Jam Dynasty, Greg the "World-Class" Gourmet Chef. With their assistance, and occasional resistance, Dave Nichol marketed ethnicity to unworldly palates. Five stories demonstrate his success.

THE SALSA MYTH

When the 1980s began, salsa — the Mexican name for a spicy blend of tomatoes, onions, garlic, and hot jalapeno peppers — was a fringe food, a veritable affront to the bland, suburban North American palate. By decade's end, however, the staple of Mexican cuisine had been embraced by the mainstream. It was ubiquitous, dispensed everywhere from Taco Bell to trendy restaurants specializing in cuisine based on the Santa Fe aesthetic. A *New York Times* article noted that between 1987 and 1991, sales of salsa more than doubled from about $300 million (U.S.) to over $640 million. This meant, according to the *Times*, that salsa had unseated ketchup — sales of which had remained flat at almost $600 million — as the country's favorite condiment.

Ketchup's overthrow was celebrated as a kind of cultural landmark: Americans were rejecting the sugary, the processed, and the bland in favor of the spicy, the natural, and the ethnic. What's more, salsa's new-found popularity, wrote *New York Times* food writer Molly O'Neill, spelled "the death knell for the sort of cooking ketchup enhances."

Thus was born the salsa myth. The source of the *Times'* story was a February 1992 study released by Packaged Facts, a New York market research firm. Like all such companies, Packaged Facts sold analysis based on selective research, extrapolations, and forecasts. Like the *Times* itself, its livelihood depended on selling a good story. The Packaged Facts study pitted ketchup against a broader Mexican food category that included salsa, picante sauce, and other sauces, including burrito, mole, and marinated jalapeno. Closer examination of the numbers revealed that, in fact, good old ketchup was still far more popular than salsa. The Packaged Facts study used dollar sales figures from U.S. supermarkets as its source, then projected sales figures for convenience stores, gourmet outlets, delicatessens, and Mexican specialty stores. Not included were sales figures from fast-food outlets, institutional clients such as hospitals, schools, and prisons, as well as restaurants, where the bulk of ketchup sales were made.

Moreover, by measuring dollar sales in supermarkets, it was inevitable that salsa would appear more popular. The average price for a quart of ketchup was $1.16; for salsa, $5.50. On whatever day dollar sales of salsa exceeded those of ketchup, the ketchup would still have been 4.74 times more popular than salsa because salsa was that much more expensive. Consumers also tended to go through salsa more quickly, since it can be used in dips, marinades, and sauces. Even David Weiss, president of Packaged Facts, later acknowledged that ketchup was still more popular than salsa overall.

But salsa's appeal, and what differentiated it from ketchup, was a nutritionally correct profile. It was lower in calories and sodium than ketchup. It was often made without preservatives. Salsa had become the condiment of fashionable choice. Ketchup was seen to be lower-class, a staple of white-trash cuisine, the perfect, acidic accompaniment to a diet of greasy, takeout fast food. Fresh, unadulterated salsa, on the other hand, became emblematic of culinary — and nutritional — awareness. By 1995, Packaged Facts predicted, Mexican sauce sales would hit the $1.3 billion range, growing by about 14% per year. Ketchup sales were expected to remain fairly flat, growing at only about 3% per year.

Salsa, in short, was a market that ketchup makers, even the mono-liths like H.J. Heinz, could not ignore. In the mid-1980s, Heinz, which had bottled ketchup commercially since 1876, tried (with British Worcestershire sauce giant Lea & Perrins) to buy Pace Foods, the San Antonio-based company that had been supplying 27% of the American salsa market and 20% of the Western Canadian market. The takeover attempt failed. Meanwhile, other food giants were storming into the salsa market. Nabisco peddled Ortega and Pet's Old El Paso; Frito Lay, which was owned by Pepsi-Cola, produced its own Chunky Salsa.

Dave Nichol came to salsa indirectly and rather reluctantly. The idea of selling a President's Choice salsa was introduced by product developer Chris Grikscheit in March 1987, after he discovered a tangy salsa made by Enrico's, a small company in Syracuse, New York, at a health food trade show in California. Grikscheit had been raised in the United States and had witnessed the growing popularity of salsa, a side effect of a burgeon-ing Hispanic population. When Grikscheit returned from California, he took the salsa to José Gutierrez, the buyer at Intersave for what was known as the ethnic food category. Within Loblaw, a company controlled primarily by Anglo-Saxon men, "ethnic" was defined as all food that did not come from North America, the United Kingdom, or Germany.

Gutierrez was a cosmopolitan man who had been Chilean trade com-missioner to Canada before joining Intersave in 1986. Impressed by Enrico's salsa, he took it to Nichol. Nichol, to no one's surprise, rejected it. Around LIM, Nichol's aversion to spicy food was well-known. It wasn't only the heat he objected to; it was what spicy food represented. "David Nichol hated Mexico as a concept," a former Loblaw employee explains. Nichol held the then prevalent attitude that the dominant use of spice, like a dom-inant use of sugar, was an indicator of lower class; it was crude.

Nichol's bias against spicy "peasant" foods had as much to do with their origin as with the actual taste. In *Class*, a 1983 examination of the symbols denoting class status, essayist Paul Fussell examines the stigma attached to spicy food. "Spicy effects return near the bottom of the status ladder, where ethnic items begin to appear: Polish sausage, hot pickles and the like," Fussell writes. "This is the main reason the middle class abjures such tastes, believing them to be associated with low people, non-Anglo-Saxon foreigners, recent immigrants and such riff-raff, who can almost always be identified by their fondness for unambiguous and ungenteel flavors." Thus Mexican food, according to Fussell, was perceived to be "irredeemably vulgar."

Nichol's attraction to the food of any given culture was based on his travels and the service he had received. For that reason, he loved France, Hawaii, Great Britain, and Brazil. He enjoyed Italian cuisine, but he disliked traveling in Italy. Part of his discomfort, no doubt, stemmed from his inability to speak anything but English. Dealing with exporters who spoke foreign languages stripped him of control.

In the late 1970s and early 1980s, Loblaw's imported foods came primarily from France. Ziggy's sold Brie cheese, pâté, escargot, béarnaise and hollandaise sauces, Dijon mustard, wine- and fruit-flavored vinegars, items that had been available only in specialty food shops. To hook status-seeking shoppers, in the *Insider's Report* Nichol would compare the goods with products he had tasted at Fauchon, the famed Parisian food emporium. But he was less comfortable with cuisine that came from farther afield. He had little interest, for example, in Indian food. When he introduced basmati rice in 1983, it was described in *Insider's Report* with Western imagery as the "Rolls-Royce" of rices.

Within LIM, Nichol became known as a man with strong social biases. For years, he refused to do business with the head of a large international food company because he regarded him as a peasant. Around the place, Nichol talked about the unwashed masses; whether a food would play to that constituency was a factor in its development. Eventually, someone pointed out that the term could be construed as élitist and offensive. Certainly it ran counter to his man-of-the-people image. "I realized it was wrong, that it would send out the wrong signal," Nichol conceded. "It was simply a turn of phrase: Do you think you'll sell that to the unwashed masses?" What he meant to ask, he said, was "whether it would play in Peoria."

Nichol understood that the WASP mentality distrusted anything too exotic. During the development of President's Choice smoked salmon, he rejected the idea of using a Chilean producer, who offered an excellent product at a lower price. "No, no, no," he told Gutierrez. "People don't perceive the Chilean product as well as the Scottish." According to entrenched taste mythology, the best salmon swam in the waters of Scotland or Norway. Nichol knew that Pinney salmon, which had the Queen's coat of arms on it, would be an easier sell.

Nichol was out of touch with the growing fashionability of Mexico and its cuisine. The popularity of salsa was a mirror of Mexico's emergence as an industrial and cultural force. In 1985, the country shed some of its Third World debtor stigma, joining the General Agreement on Tariffs and Trade. In 1988, President Carlos Salinas de Gortari and a team of Ivy League-trained technocrats launched a program of sweeping economic liberalization that yielded 5% economic growth. Mexican art came into vogue, achieving record prices at New York auction and bucking the trends of the slumping art market in the early 1990s. In May 1992, *Vendedorade*, a painting by Marxist muralist Diego Rivera, fetched $3 million(U.S.). Madonna disclosed that she collected the work of Freida Kahlo, Rivera's wife; her paintings, too, went for record sums. Decorating books featured the Hispanic style. Santa Fe cuisine gave Mexican cooking the leverage to attain gourmet and later popular status. It all took root when a young chef named Mark Miller left Berkeley's Chez Panisse in 1978 to open his own restaurant, the Fourth Street Grill, where he introduced San Francisco's upper middle class to fish grilled over mesquite, white chorizos spiced with cilantro and serrano chilis.

Despite the rise of Hispanic chic, attempts to convince Dave Nichol that salsa could be a major product met with stony resistance and even ridicule. When Nichol passed Gutierrez in the hall, he would joke, "What do you do with your salsa, José? Do you put it in your coffee?" Flinching inwardly, Gutierrez would indulge Nichol, "Yes, Mr. Nichol. It's great in coffee." All the product developers made a plea for the salsa. Finally, Nichol capitulated. Enrico's was enlisted to produce the salsa. Packaged in a 425 gram jar, La Elección del Presidente Salsa was introduced in November 1987.

The initial response was lukewarm. Sales improved slightly after President's Choice Tortilla Chips were added the following spring. Then, in conversations with store managers, Gutierrez discovered that much of the salsa was being sold to the Italian population, which used it as a pasta sauce. (Salsa, perhaps not coincidentally, is the Italian word for "sauce.") Armed with that knowledge, a two-pound jar was introduced in Christmas 1988. It became the best-selling item featured in the *Report*. The salsa was cross-merchandised in various sections of the supermarket — in the snack-food aisle, in the ethnic category with chow mein noodles and soy sauce, and with pasta sauces. By March 1992, Nichol boasted that Loblaw's La Elección del Presidente was the best-selling salsa in the country.

By then, Nichol had long since ceased to refer to it as "José's salsa." It had become "my salsa," first recommended to him, he claimed, by a lawyer on a flight from Hawaii. As for Gutierrez, he left Loblaw in 1989 to become an independent food agent, handling among other products, Enrico's salsa.

MEMORIES OF DAVE

With the success of President's Choice salsa, Nichol became more receptive to the possibilities of exotic condiments. In 1988, product developer Ladka Sweeney brought back a peanut sauce from a new product show in California. Nichol had already sampled peanut sauces at Amanpuri at Phuket, Thailand, and at Amandari at Ubud, Bali, the sublime private resorts operated by Adrian Zeeha. He was also aware of the growing popularity of Indonesian and Thai restaurants in Canada.

In late 1988, Sweeney took a sample of the sauce to Arnold Unger to duplicate. Unger and his wife, Renée, ran Excelle Brands Food Corp., a small Toronto firm that specialized in salad dressings. The couple had started producing a line called "Renée's" in 1985 and had obtained a listing to sell it at Loblaw.

Earlier in 1988, Arnold Unger had approached Nichol about becoming a supplier for President's Choice. He brought Renée to the meeting, and was surprised that Nichol ignored her throughout the discussion. "He only talked to me," Unger recalls. But that evidently was enough. Excelle secured an agreement to produce President's Choice mayonnaise.

After Sweeney's visit, Unger created a sample peanut sauce; Nichol was pleased with it and decided to call it Memories of Szechwan. The peanut sauce was introduced in the June 1989 *Insider's Report*, along with a spicy Thai sauce, also made by Unger. "We've toned down the traditional Thai 'heat' just a bit," the *Insider's Report* reassured shoppers. The name "Memories of" was appropriated from Memories of China, an expensive restaurant Nichol liked in London.

The peanut sauce was an immediate success. At some urban locations, it outsold ketchup. In 1990, it won the best new condiment award from Gorman's Publishing's *New Product News*. Unlike most President's Choice suppliers, Unger refused to sign the standard contract, which required that the recipe be given to Loblaw and that the client supply the product exclusively to the company. Most suppliers were so eager for the prestige and anticipated volumes that they agreed to these restrictions. What often happened, however, was that LIM and Intersave staff would shop the recipe to other manufacturers, seeking a lower price. "My lawyer said, 'If you sign this, you'll be committing commercial suicide,'" Unger said. Unbeknownst to Loblaw, he claims, he obtained patent for the peanut sauce. Patenting a recipe is uncommon. It is possible only if the technology or the ingredients yield a significantly different product than anything on the market.

In 1990, one of Unger's employees left Excelle, taking the recipe with him. Soon, Unger began receiving calls from his suppliers, telling him they had been approached for the ingredients of the peanut sauce. One day, Unger arrived at a meeting at Loblaw to find his former employee working there. When he returned to his office, Unger called his lawyer. The attorney approached Loblaw, explaining that Unger owned a patent. Loblaw could duplicate the recipe, the company was told, but there would be an expensive lawsuit and a fair amount of negative publicity. Arnold Unger became the first and only supplier to threaten Loblaw with a lawsuit and still keep the account. Now of questionable value, his former employee stayed with Loblaw only a few months.

Meanwhile, Excelle was free to produce a variation on his peanut sauce for A&P's Master Choice private-label program in Canada and the

Wegman's chain in the northeastern United States. Unger had won. What he did not know at the time was that he had only won the first round.

The success of the peanut and Thai condiments paved the way for a flood of other exotic-sounding sauces bottled in high-necked glass bottles. When Nichol had a winner, he couldn't let go. In time, there would be a Niagara of "Memories": Memories of Gilroy Creamy Roasted Garlic Sauce; Memories of Sonoma Dried Tomato Sauce; Memories of Jaipur Curry and Passion Fruit Sauce; Memories of Asiago Cheese Sauce, Memories of Alberta Deluxe Party Pizza; Memories of Montego Bay Jerk Marinade; Memories of Fuji Shiitake Mushroom Sauce; Memories of Canton Plum Sauce; Memories of Winnipeg Cream Cheese; Memories of Savannah Hot Red Pepper Jelly; Memories of Hong Kong Spicy Black Bean and Garlic Sauce; Memories of Cedar Springs Sage-and-Onion Stuffing (a reference to the site of Nichol's grandmother's farm); Memories of Sardinia Pasta Sauce; Memories of Ancient Damascus Sauce (based on a pomegranate sauce he found in Seattle); Memories of San Francisco Lemon Ginger Sauce; Memories of Napoli Pasta Sauce; Memories of Lyon raisin mustard sauce; Memories of Reggiano and Memories of Cheddar Cheese Sauces; and Memories of Kobe 2-Minute Marinade. By the summer of 1994, Loblaw was producing twenty-nine Memories.

Memories sauces were more than novel lures. They offered significantly higher gross profit margins than most salad dressings and sauces in that category. Kraft Miracle Whip, for example, offered a 5.3% margin — minuscule next to the 36.7% margins provided by Memories sauces and No Name salad dressings.

Collectively, the line offered a sanitized summary of Nichol's luxury travel itinerary. Memories of Bangkok bore no connection with the stench of sewage, the child hookers that were the stark realities of the Thai capital. Nichol knew his audience. "The housewife on the Kingsway [an affluent west Toronto district] isn't going to forage into cramped Chinatown shops emanating weird smells for black bean sauce," Nichol explained. In effect, Nichol was offering processed ethnicity, perfect for the harried shopper who wanted to add a little pizazz to a breast of chicken. A recipe booklet was slung around the neck of each bottle so that consumers would know how to use it.

Most of the exotic-sounding Memories sauces were made in Canada at E.D. Smith & Sons Ltd., a company best known to supermarket shoppers for its pie fillings, jams, and tomato sauces. E.D. Smith was founded in 1882 by Ernest D'Israeli Smith in the pastoral town of Winona, Ontario, smack in the centre of the Niagara fruitbelt. The Smith family had lived in Winona for seven generations. Over the years, successive sons and grandsons had managed the business. In 1983, it fell to Llewellyn (Lew) Smith, great-grandson of E.D., to assume control.

Lew Smith worked summers as a teenager at the company, picking fruit and tomatoes on its 200,000 acres. He studied business at the American College in Switzerland, and worked for a time at Nestlé and BNS SA, the giant French food company that owned Lea & Perrins. In 1976, Smith returned to Canada, convinced that if the family business did not evolve, it would die. The company's technology was obsolete. It had too many product lines, some of which, such as maraschino cherries, were no longer fashionable. It stored inventory for a year — far too long. Management was burdened with too much bureaucracy. And the food manufacturing industry was facing the advent of the Canada-U.S. free trade agreement. Smith supported this development ideologically, but he also recognized that it would hurt small Canadian food manufacturers. If he wanted the family firm to survive, if he wanted to pass it on to his three young children, he needed to specialize.

The first task, Smith knew, was to break the link with the land. Cooks were replaced by computers. The product line shifted from seasonal products, such as fruit jams, to more year-round items, such as pasta sauces, pastes, and purées. The staff of 250 was pared radically. To reduce labor costs, he hired other companies to pit and peel fruit. Instead of picking tomatoes that would sit in inventory, Smith imported paste from California and Chile. He reduced the number of product categories, eliminating so-called commodity products such as stewed tomatoes. Instead, he focused on value-added products — the same stewed tomatoes, but with added spices and onion, and transformed into ketchups and salsas for which he could charge a premium.

Smith took note that people were eating less red meat. This shift meant that the traditional mainstays of the company — products such as

HP Steak Sauce — were falling out of favor. He told product developers to focus on spicier flavor profiles — items such as salsa and teriyaki barbecue sauces for ribs and chicken. The company began supplying sauces to institutional clients; pizza sauce for the Pizza Pizza fast-food franchise and toppings for Harvey's, a hamburger chain. For the Tim Horton's doughnut chain, it made pie fillings and doughnut fillings. For Laura Secord, it made jams. Diversifying its product line, Smith added apple cinnamon and butter pecan syrups to accompany the standard maple flavor under the Aunt Jemima label.

Lew Smith, a handsome clean-cut man with a dynamic presence, made his first call on Dave Nichol in the spring of 1987. The company was already providing No Name products to Loblaw and house brands under the Zehrs and Atlantic Wholesale labels. "Lew, anything you tell me will be held against you," Nichol quipped as they shook hands. "Most companies send in sales jocks whose idea of food is a Twinkie. If you're going to do business with me, send me a *bec fin*." Smith didn't know what *bec fin* meant, so Nichol explained. "Send me people who know what they're doing. I'm demanding. I expect a lot of things. And I don't take no for an answer."

Smith went back and increased his product development staff to seven. He studied Nichol's preferences — high acidity and a balance between sweet and sour — and tailored his items accordingly. He understood that his key product line — namely, tomato-based sauces — gave him an advantage. For President's Choice, E.D. Smith developed pasta sauces, Twice the Fruit jams, and maple syrup.

Smith assigned two people to handle the Loblaw account. One was Roseanne Shortt, a friendly, hard-working woman. Several times each week, she made the hour-and-a-half trek into Toronto from Winona, often working marathon days from 6 a.m. until midnight. She dealt directly with Nichol. Once, he even called her from a boat off the Great Barrier Reef to chat about a possible sauce — something he could sell as a Memories of Australia. When they met in person, Shortt usually wore dark colors or variations on black and white. She began editing her wardrobe after LIM product developer Ladka Sweeney told her that Nichol did not respond well to bright colors. Sweeney remembered her

own first meeting with Nichol in 1986, when she had worn a bright yellow jacket. Jim White quickly pulled her aside and suggested she remove
the jacket. Deciding to test Sweeney's theory, Shortt wore red or kelly
green to a few meetings and noticed that Nichol was less receptive to her
ideas than he usually was.

Later, E.D. Smith was awarded the Memories of Singapore Passion Fruit Sauce account, and the Memories of Kobe 2-Minute Marinade. Part of what made these products acceptable, Smith knew, was
the fact that they were made in Canada. Or, more accurately, that they
were not made in a foreign country in potentially substandard conditions. "People feel comfortable with this," he explains. "It's not a flea-
bitten package." Smith also produced the Memories of Kyoto Ginger
Sauce and Glaze, based on a soy and ginger glaze that had been
launched in June 1991. Nichol had tried a similar sauce at the Tawaraya
Inn in Kyoto, Japan, proclaimed by *Esquire* as the "World's Best Hotel"
in 1985. According to Nichol, in the *Insider's Report*, the sauce "turned
chicken into a religious experience."

E.D. Smith was a significant beneficiary of the growth in private-
label house brands. By 1994, E.D. Smith had sales of almost $100 million
and several major customers. The export market constituted about 6% of
Smith's sales, of which half was President's Choice. Retailer-controlled
brands made up 34% of its business, up 61% since 1992. In 1991, A&P
launched its Master Choice line. Two years later, the Oshawa Group
chain launched Our Compliments. E.D. Smith produced products for
both. It also sold to United Grocers Inc., a buying consortium comprising
Sobey's, Federated Coop, A&P, and Overweightea. Many retailers simply
took the best-selling President's Choice product and asked E.D. Smith to
match it. Others sought products that were appreciably better.

Despite E.D. Smith's broad client base, it was most often associated with Loblaw. That's because in a self-congratulatory 1991 commercial, Nichol boasted about Loblaw's role in supporting Canadian
food manufacturers, specifically E.D. Smith, in the face of free trade.
This tactic mitigated long-circulating rumors within the industry that
the price pressure imposed by Intersave was putting small Canadian
food manufacturers out of business. Smith appreciated the plug, even

though his increasingly visible relationship with President's Choice created friction. Other retailers to whom he supplied private-label products often voiced concern about where Smith's allegiances lay. "People got the impression we were married to President's Choice," he said.

Smith's smooth relationship with Nichol notwithstanding, he failed to land several key products in the President's Choice line. For years, Smith sought to take the salsa account away from Enrico's in Syracuse, New York. LIM refused, even though E.D. Smith was hardly a salsa neophyte. In the early 1980s, it had made MexiCasa salsa for Lowry's, before that firm was bought by Unilever. The company also made salsa for A&P's Master Choice program in Canada. Winning the Loblaw account, Smith figured, would add 2% to his Canadian sales. LIM told Smith that the account would be his if his product developers matched Enrico's salsa at a lower price. E.D. Smith matched Enrico's salsa in appearance and price. But there was one flavor it couldn't duplicate. The acidity-to-sweetness ratio was off, Nichol objected. Over five years, they worked on forty formulations. Six were delivered to Nichol; he rejected them all. Smith, determined to find the answer, started thinking that Enrico's was using a secret ingredient or employing esoteric production methods.

In the meantime, E.D. Smith won the go-ahead to produce a salsa ketchup for President's Choice. Still, Smith refused to abandon the fight for the main salsa account. He bought a factory in Mississippi that had the capacity to produce 5 million cases of salsa annually. Rob Chenaux, executive vice-president of Intersave, told Smith Loblaw would be happy to switch the account, but Nichol was still not convinced about the taste. Smith wondered whether salsa had become a point of pride with Nichol, evidence that his infallible palate could discern a difference between the Enrico's and the E.D. Smith samples.

Although Nichol's pride sometimes led to intransigence, he could be surprisingly accommodating. Loblaw had been looking for ways to cut the costs of Arnold Unger's Memories of Szechwan Peanut Sauce. E.D. Smith eagerly agreed to take a stab at it. Soon after, the company returned with a cheaper version. Beginning in December 1992, the E.D. Smith-produced sauce was sold in Loblaw's Western Canada stores;

Unger's Excelle continued to make the product for the Ontario market. Unger was not informed about the switch, although he had long believed that E.D. Smith had been given his patented recipe. In fact, the two peanut sauces were from different recipes and had different flavor profiles, even though they were sold under the same label. Loblaw's plan — an uncharacteristic one — was to use Smith for 10% of the account and reserve the other 90% for Excelle. "There's a little bit of difference in the formulations of the sauce," Paul Uys, head of product development at LIM, admitted. The contract, he said, was a reward of sorts from Nichol. "E.D. Smith has worked so hard, Dave wanted to give them a little something for it." Still, for Smith, peanut sauce was a consolation prize. The elusive — lucrative — salsa was what he wanted.

THE JILTED OLIVE OIL BROKER

Bottling a President's Choice olive oil, extra virgin of course, was to Nichol a "no-brainer." By the mid-1980s, this rarefied olive extract was a staple in every gourmet's kitchen. Foodies maintained that the difference between ordinary olive oil and extra virgin was profound (the former was more acidic than the latter, containing up to 4% oleic acid while extra virgin contained no more than 1% oleic acid). Extra virgin was more flavorful, more redolent of the olive, more authentic. It was also much more expensive. A liter of cold-pressed extra virgin could cost as much as $50 in gourmet food shops. Extra virgin was de rigueur in fashionable food— in pesto, drizzled over exotic greens, even as a dip for bread. An oil's pedigree became a point of conversation. Serious oil snobs made a point of sniffing before pouring, as with wine. In more obsessive circles, it became fashionable to have your own olive oil importer.

To the broader Canadian public, however, olive oil, even the cheap stuff, was exotic. And, even though Toronto boasted the largest Italian population outside of Italy, olive oil was a product found in specialty stores. In fact, as author Nancy Verde Barr noted in *We Called It Macaroni*, a history of Italian food in North America, Italian cuisine underwent the same sort of mainstreaming early in the twentieth century that Mexican food experienced much later.

At the turn of the century, Italian immigrants encountered a hostile environment, at least gastronomically. Olive oil was costly and administered only as medicine. Bread was mushy and sweet. Grated cheeses, such as Parmesan and Romano, were unknown. Noodles were made from wheat, instead of semolina flour. Americans generally recoiled from garlic; mushrooms, eggplants, and chick peas were not even considered foods. Many immigrants were unskilled, destitute, and dark-complexioned — qualities viewed with contempt by the Anglo-Saxon establishment. Earlier Italian immigrants, mostly from the north, had found success in the hotel and restaurant business, but with French, not Italian, food. Tellingly, the first canned spaghetti dinner was produced by the Franco-American company.

The bias against Italian cuisine was reinforced by nutritional wisdom of the time, which recommended a diet high in meat and other proteins and dismissed fresh fruits and vegetables as little more than water. Spicy food was believed to debilitate the nervous system. Sausage and salami were thought to weaken the stomach. The Italian habit of mixing grains with vegetables was criticized as too confusing for the stomach, and the Italian diet in general was accused of shortening the life spans of the poor.

Then came World War I, which reshaped North American attitudes toward Italians. Italy joined the Allies in 1915, around the same time the U.S. government was urging citizens to cut down on meat for the war effort. *Good Housekeeping* praised Italians for their frugal, meatless cookery.

Yet North America's hunger for meat and its disinterest in the cultures of other nations prevailed. On this continent, Italian cuisine bore little resemblance to its roots. Distinctions between various Italian regional cuisines disappeared, while only their common ingredients — garlic, olive oil, cheese, tomatoes, onions — dominated. Meat was substituted in vegetable dishes. Tomato sauce was made from reduced paste. Cheese was melted over everything. Even names were anglicized; *maccheroni* became macaroni.

By the 1960s, Italian food had lost most of its associations with peasant cooking. Like Italian movies, Italian design, and Italian fashion, Italian cuisine was chic. Restaurants such as Toronto's now-defunct

Noodles — a sleek chrome and leather setting — served the latest in Italian fare. Dave Nichol, a regular at Noodles and a fan of modern Italian cooking, knew that a President's Choice extra virgin olive oil would add cachet to the President's Choice line. Before he had even found a supplier, he knew exactly how the bottle should look. His plan was to imitate the tall, square, dark green, one-liter bottle used by Badio a Coltibuono, one of Italy's best-selling and most prestigious brands.

The bottle, and future supplier, arrived in 1987. While visiting Toronto, Ermanno Mantova, of the respected Italian olive oil company, Fratte Mantova, set up a meeting with Andy Wallace, who worked for Loblaw International, the Intersave arm that procured products in Europe. As soon as he was seated in Wallace's office, Mantova opened his briefcase and produced a tall green bottle sealed with a cork. Wallace couldn't believe it; this was exactly what Nichol was looking for. Mantova offered documentation of the oil's quality, complete with vial samples of the first, second, and third pressings — the first pressing being the purest and most expensive. He told Wallace that he could offer any quality or combination of pressings. Wallace took Mantova to Nichol's office and the deal was done on the spot.

President's Choice Extra Virgin Olive Oil in a one-liter bottle was introduced shortly thereafter. The Intersave division bought it for $3 a bottle and sold it for $6.99 — a bargain, it would seem, on both ends, given that similar products at specialty stores cost at least three times as much. The oil was an immediate hit, more than anyone had expected. "We had no idea that people would accept the concept so quickly," Wallace recalled. That the bottle turned out to be too tall to fit in most kitchen cupboards — even that became an asset. Shoppers proudly displayed it on their kitchen counters as a badge of sophistication.

Other suppliers coveted the Loblaw olive oil account. One was a young food broker named Fabio Micacchi. Micacchi, of Italian heritage, founded an importing company called Vini Nobili Imports in 1986. Vini Nobili supplied dried pasta, bottled pesto, sundried tomatoes, balsamic vinegar, extra virgin olive oil, and tuna packed in olive oil to stores and restaurants around Toronto. Micacchi made a pitch to supply to Loblaw shortly after he set up business; he was told they weren't interested.

Then Micacchi, a short, compact, and tenacious fellow, saw an opening. Loblaw had been selling No Name olive oil produced in Spain for $1.99 a bottle. But that agreement looked a bit shaky after Spain joined the European Community in the late 1980s. Prices had jumped in line with those of other member nations, and the supply became increasingly erratic. Micacchi tried again. He called Andy Wallace but, as Micacchi remembers it, Wallace simply couldn't make up his mind.

In 1987, the resourceful Micacchi approached Dave Nichol directly. His tactic was to call Nichol's office repeatedly, each time posing as a different customer and lodging anonymous complaints about the lack of No Name olive oil on the shelves. Sensing that there might have been something wrong with the supply, Nichol granted Micacchi-the-salesman an audience. Micacchi walked away with an agreement to supply the No Name olive oil to Loblaw. In addition, Loblaw agreed to buy a blend of cold-pressed virgin and refined olive oil for $1.45 a bottle. The new No Name product that Loblaw requested, which sold for $2.59 or $2.69, was a highly processed bargain-basement product. Soon, Micacchi began to broker other oil products for President's Choice, including a light olive oil and the Lupi brand. Naturally, there were costs associated with his cherished Loblaw account, some of them hidden. One year, Micacchi recalls, an Intersave buyer called to arrange for a case (twelve bottles) of Cavelli balsamic vinegar for Nichol, a top-of-the-line product that retailed for almost $70 a bottle. Vini Nobili supplied the case, but Micacchi claimed he was never paid by Intersave. When the Intersave buyers called again the next year, Micacchi excused himself for not having the vinegar on hand.

In 1987 as well, Micacchi introduced Nichol to a pasta manufactured by the Naples-based Gerardo di Nola SpA. Until that time, Loblaw had been selling and heavily promoting the De Cecco brand, which was also produced in Italy. Jim White liked the di Nola variety. Food writer Mimi Sheraton also had given it her endorsement, which Nichol could use in the *Insider's Report*. Nichol liked both the pasta and its potential margins. By April 1988, he was trumpeting "our premium quality President's Choice pasta for the Connoisseur" in the *Insider's Report*. "It's made in Naples, Italy, by Gerardo di Nola. 99 cents a package."

Unfortunately, the pasta — sold in a cellophane bag — often became crushed in transport. LIM decided to have it boxed. Di Nola, the company's owner, didn't have the proper equipment and said it would cost an additional 7 to 9 cents per box to have the machinery installed. He was prepared to buy the equipment, at a cost of $750,000, in hopes that Loblaw would agree to a five-year contract, which he had discussed with Nichol. According to Micacchi, Loblaw suggested it could buy fifty containers a year (each fourteen-foot container held approximately 2,000 boxes of twelve pasta packages). Di Nola installed the machinery, and six months later Loblaw went elsewhere. It had found a lower-priced supplier — the American Italian Pasta Co., which operated a $50-million high-tech plant in Missouri. In 1991 Nichol introduced "The World's Best Pasta," a premium, dried product made by the U.S. firm from hard amber durum wheat. It premiered at 69 cents a box; A&P bought the same pasta for its Master Choice line and priced it at 79 cents.

About the same time, Intersave decided to cut costs by dealing directly with suppliers. That meant Micacchi's brokering services were no longer necessary. Like a lover spurned, Micacchi kept watch on the olive oil account at Loblaw's. He knew there were many unscrupulous operators in the business and that many synthetic oils were being passed off by private-label suppliers as quality goods.

Although professionals rated olive oils by their acidity levels — the less, the better — it was possible to create mechanically a low-acid olive oil that could be called extra virgin but which was in fact inferior. Fastidious consumers assumed that by paying as much as $50 a bottle in gourmet food shops, they were guaranteed quality. In fact, federal regulations that controlled the importation and labeling of olive oil were notoriously lax.

Micacchi also knew that when Loblaw launched what it claimed was a pure, cold-pressed product, the claim was false; at the price it was selling for, it simply could not have been cold-pressed. He wrote to Ottawa's Department of Consumer and Corporate Affairs to complain. The ministry subsequently asked the company to change its labeling. Micacchi also noted that Loblaw had changed the supplier of the extra virgin olive oil to lower costs. That underscored the central problem many discerning consumers had with private-label goods. Suppliers could change without warning, and so could the quality. Once buying habits and product perceptions were formed, only the most discriminating palates tended to notice changes.

Micacchi was also seething over the loss of the pasta business. Loblaw's settlement offer — $5,000 — only aggravated the wound. Early in 1993, he and Gerardo di Nola filed suit against Loblaw Companies and Dave Nichol for $8 million. (Nichol's name was later dropped.) According to Micacchi, Nichol had agreed that Loblaw would promote and sell di Nola's pasta under the President's Choice logo in Canada and the United States for five years. He never understood, he claimed, that Loblaw would terminate the arrangement if it found a better deal elsewhere. He knew fighting a Weston company would be a protracted and expensive battle. Nichol insisted that he never signed binding contracts. Period. "That's business," he said with a shrug.

THE JUMP UP SOUP STORY

During the 1980s, Toronto's restaurant mania reflected the city's faith in its never-ending prosperity. This was a decade in which the average house price jumped an astronomical 320%. Unassuming bungalows sold for more than $250,000. Homeowners were almost millionaires — on paper at least. The dominant role real estate came to play in the city was symbolized by the emergence of church-condos — neglected churches that were renovated (ecclesiastical details intact) into luxury housing complexes. The city's twin obsessions of food and real estate merged at the trendy restaurant. Every week, it seemed, a new one opened, always attempting to outdo the theatricality of the last one. Every meal had to be meaningful; every plate had to have pizazz.

The city's aspirations to world-class status were mirrored in the ascent of an inspired young chef, Greg Couillard. Couillard started his career in the 1970s at Troy's, a restaurant, since closed, that was then regarded as one of the best in Toronto. Couillard became a fixture on the hip Queen Street West scene, hopping kitchens every couple of years. He came to public attention in the early 1980s via Joanne Kates, the restaurant critic at the *Globe and Mail*. Loyal patrons followed him from place to place for his Eastern-Italian-Caribbean concoctions: Tan-

dori salmon; Bangkok chicken; beef tenderloin salad with three vinegars; three chilis, snow peas and chrysanthemums; passion fruit and
lime salmon ponzu; Osso buco boscaliola.

Like many *auteurs*, Couillard could be temperamental and erratic.
Even Kates referred to him as "the Van Gogh of the Toronto cooking
scene." In six years, he changed restaurants six times. Stories began to surface, many of them involving drugs and drink. His antics, however, only
seemed to enhance his reputation as an *artiste*. Robert de Niro, it was whispered, wanted Couillard to cook at his Manhattan restaurant, Tribeca
Grill. A group of investors even flew into town to check him out. But Couillard stayed put. According to Michael Pitnook, Couillard's agent, it was
because they wanted Couillard to work on a team. "Mr. Couillard does not
work with other chefs," he said. "Mr. Couillard is *the* chef."

An agent was not a common thing for a chef, even one as in
demand as Couillard, to have. But Couillard needed one, Pitnook
explained, to weather the vicissitudes of fame in Toronto. "It's Toronto," he said. "And it's the food business. A lot of people float a lot of
rumors and there's a lot of stories out there about Greg. We decided
there should be one source to keep things straight."

One Greg story involved his signature Jump Up soup and, indirectly, Dave Nichol. It went back to 1990, when Couillard was working at a
restaurant called China Blue. One day, a stylish woman came in for four
takeout orders of Jump Up soup. Sweet and spicy, this soup contained
Jamaican pumpkin, tomato, okra, back-eyed peas, and curried jerk chick-
en. The minute Couillard saw the woman, he decided she had to be Mrs.
Dave Nichol. It wasn't, nor did Couillard have any evidence to think it
was, but he became convinced that this Mrs. Nichol had been dispatched
to deliver the soup to the Loblaw kitchens where the recipe would
promptly be duplicated and packaged as a President's Choice product. So
paranoid was Couillard, that he demanded three pieces of identification
from the bewildered woman before he agreed to hand over the soup.

The story made the rounds. Eventually, Terri Nichol heard it.
And it got her thinking. In August 1993, she and her husband dined with
Dick Currie and his wife Beth at Couillard's latest venue, Notorious.
Shortly after, she introduced herself to Couillard and set up a meeting

between him and her husband. She even picked him up in her black BMW to deliver him to the Tower.

Unbeknownst to Couillard, LIM already had the Jump Up recipe. A product developer had copied it down during a group cooking course she had taken from Couillard two years earlier. Apart from the questionable ethics of simply copying the recipe, product development head Paul Uys knew it would be a more successful product if it had Couillard's name associated with it. The supermarket shopper, he believed, was not yet ready to embrace Jamaican recipes. If it had the endorsement of a trendy chef, that was another matter.

Couillard was keen to participate in such a venture. It would, he thought, put him in orbit with other world-class chef endorsers such as Paul (Nouvelle Cuisine) Bocuse, Paul Prudhomme, the founder of K-Paul's Louisiana Kitchen in New Orleans who endorsed a line of Magic Seasoning Blends, and Wolfgang Puck of Spago fame, who sold frozen facsimiles of the pizzas Jack Nicholson and Steven Spielberg ate.

According to Pitnook, Loblaw was not the first suitor enamored of the Jump Up soup. "Five or six companies approached us to market the soup," he claimed. "Loblaw came closest to what we wanted." By the end of 1992, LIM and Couillard had an agreement: Loblaw could use Couillard's name in marketing the soup. In return, he would be involved in its development and would earn royalties. By May 1993, they had a product everyone endorsed. Intersave spent a few months working out a lower price with the manufacturer. By then, Nichol had long lost interest in the project and was on to something new. The soup was introduced in the Christmas 1993 *Insider's Report* as part of the Too Good To Be True! nutritional line. Acceptance of the soup was warm, if not hot, and sales were high enough to keep the product on the shelf.

When the product was launched in the November *Insider's* the association with Couillard was played up, as was his Canadian heritage — an overt effort to reassure cautious supermarket shoppers: "This wizard with Caribbean-inspired flavors would be the first to admit that his recipe owes nothing to his upbringing," read the blurb. "Greg's ancestors were friends of Samuel de Champlain. He was born in Ontario, and grew up in Quebec and Manitoba." As always, Nichol knew his audience, and their anxieties, well.

THE PITA MAN

In 1984, during one of his frequent California sojourns, Nichol tasted Boboli, a round, doughy flatbread produced by baker Eugene de Christopher. Both Davidson and White had recommended it to him. "Fantastic," he said to himself after the first bite. Nichol wanted the product so badly for Loblaw that he took the unusual step of arranging for de Christopher to supply an annual case allotment to Loblaw; normally, the company did not like to lock itself into this kind of set purchasing agreement. The heads of Loblaw's in-store bakeries were skittish about the commitment, however, and Nichol soon realized that it would be easier just to make a Boboli knock-off under the President's Choice label.

To that end, Jim White approached Dough Delight, a small Toronto baked goods manufacturer that supplied Loblaw with pita bread, croissants, and coffee cakes. Dough Delight was a young, thriving enterprise formed by the Ajmera brothers — Soham, better known as Sam, and Shreyas. White knew the brothers from his food-writing days at the *Toronto Star*.

A native of Bombay, Sam Ajmera landed in Toronto by accident, after his car broke down on a trip from Detroit to Montreal. Sam and Shreyas had both recently graduated from the University of Detroit — Sam with a degree in marketing and international trade, Shreyas with a degree in financial statistics and accounting. Sam was the round, outgoing brother; Shreyas, the lean, introverted one. Noting Toronto's sizable East Indian population, Sam decided to stay. A few months later, Shreyas joined him.

The Ajmeras' parents were displeased with this development. They wanted Sam and Shreyas to return home to India, to become the third generation to run the family's watchband factory. Six times, they came to Canada to retrieve their sons. Six times, they left without them. By then, Sam and Shreyas had other plans. In 1973, when he was just twenty years old, Sam began to import pita bread from the United States. The enterprising brothers sold their product to stores from the back of their truck.

Their corporate name — Dough Delight — captured their enthusiasm for the business. Slowly, the enterprise grew. The brothers began shipping pita bread to Windsor and Montreal. In 1977, Oshawa Group supermarkets agreed to sell Dough Delight's products in eleven stores. Other supermarkets followed, including Loblaws. In time, they began importing other items, including Mexican sauces. The Ajmeras were open to opportunity; their only caveat was that, as strict adherents to Jainism, a Hindu sect that shunned animal products, they refused to handle items that contained meat. It was crucial to them that every aspect of their business conformed to their vegetarian beliefs.

Sam Ajmera met Dave Nichol in 1979 when he approached Loblaw to stock his pita bread. Nichol asked Ajmera, whom he would come to call Sam the Pita Man, to produce a pita bread for the No Name label. Ajmera was excited. Dough Delight's sales were then less than $300,000 a year. Although pita bread dated back to biblical times, it was still an oddity to most Canadians. To raise awareness, Nichol put an ad in the newspaper announcing that any shopper buying $20 worth of groceries would get a free bag of No Name pita. "If you can't get people to buy it, you give it away," he explained to Sam. Almost 20,000 bags were doled out, which netted about $7,000 to the Ajmeras. Still, the brothers, hungry for business, lost money on the deal. It cost them 42 cents a bag to produce and deliver No Name pita bread, and they were selling it to Loblaw at 38 cents a bag. Loblaw sold it for 59 cents. The same pita bread was stocked under Dough Delight's own label at the Ziggy's in-store deli counter for an uncompetitive 69 cents a package. Sam didn't know how much more success they could take.

The brothers were saved by the croissant. They had seen croissants in New York, Chicago, and San Francisco, but nobody was making them for mass distribution in Canada. They tried to import some from Chicago, only to find they went stale in transit. The solution was to prepare their own dough, which they could sell to supermarket bakeries, which in turn would do the actual baking. The operation was overseen by Paul Futtrup, a Dutch baker they had hired away from Loblaws Supermarkets in 1977. Futtrup had started the first in-store bakery at Loblaws in 1969. They wrote Nichol a letter suggesting their plan to supply croissant dough to in-store bakeries. Soon after, the price pressure eased on the pita.

In less than a decade, the Ajmera brothers parlayed their pita-importing business into a thriving, diversified bakery. By 1984, Dough Delight had grown to the point where it became an attractive acquisition target. In 1984, Corporate Foods Ltd. bought a 49% interest in Dough Delight. Corporate was owned by Maple Leaf Foods, the country's largest food-processing company and a rival to Weston Foods, the food manufacturing division of George Weston Ltd., Loblaw's parent.

When Jim White approached the brothers about making a Boboli knock-off in 1984, they had coincidentally already been at work on a similar product for several years. But it was proving tough to perfect. It was not until the spring of 1991 that Dough Delight introduced the 12-inch round flatbread named Platina under its own label. The version made for Loblaw, known as Splendido, was introduced at the same time.

To confer a gourmet imprimatur on what was essentially a convenience food, Nichol enlisted Toronto's foremost chefs to create recipes combining Splendido flatbread with other President's Choice products. A video featuring the chefs at work on their respective recipes was sold at Loblaws for $3.99. The well-known Toronto chef, Jamie Kennedy, was seen making Feta Splendido, with black olive paste. Roberto Martella of Grano Restaurant made Splendido Pizza Classic Italian and Variations. Dufflet Rosenberg, of Dufflet Pastries, made Splendido Breakfast Bread. Nichol himself made Splendido Portofino with Saint Loup cheese, butter and olive oil with hot pepper essence. Arpi Magyar of Splendido Bar & Grill made a Mushroom Splendido.

Unfortunately, Magyar assumed that the bread had been named after his restaurant, which he had opened in 1990 with Franco Prevedello, one of the city's most enterprising restaurateurs. It was an instant success. Reviewers raved about its large, boldly colored room and a kitchen that turned out rustic Italian dishes with modern California influences. Magyar's assumption about the name had a certain validity. Dave and Terri Nichol came frequently for dinner. From time to time, Jim White had talked to him about the flatbread. He had even come into the Splendido kitchen to try out recipes. Loblaw product developers who came for lunch had quizzed Magyar about various items on the menu.

When Nichol decided to create a video based on the various Splendido flatbread recipes, Magyar participated, thinking that somewhere the restaurant would be given a plug. But Nichol attributed the name to a luxurious restaurant light-years away from prosaic downtown Toronto: "Twenty years ago, I had lunch at the Terrace restaurant of the Splendido Hotel in Portofino, on the Italian Riviera," Nichol wrote in the *Insider's Report*. "I still remember the wonderful pizza-like bread they served that was crisp on the outside, and soft and moist in the centre (very typical of the Italian flatbread they call focaccia). The Splendido served it with an unctuous goat cheese spread. For 20 years, I've treasured the memory."

This miffed Magyar. He claimed to have copyrighted the Splendido name for the restaurant. Still, the last thing he wanted to do was provoke a feud with Loblaw. Believing he could settle the issue amicably with his friend Dave Nichol, he called him at home. Nichol advised him to call his lawyers. Magyar was crushed. "I worship this guy," he says. He served Loblaw with papers, but reconciled himself to the likelihood that he wouldn't win against the deep pockets of George Weston Ltd. "I would have just liked a little credit," he concluded.

Splendido flatbread was a huge success. In its first two years, more than 8 million units of the flatbread were sold. In fact, Loblaw was soon selling more in one week than they had expected to sell for the year. Its success spawned the Splendido franchise: Splendido breadsticks, individual portion Splendidos, Splendido pizza toppings, Splendido cheese mixtures, and Splendido Bundnerfleisch, an air-dried meat.

The success of Splendido added to Dough Delight's bottom line. In addition, their Platina was named the innovative product of the year by the Oshawa Group and the most outstanding new grocery product by *Canadian Grocer* in 1992. By 1993, the company was earning annual revenues of close to $75 million. From their 80,000 square-foot factory in the industrial wasteland of North York, a Toronto suburb, the Ajmera brothers produced a wide range of pre-baked products for in-store bakeries, as well as private-label goods for various supermarket chains. For President's Choice, they produced Rustico bread, President's Choice giant muffins, pita bread, bagels, jalapeno pizza pretzels, and nan flatbread. Its staff had grown to almost 900 employees working out of six

factories — five in Toronto and one in Montreal. "God has been gracious," said Sam, humbly. Forty company-owned trailers transported
baked goods; about a third of them were shipped to the United States.
"The cow that goes further in the field," philosophized Shreyas, "eats
more green grass." Always looking ahead, the Ajmeras registered the
name "Flatbreads of the World" in the hope that they would one day
dominate that business. "Every culture has a flatbread," Sam said. "Anything flat, made out of flour, and we're there."

The Ajmeras' success reflected the extent to which tastes had
shifted from the WASP white-bread aesthetic that had helped create the
George Weston empire. Dough Delight's diversified product mix —
everything from Jewish bagels, its number one selling product, to Italian focaccia to Indian nan bread to German strudel to Arabian pita —
reflected the extent to which ethnic had been mainstreamed into popular taste. For the brothers, the scone, once a WASP staple, was just
another ethnic market niche.

It did not escape the notice of Weston executives that many of the
best-selling bakery products in Loblaws stores were being produced outside the Weston fold. The baking division had a special resonance for
Galen Weston; it was the foundation of the family dynasty. Moreover,
Dough Delight's parent company, Corporate Foods, was 68%-owned by
Maple Leaf Foods, the largest food company in Canada. Maple Leaf, in
turn, was owned by Hillsdown Holdings PLC of the United Kingdom, an
$11-billion conglomerate and one of Weston's major overseas competitors.

Weston Foods' bakery division, Interbake, made a pitch to produce Rustico, a bread copied from a British product. Nichol tried the
product and rejected it, claiming the quality of the Weston-made bread
inferior. Even so, Sam Ajmera knew it was only a matter of time before
Weston appropriated some of his Loblaw business. Ajmera was not
naïve to the ways of the food business. In 1988, Brian Davidson suggested to Ajmera that rather than deal directly with Loblaw, it might be
more prudent to have food broker Simon Zucker mediate his dealings.
Zucker, who had earlier worked with Davidson at Shopsy's Delicatessen, brokered No Name and President's Choice products for many
suppliers. Zucker had also been close to Nichol; for a time, the two

played squash every Friday night. Then a rift developed, which neither would discuss. In return for 2 to 5% of sales, Zucker could help Dough Delight keep the Loblaw accounts. Predictably, Ajmera was less than enthusiastic about ceding a percentage of his sales to a broker, but he accepted it, explaining, "It's the way the world works."

Sam Ajmera also had to contend with growing conflict with Corporate Foods. In 1992, Ajmera decided to flex his muscle under Corporate's often bullying domination. He purchased a bread plant from Safeway Stores in Houston that had ceased operation. He dispatched a convoy of eighty-five trucks to Texas to dismantle the operation, pack it on the trucks, roll back to Toronto, and install it in a 100,000-square-foot Toronto factory. "It was the fastest bakery assembly in history," Ajmera boasted. Ajmera's bold move was motivated by cost-effectiveness, but it had another consequence. Dough Delight could now underbid Corporate on some of its accounts. One grocery executive recalls that the brothers went to Oshawa Group to bid on their private-label white breads, which were being supplied by Corporate at 69 cents a loaf. Dough Delight bid 49 cents a loaf. Ajmera was playing hardball.

Corporate Foods was not amused. In the summer of 1993, it purchased the Ajmeras' remaining stake in Dough Delight for an amount rumored to have ranged between $40 million and $90 million. On this subject, Sam Ajmera was uncharacteristically silent. "It's a land of giants," he said softly. "The small cannot survive." Big fish eat little fish. As it is in the food chain, so it is in corporate life. It's perfectly natural. And even if it were unnatural, it didn't matter. That was simply the way it was.

CHAPTER NINE

THE DOGFATHER

B y the thirtieth batch of President's Choice Gourmet Italian Dog Food, the people at Menu Foods Ltd. were mighty fed up. It had been a laborious process of trial and error to figure out the precise mixture of oregano, basil, marjoram, and garlic to please the canine palate. Then they had had to tackle the aesthetic problems — the unwanted tomato paste crust, the shriveled-up meat, and the unhydrated pasta that fell to the bottom of the can. The average mutt might not balk at such imperfections, but the average dog owner — the person who paid for the stuff — surely would.

The culinary angst engendered by Italian dog food was almost too much for Menu's president, Robert Bras, who more than once, fantasized about pulling the plug on the project. But it had been commissioned by Dave Nichol, with whom Bras had shared considerable history. Bras worked for Loblaw for a few years before joining Menu Foods in 1977. Menu, which had made canned pet food since 1974, had been a major beneficiary of the growing popularity of premium store brands. Nichol was the reigning dogfather of gourmet pet food. "If it hadn't been Dave who asked us to do it," Bras conceded, "we would have given up." If Dave wanted trattoria fare for pooches, then that's what Dave would get.

The Italian dog food saga began in the fall of 1987 when Nichol read a column written by Gary Lautens in the *Toronto Star*. "I have never met a dog that didn't love Italian food," Lautens wrote. Nichol immediately called Bras and read him the column. "Wake up," Nichol barked at

Bras. "Let's do something here."

Pleasing pet owners had been crucial to Nichol from the outset of Loblaw's private-label program. For one thing, the typical pet food buyer represented a demographic ideal for supermarkets: female, aged between twenty-five and forty-five, a college graduate who was employed full- or part-time, with a household income of $40,000 or more. Pets were typically owned by dual-income households, composed of three or more people, including children. On average, this group spent close to 3% of their grocery bill on food for Lassie or Tiger, making pet food the third largest category in the supermarket, behind flavored soft drinks and ready-to-eat cereals. Most supermarkets devoted an entire aisle to pet food, more space than was allocated for any single category of human food.

Then there was the not insignificant matter of profit: margins on canned pet food were 35% — seventy times the average net profit margin of supermarkets in general. And there was the marquee appeal. Italian dog food was precisely the sort of lunatic, attention-grabbing product that would entice shoppers to do their entire shopping run at Loblaw. It was for concepts like this that Dave Nichol lived.

Menu's first five-pound lab test had been a breeze — the macaroni in tomato-meat sauce looked and smelled exactly like something served in an Italian restaurant. When it came time to industrialize the recipe, though, problems began. Unlike processed canned Italian food consumed by humans, which contained as little as 2% meat, Menu's recipe was more than 50% meat and meat by-products. The acids in the meat fought with the acids in the tomatoes, which had been imported from Israel and California, creating an unsightly crust on the edge of the can. The oleic acid in the olive oil only exacerbated the condition. Nichol insisted on using pure olive oil because it was believed to improve the shine of a dog's coat. Besides, what respectable Italian food was made without olive oil? "It looked really gross," recalls Al Tourney, Menu's head of research and development.

Development took almost a year. As always, Nichol was terrier-like in pursuit of progress, calling Bras frequently to seek news of the latest tests and accusing him of dragging his feet. After almost forty plant trials — the costs of which Menu absorbed — the company arrived at a product that met nutritional lab standards and could be taken to a focus group of quadruped taste-testers. One professional kennel served the Italian dog food alongside a competitive brand for two days. The animals were carefully monitored to see which bowl they approached first, which they ate from first, and whether their attention flagged while dining.

Test samples were also sent out to twenty-eight volunteer households to elicit subjective observations about both the animals' and the owners' responses — such as how the animals' digestive systems responded to the food, as well as the owners' opinions about its appearance, odor, texture, and convenience. Response to the Gourmet Italian fare was overwhelmingly positive. "Awesome," declared a householder. "I can't cook this well," one woman confessed. "Even my cats were fighting over it," a third declared.

Bras delivered the final product to Nichol, who took it home for the benediction of his French bulldog, Georgie Girl, and her progeny — her daughter, Bonnie; granddaughter, Kathryn, known as Stinkie; Stinkie's son, The Great Buckaroo; and Buckaroo's daughter, The Jazz. They all lapped it up. And so in April 1988, Gourmet Italian Dog Food — Bolognese-style (with beef) and cacciatore-style (with chicken) hit Loblaws' shelves in green, red, and white packaging, the colors of the Italian flag. At 79 cents for a fourteen-ounce tin, it was more expensive than some processed Italian food for bipeds. Not surprisingly, it was a strong seller. Two of the first cartons off the line were shipped directly to Gary Lautens, who penned a glowing endorsement. "Dave Nichol," he accurately predicted, "is going to clean up on this canine breakthrough."

The Gourmet Italian Dog Food story may seem like a fleeting moment of wretched excess in the history of commercial pet food, but its meaning is far more complicated than that. For Streetsville, Ontario-based Menu Foods, for example, the exercise marked another step on its long ascent from the abyss of near-bankruptcy to top dog in the private brand pet food category. By 1993, the privately owned business was using nine hundred formulas to produce 2,200 labels, including Nutra Menu, Health Diet, Performatrin, Veterinary Medical Diet, Waggles,

Zels, Mother's Natural Pet Food, and Rainbow. It employed 120 people in Canada, another 110 at a factory in Pennsauken, New Jersey, which it purchased in 1991. Its annual revenues were approaching $100 million.

At Menu's pristine 176,000-square-foot factory on the western outskirts of Toronto, pallets held tins stacked thirty feet high, ready for shipment to retail customers around the world. In addition to the seventy-five President's Choice and twenty No Name and Zehrs label pet foods Menus produced for Loblaw, the company developed and manufactured store brands for food retailers such as A&P and IGA in Canada, and Safeway, Wegman's, and Finast in the United States. For the Amway network, it also produced the Prominance label. Menu shipped Seiyu and Let's Mee brands to Japan; Miamore and Diva to Germany; Stuzzy Gold to Italy; and Town & Country to the United Kingdom. By 1993, more than 43% of Menu's sales were to the United States, 37% were in Canada, 13% to Japan, and 5% went to Europe and New Zealand.

Bras's company was an upstart in the cutthroat, highly lucrative industry. By the early 1990s, sales of pet food in Canada were estimated in the area of $750 million. "Nobody really knows how big [the market] is," explains Dave Mitchell, manager of the Pet Food Association of Canada. Lack of hard numbers, in part, stemmed from the fact that close to 80% of the market was dominated by a handful of multinationals — Switzerland's Nestlé S.A. (Fancy Feast, Dr. Ballard's); U.S candy giant Mars Inc. (Pedigree Pal, Kal Kan, Whiskas); Ralston Purina of St. Louis (Purina Dog and Cat Chow, Purina Tender Vittles); and Chicago's Quaker Oats Co. (Ken-l Ration, Puss 'n Boots). All were notoriously tightlipped with market share information. The rest of the market was divided among dozens of niche producers — Maple Leaf Foods Inc., H.J. Heinz Co. of Canada Ltd., Iam's Canada Inc., Colgate-Palmolive Canada Inc., and Sun Pac Foods of Brampton, Ontario, which produced Purr, the number one economy cat food in Canada.

"It's a brutal, competitive market," concedes Shelley Martin, business director of Friskies PetCare, the pet food division of Nestlé Canada Inc. The major players competed muzzle-to-muzzle in international markets, using the same brands. Traditionally, the battle among pet food companies had been fought on supermarket shelves. But the advent of specialty pet food stores in the late 1980s carved a major chunk from these sales, as finicky pet owners looked for service, information, and high-end brands not available in grocery stores. By 1993, only 60% of all pet food sales were recorded in supermarkets. Grocers fought back against the trend with new store brands. Even the giant national brands acknowledged the growing acceptance of private labels. "It can be as good quality as the national brands," acknowledged Nestlé's Martin. Several brand name giants — Nabisco Brands Ltd., Sun Pac, Quaker Oats — even tried their hand at private-label pet food. The experiments were short-lived. "Nobody can produce at a better cost than we can," boasted Bras. By 1994, private labels made up about one-third of total canned pet food sales in Canada; Menu claimed about 95% of that. In the United States, where pet food represented a $5.5 billion industry, private-label penetration was only about 5% of the market. "The per-ception [there] is that the quality of private label isn't as good," Bras said. He was determined to change that.

In his late forties, the still-youthful Robert Bras exudes the glossy demeanor of a well-fed Labrador. Born in New York City, Bras moved to Toronto as a teenager and later attended the University of Western Ontario, in London, where he earned an undergraduate degree in Eng-lish. After a short period in advertising, he went back to school for an MBA, then joined management consultant McKinsey & Co. in Toron-to; there, he specialized in retail and distribution. In 1974, at the sug-gestion of his former McKinsey colleague Serge Darkazanli, Bras called Nichol, who was busy recruiting Loblaw management. The following year, Bras was hired at Intersave, Loblaw's procurement arm. In early 1976, Bras learned that Loblaw's house brand was the best seller in the pet food category. Menu Foods was the manufacturer.

His curiosity piqued, Bras called Menu president Donald Green and inadvertently stumbled onto a new career. Founded by Green in 1971, Menu was an outfit in urgent need of an overhaul. Revenues were stagnant at $900,000. Its product lines were unfocused. It was producing not only pet food — under its own and other labels — but cat litter, bleach, anything thought capable of turning a profit.

In 1977, Bras bought a 50% stake in Menu and began stripping away extraneous product lines. There were then few signs that store brands would ever shed their stigma as cheap imitators and gain pedigree. But Bras saw their future differently. The work he had done at McKinsey on house brands for Dominion Stores convinced him that a market for quality retailer branded products would emerge. "I saw that you couldn't succeed as a retailer if you let the brands tell you what to do," he said, reflecting the Loblaw philosophy. Bras was also aware of how committed Loblaw was to setting up a private-label program, which would cut advertising and distribution costs that inflated the prices to retailers of national brands. A private-label pet food, Bras and Nichol believed, would do more than break the tyranny of the national brand giants. Pet food was one of the few products consumers used every day, a high-frequency purchase that brought shoppers into the stores. If he could create brand recognition for a pet food line, Nichol knew, he could cultivate new customer loyalty to Loblaw.

For the first few years, private-label production represented only one-fifth of Menu's business. Bras's big break came in 1979, courtesy of Loblaw, when Menu began producing its low-priced No Name canned pet food. The first effort, a No Name Luxury meat mix, claimed to match brand leader Dr. Ballard's formula, but at a lower price. The "luxury" reference was designed to seduce pet owners into buying status for the same price as maintenance, the industry term for the standard product. Within six months, the Menu product was the number one selling dog food in Loblaws stores in Ontario.

Menu built its business by matching the national brand or developing other unique premium products. Bras was resourceful. When an east coast fishery went out of business in 1982, 500,000 pounds of frozen cooked lobster meat was found in its freezer. It was stale-dated for human consumption, but Bras saw the prospect for No Name gourmet lobster cat food. In fact, the lobster was so good that employees at the processing plant were stealing it to take home.

That same year, Menu moved into larger, state-of-the art quarters. Throughout the decade, sales grew by an average of 25% a year. In June 1992, Don Green sold half of his 50% share to Cott Corp., which produced PC cola. With both companies looking to expand their private-label operations, Bras and Pencer worked together on accounts such as Wegman's in the United States. Cott also opened doors for Menu at Safeway in California. Bras was friendly with both Nichol and Pencer and occasionally socialized with them. But he nursed a few reservations about their bombastic, flamboyant style. "Dave and Gerry, they talk too much," Bras would say. "They want to rub everybody's noses in their success. I think we should keep a low profile."

According to the Pet Food Association of Canada, there were more than 3 million dogs and 4 million cats in Canada in 1993. More than 27% of Canadian households owned at least one dog; 28% owned one or more cats. Like parents, pet owners inevitably wanted the best for their animals; in return, they expected their pets to reflect their own values, even their neuroses. Pet food manufacturers gleefully referred to this as an appeal to "anthropomorphic emotions."

Gleefully, because these characteristics tend to yield big profits. Manufacturers like to compare "pet lovers" to the average "pet owner." Pet lovers are obsessive about the nutritional composition of the food their animals ate. They spend copiously to keep their animals healthy, glossy, well-fed, fragrant, and well-adjusted. Pet owners like to serve their animals food they can relate to personally, food that reflected their own dietary concerns and culinary dispositions. Hence, pet food had come to be designed to mimic human food — meat was served in large chunks with gravy or mint-flavored dog bones that appealed to the human fondness for the taste of mint and the belief in its cleansing power. Pet owners who spurned chemicals and additives in their own food eschewed them in pet food as well. Diet pet food catered to the growing ranks of fat-conscious owners. It is possible to buy not only hypo-allergenic vegetarian and kosher pet food, but an avocado-based line that promised to improve canine complexions.

Most manufacturers offered at least ten flavor profiles, on the theory that because people craved variety in their own diets, so too must animals. Indeed, there were more SKUs (stock-keeping units) in pet food than in any other supermarket category — ironic, considering the continuing scientific debate about whether dogs and cats actually possessed taste buds. Some 15% of all pet food sales fell into the category broadly referred to as treats or snack foods — more evidence that marketing campaigns were targeted squarely at owners. According to Nestlé's Martin, people bought treats out of guilt. "They've been away from their pets all day, and the treat says, 'Don't be mad at me.'" Treats, she said, were more "interactive" than pet food. Treats were "relationship builders."

What pets ate, of course, was at least partly determined by what a pet was — a role that has changed over time. For centuries, domestic animals ate the scraps left over from their masters' meals. It wasn't until the mid-nineteenth century that cooked biscuits made from cereal products were introduced in England, to take on the hunt. The next innovation was kibbled dog food, which easily absorbed water to make it palatable. In 1922, the first canned dog food, a by-product of meat packing, was sold in the United States. Pet food became a profitable means of disposing of surplus horsemeat and offal. In 1926, Ralston Purina Co. of St. Louis, originally an agricultural feed company, introduced Checkers, the first commercial dog food in North America. In 1933, Admiral Richard Byrd took fifty tonnes of Ralston Purina dog food on his second expedition to the South Pole.

In 1928, the first canned dog food was sold in Canada — created by Dr. W.R. Ballard, a veterinary surgeon born in Grenfell, Saskatchewan. Ballard's wife and daughters cooked the recipe at home. By 1932, Ballard had moved to Vancouver and was devoted to the full-time manufacture of dog food. (Ballard sold the company in 1955 to Standard Brands, which became Nabisco. Nestlé Enterprises bought the brand in 1987.)

During World War II, the Canadian government declared pet food a non-essential item and refused to allow it to be packaged in tins, which were needed for the war effort. But with the armistice, sales exploded. In the 1950s, U.S. veterinary nutritionist Jim Corbin created the first homogenized and nutrient-balanced dry dog food. The role of pets was changing too. More than a recreation, pets were increasingly perceived as members of the family, an antidote to the loneliness and insecurity of contemporary urban society. As more and more people moved into cities, cats and dogs became companionable reminders of the rural life and of a simpler time.

The evolution and success of President's Choice pet food was heavily influenced by Nichol's obsession with his own canine family. Georgie Girl became part of his public persona, appearing on television commercials and in the *Insider's Report* advertising supplement. It was Mortimer Lowell, an ex-Madison Avenue ad executive and second husband to Nichol's mother, Gladys, who suggested turning the animal into a canine prop. "Use a dog," he told Nichol, after viewing a selection of thirty-second spots in the early 1980s. "It'll humanize you. You need something to soften your aggressive personality." Georgie Girl made her professional debut under Nichol's arm on the cover of the first *Insider's Report* in November 1983.

Georgie Girl was actually the second French bulldog Nichol owned. The first was George, her brother. When it comes to canines, Nichol was brand loyal. His infatuation with the breed dated back to 1979, when he spotted George at a Loblaw-sponsored Top Dog dog show. Loblaw had become involved in the dog-show circuit in the mid-1970s and used it as a marketing platform. Top dogs, of course, ate Loblaw-brand dog food. Two prominent dog show organizers, Fred Peddie and Herb Williams, consulted on Loblaw's pet food program. Peddie and Williams, a flamboyant duo, were known around LIM as Fred and Ethel. Peddie, who favored expensive, oversized zoot suits, was the louder, more aggressive of the two. Within the industry, he came to be known as the Liberace of pet promotion. In the mid-1980s, Williams conceived the Superdog show at which dogs selected from fairs across Canada would perform — navigating obstacle courses, through tunnels, up walls, and down — against the clock. In 1991, the Superdogs were introduced to Ontario's Royal Winter Fair. It was a major crowd pleaser.

The rapport between Nichol and George was immediate. Nichol loved the breed's demeanor — determined, pug-nosed, stocky, yet good-natured, and manageable in size. He took a perverse pleasure in the unmistakable physical similarity between himself and the breed. He also liked the fact that in breeding circles, French bulldogs were known as "philosophers in clown's clothing." George, however, lived only three months with the Nichols. His short life ended tragically one December evening — the din of a boisterous Christmas party in the background —

the result of an accidental drowning in the hot tub. His legs were too short to cope with the treacherous currents. A year later, Georgie Girl joined the Nichol household. As a pup, she had fallen and broken her jaw, ending her prospects as a career show dog. But Nichol doted on the dog and was transformed in her presence, becoming relaxed and affectionate in a way he rarely was with people. Whenever he took a Tums to settle his acidic stomach, he fed one to the dog. On one occasion, Georgie Girl was brought into the LIM studio to be filmed for an MGM-style opening credit in which she roared. Nichol stood behind the cameras, urging her to "do it for Daddy."

For pet lovers, the presence of Georgie Girl offered assurance that Nichol was a kindred spirit. The dog quickly learned to be cooperative in front of cameras, sitting passively take after take. "When the cameras rolled," Nichol told the editors of *Urban Pet* magazine in 1992, "she was a natural actor." She appeared in a variety of zany formats in *Insider's Report*: in a Santa Claus hat at Christmas; in sunglasses and a barbecue chef's hat in the summer; in bunny ears and eyeglasses, reading a newspaper; and with Nichol, he in formal attire, she attired in a dog-sized tuxedo. She also appeared on the gourmet dog food package, and on a treats package — riding a skateboard in little white boots. When Georgie Girl was finally put to sleep in April 1992, at the elderly dog age of eighty-four, Nichol ordered a last-minute reassembly of *Insider's Report* and ran a tribute on page one, complete with a color picture of the dog and her progeny.

If in life Georgie Girl was beloved to the point of fetish, in death she was canonized. Loblaw customers sent letters of condolence and flowers to Nichol's house. There, under The Dome, her ashes sat — in a bulldog-shaped bronze urn ten feet from Nichol's dining-room table. Her image continued to show up in subsequent *Reports*, superimposed in photographs and cartoons. A Memories of Georgie Girl commercial ran at Christmas. Nichol himself often wore a tie silk-screened with images of French bulldogs. And for his birthday in 1993, the art department gave him a varsity-style jacket with a cartoon of Georgie Girl on the back. But the apotheosis of dog worship may have been the memorial video put together in the spring of 1992 by Robin Periana at the

company's in-house studio. Entitled "Best Friends," the ten-minute production was a montage of photographs of Georgie Girl and Nichol, set
to a soundtrack featuring "Hey There, Georgy Girl," Nat King Cole's
"Unforgettable," and Tina Turner's "Only the Best." For visitors to the
Nichol house, "Best Friends" became obligatory viewing.

The development of President's Choice premium line of pet food
mirrored the pathology of the devoted pet owner through the 1980s. In
1984, Nichol introduced a no soya dog food. Soya was a common filler
used as a protein base in pet food that had the unfortunate side effect of
producing flatulence. Nichol's dog Stinkie helped to introduce Nichol to
the need for the product. Later that year came a canned Christmas dinner for pets — so owners wouldn't feel guilty about feasting while their
animal was limited to his regular diet. Cats supped on luxury turkey
with giblets and dressing that smelled "like real turkey," while dogs
were offered luxury English mixed grill, with beef, lamb, bacon, ham,
sausage, and liver.

From then on, each year seemed to bring a new niche product. With
the birth of Bonnie's puppies in 1985 — Georgie Girl's granddoggies —
Nichol perceived the need for Puplum, a mild, transitional cereal somewhere between milk and solids. Human infants had their own food; why
shouldn't infant dogs? The following year, President's Choice introduced
low-ash, low-magnesium dry cat food, which claimed the ability to help
prevent urinary tract infections and gallstones. Recognizing the increasing
focus on nutrition, Nichol hired Dr. Jim Corbin — creator of extruded
dry dog food — to develop President's Choice Superior Dog Food.

In 1987, Superior Cat Food with less cereal and more fish was
introduced, along with Senior Dog Food for older pets. Perhaps in
penance for the indulgence of ethnic gourmet Italian dog food, Loblaw
introduced "body friendly" pet foods in 1989, in association with the
launch of its G.R.E.E.N. products. Included in this salutary line were all-
natural dog biscuits, to prevent tartar build-up and bad breath, and Slim
'N Trim dog and cat foods, with one-third less fat than the leading
brands. There was more to come. In 1991, as pet owners fretted about
their own cholesterol levels, Loblaw developed Nutritional Breakthrough Dry Dog Food, to compete in the new high-tech, super-premium

market dominated by Science Diet and Iams. Although the canned version sold for more than $1.50 a tin, super-premiums soon became the fastest growing segment of the industry. For manufacturers, it offered a particularly attractive niche, with margins as high as 25%, compared to 10% for standard brands. By 1993, Loblaw was selling 144 separate No Name and President's Choice pet food labels.

Back at Menu, the reign of cats and dogs continued. Cat food made up 60% of Menu's overall business, virtually all of it "ultraluxury" or "gourmet" lines (read: high meat content). Potentially, the cat side of the pet food ledger was even more profitable. Finicky eaters, cats ate twice as much canned foods as dogs. Dogs, of course, consumed far more volume, but they ate more dried meal and kibble, which was less expensive. However, Bras was never under pressure to create PC Gourmet Italian for cats. The reason was simple. Dave Nichol had no interest in cats. "Over all these years," Bras says, "I don't once remember Dave coming to me for an innovative product in this category."

Robert Bras is blessed with a sense of humor that allows him to see the paradoxes and lunacies of the industry. "This business is completely counter-economic," he says. "You can't sell pet food on price alone. If your dog or cat isn't going to eat it, you're not going to buy it." Content was the number one thing people looked for when buying pet food, said Susan Pearce, editor of *Dogs in Canada*. "If pet owners believe they can improve the health and extend the life of their pet," says Pearce, "they'll spend the extra few cents on premium." Nichol was aware of this proclivity when he commissioned President's Choice Extra Meaty Dog Food to take on Mars's Pedigree Pal. "He said, 'Forget the economics, just give me the best,'" Bras recalls. "We could have made dog food twenty cents less expensive than the national brand, but he had the guts to go for it. He said, 'Just make it the best on the market.' I'll take the credit for production, but Dave knew the dog owner would go for it."

Nichol was right. The growth in the pet food market during the 1980s was almost entirely in the premium and then the super-premium end of the market. Among other virtues, these upscale lines were purged of artificial flavors and colors, as well as of chemical preservatives and additives. By 1991, 86% of canned cat food, which made up more than half of all cat food sales, was in the luxury category; only 14% was maintenance. In canned dog food, which amounted to less than one-third of all sales, 63% was luxury, 37% maintenance.

The fastest-selling format, according to Bras, was a tiny three-ounce tin of luxury cat food that retailed for between 49 and 69 cents. "That works out to about $4.75 a pound," Bras said. "There's all sorts of nummy stuff you could buy for your pet for that money. Real livers." The larger, six-ounce can sold for the same price. "But if you have one cat, you're going to buy the smaller size," says Bras. "It's one serving. It's cleaner. It's easier." It also had a convenient pull-off tab; people did not like using their own can opener to open pet products.

Despite the money people are willing to spend on pet food, a certain stigma continues to surround it. Most pet food is still composed of the unsavory remains of meat processing, otherwise known as "by-products," bulked up with bonemeal, fishmeal, or cereal. "By-products" can include lungs, ox lips, cow's cheeks, udders, heads, assorted offal, and chicken backs and necks. Often, it includes meat that has fallen below human consumption grade — for reasons best left unpondered. In the "meat room" at Menu's processing plant — not a place to hang out if your sense of smell is intact — tonnes of frozen meat sit denatured with charcoal, a process by which packers identify meat and by-products as unfit for human consumption and assure that it does not reach supermarkets or the black market.

Surprisingly, there are no regulations governing pet food production in North America. The Department of Consumer and Corporate Affairs monitors labeling, so that manufacturers cannot claim a product is beef if it is in fact horsemeat. But pet owners have become increasingly vigilant about nutrition. In 1984, the Canadian Veterinary Medical Association conferred a seal that said the product met certain nutritional standards. And the Pet Food Association of Canada has implemented a voluntary nutritional assurance program, indicating that the brand satisfies the animal's requirements at a particular stage of its life.

Within the industry, it is taken as gospel that "premium" pet products enhanced with supplementary minerals and vitamins are more nutritious than processed food for people. "Even in common brands, pets get more nutrients than people," claims *Dogs in Canada*'s Pearce. Bras concurs, noting that "standards are far more onerous than in human food." He takes great pride in showing off the quality of his products. In Menu's white lab, overlooking the assembly line, Bras liked to open a tin of President's Choice Extra Meaty Lamb and Rice luxury dinner and say, "Just smell that. It smells like something you'd get in a restaurant." Then, he would pour out the contents of cans of Beefaroni (for humans) and President's Choice Italian Gourmet (for dogs) and ask guests to compare. The canine food looked more like homemade pasta sauce. The primary ingredient of Beefaroni (99 cents) was water; the main ingredient of Italian Gourmet ($1.59) was beef. "It's hard to find the meat," Bras would say, combing the Beefaroni with a fork. The canned pasta manufacturer uses mechanically boned meat. "You couldn't call it beef in the United States if you were making dog food," Bras insists. "It wouldn't make it as a pet food. It's high in fat, carbohydrates. It's a nasty product." Bras's partner, Gerry Pencer, was even more enthusiastic. "You could put PC Italian Dog Food next to Chef Boy-ar-dee in a blind taste test," he says, "and PC would win."

The gourmet Italian line met with greater acceptance in the United States than in Canada; Chicago and Philadelphia were particularly strong markets. More than one national brand attempted to duplicate the product; none made it to market. Its success encouraged Bras to be always on the lookout for new flavors to snag the pet owner's imagination. In 1992, Menu introduced gumbo for chain in the United States. In late 1992, Bras went to Jim White for a new Italian dog food flavor to pitch to Great Dane gourmands and their masters. White was by then under contract for Retail Brands, the marketing arm of Cott. He and Bras are good friends.

White suggested turkey pasta primavera — a practical suggestion, because processing a turkey created a lot of leftovers. It was an idea also calculated to please Nichol. White knew that Nichol would respond favorably to primavera-flavored dog food. Years earlier, Nichol had taken White to the revered New York restaurant Le Cirque and had insisted that White order pasta primavera, a signature house dish made with fresh vegetables over pasta. Turkey primavera, however, posed its own production nightmares at Menu. One day, Bras was informed that production had been delayed because the broccoli florets were turning to mush during the cooking process. "Broccoli florets?" he asked. "This is dog food, for God's sake. What's going on here?" But White had insisted that the carrots and broccoli had to be discernible. "The large particularization of florets was important," he maintained. "You can't have turkey primavera without vegetables." A compromise was later reached. White was chockablock with other ideas he regularly relayed to Bras, including Gatorade for pets and tiramisu crackers for dessert after a gourmet Italian meal. Bras refused to do pet treats. "I don't believe in them," he said.

Bras also drew the line at Kobe beef dog food, an idea Nichol approached him with in late 1992. Kobe beef, a Japanese delicacy, retailed for $150 (U.S.) a kilogram. It was not available in Canada; a special dispensation was required to import it. For New Year's Eve 1992, Nichol arranged for delivery of a side of Kobe beef to a dinner party at his house. Bras was invited to the event but, by the time he arrived, the beef had been devoured. "Why don't you go to Japan, Bob," Nichol suggested. "Get what's left over from producing Kobe beef, and make dog food from it?" Bras shook his head. This was too much. Over the top. "There's no way," he said.

As a compromise, Menu did embark on the development of Ter-riyaki Dog Food, flavored with President's Choice Memories of Kobe Tamari Garlic Marinade. Again, production was problem-plagued. The texture of the first batches was slimy. The flavorings posed a major headache. "The sauce they want us to use costs as much as Dom Perignon," Bras complained. But not too loudly. Robert Bras and Menu Foods owed a lot to Dave Nichol. Besides, he didn't need to plant more doggone ideas — Bubbly for the Great Buckaroo, maybe — in Nichol's already overheated imagination.

CHAPTER TEN

"YOU'RE GREEN, I'M GREED"

Early one bright, crisp Sunday morning in October 1988, just as Patrick Carson was leaving for church, the telephone rang at his home in Nobleton, a small town northwest of Toronto. It was Dave Nichol, calling from his suite at the George V Hotel in Paris. Nichol, as usual, got right to the point. "Pat, let's do it. Be in my office first thing Wednesday morning." Carson had waited months to hear those words. They signaled Nichol's blessing for development of an "environmentally friendly" line of President's Choice products, the first of its kind in Canada. Nichol then kept Carson, a devout Catholic, on the line for so long that he had to drive into Toronto to find an afternoon Mass.

A dark-haired man with a craggy, lived-in face, Carson is Loblaw's in-house strategist on environmental matters. He comes across like a tough leprechaun, speaking in a lilting Irish cadence, with rhythms as plush as wide-wale corduroy. Carson possesses that indigenous Irish knack for storytelling, a skill that in no small part makes him the perfect man for his job. There was, after all, no more compelling story in the late 1980s than environmental distress.

Carson — Paddy to his friends — was born in Belfast, Northern Ireland, in 1939, into a working-class family. His parents ran a pub, where, as Carson wryly remarks, "my father was the best customer." His father, known as Bull, was also a boxer who taught his sons — with the exception of Patrick — how to fight. "I lacked the killer instinct,"

Carson would confess, with the sort of ingenuous charm that punctuates his conversation.

Life in Belfast was difficult. Carson didn't finish eighth grade, a limitation that did little to dampen his agile intellect or ambition. When Carson was twenty-one, a friend got him a job at the Ford Motor Co., where he tracked the efficiency of assembly-line procedures. He was destined for management, but could not envisage living out his life in Northern Ireland, which was fast becoming a Celtic Beirut. In 1974, he emigrated to Canada with his wife, Deirdre, a teacher. After a short stint as a consultant, Carson joined Loblaw in 1977, making use of the quality-control lessons he had learned in the auto industry. In 1980, Carson was named a vice-president in the Intersave division, responsible for waste management. The following year, he instituted changes that reduced Loblaw's garbage bill from $1.2 million to $570,000.

In February 1988, Loblaw president Dick Currie instructed Carson to develop a corporate strategy to deal with environmental issues. However belatedly, Currie was becoming concerned with the unrelenting barrage of news chronicling the greenhouse effect, the depletion of the ozone layer, the stripping of the world's rain forests, the swelling of landfill sites, and the effects of pesticides in food production. In 1977, the *Globe and Mail* had published exactly twelve major stories on these issues; a decade later, in 1987, it published 1,074. Currie's daughters, sensitized to ecological issues, were beginning to ask their father questions about the way Loblaw did business. The subject could no longer be ignored. Currie told Carson that he wanted to anticipate the fallout of environmental problems on the company.

Carson soon became conversant with the major issues. He learned how quickly the Amazon rain forest was being cut down and how drift-net fishing in the Atlantic Ocean was causing the indiscriminate slaughter of marine life. He subscribed to left-wing publications such as *The New Internationalist*, and environmental magazines *Buzzworm* and *Garbage*. His thinking was most profoundly influenced by the 1987 report of the World Commission on Environment and Development, more commonly known as the Brundtland report, after its chairman, Norwegian Prime Minister Gro Harlem Brundtland. The document conferred credibility on the claim that the affluent 20% of the world was consuming 80% of its resources. And it warned that developing countries such as India and China had no intention of depriving their people of the fruits of industrialization — cars, microwaves, refrigerators, etc. — that the rest of the world took for granted. Brundtland's vision was a scary one for Western world readers: just how long would it take for that less-affluent 80% to run through the remaining 20% of its resources?

The report introduced Carson to the notion of "sustainable development," a vague, somewhat ambiguous theory that had been kicking around in Third World development circles. According to Brundtland, economic growth had to be based on policies that sustained and expanded the environmental resource base. Yes, environmental questions had to be viewed from a business perspective. But if business failed to eliminate sources of ecological distress, then not only would the environment be at risk — so too would continued economic well-being. Sustainable development, therefore, had something for everyone: the "sustainable" part reassured those concerned about depletion of the world's resources; the "development" part buoyed the hopes of those who wanted to profit from it. That linkage was crucial to the growing fashionability of eco-concern within the business community.

Many environmental groups were initially suspicious of Carson, even hostile. But his wit and salt-of-the-earth character cracked much of the early skepticism and resistance. At many gatherings, including The World Conference on Changing Atmosphere held in Toronto in June 1988, and the Earth Day Festival held in Halifax, his would be the only suit in attendance. Carson stayed in touch with the eco-fringe, noting that "radicals had changed the course of human history," but he also assiduously cultivated government contacts, most notably in the swelling federal and provincial ministries of the environment.

It was during that summer of 1988 that Carson met Warner Troyer, a journalist and pioneering environmental activist. Troyer's 1975 book, *No Safe Place*, had chronicled the tragedy of mercury poisoning in the waters that ran through northern Ontario Indian reserves. Currie had suggested Carson talk to Troyer after Tom McMillan, then federal minister of the environment, had called Currie to ask for assistance in shaping Ottawa's newly formed Environmentally Friendly Products Program. The idea behind the program, modeled on a plan in Germany known as Blue Angel, was to identify and endorse products believed to have been manufactured with minimal environmental damage. Troyer was among McMillan's group of consultants. The federal program ultimately went nowhere, but Carson was quite impressed by Troyer. To Loblaw senior managers, he handed out copies of another Troyer book, *Preserving Our World*, which contained a 100-page synopsis of the Brundtland report. Troyer soon became something of a fixture around Loblaw, and the two men began discussing publishing a Canadian version of *The Green Consumer Guide*, a best-selling handbook published in Britain in 1987.

Concern about the environment had by this time gone mainstream. In a survey taken by Decima Research for *Maclean's* magazine, Canadians cited the environment as the number one problem facing the country, far ahead of unemployment, free trade, or the deficit. Poll respondents declared their willingness to pay 20% more for products perceived as salutary for earth, air, and water. Later, it was discovered that people actually expected to pay *less* for products that used fewer resources and less packaging. At the time, however, it would have seemed uncaring, and politically incorrect, not to declare that you would do anything you could to help The Planet.

Implicit in this attitude was the burgeoning sense of collective guilt, a fear that if more virtuous attitudes were not soon adopted, there would be grandscale retribution for the cavalier abuse that had been heaped upon the Earth. The world seemed to be running on empty. This pressure to return to what was seen as a simpler, more honest way of life — spurred in great part by economic uncertainty — spawned the emergence of Bunker Chic. Down-market was suddenly in. Barbecue and Cajun foods replaced sushi in food fashion. Meat loaf and mashed potatoes showed up on the menus of smart dining establishments, disguised as "bistro fare." Country music went mainstream; organic cotton replaced silk in status. Television did a 180-degree reversal — from resource-consuming, eco-barbarians on *Dallas* to the blue-collar, financially strapped family on *Roseanne*.

The need to be perceived as sensitive to environmental issues was dawning on business, particularly the retail sector. But public relations aside, there was also big money in going green, as the staggering success of an unusual British soap store demonstrated. The Body Shop, founded by Anita Roddick in Brighton in 1976, had become a $600-million-a-year giant, selling offbeat hair and skin products with names such as Seaweed and Birch Shampoo, Banana Hair Putty, and Passion Fruit Face Cleanser. All the ingredients, such as jojoba oil, cocoa butter, and aloe vera, were natural. Roddick herself was celebrated as the doyenne of virtuous consumption, a cross between Mother Teresa and Estée Lauder. The Body Shop gained a reputation as a company with a social conscience: it refused to test products on animals, used refillable and recyclable plastic containers, spent absolutely nothing on advertising, and was actively involved in various causes and charities, including AIDS awareness, saving whales, day care for its female work force, and an orphanage in Romania. When it built a soap factory in Easterhouse, a depressed area outside Glasgow, it put 25% of the profits back into the community. Roddick explained her philosophy in her best-selling autobiography, *Body and Soul*: "I am still looking for the modern-day equivalent of those Quakers who ran successful businesses, made money because they offered honest products, and treated their people decently, worked hard, spent honestly, saved honestly, gave honest value for money, put more in than they took out and told no lies." By 1988, Body Shop's bright green stores dotted the urban landscape in thirty-eight countries; in North America, they had become almost as common as 7-Elevens.

The notion that Loblaw too could blaze a trail in green marketing began percolating in Dave Nichol's head in the fall of 1987, in the wake of the egg-carton incident. Earlier that year, the Ottawa chapter of the environmental lobby group Friends of the Earth had approached Loblaw, along with twelve other major grocery chains, urging them to get rid of foam egg containers, which were made using chlorofluorocarbons (CFCs), and to replace them with pulp. Loblaw ignored their appeal. "Egg cartons don't interest Dave Nichol," Carson would explain. "There's no drama there. He's more interested in being the first person to market with an organic chicken that can lay an organic egg."

But Nichol had misread the prevailing zeitgeist. When Friends of the Earth and Quebec's Provigo jointly declared that the supermarket chain would be switching to pulp egg cartons, the announcement generated a huge amount of positive publicity.

While reading an article on biodegradability in the October 5, 1987, *Globe and Mail* newspaper, Nichol jotted a note at the top of the page and sent it to Larry Griffin, in Quality Assurance. "Let's be the first in Canada with a biodegradable green garbage bag," he wrote. "Launch date spring 1988 *Insider's*." The deadline was optimistic. It took nearly ten months to develop the bio- and photo-degradable garbage bag, using St. Lawrence Starch's "Ecostar" system. (Cornstarch is commonly used to accelerate biodegradability in plastic; ironically, extra plastic must be used to compensate for the presence of the cornstarch.) The product was previewed in the fall of 1988 under a new trademark, "Nature's Choice." The process was also used to create the "88% biodegradable" plastic shell that covered Teddy's Choice Ultra Diapers. The garbage bag included a convenient, though non-biodegradable, drawstring tie, which meant that it could be flogged as only "94% biodegradable." The September 1988 *Insider's Report* touted it as "the same quality as Glad garbage bags (which AREN'T biodegradable and DON'T have draw-strings)." The Nature's Choice logo and the word "biodegradable" were stamped in white on the dark green bag, providing curbside evidence of its owner's sensitivity to the ecosystem.

In what would be a foreshadowing of the circus to follow, between the time the project began and its commercial launch, the right-eousness of biodegradability had come under scrutiny in scientific cir-cles. Some critics compared the term itself to "lite" and "non-toxic" — soothing advertising palaver, but not terribly meaningful. Ultimately, it would come to mean that the biodegradable jug in which consumers bought milk or orange juice would take a mere 500 years to disintegrate, instead of a million, and that while it was decomposing, it might break into bits of plastic that would poison birds and contaminate groundwa-ter. While biodegradable plastic bags could eventually disintegrate (that is, with help from sunlight, a scarce commodity in landfills), its contents retained much of their bulk and occupied as much space as with regular plastic. Even a spokesman for Mobil Chemical Co., in an interview with the Tallahassee (Fla.) *Democrat*, called biodegradability "a marketing tool," adding: "We're talking out of both sides of our mouths because we want to sell bags. I don't think the average consumer even knows what biodegradability means. Customers don't care if it solves the solid waste program. It just makes them feel good." The bags sold well at Loblaw-run supermarkets but, as Carson later conceded, "the technology was of dubious merit." Nichol eventually instructed him to take them off the shelves.

It was later that year, while the garbage bag was still in development, that Carson approached Griffin and Nichol about setting up a line of products they could market as ecologically sensitive. A Loblaw survey revealed that 93% of shoppers were "extremely," "quite," or "somewhat" concerned about the environment. Some 92% said they were "very" or "somewhat" likely to buy environmentally friendly products and would pay an extra 47 cents on average for the privilege. Nichol liked the sound of this. Green could be a "hook," unique products that brought people into the store. The bombardment of media stories that "values" were changing forced him to believe that if he was to attract shoppers, Loblaw needed to differentiate its products.

Nichol's growing interest in marketing a line of so-called environmentally friendly products was given a big nudge during a trip to Europe in the spring of 1988. While in England, he discovered that 15% of the electorate had voted for the Green Party in the 1987 election. Ten percent of the European Community parliament was occupied by Greens. Tesco, the largest food retailer in the United Kingdom, had enjoyed huge success with its "healthy eating" products. While browsing in a Knightsbridge bookstore, Nichol came across *The Green Consumer Guide*, by John Elkington and Julia Hailes. At first, he dismissed it as the sort of book only the authors' parents would buy. When he noticed it was on the best-seller chart and had sold more than 300,000 copies, he bought a dozen copies to bring back to Loblaw.

Nichol began to look at everything through a "green" filter. During the final leg of his trip, in Thailand, he noticed there were fewer trees than during his last visit. Nature itself seemed to have gone berserk that year. North America had recorded record high temperatures, raising anxiety about the greenhouse effect. Seals were dying mysteriously in the heavily polluted North Sea. Hurricane Gilbert had wreaked havoc in the Caribbean. Bangladesh was ravaged by floods. It all seemed to add up to a frightening cosmic omen.

The Wednesday following his call to Carson from Paris, Nichol met with Griffin and Carson in his office. Carson recollects Nichol recounting his exposure to the green frenzy in Europe. "In Sweden, it is now virtually impossible to sell a whiter-than-white chlorine-bleached disposable diaper," he said. "In England, the introduction of non-chlorine-bleached diapers quickly captured over one-third of the market, and even Pampers was forced to change to non-chlorine-bleached fluff pulp. What if consumers refused to buy our products for environmental reasons? Utter pandemonium! What if our governments banned products such as disposable diapers, as they are contemplating doing in some U.S. states? An entire market could be legislated away, with the stroke of a pen. It won't be long before the environment is the number one issue here, and we better be ready for it. Our green products will dominate the category if we act now. What's the key ingredient that will make this thing fly?"

"Secrecy," Carson replied. "No one else can catch wind of it."

"What happens if this doesn't work?" Nichol asked.

"You'll get a call from Ireland," Carson quipped. "That's where I'll be."

By and large, Carson and Nichol had an amiable relationship. After Nichol had been deposed as president of Loblaw Supermarkets, Carson gave him a copy of Churchill's memoirs, recommending that he pay particular attention to one chapter, "The Dark Years." For months, Nichol kept the book on his desk, alongside the *Oxford English Dictionary* and a photograph of Terri. But when it came to green products, Nichol was never an easy sell. During much of the original planning, he would snipe at Carson: "Convince me that this will work." "He'd always ask us what can we do for him," Carson recalled. "He'd say, 'You're green, I'm greed' — deliberately, to antagonize me." Carson was occasionally stung by Nichol's criticism. Once, after a major disagreement, Terri had to call to effect a rapprochement.

Nichol was concerned about where Loblaw would find the expertise needed to help with product development. When Carson suggested working with environmental groups, Nichol balked, but Carson persisted. Not only would such groups give Loblaw ideas it could commercialize, they could reach out to the public in ways a business could not. The endorsement of a respected environmental lobby would reassure shoppers and confer instant credibility on the products.

Finding environmentalists willing to cozy up to a billion-dollar conglomerate, unsurprisingly, was no simple task. For many such groups, an adversarial stance toward business was central to their self-definition. In 1988, Carson asked Julia Langer, head of the Ottawa-based arm of Friends of the Earth, if the organization would be interested in endorsing Loblaw products, as some U.K. groups were doing with European products. Langer was wary about a full-throttle commercial endorsement, but Friends of the Earth did agree to consult, helping Loblaw identify products that posed the greatest environmental risk. The Toronto-based Pollution Probe Foundation, the largest environmental lobby in Canada, also agreed to review the supermarket shelves. Both groups focused on the dangers of detergents with high phosphate levels, paper products made from non-recyclable paper, diapers made from chlorinated paper, and food produced with pesticides.

In search of endorsements, Carson contacted more than ten high-profile environmental agencies across the United States and United Kingdom, only to be turned down by them all. He received a more encouraging response from Colin Isaacs, the then executive director of Pollution Probe. The rotund British-born Isaacs, a former New Democrat MPP in Ontario, was an often-blunt pragmatist who had been with Pollution Probe since 1982. He saw a relationship with Loblaw as a potential way to bridge the gulf between industry and environmental activists. Both sides stood to gain from the arrangement — Loblaw in credibility for its products, Pollution Probe in finding a source of much-needed cash to help reduce the agency's $60,000 deficit.

Pushing hard, Nichol set a deadline of June 1989 for the launch. That left a mere six months to source existing products, or develop and manufacture new ones, and package and ship them to the stores. Some

$10 million was allocated for research and development. The George Weston Diversified Lab was used to test things such as plastic bags and coffee filters. The product development team visited trade shows and combed through health and specialty stores, where so-called "greener" products had been sold for years. They pored over green consumer guides from Britain and the United States. At the suggestion of Friends of the Earth, Loblaw's Intersave division secured Ecover's cleaning products from Belgium and "acid-reduced" gourmet coffee from Germany.

In late 1988, Pollution Probe agreed to help develop a fertilizer and lawn dressing. Doug Harpur, who ran Organix, a company that sold composters, asked Stuart Hill, a professor of agricultural ecology at McGill University, to brainstorm with the formulation. Hill was wary of Isaacs's suggestions for ingredients — among them, bat waste from South Africa — that might have run the risk of disease, but stayed with the project, which resulted in the first "green" product.

For Loblaw, the big question became whether Pollution Probe would consent to use its name endorsing the product on the outside package. After some wrangling with the wording, Isaacs agreed. In fact, the foundation signed on to work on eight products: the organic topsoil dressing, soil conditioner made from wood pulp paste, organic fertilizer, phosphate-free laundry detergent, phosphate-free dishwashing soap, unbleached sanitary napkins, re-refined motor oil, and unbleached disposable diapers. Before issuing a final endorsement, Pollution Probe insisted that less raw material be used in manufacturing, that a toxic component standard in competing brands be eliminated, and that recycled materials be used in the packaging.

For Pollution Probe, the relationship with Loblaw was a source of friction from the outset. Conflict was nothing new to the foundation; it had long been racked by internal dissent. Founded in 1969 by a group of ecology activists, the independent, non-profit, research-based organization had set itself up as an unofficial pollution watchdog. This was before the birth of any public awareness of acid rain, the depleting ozone layer or polychlorinated biphenyls (PCBs), before even the creation of government-run ministries of the environment. As awareness grew, so did Pollution Probe, so quickly that it lacked a proper management structure to support it. It continued to operate largely by consensus, which slowed the decision-making process. In the fall of 1988, the organization almost imploded over what its public stance on the Canada-U.S. Free Trade Agreement should be. The board and staff complained that Isaacs was acting unilaterally, without board approval. In December of that year, a consultant was hired to implement a new management structure. The plan was taken to the board in January, but Isaacs would later gripe that he was never given the authority to implement it.

And then there was this giant supermarket chain looking to the foundation for some kind of corporate redemption. Almost all of Pollution Probe's staff opposed taking money from Loblaw for product endorsements, arguing that such a step would compromise its objectivity. Joint ventures between environmental and business groups were standard in the United States, but in Canada they were tantamount to sleeping with the enemy. Some Pollution Probe staff feared that the Loblaw connection would force the foundation into the maw of the mainstream. Others worried that the alliance would paint the group as promoting consumption, when what they wanted was to teach people how to consume less. Corridor arguments were common. Although the all-volunteer board, responsible for keeping the agency solvent, was supportive of Isaacs, he began receiving anonymous notes. One message, neatly printed on computer paper, was succinct: "RESIGN."

Isaacs stood firm. He argued that the money from Loblaw could be used for research and would not affect the agency's independent status. "We've been taking fund-raising money from business for twenty years, from natural resource companies like Inco and Noranda," he reminded the group. In 1982, the agency had published *Profit from Pollution Prevention*, a book that cited four hundred examples of successful corporate waste-recovery projects. He likened the endorsement to the American Dental Association accepting money to sanction a toothpaste. To appease the board, Isaacs did decline certain endorsements, including a bottled water produced with reverse-osmosis technology. The organization held the view that no one should have to buy bottled water, and that municipalities should be installing reverse-osmosis processes in all water-filtration plants.

Loblaw agreed to pay Pollution Probe a fee for every item it endorsed, up to $150,000. On lower cost products, such as dishwashing liquid, it would receive 1 cent per unit sold; on the fertilizer, 10 cents a bag. The foundation estimated that annual revenues would run between $75,000 and $150,000. Friends of the Earth, which agreed to endorse a baking soda repackaged as a household cleaner, earned a penny per package. The agency also received 25 cents per bag sold of a natural-source rose food developed by Loblaw, based on a formula found in its book, *How to Get Your Lawn and Garden Off Drugs*. The organization had also lobbied the company to package a reusable mesh coffee filter — instead of paper filters — but the economics weren't favorable and the idea was abandoned. Its two endorsements ultimately netted the organization less than $3,000. Not wanting to be seen as backing a complete line, Friends of the Earth ended the relationship there.

Designer Don Watt was brought in to consult on the look. Package image was crucial, an irony, given that packaging itself was a major environmental villain. Nichol's goal was to be the owner of the term "green." Watt suggested that Loblaw could copyright the name by inserting periods between the letters — G.R.E.E.N. — making it a graphic wordmark. He chose an old-fashioned typeface to reflect, as he put it, "a more traditional look, a moving backward not forward, not brave new worlds."

Pollution Probe staff frequently bickered over the copy used on packaging to explain why the product was regarded as environmentally friendly. The soft, simplistic, self-congratulatory tone of some of the descriptions annoyed many. For example, the 100% chlorine-free coffee filters box told shoppers: "Unlike most North American coffee filters which are bleached with environmentally-harmful chlorine, these premium quality filters have never been bleached; their natural creamy tan colour is an indication of their environmentally-friendly manufacturing process and will not alter the taste of your coffee. Now you can drink coffee while doing something good for the environment."

Approaching the June launch date, Nichol began showing up on television in his new role of environmentally sensitive retailer. In May 1989, he appeared on the CBC's news program "The Journal" on a panel discussion of the use of pesticides and the claims of organic farming. "Nobody can say that organic is free of pesticides," Nichol maintained. "What we can say is that there is a likelihood they don't have them." A week later, three weeks before G.R.E.E.N.'s official unveiling, Nichol was invited to a press lunch at Toronto's Four Seasons Hotel for Sting, the British pop superstar and self-styled champion of the endangered Brazilian rain forest. Sting was on a fourteen-city press tour for his book, *Jungle Stories: The Fight for the Amazon*, co-written with Belgian film maker Jean-Pierre Ditilleux. The tour was also a fund raiser for his newly formed Rainforest Foundation. Accompanying him were two disk-lipped Kaiapo Indian chiefs, Raoni and Megaron, whose arresting presence flanked the singer at every photo op, lending authenticity to his cause.

Shunning any publicity events that put others at center stage, Nichol turned the invitation down. Then he had a better idea. He called Sarah MacLachlan, a publicist with Little, Brown and Co. Canada, the publishing house handling the Canadian leg of Sting's tour, and asked for fifteen minutes of Sting's time before the lunch. What he was doing was unique in environmentally aware retailing, he told her. She granted Nichol an audience with Sting minus entourage. Nichol booked a meeting room atop the hotel to present his "G.R.E.E.N." slide show.

In the context of the summer of 1989, the Sting-Dave Nichol meeting had a bizarre but logical symmetry. Where the logic collapsed was that Nichol, consummate consumer, was being upheld as the personification of environmental activism in Canada. It was no surprise that the endeavor was destined to detonate.

At 11:30, Sting made his appearance, accompanied by MacLachlan and Don Green, co-owner of Roots Canada, which was co-sponsoring the Sting lunch. Green and his business partner Michael Budman were known as the Roots guys, perennially hip and healthy founders of a chain that made and sold shoes, purses, and clothing under the Roots label. Their success derived from an ability to tie the merchandising and marketing of their wares with their vision of the Canadian wilderness, a sensibility developed in the 1960s when, as teenagers from Detroit, they both attended summer camp in Algonquin Park. Roots' marketing capitalized on the mythology of Canada as outsiders often saw it — clear running waters, wide-open outdoors, and birchbark canoes. The Roots logo was a stylized beaver. Its success in markets outside Canada was also tied to their celebrity connections. They chummed around with Dan Aykroyd and John Candy. The Roots guys understood the allure of celebrity tie-ins.

The environmental movement dovetailed nicely with their image. They had heard about G.R.E.E.N. through several channels. Don Watt had worked on their stores and Warner Troyer was their summer neighbor on Smoke Lake in Algonquin Park, where both Budman and Green owned cottages. Earlier that spring, they had approached Nichol seeking permission to market T-shirts and sweatshirts with an emerald green G.R.E.E.N. logo through their stores.

As for Sting, he was impressed by Nichol's pitch, which included slides of demographic patterns, consumers' concerns about the environment, and how the G.R.E.E.N. line had been developed. Nichol was taken by Sting's polite manners. The rock star and the supermarket executive discussed how their efforts could complement one another. Sting could publicize the products. Nichol could offer financial backing to Sting's foundation. Nichol then flung open the door to an adjoining anteroom filled with G.R.E.E.N. products — phosphate-free detergent, Ecover washing powder, unbleached coffee filters, disposable diapers, fabric softener, peanut butter produced without mono and diglycerides. Sting browsed. He was particularly taken with the diapers. He asked if he could have them. "Absolutely," Nichol said. At the press conference following the lunch, Sting praised Loblaw's efforts and raised the diaper package. "You have a retailer right here in this country who is trying to do something about the environment," he told the crowd. "He should be supported." Later, one of Sting's people called Nichol about making a donation to the Rainforest Foundation. Nichol turned him down.

Printed on recycled paper, a G.R.E.E.N.-product *Insider's Report* was distributed across Canada on June 3, 1989; for this edition, green replaced the usual yellow highlights. The front page featured Nichol and Georgie Girl, both outfitted in green sweatshirts, with white G.R.E.E.N. logos (for sale at $9.99, $1 going to Pollution Probe). Above their heads was printed the slogan "Something Can Be Done." Below was a letter to consumers from Nichol. "Some may accuse us of being environmental opportunists," he said with prescience. "WE SEE OUR ROLES AS PROVIDING PRODUCTS PEOPLE WANT." He concluded: "If G.R.E.E.N. products do nothing more than help raise awareness of the need to address environmental issues NOW, and give Canadians hope that SOMETHING CAN BE DONE, then in the end, they will have made a positive contribution."

The *Report* abandoned its standard practice of invoking the names of fashionable restaurants and chefs. Instead, it dropped the names of environmental groups and trendy eco-issues. Greenpeace, a group that had nothing to do with G.R.E.E.N., was mentioned in conjunction with its stance on tuna fishing that imperiled dolphins — in a plug for President's Choice canned tuna. The G.R.E.E.N. lineup offered shoppers redemption without requiring them to change their habits. There was a phosphate-free detergent; a 100% natural source lawn and garden fertilizer; a high-performance motor oil that had been re-refined and "hydrotreated" to remove impurities; all natural, non-toxic pesticides; and G.R.E.E.N. foam disposable picnic plates, made without chlorofluorocarbons. There was also Rainforest Mix, an ecologically correct snack of caramel-coated pecans and Brazil nuts from South America; the nuts were a cash crop that gave the rain forests an economic *raison d'être*. Most of the 100 G.R.E.E.N. products were priced at or below the national brand in their category.

Backed by a $3-million television and print promotion campaign, the G.R.E.E.N. launch also encompassed a sister line of "Body Friendly" products, including The Virtuous Cooking Spray made from canola oil and packaged in a CFC-free container; The Virtuous Soda Cracker, with no cholesterol and unsalted or lightly salted tops; Leaner than Lean Processed Meats; Nature's Perfect Fruit Snack, a chewy apple roll-up; olive oil and salad dressings containing no MSG or preservatives; high-fiber corn flakes; Cox's Orange Pippin Apple Juice, a pesticide- and herbicide-free product made from Alar-free New Zealand apples; If the World Were Perfect Water; low-ash cat food, and Slim 'N Trim Dog and Cat Food, with no preservatives or artificial flavors or colors.

The line received further exposure that same day via Loblaw's sponsorship of a five-hour international TV special on "Earth Day" focusing on the earth's environment and development. Linked by satellite, the show featured Elton John, Diana Ross, the Moscow Symphony, and, of course, Sting, as well as Richard Gere, John Denver, Christopher Reeve, and a cadre of politicians — George Bush, Rajiv Gandhi, Brian Mulroney, Margaret Thatcher and Gro Harlem Brundtland.

The initial response to G.R.E.E.N. products was overwhelming. In four weeks, Loblaw sold $5 million worth, double the projected sales. After two months, G.R.E.E.N. accounted for 5.1% of corporate brand sales. Loblaw couldn't keep the products on the shelf. The phosphate-free detergent outsold Tide. G.R.E.E.N. bathroom tissue stole 50% of the category. The launch was covered by the *New York Times* and news of it spread as far as the U.S.S.R. and mainland China. The publicity value was estimated at $100 million. Loblaw's survey showed that 82% of Canadians were aware of the line and 27% of the population had tried a G.R.E.E.N. product, even though the products were available only at Loblaw-run stores. Optimism, understandably, ran high. "In a year, Canada is going to be green," declared a buoyant Dave Nichol in one interview. "We're going to be the most environmentally conscious country because of these types of programs....It's a green wave that's going to come crashing down on those retailers and manufacturers who have not 'greened' their company and their product lines."

Nichol was correct. The green wave did come crashing down, crashing down right on Loblaw. The first blow came from Friends of the Earth, which criticized the inclusion of products it regarded as inconsistent or irrelevant to a green philosophy — recycled yet chlorine-bleached toilet paper, throwaway foam plates, and household cleaners containing Bitrex, a bitter-tasting substance that discouraged children from ingesting it. Julia Langer wrote Colin Isaacs advising Pollution Probe not to endorse any Loblaw products. Overconsumption was the problem, she pointed out. Changing consumption patterns, not brands, was the answer. Friends of the Earth let the contract for its endorsements lapse.

Famed environmentalist David Suzuki, a Pollution Probe board member, added his voice to the debate in late June. Firms like Loblaw should be applauded for manufacturing environmentally safe products, Suzuki said. But by endorsing products for cash, Pollution Probe had seriously compromised its integrity. "I'm very disturbed by it," he told the *Toronto Star*. "By doing this, you now have a vested interest that takes you away from being an objective observer."

The final straw was the Diaper Dilemma. In retrospect, this should not have been a surprise. In the late 1980s, there was no more potent or pungent symbol of the North American garbage crisis than the disposable diaper. Although versions of the throwaway diaper had existed since World War II, it wasn't until 1961 that Procter & Gamble applied for the patent on Pampers, which became the best-selling baby bum-wrap in history. Three decades later, P&G and Kimberly-Clark produced almost 80% of the 16 billion disposable diapers used each year. (This did not include the market niche for adult incontinence, which made up another billion diapers.) One U.S. study declared that disposable diapers constituted 12% of total trash in landfills.

The truth about disposable diapers remains unclear. Are the thousands of disposable diapers that an average child consumes in infancy — 4,907, according to one study, 5,840, according to another — more detrimental than the cloth diaper, given the same number of wearings and thus washings, and accounting for soap and energy? Studies, most of them commissioned either by companies that produced disposables or by diaper-washing services, failed to offer definitive guidance. Often they descended into arcane arguments over how much more energy was created by burning a dry cloth diaper or a sodden Pamper, or how many people rinsed diapers before throwing them away, or how many parents double-diapered their babies when using cloth.

Pollution Probe's official diaper position was that cloth was preferable to disposable. Within the organization, those opposed to the Loblaw campaign said it did not matter how good the diaper was compared to what else was on the market: the agency should be pushing for a complete ban. Isaacs took the more pragmatic approach. Consumers were interested in comfort, he argued. They were not interested in a ban. At least Loblaw's diapers were made with fluff pulp bleached with hydrogen peroxide, instead of the more threatening chlorine. They were therefore believed to be free of the dioxins found in trace amounts in almost all chlorine-bleached pulp and paper products.

Loblaw wanted to call its disposable diaper biodegradable. Pollution Probe would not consent. Nothing, the agency insisted, was biodegradable. In a Loblaw commercial for the diaper, Isaacs told viewers, "In the best of all worlds, everyone would use cloth diapers. But cloth diapers aren't always convenient." Nichol, seated beside him, explained why the disposable diapers were environmentally friendly. Isaacs ended with, "If you must use disposable diapers, use this one." Two Probe staff members promptly resigned and vented their frustration to the media. Colin Isaacs could see no way out. On June 29, he submitted his resignation to the board. His departure, he claimed, had little to do with the endorsements, except to call into question his support on the board. Isaacs then joined the ranks of consultants working within corporate suites to effect environmental change. Loblaw became a client. Pollution Probe pulled its name from the diaper endorsement, but continued to stand behind seven other products until its initial agreement lapsed the following June.

Nichol vigorously defended the diaper decision. Two years earlier, he pointed out, a Greenpeace expert had toured Canada, promoting non-bleached dioxin-free paper products, including disposable diapers. "You can't have it both ways," Nichol told the press. "We delivered what Greenpeace advocated. We did the same with energy-efficient light bulbs. And now the environmental groups are saying that this, too, is not enough. Well, I say they are a good start and we are going to do more."

Nichol also defended Isaacs. "[He] raised his head above the masses, and in Canada, when you do that, somebody always tries to blow it off, because we want to be a grey, amorphous mass. This is why we have never even begun to approach our potential as a nation." The whole episode, Nichol thought, was yet more evidence of the passive, guilt-ridden Canadian archetype. "According to most environmentalists, there is nothing that can be done, so what we're supposed to do is put on a hair shirt and whip ourselves," he said. "Don't do anything except feel incredibly guilty about what we've done to the environment. That's a very Canadian attitude."

But the ecological die had been cast. As soon as Pollution Probe's credibility was brought into question, so too was Loblaw's. Greenpeace, quiet to this point, announced that its test of two samples of Loblaw's organic fertilizer had revealed minute amounts of chlorinated organic compounds, which can include dioxins. Greenpeace asked the grocery chain to remove it from the shelves and publish test results for other products. Nichol refused; the company had spent $50,000 testing for dioxin alone, he claimed, and had found no toxins. He was convinced that if he released the complete fertilizer study, it would be used against the company. The allegations were neither proved nor disproved, but left a lingering uncertainty in shoppers' minds.

Another assault on G.R.E.E.N. was launched by the Consumers' Association of Canada. It claimed Loblaw's advertising was misleading. It questioned how a diaper that took 300 years to break down in a land-fill could benefit the environment. It questioned why unsalted crackers should be packaged under the environmentally friendly banner. Suppliers, who had deluged Loblaw with bids to produce G.R.E.E.N. products, stopped calling. The media adopted a critical tone. Attempting to reassure Loblaw executives, Dick Currie sent out an excerpt from Machiavelli's *The Prince*: "It should be borne in mind that there is nothing more difficult to arrange, more doubtful of success and more dangerous to carry through than instigating changes....The innovator makes enemies of all those who prospered under the old order and only lukewarm support is forthcoming from those who would prosper under him. Their support is lukewarm partly for fear of their adversaries, who have the existing laws on their side, and partly men are incredulous, never really trusting new things unless they have tested them by experience."

When interviewed again on "The Journal," an embattled Nichol was asked whether he felt any sense of responsibility to his customers or to the environment. Nichol fumbled, uncharacteristically. "Responsibility...I feel responsible for, uh, you know. To be not concerned about the environment you'd have to be some sort of cretin....Okay, I do not feel myself to be cretinous....And I'm proud to be involved in having brought the G.R.E.E.N. products and green awareness to Canada and it's also great that, you know, caring about the environment is really good business. It's lovely that the two things are compatible."

That fall, Nichol spoke at Our World, a summit on the environment organized by Carson and Dennis Mills, a Liberal MP. By then, however, the earnestness of it all was beginning to get to him. "I was careful not to position myself as an environmentalist," he would later insist. "I give people products they want to buy. And 'The Journal' gets me on the air and they put hot lights on you. And the first question is 'Dave Nichol, are you an environmentalist?' And I say, 'No, I'm not, I'm a person who brings people products that they want. The reason I do that is because I want them to switch to our supermarkets.' I think they forget that's the way our society works. People buy products. People produce products. People sell products."

Paradoxically, this was not the viewpoint expressed in the Canadian version of *The Green Consumer Guide*, prepared by Pollution Probe, designed by The Watt Group and published in November 1989 by McClelland & Stewart Inc. Avie Bennett, M&S's chairman, had secured Canadian rights for the book at the Frankfurt Book Fair and in early 1988 approached Pollution Probe about preparing a Canadian edition. When Isaacs informed Carson of the project, Carson told him that Loblaw was working on a similar book to be written by Warner Troyer and published by Doubleday (Canada). Bennett stepped in to broker a deal with Loblaw. Troyer and Pollution Probe would collaborate; Probe was to get the "prepared by" credit; Troyer and his wife, Glenys Moss, would be cited on the cover as consultants. Troyer drafted the foreword. Novelist Margaret Atwood, the superstar in McClelland & Stewart's firmament, wrote the preface.

From the beginning, the project was marred by whiny discord. "A nightmare," is how Isaacs later remembered it. Troyer and Pollution Probe soon were at loggerheads over the book's focus. Troyer wanted to emphasize health-related issues such as pesticides, irradiation of food, hormones and antibiotics used in the production of meat, or what he called the internal environment. Pollution Probe wanted to focus on other issues such as acid rain, waste management, transportation, packaging, non-toxic cleansers. The organization feared that straying too far from mainstream concerns would reduce the guide's authority and credibility. Personal relations were also tense. Troyer, then undergoing chemotherapy for the cancer that would take his life in September 1991, persisted in smoking at meetings, much to the irritation of some Pollution Probe members.

Eventually, the book was written. Loblaw guaranteed sales of 60,000 copies at $14.95 apiece through its stores. There were no G.R.E.E.N. product endorsements to be found, nor any mention of the line. Yet the tie-in between book and products was explicit; the Watt-designed cover used the same lettering as the G.R.E.E.N. logo, minus periods between the letters. Green and red were the book's principal colors, just like the G.R.E.E.N. packaging. And with every sale, Loblaw offered shoppers a booklet of coupons worth $20 on selected G.R.E.E.N. products.

Philosophically, the guide had a mantra: reduce, reuse, recycle, refuse. It explained the major problems and how people could change their behavior to make a difference. Don't use Tetra Pak, blister, single-serving, or microwavable packaging. Don't use abrasive cleaning substances. Shop at an enlightened retailer. It was a message for its time; the book hit the best-seller charts, sold more than 175,000 copies and was reprinted once. But its time passed, quickly. Only a few years later, Bennett would say, "Green is pretty much dead in publishing."

Part of the problem was data. Emerging research disputed some of the book's conclusions. But there was an even more glaring problem — the basic contradiction between the tenets of an environmentally correct life as defined by *The Green Consumer Guide* on the one hand and the supermarket culture, which celebrated packaging, convenience, and choice on the other. True, green would be at the forefront of a new product wave led by detergent and diaper manufacturers. Procter & Gamble set up a pilot project to recycle disposable diapers into reusable pulp and plastic. Household detergents were issued in thin recycled plastic pouches, instead of more wasteful plastic bottles. Cereal makers such as General Mills used recycled paper in their boxes.

But much of the change took place at the margins. The conditioned supermarket shopper still wanted whites whiter than white (something phosphate-free soaps could not deliver), single-serving portions, "new and improved," flawless fruits and vegetables. Products were supposed to solve problems, not create them. Moreover, as many environmentalists complained, the hype generated by modestly laudable "green" products tended to divert attention from a company's or manufacturer's more serious environmental transgressions.

The birth of G.R.E.E.N., therefore, marked not so much the dawn of a new consumer consciousness as a refocusing of the old one. As was the case with No Name and President's Choice, the success of the G.R.E.E.N. label hinged on consumers' perception that buying the brand would improve the quality of their lives. For those who defined themselves as committed environmentalists, the line implied that buying phosphate-free detergent, for example, would slow the formation of pollutive algae in lakes and oceans; that chlorofluorocarbon-free aerosol sprays would protect the ozone layer (another claim later subject to dispute); and that coffee filters, paper towels, and toilet paper made with non-chlorine-bleached fluff pulp would reduce dioxins and other wastes arising from industrial pollution. It was a naïve approach, one that seemed to lull consumers into environmental complacency: having bought "green," they did not need to do anything else. As journalist Wayne Ellwood had predicted in *The New Internationalist*, "Consumers, finally satisfied that they can 'do something,' may seek no further than their shopping baskets." Paradoxically, the best "green consumer does not consume at all, or reduces consumption and waste to a minimum while selecting essentials for living."

But G.R.E.E.N. also offered more immediate gratification: it made purchasers feel virtuous. It offered emotional fulfillment for buying goods seen to be straightforward, honest, and reliable. It assuaged the guilt that had come to be associated with consumption. And it gratified the desire for a new self-image. As Canadian anthropologist Grant McCracken points out, consumers tended to define themselves socially through the things they chose to buy and not to buy. As such, consumer goods were, as he put it, "mediums of culture." In a society that placed a premium on individuality, choosing to spend $100 on a cotton T-shirt with a designer label or to buy detergent made without phosphates provided consumers with an opportunity to establish their identities.

To the middle class, the G.R.E.E.N. line packaged the illusion of consumer activism. Many of its members had never given a thought to the politics of shopping. Now, buying G.R.E.E.N., shoppers believed they could effect changes that the political process could not achieve. Handbooks such as the British *Green Consumer Guide* and *Shopping for a Better Planet* fostered active consumerism by making it clear that everything bought had political ramifications. Ultimately, these books taught, buying a single carton of Tide implied support for the store that sold it, the company that manufactured or supplied it, and the political regime of the country that produced it.

Such views fostered a radical shift in consumer consciousness. For more than two hundred years, beginning with the American colonists' protest of the 1775 Stamp Act and a refusal to buy British-made goods, the power of consumers had been expressed not by what was bought, but by what was boycotted. (The word derived its name from Captain Charles Boycott, a nineteenth-century land agent in County Mayo, Ireland, who was forced to flee after the local population refused to accept lower wages for work.) The premise of the boycott was that it would generate enough support to drive down demand. The supermarket had been a logical and frequent arena of modern boycotts, most prominently the mass boycott of California grapes and lettuce organized in the 1960s by the late César Chavez to protest the conditions of migrant farm workers. In the 1970s, the campaigns mounted by consumer advocate Ralph Nader broadened the very definition of "consumer" until it was synonymous with citizen.

Typically, the damage inflicted by boycotts had less to do with sales revenues than with image. After a five-year campaign supported by church groups in the 1980s, Nestlé removed its infant formula from Third World countries. Opponents argued that formula, although convenient, was less beneficial than mother's milk, which contained among other things antibodies to fight infection. Moreover, the water that would be used to make the formula was often untreated, posing a potential risk for infants. Sales of the formula, which made up only 2 to 3% of the multinational giant's business, actually rose during the period of the boycott. But Nestlé felt the need to avoid negative publicity. In Canada, a protest by schoolchildren to force McDonald's to replace polystyrene hamburger containers with paper was successful — even though many environmentalists maintained that Styrofoam was "greener" because it did not consume trees. Similarly, Heinz announced in 1990 that its StarKist tuna was "dolphin safe," after consumer groups complained that nets used to snare tuna were simultaneously killing dolphins.

Pat Carson liked to call the process of principled purchasing a "buycott." Buycotts not only restored a measure of control to shoppers, they also opened a new avenue of consumerism that demonstrated social concern — from buying Rainforest Mix candy to taking eco-tour vacations in endangered regions of the world. By decade's end, Body Shop values had become so pervasive that even stodgy chartered banks were paying lip service to the notion of "giving back" to the community. Other manufacturers followed the lead of ice-cream titan Ben & Jerry's, which created a $96-million-a-year empire catering to the aging Woodstock generation, while donating 7.5% of its profits to charity.

Despite the backlash, Loblaw continued green product development in some areas. Larry Griffin took his search for a cloth diaper to manufacturers in Korea and Mexico. Early in 1990, he was approached by Rhonda Windsor (formerly Maxwell), who had appeared as a consumer spokeswoman in company commercials in 1979. Now, she re-entered the Loblaw universe with a reusable cotton diaper made by her own company, Dimples Diaper Inc. For the next eight months, she and Griffin discussed development of a private-label diaper for Loblaw under G.R.E.E.N. She was not therefore amused when The Alternative Diaper, made by another manufacturer, previewed in the Christmas 1990 *Insider's Report*. "They took my ideas and bastardized them," Windsor complained. "They put metal snaps on them, for God's sake. Why they would do that I don't know. They're cold. They made them in different sizes, which kills the one-size-fits-all theory. And they cased them in plastic. You can't get more anti-environment than that." Griffin said Loblaw had already hooked up with the other manufacturer before Windsor approached them.

(Loblaw was the least of Windsor's concerns. When Dimples developed problems with deteriorating plastic, elastic, and the snaps, it was taken off shelves. Nor did it end there. According to Windsor, the company was effectively stolen from her by consultants brought in to promote Dimples stock. The stock price did rise — to more than $8 a share — but by then, she claimed, $20 million had been siphoned from the treasury. In a story that could have been turned into a made-for-TV movie, Windsor alleged that she was followed, was sent threatening letters, had the tires of her leased Jaguar XJS convertible slashed, and was made the target of an attempted poisoning. Somehow, she believed, a religious cult was involved. What was clear was that she kept strange company: her business partner and boyfriend, Tony Boydon, had been jailed in September 1991 for counselling the attempted murder of the husband of a former paramour. Another Dimples principal, Bob Reid, was also jailed — for an earlier stock fraud. By 1993, Dimples was in the hands of Doug Elliott, a former tax-shelter salesman; it traded on the Vancouver Stock Exchange for pennies. Ever resilient, the self-proclaimed Diaper Queen of Canada started over. In the fall of 1992, Windsor founded Sunburst Ltd., marketing two products in sync with the times: watches that beeped when people had absorbed their quota of ultraviolet rays; and a homeopathic zinc-based lozenge that claimed to reduce the severity of common cold symptoms.)

Fighting a barrage of negative publicity, the G.R.E.E.N. line lost money in the first year, with sales of $60 million. Of that amount, Pollution Probe was paid $75,000. Currie told the company's annual meeting in May 1990 that the line would have to make $100 million to break even. Sales finally reached that level in 1991, reflecting continuing consumer interest in environmentally sensitive products.

Nichol liked winners, and G.R.E.E.N. was not proving to be fertile territory. "The problem with green products," he lamented, "is that they're so darn hard to find." He longed for another hit like the energy-efficient light bulb. "When I told my people I wanted to sell a $20 light bulb, they told me I was crazy," Nichol recalled. "Carson said, 'That's a problem.' I told him, 'It's not a problem. It's controversial.' Nobody would sell a $20 light bulb unless it works. It had a heck of a story, which was that if everybody in Canada took three ordinary light bulbs and replaced them with three of these, we could light the Ottawa-Hull area for a year. We got Hydro to support us with a $5 rebate per bulb. We sold 2 million right away. People were signing up for them at stores. That was good stuff." The bulbs sold out, but Loblaw did not repeat the offer. There were other additions to the line in 1990 — a complete water filtration system in a box; an alternative bleach that did not use chlorine; a low-ash cat food without preservatives; a universal battery recharger, billed as "the one G.R.E.E.N. product everyone agrees on"; Christmas lights; and The Alternative Diaper. The following year, Nichol launched all-natural dog biscuits, baby shampoo, paper towels made from recycled Yellow Pages, and a President's Choice 100% organic compost accelerator. But green products *were* hard to find. New product development eventually slowed to a standstill. Only three G.R.E.E.N. products were introduced in 1992, as the emphasis turned to healthful products.

Nichol's growing disillusionment mirrored that of the average Canadian consumer. By the fall of 1992, three years after G.R.E.E.N.'s launch, a federal study revealed that Canadians were suffering from "environmental fatigue" and had little appetite for learning more or taking further action. People said they were content with what they had done about the environment, confused by information overload, and ill-informed on some issues. One in four regularly put hazardous waste in regular garbage, few conserved water, and fewer still wanted more park land created. There was at once too little information and too much.

What was abundantly clear was that you could not shop to save the planet. Or if you could, salvation was too slow arriving. Canadians wanted garbage gone by the end of the week, if not in their lifetimes. In the beginning, green had been chic in a Euro-peasant kind of way. A composter in the back yard was a badge of awareness. Eliminating paper napkins wasn't a problem — they were *déclassé* anyway. But then came the problem of not washing cloth table napkins with every use. Shoppers seemed to miss the reassuring grinning babies and blonde housewives on the packages of products they were used to seeing on the shelves.

No wonder the environment was a mess. It was all so confusing. Just because a product claimed to be biodegradable did not make it ecologically benign. It was not clear where recycled products came from. Using a non-aerosol spray deodorant did not remove the threat of a thinning ozone layer. In fact, the replacement propellants had been found to contribute to low-level smog. Compostable sounded good, but meant nothing if there were no facilities available. Detergents without phosphates failed to get shirts as white as algae-causing detergents once did. And scary preservatives did help things last longer.

What finally became apparent to consumers was that there was no such thing as a truly environmentally friendly product, just products that were less damaging to the environment than others. In the meantime, with no standards or defined terms in environmental labeling, many manufacturers indulged in "greenwashing," using bogus claims to position their products as environmentally pure. In that climate, it was hard for many consumers to shake the what-difference-does-it-all-make attitude. If a sponge were used to clean up a kitchen spill, instead of a huge clump of paper toweling, would it actually save a single tree in the forest?

Ironically, *The G.R.E.E.N. Insider's Report* helped to breed confusion and fear. It introduced shoppers to a new set of worries — the lack of guidelines for the manufacture of peanut butter, the effects of the chemical Alar (or daminozide) used to spray apple trees on apple juice, and the lax treatment of toxic chemicals in drinking water. Putting body-friendly products under the environmental banner added to the confusion, since shoppers were conditioned to seeing the environment as something outside, a separate entity. The G.R.E.E.N. fallout also tainted the eco-lobbies. The public wanted their environmental activists pure, wrapped in an eco-bubble, unmarked by commercialism or self-interest. Now, Pollution Probe and others had been exposed as vulnerable to the same political self-interest and petty bickering as any other organization.

Within Loblaw, Carson came to view himself as a "fifth columnist" — a self-proclaimed traitor and spy, teaching people how to change their habits. He likened himself to a Trappist monk leading the way through a modern Dark Ages. Inevitably, his work created friction. After Carson's appearance at a farmers' protest meeting, Nichol accused Carson of trying to embarrass him. "No," Carson responded, "I'm trying to protect you." Indeed, he regarded Nichol as his silent co-conspirator. "He's trying to counter what he's doing. And he's letting me do it. He'll say he's only in it for the money. So how come he's increasing my budget all the time?"

With writer Julia Moulden, Carson wrote *Green Is Gold*, a primer for businesses interested in going green; published in 1991, it enjoyed a modest success. Half of his time was spent on the road, speaking to schools, businesses, industry associations, and governments. He often began speeches with a story about visiting his mother, Josephine, in Ireland. She questioned him about the meaning of consumerism. "I thought consumption was a disease," she told him. "Does that mean that consumerism is a disease of the mind?" Thereafter, Carson referred to consumerism as a disease of the mind. At times, in the full flight of oratory, he sounded like someone plotting the end of consumer society. "In Ireland, when you see a sign that says garage sale, they're selling the garage," he would tell audiences. "I couldn't believe the amount of waste when I came to this country."

Much of his address was devoted to Big Questions — overpopulation, depletion of natural resources, the need for undeveloped nations to build a sustainable agricultural base, the contamination of food by pesticides, herbicides, insecticides. He warned of global nuclear war if some sort of order were not imposed. "We're living off the backs of the less fortunate," he insisted. "How do we get China and India to avoid the industrial revolution? The inventory of resources is depleting." He talked about turning Loblaw into a multi-domestic company — selling its know-how to many countries, but using foreign resources to make products within those countries.

When he was not forecasting the end of the modern shopping ethic, Carson devoted his time to saving Loblaw money by installing energy-efficient lighting, introducing recycling programs, reducing packing and bags at checkout. He developed the green box pilot program — stacked green containers on wheels that substituted for shopping carts and allowed shoppers to sort food, have it scanned at checkout without unloading it, and take it home, eliminating the need for plastic shopping bags. Carson fantasized about a self-contained "store of the future" that used solar energy and would be built with non-toxic materials. Never losing sight of the bottom line, Carson estimated it would cut heating, air conditioning, and building costs by 50% each. In an effort to sell the concept to Dick Currie, he used the motto "Build it and they will come," a line borrowed from *Field of Dreams*, Currie's favorite movie.

Despite the setbacks, Carson continued to believe in "green." "The green revolution is as competitive as the industrial or technological revolution," he maintained. "If you behave in an ecological manner, you are going to get the customers." He continued to remain loyal to Nichol. "Dave Nichol," Carson liked to say, "is the most ethical guy I've ever worked for."

When Nichol thought about G.R.E.E.N. which was infrequently, he took solace in the sales numbers for the Club Pack Toilet Tissue, the best-selling G.R.E.E.N. product. In the years to come, it would become the number three selling President's Choice product, after PC Cola and The Decadent Chocolate Chip Cookie. But the inherent clash between an environmental message that implicitly condemned consumption and his larger mission to supply products and constantly whet the appetite for new ones created stasis, an intolerable condition to Nichol. He began to focus his attention on developing products for another burgeoning mass-market anxiety: fear of food. Public obsessions had shifted from the political to the personal, from altruism to self-interest, from ozone levels to cholesterol levels. A new market niche was opening, a potentially large one. Dave Nichol, as always, wanted to be there first.

CHAPTER ELEVEN

DR. J. AND BARBIE

A polite and proper Englishman, David Jenkins would seem quite at home walking across the quad of Merton College, Oxford, a black gown fluttering behind him. Certainly to look at him, no one would ever guess that he had squirreled away 300 kilograms of human excrement in his freezer. But, by April 1993, thanks in good part to Dave Nichol, that is exactly what Jenkins had amassed — 650 pounds of poop, carefully packed in ice. And very thankful Dr. Jenkins was; for the waste, he believed, contained answers he had been seeking for twenty years.

Jenkins, who was born in England in 1942, had earned a Ph.D. in human physiology and nutrition in 1970 from Oxford University. A decade later, he moved to Toronto with his family and joined the faculty of the University of Toronto as a professor of nutritional science. Jenkins's life's work — his passion — was investigating the effects of dietary fiber on health. In fiber, Jenkins was convinced, lay the answers to the host of ills that plagued Western society.

He had come to this mission while working at a teaching hospital in London in the mid-seventies. There he met Dennis Burkit, known in medical circles as "the bran man." Burkit, well-respected for his cancer research, had written a paper on the salutary effects of fiber on diet in Africa. Based on research undertaken in Uganda in the thirties and forties, the paper was the talk of the British scientific community. In it, Burkit observed that villagers who routinely consumed fiber had bowel

217

movements nearly five times as heavy as sailors in the British navy. This fact may not be the stuff of cocktail party chitchat, but for Burkit it was a revelation. People who consumed high-fiber diets, he concluded, had more efficient digestive systems, which in turn made them less prone to certain diseases. One of the first studies to link nutrition to the prevention of disease, Burkit's work demonstrated that what the body did not absorb was just as important as what it did.

David Jenkins is something of a dietary zealot, in a mild-mannered way. He hates fat with a fervor. He has not eaten meat since he was thirteen. He knows that his fiber obsession is not widely shared. "Everybody thinks I'm a flake," he says calmly. But it is people who adhere to a high-fat meat and dairy diet whom Jenkins finds absurd. "Here we are, living sedentary lives in houses warmed by central heating, driving cars everywhere, while we continue to eat the same food as our tribal herdsmen-hunter ancestors," he says. Small wonder heart disease is the number one killer in North America.

Jim White came to know Jenkins in the early 1980s while writing about food for the *Toronto Star*. When he needed an expert to quote on nutrition, White often turned to Jenkins. White, too, was a big fan of fiber and extolled its benefits in print from time to time. Shortly after joining Loblaw in 1984, he persuaded Nichol to create a No Name high-fiber cereal — no small achievement on White's part, since Nichol considered fiber-rich foods about as tasty as plywood. White then suggested to Larry Griffin, vice-president of Quality Assurance, that he ask Jenkins to help analyze the test results. Jenkins agreed. When the cereal was launched in September 1984, it was touted in *Insider's Report* as tasting better and having more fiber than Kellogg's All Bran. Much to White's disappointment, the cereal was delisted within a year, a victim of poor demand.

But if the mass marketplace had not yet embraced fiber, nutritional concerns were surfacing, directed principally toward fat and the chemicals used in food production. Food on supermarket shelves contained a dubious mélange of chemical additives, artificial colorings and flavorings. Anti-caking substances were used to prolong shelf life. Sequestrants were added to prevent trace minerals from clouding soft drinks, or fats and oils from turning rancid. Artificial emulsifiers helped homogenize milk and shortenings.

Indeed, much of the food technology heralded in the 1950s as miracles of modern science had, by the 1980s, become suspect, if not undesirable. In the late 1960s, monosodium glutamate (MSG), an extract of seaweed, had been found to cause brain damage in infant mice. Baby-food manufacturers were forced to stop using it, but it continued to be a staple in other processed foods. Throughout the 1970s, owing in part to the writings of Rachel Carson, Adelle Davis, and Ralph Nader, chemical scare stories spread: there were lethal levels of DDT in animal fat, mercury in fish, arsenic in chicken feed, hormones and antibiotics in beef, salmonella bacteria in eggs and chicken, nitrates in bacon and ham. Fruit and vegetables were dependent on pesticides, fungicides, growth enhancers, shine enhancers, and ripeners. Radiating food with gamma rays to retard spoilage and extend shelf life created new questions and new fears. The supermarket, it seemed, had become a potential deathtrap. So-called "health" foods had their own shelf, distinct from everything else.

The task of addressing toxicity in food production was so overwhelming that food manufacturers chose to shift their focus to the growing fear of fat and high cholesterol fostered by medical studies. This trend was nowhere better illustrated than in the explosion of "light," "lite," or "lo-fat" products. The market for light was pretty much inevitable after nutritionists began to argue that it was fat grams, not calories, that weight-conscious eaters should count. More important than the calorie per se was its composition. No more than 30% of calories consumed, it was suggested, should come from fat.

But like "healthy" and "natural," it was never precisely clear just what the term "light" actually meant. Officially, it was applied to labels of any food that had undergone a 50% reduction in calories from its original form, or that had a minimum 25% reduction in fat or proteins. But light was also used to describe a change in texture. Oils, breads, and cakes were called light if their *color* was lighter than the original. Light meats were not lower in fat content, but in sodium — by at least 25%. Light wine had less than 9% alcohol; light liquor carried an alcohol reduction of at least 25%. Light ice cream consisted of 3 to 5% fat from milk solids, compared with a minimum of 10% in regular ice cream.

Ironically, light existed only in foods that in original form were of questionable nutritional merit. One company, Hostess, actually brought a Twinkie Lite to market. Light, in short, did not necessarily mean healthy; it was simply less of a nutritional burden than the original. For example, a single two-tablespoon serving of the "light" version of Kraft Cheez Whiz, not one of mankind's more salutary spreads, contained seventy-seven calories, compared with ninety-three for ordinary Cheez Whiz. The light version had 4.8 grams of fat, (vs. 7.2 in the original), 3.0 grams of carbohydrate (vs. 2.9), and 5.5 grams of protein (vs. 4.2).

Despite the ambiguities, light was broadly interpreted as a good thing. By the early nineties, light and diet foods made up more than 20% of all food sold in North American supermarkets. And the category was growing a hundred times faster than any other. Inevitably, Nichol wanted a share of the market. In June 1985, President's Choice launched its light mayonnaise, with 18% less fat, to compete with Kraft's Miracle Whip Light. Shortly after, No Name Light Margarine, Light Sour Cream, Light Cottage Cheese, and Light Cream Cheese were introduced.

Light, however, was only one marketing thrust. Nestled among the raspberry vinegar and Brie cheese in the June 1985 *Insider's Report* was low-sodium tinned tuna (for those fearful of salt), safflower oil (billed as a healthful alternative to sunflower oil), with 79% polyunsaturated fats and 8% saturated fats, and unsweetened, unflavored yogurt. Jim White, who possessed a missionary-like zeal to eradicate additives, preservatives, and artificial flavors from the President's Choice line, had returned from a conference on gastronomy in California high on yogurt. In Asia, nonagenarian Georgians and Azerbaijani ate it every day and credited it for their long lives. White borrowed other ideas from the shelves of health food stores. President's Choice muesli and rice cakes were available by the fall of 1987. A year later, *Insider's Report* launched canola oil. In the absence of federal labeling legislation, it was never explained why canola oil, made from rapeseed, was so wondrous. Instead, Nichol referred readers to press coverage in the United States, including a Jane Brody column in the *New York Times*, which explained that canola contained fewer saturates.

For Dave Nichol, the development of nutritionally correct products ran against instinct. He privately referred to Brody and others like
her as members of "the food police" (a term also employed by Julia
Child), and he dismissed most of their ideas out of hand. His first objection — an insurmountable one — had to do with taste. His second
objection had to do with style. For him, health food advocates conjured
up images of arid, earnest characters who wore socks with their sandals
and cared nothing about pleasure.

The food police were not a new phenomenon. On September 19,
1899, ten women and one man (Melvil Dewey, developer of the Dewey
Decimal System) had gathered at an informal conference in Lake Placid,
New York, to establish a new discipline called domestic economy, later
known as home economics. Its arrival dovetailed with the emergence of
the Progressive era, which sought reforms needed to deal with the new,
urban-industrial order. And it provided yet further evidence that the
authority of religion had given way to the authority of science.

One clear mandate of domestic economy was to curb the subjective palate in favor of objective nutritional standards. A favorite device
was to imply that there was something suspiciously sensual about a too
enthusiastic enjoyment of food. Choosing food on the basis of whim or
habit or because it tasted good was said to lead people away from the
higher life. Denial was a virtue; the less memorable the meal, the better.
Soon, the taste bud ceased to be the determining measure of the American diet. In *The Taste of America*, writers John and Karen Hess referred
to this as "the rape of the palate." Heavily influenced by advertising and
food manufacturers, women who had routinely ground their own coffee
were now persuaded to buy it canned, vacuum-packed, and already
ground. Convenience took precedence over flavor. It was the beginning
of the chasm that would open between food that was perceived to be
good for you and food people believed tasted good — a chasm that,
almost a century later, Dave Nichol perceived an opportunity to bridge.

In April 1988, LIM launched President's Choice Under 300 Calories frozen
entrées. The aim was to take a run at Stouffer's Lean Cuisine, a line that

had dominated the low-calorie frozen entrée category since 1981. This category was crucial to crack, because it was the largest in the growing diet-food market, with close to 25% of the share. The very creation of diet products — foods you needed to consume in order to lose weight — was a marketer's fantasy. The dieter was the ideal consumer, never satisfied, always possessed with the desire to consume more to reach an impossible goal. The diet industry was born in Queens, New York, in May 1963 when Jean Nidetch and Albert Lippert founded Weight Watchers International. Since then, diet-food sales have climbed steadily, enhanced by the powerful images of the fashion industry and by an endless catwalk of waif-like models, from the eponymous Twiggy in the sixties to Kate Moss in the nineties. By the start of the decade, according to the National Eating Disorder Information Centre at Toronto General Hospital, 80% of all girls had been on at least one diet by age eighteen. Among teenagers of all races, classes, and educational levels, anorexia and bulimia were running at near-epidemic levels.

Sales of the Under 300 Calories line were sluggish. Paul Tepperman, George Weston Ltd.'s in-house physician, whom Nichol dubbed Dr. Smoothy for his laid-back California demeanor, suggested they contact Dr. George Steiner, an internationally renowned blood fat specialist. Steiner, who ran the Lipid Research Clinic Program at Toronto General Hospital, agreed to consult on development of a new frozen entrée line in late 1988. In return, Loblaw agreed to make a grant to the hospital. Steiner's first comment was that three hundred calories did not offer enough substance. He recommended that entrées contain 350 to 500 calories and that the volume be increased from 300 to 400 grams. In Steiner's view, the source of the food energy was more important than the calorie count. A maximum of 25% of calories should come from fat. The product developers, with help from Terri Nichol, then went to work on five flavor profiles: spinach lasagne, Oriental lemon chicken with lychees, chicken cacciatore, spicy Thai chicken, and turkey chili.

Getting a plug from the leading specialist in a field — even if the field was lipids — was crucial. Nichol was not concerned about a repeat of the Pollution Probe debacle. The shopper was accustomed to medical endorsements and had come to trust them. In due course, Loblaw submitted the package to Consumer and Corporate Affairs for approval. But the ministry said no: the hospital, it said, could not engage in a commercial endorsement. Minus Steiner's plug, the microwavable frozen entrées were launched in November 1989 as the beginning of the G.R.E.E.N. Gourmet line. Turkeys raised on an all-vegetable diet, with no antibiotics, artificial additives, or growth accelerators were also introduced.

In August 1989, in the middle of the G.R.E.E.N. backlash, David Jenkins met with Griffin and Nichol to discuss his project: the effects of dietary fiber on serum cholesterol in people with high cholesterol levels. Jenkins was already a known commodity at LIM. He had stayed in touch with product developers over the years and, in 1986, had been brought in to discuss the composition of certain PC products. Nichol had wanted to know exactly how decadent The Decadent Chocolate Chip Cookie was. (Jenkins told him it was not very decadent at all; from a fat and fiber point of view, it was quite respectable, for a cookie.) Jenkins appreciated Nichol's curiosity and intensive questioning. After that meeting, Nichol would refer to Jenkins as Dr. J., after the former pro basketball star Julius Irving.

For his new project, Jenkins had already received a grant from the National Institutes of Health, in Bethesda, Maryland. That grant, however, covered only half his costs; Jenkins asked Nichol for the other 50%. He expected the three-year study to cost $1.2 million. (In the end, it cost closer to $2.4 million. Loblaw provided funding of $450,000 plus space and product development services, which Jenkins says were worth around $300,000 to him.) He also asked Loblaw to help him produce the food to be used in the study. Nichol immediately saw the marketing benefits of associating President's Choice with such high profile research. Jenkins could confer credibility on the line. Nichol got up from the table and immediately called Dick Currie for the go-ahead.

The link with a respected medical authority had become a key component of food marketing. Increasingly, the medical press, notably the *New England Journal of Medicine*, had become the source of nutritional truths used by food manufacturers to flog their "healthy" offerings. It didn't seem to matter that these truths seemed to swing like a revolving door. In the 1950s, whole milk and steak were in, and margarine was considered better than butter. In the 1960s, coffee was bad, whole milk was out, calories became the culprit, and cyclamates were embraced by dieters. In the 1970s, cyclamates were out, interest in fiber was developing, bottled water was in, salt was out, 2% milk was in, and caffeinated coffee was once again good for you. The 1980s brought oat bran into vogue, along with decaffeinated coffee, canola oil, and skim milk. Chicken was in, red meat was out, Slim Fast in. Fat was reviled, fried foods were out, grilled fish was in. Cholesterol intake was linked to heart attacks. By the late 1980s, due in part to the Reagan administration's relaxation of food labeling requirements, 40% of new supermarket products touted health claims. Most of these had little nutritional grounding, but they reassured shoppers who saw food as a source of control and longevity.

The 1990s began with studies announcing that decaffeinated coffee raised cholesterol levels. Perrier, *the* icon of the 1980s, was out, then in. Organic foods were in and sold at a premium, despite confusion about what organic really meant. Fiber was in again. Shellfish, tuna, and swordfish were out, victimized by mercury scares. Even the barbecue was a deathtrap when studies showed that grilling foods at high heat gave rise to cancer-causing heterocylic aromatic amines. Increasingly, the conventional Western diet was shrouded in fear and anxiety. The questions changed by the week — and so did the answers: Was milk good or bad for one's health? Was protein dangerous? Which was the superior cholesterol fighter — oat bran or psyllium — a grain said to contain eight times as much soluble fiber as oat bran? There were no firm guidelines — or rather, there were new guidelines and new gurus every month.

Like many medical researchers, Jenkins relied on corporate sponsorship to fund his projects. Kellogg, the cereal giant, had funded some of Jenkins's work, in concert with the Natural Sciences and Engineering Research Council. Kellogg's support, while clearly market-driven, also harkened to its past. William Kellogg, the doctor who founded Kellogg at the turn of the century, had been a Seventh Day Adventist. He and his brother John operated a health sanatorium at Battle Creek, Michigan, for members of their faith. Because the religion shunned meat, lest it stir unwelcome passions such as sexuality, the brothers created meat substitutes for the sanatorium's menu. John Kellogg experimented with nut

meats made from peanuts and gluten. Another church member transformed soybean into a semblance of bacon bits called smoein. They created granula, an early version of granola made with dried bread and
wheat flakes. Will, the more commercially minded of the two, wanted
to add sugar and sell the cereal to the masses. Brother John preferred to
stick to a strict health food regimen. When they split up near the turn of
the century, Kellogg's corn flakes was born. By the 1980s, Kellogg, along
with every other cereal manufacturer, positioned its products as nutritionally virtuous. Cereal was an $8-billion, cutthroat market. Medical
research became a marketing tool.

Just as Jenkins's project was getting started in January 1990, the
New England Journal of Medicine published a study that contradicted
the prevailing view that fiber reduced cholesterol levels. People who ate
a lot of oat bran, it concluded, had lower cholesterol levels not because
it had magical properties, but simply because they had filled up on oat
bran. The press was all over the story. Cereal makers were miffed. This
was not what they wanted to hear after having invested heavily in
countless studies that confirmed the benefits of oat bran and plastering
its praises all over their packages. The benefits of fiber itself came into
question. One study even posited that eating too much roughage could
interfere with the body's ability to absorb nutrients.

Jenkins was unmoved. The *New England Journal*'s study was not
conclusive, he explained to Larry Griffin. His study would focus on other
types of soluble fiber — vegetable proteins and beans — not just oat bran.
Besides, the subjects in the study had registered normal cholesterol levels.
His subjects had *high* cholesterol levels. Jenkins continued to look for
appropriate products to feed his own subjects. He discovered dehydrated
split pea and black bean soups, made by Fantastic Foods in California.
LIM's product development team reformulated them into high-fiber, low-
fat, under 250-calorie dried soups, added spices and came up with soups
such as Leek and Potato, Black Bean, and Curried Lentil. Jenkins advised
the company to avoid animal proteins and opt for textured vegetable proteins. Nichol was skeptical. "People won't eat this," he argued, biting into
a mealy soybean patty. Later, a vegetarian chili was developed with textured vegetable proteins. Duplicating the taste of meat was difficult.

When they were satisfied that they had the right formula, long-time Loblaw meat specialist Bill Clubine was summoned to the test kitchen. Clubine could not decide whether the meat was lean or regular grind. The deception cheered Nichol, who dined out on that story for a long time.

The food created for Jenkins's research was the basis of what became Loblaw's Too Good To Be True! line. The products allowed Jenkins to provide a controlled diet in the experiment, a research first. "We have never had packaged, weight-adjusted products that allowed us to make an accurate determination of what people ate," he said. Even so, the study was arduous. Jenkins worked with forty-three volunteers, divided into three groups. Each group ate a prescribed diet over an eight-month period, supplied by Loblaws. For four months, patients were served mainly high-soluble foods — heavy on peas, beans, lentils, barley, oat bran, and cereals rich in psyllium. Then they switched to foods high in insoluble fiber — wheat, bran, wholewheat bread, high-fiber crackers. The diet was mostly vegetarian, although chicken was allowed. Volunteers were not allowed to deviate in their diet. Food was couriered to their homes weekly. When a local expressway was closed or a winter storm hampered delivery, Jenkins was frantic with worry. He knew if his subjects missed even a single meal, the credibility of the entire study would be in question.

Nichol, meanwhile, was wrestling with an image problem. To sell a nutritional line, he knew, he needed a spokesperson, someone who knew the language of nutritional correctness yet had style. Dr. J. just wouldn't do. After some searching, he found what he was seeking in the well-articulated form of Toronto nutritionist Barbie Casselman. In another generation, a degree in nutritional science earned you a job in a hospital kitchen or as a home economics teacher, training young girls to make cheese dreams with processed cheese slices and pineapple rings. But times had changed. Barbie Casselman parlayed her 1979 degree in nutrition from Ryerson Polytechnical Institute into a thriving consulting practice. From her office in the financial district, she counseled businessmen, lawyers, accountants, and rich wives, who feared their husbands would trade them in for younger models if they failed to keep up.

By the end of the decade, personal nutritionists rivaled personal trainers as status accessories. Increasingly, dieting became defined by class lines. The poor never had the luxury of actively not eating. The middle class joined Weight Watchers, avoiding calories in mutual support groups. And the rich hired experts to plan dining schedules — in effect, to *not eat* with them. Leanness was a virtue, or at least confused with one. Hard and defined was the image to present to the world, particularly in business. The corporate world was downsizing, literally and figuratively. Restraint was crucial; to be soft was slothful, to be fat was self-indulgent, a symptom of waste, weakness, inefficiency. Fitness became a corollary to food obsession.

Casselman, born in 1955, was a hundred pounds of tautly manicured muscle. A tiny five-foot-two, her blonde hair cut pixie short, she had the demeanor of a trendy Tinkerbell. This was entirely misleading. Barbie Casselman was no pushover. Her clients were subjected to a bootcamp-like regime in which they filled out a chart after every meal. Progress was monitored in weekly five-minute meetings, which included the weigh-in. For Casselman, it was portions, not total calories, that mattered. Her diet allowed six protein portions and five starches. Clients could eat endless amounts of certain vegetables such as carrots and broccoli; others, such as corn on the cob, were limited. Like Jenkins, Casselman loathed fat. Clients were not permitted even to look at a potato chip. If you slacked off, you were out, fast. Casselman's dominatrix act won many disciples. Her reputation spread. By 1993, more than 5,000 people had passed through her office.

Terri Nichol consulted with Casselman early in 1989, when she realized that a life of marathon eating was taking its toll. Ironically, given Casselman's contempt for junk food, Terri had heard about Casselman from Joseph Murphy, owner of Murphy's Potato Chips, a supplier to No Name and President's Choice. She was impressed by Casselman's energy and discipline. More importantly, perhaps, she lost weight. Occasionally, while helping formulate the G.R.E.E.N. Gourmet line of entrées, Terri would call Casselman for suggestions and advice on such things as how to prevent low-fat sauces from curdling.

Seeking to expand her own business, Casselman that same year developed a line dubbed Barbie Casselman's Spa Cuisine. Sold at the upscale David Wood Food Shop in downtown Toronto, it included black bean soup, gazpacho, roasted eggplant salad, and grilled fish entrées. The term "spa cuisine" was a marketing device, meant to lend an air of refinement and luxury to low-calorie, low-fat, low-sodium products. It was diet food for the rich. The first North American spa, Rancho La Puerta of Baja California, had been opened in the 1940s by Dr. Edmond Bordeaux Szekely and his wife, Deborah. Spas went upscale in 1958, when the Szekelys opened the posh Golden Door in California. By the time real estate developer Mel Zukerman opened the sybaritic Canyon Ranch Spa in Tucson, Arizona, in 1978, spas had become meccas for the overworked upper classes. People paid thousands of dollars a week to attend New Age bootcamps, where intense exercise and a spartan diet were interspersed with biofeedback, shiatsu massage, stress management, loofah salt rubdowns, and rosemary and eucalyptus herbal wraps.

Spas accelerated the fusion of gourmet cooking and health concerns that had been twenty years in the making. Meat-and-cream-based fare such as Beef Wellington, foie gras en brioche, and coeur à la crème were blown off the table in the early 1970s by nouvelle cuisine, a mode of preparation that disparaged rich, processed foods and espoused freshness and perfection of ingredients. Nouvelle cuisine, a term coined in 1973 by French food critics Henri Gault and Christian Millau in their magazine *Le Nouveau Guide to Gault-Millau*, was a reaction to rich and heavy concoctions of *la grande cuisine*. Tiny portions made it possible to eat in three-star restaurants without worrying about gaining weight. The sauces were lighter, often made with puréed vegetables. In a way, it was the ultimate indulgence — paying the most to eat so little. Perhaps it was only coincidental that nouvelle arrived in the wake of the Bangladeshi famine.

Advocates of nouvelle cuisine soon became celebrities. At the forefront was Paul Bocuse, the first chef-businessman, who wrote books, hired public relations advisers, took ownership stakes in restaurants, starred in television programs, and consulted for airlines. Bocuse even appeared on the cover of *Time*. A visit to his restaurant at Collonges-au-Mont-d'Or, near Paris, was the foodie equivalent of a supplicant's trip to Lourdes. French chef Michel Guerard took nouvelle cuisine one step further. He developed *cuisine minceur*, the "cookery of slimness" for dieters at his health farm at Eugénie-les-Bains. Guerard banished all butter, oil, cream, starches, and refined sugar. Food was baked, poached, roasted, or steamed; frying and sautéeing were taboo.

California cuisine, the basis for a food sensibility later to be dubbed New American, was the American take on nouvelle cuisine. It too was obsessed with freshness and simple preparation — natural foods, preferably organically grown, untainted by polysyllabic preservatives and artificial ingredients. As the *Foodie Handbook*, a primer for the new class of food-obsessed, pointed out in 1984, the Industrial Revolution was over. "The cooking methods suited to coal were out. Even veal was out. The animal fats and flour that fueled you through long winters were out." The cooking of the Third World was gaining a foothold in the First World, where the agricultural and food economy had been based on the primacy of beef and milk.

A dilemma emerged in that as increasingly health-hyped North Americans altered their eating habits, they refused to give up flavor. The problem with the food David Jenkins was recommending for development was that most of it tasted like the Sahara. Jenkins was a purist, a theorist, interested only in efficacy. Terri Nichol sensed that Casselman could infuse the nutritional line with a touch of glamour. Casselman, who had been chubby as a teenager, understood that people looked to food for comfort and flavor. Terri introduced Casselman to Nichol. "Give me one good idea," he requested of Casselman in the spring of 1990 while she was visiting the Loblaw kitchen. She suggested low-fat tzatziki, a yogurt-garlic dip. A company called Astro was commissioned to make it. It premiered in the June 1990 *Insider's Report* and sold well.

About that time, Consumer and Corporate Affairs advised Larry Griffin that the term "body-friendly" was a health claim and had to be removed from the products. Nichol lashed out in a news story that appeared in the *Globe and Mail*. "Too many people think of the consumer as a slobbering cretin who needs to be protected in every way by another battalion of bureaucrats. We think the consumer is pretty darn clever." Body-friendly products were then folded into the G.R.E.E.N. Gourmet line and promoted in the June *Report*. The expanded line featured new products such as vinegar made from spring water and naturally fermented grain mash; Slim 'N Trim Dry Dog (and Cat) Food, for people who wanted to avoid the shame of owning obese pets; and fat-free yogurt, mini-rice cakes, and high-fiber crackers.

Casselman formally entered the Loblaw development process in early 1991, after the dehydrated soups had been introduced. She devised menus with recipes based on accepted nutritional wisdom: no more than 30% of the calories could come from fat, and at least 55% of the diet would be composed of complex carbohydrates. The Too Good To Be True! name, coined — by Nichol, it is generally agreed — during a packaging meeting that summer, captured perfectly the dogma of nutritional correctness, which had come to span the high and low ends of the food chain as a form of edible morality. Fat was villainous. Cholesterol was a very bad thing. Sodium was taboo. Refined sugar was unacceptable. Meat was a cause for uncertainty, even hysteria. Fruits and vegetables, if organically grown, were sacrosanct. The world seemed to be lacking fiber, both nutritionally and morally. By 1993, President's Choice product names were beginning to read like a morality play. In addition to Too Good Too Be True!, there was the Decadent line, the Temptation line of sandwich creme cookies, not to mention Virtuous Oil, Virtuous Cooking Spray, and the shelves of low-fat Too Good To Be True! products.

Too Good To Be True! was officially launched (with close to fifty products) in the November 1991 *Insider's Report*. It did not, however, merit the front page, an honor accorded to The Decadent Chocolate Fudge Crackle Ice Cream. Elsewhere, the issue was enthusiastic about Decadent #2, a short-lived marshmallow cookie, a couple of new "Memories of" sauces, and peanut butter-filled pretzels. There were recipes for the World's Best Brownie and for tiramisu, a fat-filled Italian dessert. Tucked inside the *Report* was a photograph of Casselman, who was described as the nutritionist to "the rich and famous."

Essentially, the Too Good To Be True! line followed the lead of products culled from health food stores, which were increasingly a testing ground for mass-market tastes. Food once regarded as fringe — granola, yogurt, rice cakes, canola oil, bean sprouts, algae, new grains,

organically grown foods — now offered serious profit potential. Suddenly, cereals boasted of containing amaranth, a high-protein grain with
a woodsy flavor that had been used by the Aztecs. Loblaw launched its
own Ancient Grains cereal in the fall of 1992; a picture of an Aztec mask
was on the package. This cereal contained spelt (a grain tolerated by
people who were allergic to wheat), millet, kamut, and quinoa, a staple
of the Inca empire. Beta carotene, a substance found in vegetables that
transmuted in the body to Vitamin A, was getting attention as a cancer-
inhibiting agent. The Loblaw product developers created the Beta Blast
Beta Carotene Cocktail, sourced with Beta III carrots containing twice
the regular amount of beta carotene.

The food establishment's latter-day embrace of so-called health
foods was richly ironic, considering that the birth of the health food
industry had been a reaction against supermarkets and processed foods
and a reaction to fears of unsafe food production. In the 1960s, brown
rice and brown bread became symbols of a hip, anti-establishment
stance. "Don't eat white; eat right and fight" was an underground slogan directed against Cool Whip and Wonder Bread. More broadly, it
was a protest against white-collar society and mainstream politics, as
symbolized by the White House. White was suspect, overprocessed,
bland, the color of sugar, salt, and saccharine. Brown was genuine,
earthy, tasty, the color of whole wheat, soy sauce, wildflower honey.

Within the space of two decades, health food went from fringe to
mainstream, perceived as the path to redemption. In 1970, according to
the *Wall Street Journal*, there were only 1,500 to 2,000 health food
stores in the United States. By 1979, the health food market, including
restaurants, had grown to $1 billion. By the mid-eighties, there were
8,000 health or natural food stores, with total sales of more than $4 bil-
lion. "I sure wish I had bought stock in that little yogurt company,"
sighed an editorial in a 1993 edition of *Bon Appétit*. In 1975, Bostonians
Anthony and Susan Harnett bought Bread & Circus, a small health food
store, for $30,000. Turning it into a profitable bully pulpit for food and
agriculture ethics, they banned all refined sugars, artificial preservatives,
colors, flavors, and growth hormones. The chain grew to six successful
stores. In 1993, the Harnetts sold the business for $26.2 million to a

231

Texas-based organic and natural foods supermarket chain, Whole Foods Market Inc.

That transaction, among others, underscored the growing ranks of vegetarians in the North American population. In 1973, the Oak Park, Michigan-based *Vegetarian Times* had been a simple four-page, Xeroxed newsletter. By 1993, it was a glossy, 100-page-plus publication with the kind of advertising-editorial ratio publishers dream about, and more than 300,000 subscribers. By the mid-nineties, an estimated 14 million Americans defined themselves as vegetarians, a discipline now considered as radical as Rotarianism. Backed by the endorsements of such vocal vegi-celebs as k.d. lang, Paul McCartney, Brian Adams, Sting, Twiggy, Mr. Rogers, and Def Leppard guitarist Phil Collen, vegetarianism had gone mainstream, in tandem with the green movement. It was a way of eating one's politics. And one's health: on a diet of legumes, tofu, grains, and root vegetables, vegetarians were believed to have reduced rates of heart disease and cancer, plus lower cholesterol and blood pressure levels.

As the quest for healthful food gathered momentum, the avant garde eagerly embraced ingredients that not long before had been considered fringe, even peasant. In June 1993, *New York* magazine food critic Gael Greene raved about Luma, a Manhattan restaurant that eschewed preservatives, chemicals, eggs, sugar, and dairy. Luma counted celebrities Robert Redford, Gloria Steinem, Barbra Streisand, and Madonna among its regular clientele, all presumably seeking that politically copacetic, beta-carotene glow. Devotees happily shelled out upwards of $100 a couple (including organic wine) for a meal that only twenty years ago would have been considered Third World fare — tot soi (Japanese lettuce), tofu feta in sweet miso dressing and arame (seaweed), and tempeh scaloppine (fermented soybean).

Early in 1992, Yves Potvin approached Paul Uys about making a meatless weiner. Potvin ran Yves Veggie Cuisine Inc., based in Vancouver. A former chef at that city's Le Chef et sa Femme, Potvin hung up his apron in 1985 to create healthy fast food. In 1992, his business employed forty people and recorded $4.5 million in sales, 40% in the United States. In his 16,000-square-foot factory, he made tofu hot dogs and garden vegetable patties. Potvin developed a prototype weiner for Uys and, after a bit of tinkering with the recipe, it was added to the line; it sold well, both in the meat and the produce sections.

In fact, tofu and analogues made from simulated vegetable proteins constituted an important part of the Too Good To Be True! line. (Tofu is made from soybeans processed into liquid soymilk, then mixed with calcium sulfate, an ancient Chinese curdling agent.) Such additions allowed the product to be shelf-stabilized, which meant it did not occupy valuable refrigerator space and posed less risk of spoilage. It was also less expensive to source. These foods themselves were not new. Kosher dairy restaurants, Catholics observing Lenten food rules, and vegetarians had long since improvised steak and cutlet analogues out of grains, beans and seasonings. Now, they were going mainstream, quelling concerns about cholesterol and other food additives. Paradoxically, the complete unnaturalness of the product made it safe.

Before any product could carry the Too Good To Be True! logo, it had to be approved by Jenkins and Casselman. Jenkins passed judgment on fat and fiber content. Casselman told the product development team what was required to make it conform to the Too Good To Be True! format. It was up to the product developers to work on the flavor. Jenkins and Casselman never met, but talked on the phone from time to time. Occasionally they would bicker over taste. "He couldn't come up with what was tasty meeting his criteria," Casselman complained. "He's not a chef." No Name light dairy products could not qualify, for instance, because they exceeded the not-more-than-30%-calories-from-fat rule. And when fat wasn't the problem, sugar was. Early in 1993, the two consultants clashed over the no-fat cookie. Jenkins was content because the cookie had no fat. Casselman objected to the excess calories from sugar. It was eventually launched, but under the President's Choice label, not Too Good To Be True!

Adhering to a nutritional discipline created taste problems that often took years to resolve. The twenty-bean soup, for example, took two years. The original recipe had come from Terri Nichol and contained seven types of beans. In the summer of 1990, Nichol brought the recipe into the test kitchen for chef Alison Jarvest. Everyone agreed it tasted great. Then Nichol decided that seven was a paltry number of beans. Double it, he commanded. Once a soup contained fourteen different kinds of beans, it became, in the language of LIM, "bean-oriented." It was then a logical candidate for the burgeoning nutritional line. However, to meet the criteria, its fat and sodium counts had to be lowered, so they took out the ham hock. But without the ham hock, a metallic taste prevailed — "a high acid note," as it was known in food development lingo.

Months passed. While Uys grappled with the acidity problem, Brian Farb in the packaging department had his own set of worries. Since Nichol liked the look of all those different beans, it was decided to put the soup in a glass jar. They found the right jar, but then had to find a company that did retorting, a process that sealed bottles by submerging them in hot water. But when the pre-cooked beans were immersed in hot water, they turned to mush. The recipe was reformulated, so that the beans were slightly undercooked.

A full year passed. The momentum had been lost for introduction at Christmas 1991. The following April, Nichol decided that the soup should contain seventeen beans. Then he changed his mind again: twenty beans would be more of a story. Seventeen-bean soup didn't have much romance. Twenty became the new magic number. The product developers were entering uncharted bean territory. The soup now contained a battery of beans: navy, yellow pea, green pea, pink, black turtle, mung, great northern, pinto, red kidney, baby lima, black-eyed, green lentil, white kidney, small red, Swedish brown, yellow-eyed, romano, adzuki, red lentil, and soya. But some of the newer, more exotic beans made the mixture taste metallic again. Someone suggested adding balsamic vinegar. To cut the acidity, Loblaw imported tomatoes from Chile — less acidic than those grown in North America. Finally, in the summer of 1992, it all came together. Twenty-bean soup was launched that fall.

These ordeals sometimes strained Casselman's relationship with Nichol. Working with him, she would complain to clients, was no picnic. But Casselman was pragmatic. She had a three-year contract. In turn, Casselman's flair for self-promotion did not always please Nichol. He liked his employees, even those on contract, to be subservient. He was not amused when Casselman, for the Christmas party of 1991, called chef Jamie Kennedy and asked him to prepare fish for her — instead of the beef Nichol had requested while planning the menu.

More troubling was her cookbook, *Barbie Casselman's Good-for-You Cooking*, released in the spring of 1993. As part of the pre-publication promotion, she was interviewed by *Toronto Life* magazine. The article was accompanied by a photograph of Casselman posed in a white negligée on her kitchen floor, lying languidly in front of an open refrigerator, feeding strawberries to her muscular husband and business manager, Brian, attired in an undershirt. Writer Robert Hough asked Casselman the calorie count of ejaculate. Twelve, she told him sprightly. Word of the story quickly traveled to the ninth floor at Loblaw. Nichol was not amused. This was not the sort of image he wanted associated with his seemingly wholesome, healthy line. Boris Polakow was so incensed with the perceived indiscretion that he called Casselman's lawyer, David Himelfarb, to complain.

Eventually, the rift settled. In its wake, Casselman arranged a dinner party in the kitchen at the former Sutton Place Hotel in April 1992 with a small group that included Robin Leach, the adenoidal huckster-host of "Lifestyles of the Rich and Famous," who was in town shilling for the Last Minute Travel Club. Casselman and Leach shared the same lawyer, David Himelfarb, in Toronto. Nichol presented Leach with a black silk kimono and a pair of boxer shorts with President's Choice cookie logos scattered all over them, part of a clothing line he was working on. Over dinner, Nichol and Leach discussed their favorite hotels and restaurants with a fetishistic frenzy.

While Casselman was deflecting the semen furore, David Jenkins was at last coming to terms with other bodily emissions. After analyzing urine, feces, and blood samples, he discovered that his participants recorded an additional 5% reduction in total blood cholesterol by eating foods high in soluble fiber content. Such a diet, he concluded, could significantly lower cholesterol levels, even for people who already ate low-fat, low-cholesterol foods. It would also, he believed, translate into a reduced risk of heart attack. His study was published in the July 1, 1993, *New England Journal of Medicine*. Jenkins framed his findings in the context of mounting financial pressures on universal medicare in Canada. "At least healthy diets can empower individuals to take care of their health on their own," he told the *Globe and Mail*. "That may be important to my children, who will not have all the health care we have when they get to fifty." Jenkins also expressed hope that his study would end the fiber-cholesterol controversy once and for all. As for Too Good To Be True!, he had expectations that the line could be sold to airlines, hospitals, and other institutions and would "be our contribution to public health."

The response to Casselman's cookbook was more controversial. The book featured an endorsement from David Jenkins on the back. It was also peppered with references to the benefits of President's Choice products, although Casselman provided this caveat: "I am not advertising for Loblaws and I have not received compensation for these recommendations." Dick Currie received letters from the Farm Animal Council and the Meat Marketing Board, protesting what they called Casselman's anti-meat stance. They didn't like references to possible contaminants in meat or her rejection of high-fat content meats such as pastrami, sausage, and hot dogs. They felt that Loblaw was supporting her position by using her as a consultant. The Ontario Dietetic Association was also exercised. It resented the fact that a non-member had been given a pulpit to preach nutritional truths. It questioned her qualifications and conclusions. The complaints were referred to Quality Assurance vice-president Larry Griffin, who told one and all to take the issue up with Casselman.

By the spring of 1994, more than a hundred Too Good To Be True! products lined the shelves. Loblaw could not keep its dehydrated soups in stock. The Twice the Fruit "jam-type" spread was also a hit. The margarine that took a run at best-selling Becel was a hit, as were the Ancient Grains and 7-Reasons cereals, and Too Good To Be True! Memories sauces with half the calories of the original formulation.

Although Nichol recognized that nutritional concerns increasingly colored shoppers' perceptions of food, his impatience with the food police continued. "We're going to find out that it's all circular," he predicted. "Fat will cure cancer, not beta carotene. Everybody wants to be a big guy and tell everyone else what to do." It also bothered him that the one Too Good To Be True! product he was genuinely enthusiastic about had failed in the market. This was a variation on a yogurt-like food seen in England. Called The French Alternative — Fromage Frais, it had an 8% butterfat content and was meant to replace whipping cream (35% fat) in recipes. Maybe it was the name. Cheese was regarded as unhealthy, unless it was light. Others blamed its failure on location — in the dairy counter. It was tough to launch new dairy products. Whatever the cause of its unpopularity, Fromage Frais was soon taken off the shelf. So was tofu, a food considered too fringe for the supermarket shopper.

Casselman continued to consult to Loblaw, but her profile declined. "Let's just say she's not the flavor of the month around here anymore," one product developer said in the fall of 1993. But if Cassel-man was in eclipse, David Jenkins was a still-rising star. Uys, for one, foresaw an increasing need for Dr. J.'s technical expertise. The benefits of soluble fiber as spelled out in Jenkins's study were prominently fea-tured in a mini-*Insider's Report*, published in January 1994.

With the introduction of Too Good To Be True!, Loblaw was able to cover modern food fetishes at both ends of the market, offering sin and then redemption. But Nichol's principal interest remained the develop-ment of high caloric, "decadent" President Choice products — Peanut But-ter Decadence Chocolate Fudge Crackle Ice Cream, a Key Lime Pie found in a Florida restaurant, Terri's Chocolate Bavarian Torte, a chocolate mousse cake. Increasingly, however, Nichol's focus was less on adding share in the Canadian market. He had a new crusade, one that began to consume him night and day: to propel the private-label revolution — and his name — into the United States marketplace. That would be step two of his master plan to take President's Choice to the world. In this immod-est quest he was spurred by his new best friend and come-lately comrade in the private-label war, Gerry Pencer.

CHAPTER TWELVE

THE CROWN JEWELS

W hen Dave Nichol met Gerry Pencer in the spring of 1989, neither had an inkling that their routine business meeting would spark a chain of events that would markedly change each of their careers and link their futures inextricably. To Nichol, Pencer was nothing more than a supplier — and a supplier of an inferior product at that. Pencer was the chairman of Cott Beverages, a small family-run outfit that produced President's Choice soft drinks and mineral water; the company had bottled President's Choice Cola for the Connoisseur since 1987, under a deal worked out with Sam Pencer, Gerry's older brother. Cott handled only part of the President's Choice soft drink program; the rest was handled by an Edmonton company called HPI, or Happy Pop. Nichol was not pleased with the quality of either cola. Gerry, the genius salesman of the Pencer clan, was sent in to fix the problem.

The meeting occurred during a time of transition in the lives of both men. Nichol was restless, coming off the development of the G.R.E.E.N. line, looking for his next big hit. He had also become increasingly frustrated by the constraints placed on him by Loblaw president Dick Currie. Pencer had just taken over the helm of Cott, following the humiliating demise of his last business venture, Financial Trustco Capital Ltd., which flamed out spectacularly in the wake of the 1987 stock market crash. He, too, needed a new venture, a new goal.

Pencer, short and round and bald, with a salt and pepper beard, is an effusive man — seemingly open about everything, from his failed attempts to lose weight to his last visit to his shrink. His expressive brown eyes are conspicuous barometers of his mood swings, welling with tears when he is troubled or sad, twinkling merrily when he's happy. He speaks slowly and softly with a slight lateral lisp, his inflection rising at the end of each sentence as though he were asking a question. The overall effect is of a very wise man, a prophet. That soft, mystical Cabbage Patch-doll demeanor is misleading, however. Gerry Pencer is one brilliant operator, a spellbinding promoter, a master persuader. "Gerry Pencer," as one Toronto financial analyst put it, "could sell you your shoes while you're still wearing them."

Pencer looks older than his forty-nine years, which was not surprising given the number of triumphs and reversals he has crammed into one life. He was born in 1945 in Montreal, the son of Harry Pencer, who was in the shmatta business. One summer, Harry's three young sons — Gerry, Sam, and Bill — returned from Camp Winaukee on Lake Winnipesaukee, New Hampshire, extolling Cott soda pop. There were "seventeen heavenly delicious flavors," the Pencer boys told him, including a killer sweet black raspberry and black cherry. Harry decided to import it. Initially, it was just a sideline, and cases of pop were stacked among the coats and dresses. But in 1955, Harry Pencer became a full-fledged bottler, acquiring the Stewart Bottling Co. of Montreal.

During the next two decades, the Cott label became a presence in Quebec and Ontario, as did its corny slogan, "It's Cott to be good." Yet Cott was never a big money maker. In 1983, the year Harry died, Cott lost $367,000. The auditors advised Sam and Bill Pencer, who were running the operation, to liquidate. The brothers ignored the advice. Instead, they decided to rebuild their inheritance by slashing prices. They convinced customers to pick up their own pop, thus eliminating store-to-store delivery. The price of six bottles of Cott soda dropped from $2.49 to 99 cents. They also got into producing private-label pop for supermarkets. The Steinberg grocery chain became their first customer. By 1986, the company was generating sales of about $20 million and a net profit of about $1 million. That year, the Pencer brothers took the company public, selling a minority interest through the Quebec Stock Savings Plan. Cott stock came to market at $7 per share and promptly plummeted to half that value within months.

A career in the family soft drink business had never been part of Gerry Pencer's plan. In 1963, at eighteen, he enrolled in pharmacology at the University of Montreal. As a sideline, he set up machines around campus and the city that dispensed gum, cashews, peanuts, and plastic charms. Before long, he was clearing $100 a week. The prospect of a life dispensing pills started to look pretty dull. He switched to commerce at Sir George Williams College (now Concordia University), but again felt the tug of entrepreneurial ambition. He dropped out of school to start a catering company, Maisonneuve Food Services Inc., and quickly secured contracts with big clients such as Rolls-Royce, Canadian National Railways, and Northern Electric. In 1968, Pencer won a $1-million contract to supply cafeterias at McGill, after an inspired pitch to the executive council in which he promised to set up a deli counter and a vegetarian buffet. By the time he was twenty-five, Maisonneuve was the largest institutional caterer in Montreal. Then, in what was to be a career trademark, controversy arose. McGill students began complaining about some of Maisonneuve's practices. Eventually, Maisonneuve lost the contract and left the campus in 1972.

That same year, Pencer formed a partnership in a Montreal restaurant, which he built into a chain called Curly Joe's. A few years later, he diversified, buying a local meat-packing plant. In 1975, after striking a deal with a large Calgary packer called Burns Foods, he moved his wife, Nancy, and family to Calgary to create Burns H.R.I. Ltd., which supplied meat to restaurants, hotels, and institutions. Pencer became president.

This venture, too, was tinged with controversy. Pencer had formed another company called Fortress Foods, which he owned with former Burns employees. The buzz around Calgary was that a dispute arose between Fortress and Burns involving the buying and selling of frozen New Zealand beef. In the ensuing fallout, Pencer resigned from Burns; Burns sued Fortress, Fortress wound down operations, and in 1978 Burns filed a civil lawsuit of $1 million against Pencer. It was said to have been settled out of court.

Resilient and versatile as ever, Pencer then set up Bow River Cap-

ital, a real estate company that invested the money of wealthy Montreal-
ers in mortgages. The late 1970s were boom times in Calgary, and the
city was bulging with opportunity. In 1980, Pencer and three other partners bought a majority interest in Turner Valley Holdings Ltd. Over the
next few years, Pencer used Turner Valley to shuffle businesses with the
virtuosity of a Vegas blackjack dealer, trading car dealerships, real estate
assets, food companies, a courier service, oil and gas firms. He loved the
play of it all. He even tried to get into the supermarket business. In 1984,
he approached John Toma, then president of Dominion, to organize a
management buy-out of the beleaguered chain; it never gelled.

What did gel was a two-branch trust company called Financial
Trust Co., which he bought in 1981 for $3.8 million. In July 1983, the
company changed its name to Financial Trustco Capital Ltd. Its rise was
meteoric. Starting with a profit of a mere $1.6 million in 1982, Financial
Trustco built assets of $2 billion and annual profits of $18 million by
1987. Deposits rose from $30 million in 1980 to $269 million by mid-1983.

Ready for Bay Street, Pencer moved his family to Toronto in 1986.
He purchased one of the largest properties in the affluent Forest Hill district — not far from where Galen Weston and Dick Currie live — and
spent millions on renovations, adding a swimming pool and tennis
court. The next spring, at Sotheby's in Toronto, he bought a Cornelius
Kreighoff winter scene for $230,000, a record selling price for the artist's
work. Paying top dollar for a Kreighoff had become almost a rite of corporate passage in Canada. What Pencer did not then realize was that his
days as a conglomerateur were numbered.

Much of Financial Trustco's growth was fueled by junk bonds,
Wall Street slang for high-risk but high potential yield corporate bonds.
Junk had become a common form of financing leveraged buy-outs. In
such deals, acquisitors bought companies with only a small percentage
of cash up front, often as little as 10%. The rest was financed with borrowed money. For many years, this debt was financed by insurance
companies, which tended to be conservative in their lending practices.
But in 1984, Michael Milken, a bond salesman at investment dealer
Drexel Burnham Lambert Inc. in New York, came up with what was
believed to be a no-lose technique: he began using high-risk corporate

bonds to replace these funds. Soon, everyone was doing it. By 1985, there had been eighteen separate leveraged buy-outs valued at $1 billion or more. Drexel Burnham Lambert was Financial Trustco's New York underwriter. Pencer boasted that Milken had personally raised more than $100 million for the firm.

Then came October 1987. The market crash eroded the value of Financial Trustco's underlying assets. The company had too little cash flow coming in to cover its massive debt payments. Regulators became nervous about Financial Trustco's aggressive accounting practices and the non-arm's-length deals among Pencer's myriad holdings. In 1988, the federal government and provincial governments in Ontario and Quebec stepped in with an $84-million bailout. Central Capital Corp. was given almost instant approval to absorb Financial Trustco. On Bay Street, it was rumored that the government had played a role in the negotiations. Lawyer Sam Wakim, a close friend of then Prime Minister Brian Mulroney, sat on the Trustco board, as did Senator Jack Austin. Regulators were so concerned about the contents of a soon-to-be-published *Financial Post* story that they asked that it be delayed until after the Central Capital deal was completed. They feared that Pencer's background would unnerve depositors, who would make a run on the institution. The *Post*'s story, by Philip Mathias, reported that Pencer had been bankrolled in his early days by William Obront, alleged to be a prominent figure in Montreal's organized crime circles. (Obront was subsequently convicted of drug trafficking.)

In the ensuing months, Financial Trustco was dismantled, its assets sold or wound down. Pencer dropped out of sight. He refused to talk to the press. He was bruised by the *Financial Post* story and other rumors associated with the Trustco debacle. It was said that he had lost almost $50 million on paper. Facing personal bankruptcy, he sold a few paintings — an Emily Carr, a Riopelle, a Franklin Carmichael — and walked away with three, maybe four, million dollars.

One asset untouched by the affair was Pencer's one-third interest in Cott Beverages. He had been its chairman since 1986, the year the company went public, although day-to-day operations were managed by his brothers, Sam and Bill. In the fall of 1989, Gerald Pencer finally resurfaced at Cott. He devoutly hoped to shed the rumor and innuendo that had surrounded his business dealings, something that wasn't to be. He said he was humbled and changed by the trust company fiasco. Never again would he get into debt, he promised himself. "Canadians are terrified of failure," he says. "I'm proud of having failed because I learned something from it." Bay Street, wary of brash entrepreneurs, particularly those whose grasp exceeded their reach, were not sympathetic. Pencer would remain an outsider, an unforgiven outsider.

Dave Nichol did not care about Pencer's history, the little he knew of it. All he wanted was a successful cola. Cola had been a sore point with Nichol for years. It was supermarket practice to run Coke and Pepsi promotions as loss leaders to draw customers into the store. This seemed to him a squandered opportunity. Cola — essentially sugar, caramel, water, and dissolved carbon dioxide gas — was sold at huge premiums; it could therefore provide huge margins if it could be successfully packaged under the President's Choice label.

The objective facts supported his contention. The public's thirst for cola, the most marketed taste in history, seemed unquenchable. Coca-Cola was an American institution, its logo the most pervasive commercial icon in the world. Distributed to 155 countries, Coke was consumed more than 350 million times a day. It was American ingenuity made manifest: carbonated, sweetened brown water, bottled and sold at an exponential markup. A single can of Coke cost less than 10 cents to produce; on the supermarket shelf, it sold for 75 cents or more. So valuable was it in North America that shoppers happily paid more for it than they did gasoline, a non-renewable resource.

The liquid that became famous as Coca-Cola had its roots in a recipe patented by Atlanta pharmacist John Pemberton in 1885. The original concoction contained wine and extracts from coca, the Bolivian Indian leaf from which cocaine is derived. Pemberton called it French Wine Cola—Ideal Nerve and Tonic Stimulant. The following year, he removed the wine, added caffeine and flavored it with extract of the kola nut. His bookkeeper, Frank Robinson, recommended that the name be changed to Coca-Cola, thinking that the two C's written in an italic script would look better in advertising. Coca-Cola was first served on May 8, 1886 at Jacob's Pharmacy in downtown Atlanta. It was later peddled by traveling salesmen as a cure for hangovers and headaches.

Georgia businessman Asa Griggs Candler bought the rights to Coca-Cola in 1889. A devout Methodist and skilled promoter, Candler sold Coca-Cola as a "soft" drink: non-alcoholic, thus pure, safe, and wholesome. He also laid the groundwork for the mammoth Coca-Cola infrastructure that exists today. He sold the syrup to wholesalers, who in turn sold it to drugstores to be mixed at soda fountains, which were gaining popularity as social gathering places. Later that year, he set up contracts with bottlers for exclusive territory rights. The drink was introduced in Canada in 1892. In 1903, after medical journals decried the effects of cocaine, the company removed the ingredient. In 1919, the Coke franchise was sold for $25 million to Ernest Woodruff, president of the Commercial Travelers Savings Bank, later the Trust Company of Georgia. According to Coca-Cola corporate lore, the recipe for Coke is still contained in its vaults. Coke's formulation has always been a carefully guarded secret. Over the years, 99% of the ingredients have been identified. But one — known as 7X — remains a secret, part of the Coca-Cola mythology.

By 1930, Coke was an international commodity, synonymous with America around the world. It was sold as the solution to thirst and as a reward for hard work. Its slogan was "Within arm's reach of desire." Coke was everywhere, in factories and offices, in movie theaters and sports stadiums, at gas stations. During World War II, it was an emblem of democracy for homesick soldiers; GIs were given Coke for 5 cents a bottle. In 1943, General Dwight Eisenhower asked the War Department to provide machinery and personnel for ten Coke bottling plants in Allied-controlled zones in North Africa and Italy. By the end of the war, the U.S. government had financed sixty-four bottling plants worldwide, which Coca-Cola later incorporated without cost.

The post-war period saw further expansion. Coca-Cola bought the Minute Maid Corp. and the Duncan Hines Food Corp., and formed Coca-Cola Foods. In the 1970s, however, the company encountered trouble. It had been locked into agreements to supply all the ingredients for the syrup, with the exception of sugar, at fixed prices. With hyperinfla-tion, these costs skyrocketed. Then the government complained that con-tracts granting bottlers territorial exclusivity restricted competition.

Coca-Cola's marketing methodology was also starting to meet resistance. The trumpeted virtue of Coke — that it was a single product from a single source — became a liability in a decade that began to cel-ebrate ethnicity and diversity. Norman Rockwell's *Saturday Evening Post* images used in Coca-Cola advertising were suddenly square. So was the product's affiliation with the establishment, through ads fea-turing photos of Eisenhower, John F. Kennedy, Lyndon B. Johnson, even Fidel Castro. Exploiting this weakness, rival Pepsi-Cola anointed the "Pepsi Generation" in 1963. This slogan broke advertising ground in referring not to the product, but to the user. Coke retaliated with "The Real Thing," a phrase it had resurrected from the 1940s.

By the 1980s, the marketing war intensified with the use of multi-million-dollar celebrity endorsements. Pepsi signed Michael Jackson for $5 million, after Coke had rejected the performer as too androgynous for its all-American image. Bill Cosby — an establishment black come-dian — was signed to promote Coca-Cola. The virtually indistinguish-able taste of the two beverages was trotted out as a battleground. Pepsi concocted its Pepsi Challenge, in which blindfolded tasters showed a marginal preference for Pepsi-Cola. By the middle of the decade, the rival had edged ahead of Coke in supermarket sales.

Inside Coke's Atlanta headquarters, this elicited mounting con-cern. Tastes were changing, but Coke's formulation had remained the same for more than a century. Pepsi, on the other hand, had revamped its taste profile several times. "Maybe the principal characteristics that made Coke distinctive, like its bite, consumers now describe as harsh," suggested Brian Dyson, president of Coke's U.S. operation, in 1978. "And when you mention words like 'rounded' and 'smooth,' they say Pepsi. Maybe the way we assuage our thirst has changed."

Coca-Cola went about reformulating Coke with the sort of mili-taristic fervor for which the company was known. The campaign was dubbed Project Kansas. The new beverage was sweeter, smoother, and less carbonated than Pepsi. But the whole endeavor backfired. A hue and cry erupted with the launch of the new Coke in 1985, but it had little to do with taste. The American public was outraged that the company could tamper with a national emblem. "Next week, they'll be chiseling Teddy Roosevelt off the side of Mount Rushmore," groused *Washington Post* columnist Michael Kernan. The "MacNeil-Lehrer Newshour" did a twenty-minute spot, during which people emptied cans of new Coke on the street.

Although 200,000 people had sampled the new Coke prior to its launch, the company had failed to tell them that it planned to replace the old formula. The democratic premise of Coke had been shattered. On July 11, 1985, Coca-Cola chairman and CEO Roberto C. Goizueta formally apologized to the American public for the new Coke and reintroduced the old Coke as Coke Classic. The new Coke launch was widely proclaimed the greatest marketing blunder of the twentieth century. More cynical observers regarded it as a calculated ploy, designed to draw attention to the drink and reconfirm its value as a classic icon of American life.

Controversy aside, it was clear that the appetite for soft drinks had tripled since the 1950s. Soft drinks are the largest category in the supermarket; 72.2% of Canadian households buy their cola there. Canadians drank ninety-six liters of soda pop per capita on average in 1991, up from eighty-six in 1986. In the United States, per capita consumption was 169 liters per year. There, more than 15% of the cola was consumed before nine a.m. Over half of the soft drinks sold in Canada — a $1-billion market — were cola-flavored. In the United States, where cola culture was more deeply entrenched, 70% of soft drinks sold — a $45-billion market — were colas.

Dave Nichol knew that he would never build a dominant store brand until he cracked the cola category. He believed cola could be a mammoth profit center, if he could strike the right formulation and price. But creating a successful cola had eluded him. The No Name cola, launched in 1978 and supplied by Coca-Cola, had bombed. Coke had come to the project at the last minute. A deal had been worked out with Sam Pencer for Cott to bottle it, but Neville Kirchmann, then president of Coca-Cola Beverages, the Canadian arm of Coca-Cola, made an impassioned

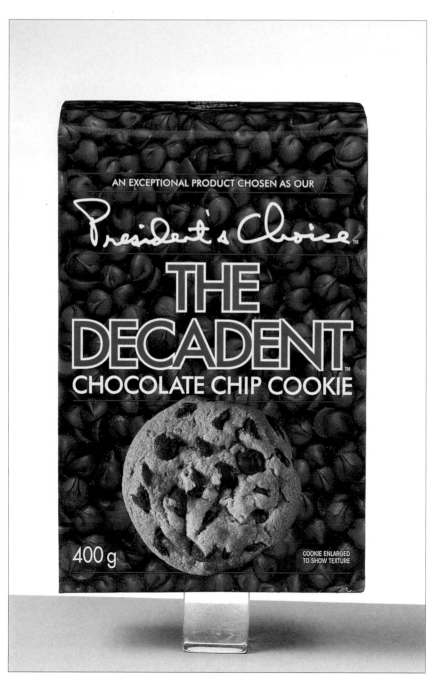

THE ULTIMATE RETAIL WEAPON:
THE DECADENT CHOCOLATE CHIP COOKIE

PRESIDENT'S CHOICE GOURMET ITALIAN DOG FOOD
FOR THE CULTIVATED CANINE

Dave Nichol with a few of his favorite "children"
in the Loblaw test kitchen

LOBLAW'S G.R.E.E.N. PERIOD: A SAMPLE OF
THE PRODUCTS THAT SPARKED THE FUROR

HAPPIER DAYS: DICK CURRIE, GALEN WESTON, AND
DAVE NICHOL CELEBRATE WESTON'S FIFTIETH BIRTHDAY
UNDER THE DOME IN 1990

LIFESTYLES OF THE RICH AND FAMOUS: DAVE NICHOL SHOWS OFF
HIS PRESIDENT'S CHOICE SILKS TO ROBIN LEACH

MORE LIFESTYLES OF THE RICH AND FAMOUS: COTT CORPORATION CHAIRMAN GERRY PENCER, TERRI AND DAVE NICHOL, AND NANCY PENCER ON HOLIDAY

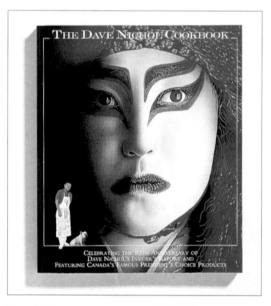

THE FACE THAT LAUNCHED 200,000 COOKBOOKS:
THE DAVE NICHOL COOKBOOK, ADORNED WITH ONE OF
NICHOL'S FAVORITE PACKAGING IMAGES

SUPERMARKET HERO: NICHOL AND PRESIDENT'S CHOICE
GROUPIES AT AN IN-STORE SIGNING OF HIS COOKBOOK

THE PRESIDENT'S FINAL CHOICE: DAVE AND TERRI NICHOL
AMID FLOWERING MUSTARD IN THE NAPA VALLEY

eleventh-hour appeal to Nichol, Brian Davidson, and Doug Lunau of Intersave. Coke was not above producing private-label pop; it made Becker's house brand. Kirchmann promised to match Cott's price. The trio agreed to give Coke the contract.

There were problems from the beginning. Within Loblaw, they questioned whether the cola being produced was the same as the first samples they had tasted. There were also constant problems with inventory depletion. "It was a nightmare," one Loblaw executive remembers. "The stuff tasted like bellywash. It put us back two years in the cola business." Loblaw took No Name cola off the shelf within a year.

In 1985, Nichol decided to try again. LIM product developer Ladka Sweeney was dispatched to buy eleven cans of Coke from different stores around the city. In a blind taste test, the product developers identified them as different brands. The lesson was that each bottler treated the syrup differently. If they couldn't identify the cola in a comparison test, how could consumers, who would be drinking only one at a time? Nichol decided to work on the cola formulation.

Sweeney asked Universal Flavors in Toronto to create a syrup that could be used as a base. Universal was what was known in the industry as a flavor house. Flavor houses design the tastes of processed foods — the peppermint in chewing gum, the strawberry in yogurt, the chicken in chicken noodle soup. The flavors are derived from both natural and synthetic sources. Natural flavors, which were more expensive to produce, also tended to be weaker and thus more difficult to control.

Flavor was only one component of the taste of carbonated beverages. Soda pop is an amalgam of water, sugar (or aspartame in diet varieties), natural and artificial flavorings, natural and artificial colorings, acidifying agents, buffering agents, emulsifying and stabilizing agents, viscosity-producing or viscosity-lessening agents, foaming agents, and chemical preservatives. During the testing process, Universal developed different emulsifiers needed to keep the carbonation droplets suspended, including both a synthetic kind and one made from the gum of acacia trees. After several trials, Nichol decided he preferred the natural, and more expensive, version. It took a year and thirty testings before an acceptable cola flavoring was found. Universal absorbed the cost of the research.

The reformulated cola was launched in the summer of 1987 as "The Cola for the Connoisseur." Cott was given an agreement to provide it, with the provision that it meet initial projections of 500,000 cases a year. In 1988, Loblaw sold 670,000 cases. Even so, Nichol believed the cola could be improved. The taste was inconsistent. Some batches tasted like root beer. Around this time Gerry Pencer landed at Cott. Brian Davidson suggested that Nichol meet Pencer. Davidson and Pencer were similar in many ways — personable, street-smart, natural deal makers. "He'll solve the problem," Davidson said.

That first meeting between Nichol and Pencer in the LIM board room lasted just over four minutes. It was the standard Nichol-to-supplier rant. Nichol told Pencer that if the product couldn't be improved, he'd take the business elsewhere. What he wanted, he said, was a cola indistinguishable from Coke or Pepsi. He believed that if the cola was properly packaged to compete with the national brands and priced $1.50 less than a twenty-four-can case of Coca-Cola, Loblaw could dominate the category.

Pencer returned days later with a sample of Royal Crown Cola. For years, Cott had owned the rights to bottle RC Cola and Diet Rite cola in Canada. Royal Crown's weakness — a lethal one in the cola business — was poor marketing. It fared well in consumer taste tests, but shoppers perceived it as the poor cousin to Coke and Pepsi. The beverage was so cheap and unfashionable that David Letterman used "Time to switch to RC Cola" in a Top Ten list of euphemisms for the recession.

After tasting it, Nichol made four demands. "I want more acidity. I want more carbonation. I want more citrus tone. And I want you to use more syrup so it has more body." Cott altered the RC formula to meet Nichol's specifications. Pencer then flew to Miami Beach to meet Victor Posner, the corporate raider who was running Royal Crown Cola. He needed Posner's permission to amend the RC formula for customer specifications and use it as the base for Cott's colas. Gerry the genius salesman walked away with a twenty-year arrangement under which RC Cola Co. not only provided Cott with concentrates for private-brand colas, but gave Cott access to its U.S. bottling network. Cott took over total production of President's Choice soft drinks.

The relaunch of PC cola was handled carefully. This was Nichol's third attempt; he could not afford to strike out. He sent Pencer to Don Watt to have the package redesigned. Patty Watt came up with a red can with a stylized white PC logo on it, the same colors used by Coca-Cola. To get customers to taste the product, sample booths were set up in every store over a two-week period. Vending machines offering lower-priced PC pop, were also installed. In the June 1990 *Insider's Report*, Nichol gave it his formal benediction: "My taste buds told me that 'The Decadent' Chocolate Chip Cookie, the President's Blend Coffee, 'The Decadent' Apple Pie and our Szechwan Peanut Sauce & Dressing were superior to any other products on the market. And now they're telling me in no uncertain terms that our new PC COLA is better than Coke or Pepsi. SURELY YOU DON'T INTEND TO SPEND THE SUMMER CHASING FROM SUPERMARKET TO SUPERMARKET, COLA COUPONS CLUTCHED IN YOUR HAND, JUST TO GET ONE MEASLY CASE OF NATIONALLY BRANDED COLA!"

"If you can't taste the difference, why pay the difference," became Nichol's mantra. Cott offered retailers a margin of 85 to 90 cents a case in Ontario, minus the cost of transportation, which ran 20 cents a case. Coke and Pepsi were offering margins of 15 to 25 cents, depending on the customer. A case of PC cola sold for $5.99 compared to $8.99 for the national brands. When Coke and Pepsi dropped their prices to $5.99 to compete, Loblaw cut its price to $4.99. In 1990, Loblaw sold 4 million cases of the new cola. Two years later, it sold 10 million cases. Cola became the best-selling President's Choice product and, with The Decadent cookie, the cornerstone of the President's Choice line. Nichol would refer to the cola as "the crown jewels." Pencer shrewdly capitalized on the value of the cola to Loblaw. In 1991, he signed a contract with Brian Davidson that gave Cott a three-year contract with two two-year renewal clauses to produce President's Choice soft drinks for Loblaw Companies supermarkets as well as companies for which Loblaw acted as supplier. It was unheard of for Loblaw to make this kind of commitment with a supplier, but cola was unique, the crown jewels. The agreement established a minimum annual order and gave Cott the exclusive right to use the PC logo on beverages.*

*Loblaw counsel John McCullough refused to comment on the existence of such an agreement.

It was not within Gerry Pencer's makeup to think small. His success with President's Choice cola, he realized, could pave his way to corporate and financial redemption. In characteristic fashion, he had big plans for Cott. Pencer was possessed by his new vision. He was going to transform a small-time bottler of budget-priced pop and take on the biggest brand name in the world.

Pencer started building again. Fraser Latta, a former executive VP at Financial Trustco, became vice-chairman and chief operating officer. Executive talent was hired away from Pepsi-Cola. Pencer bought and upgraded a Pepsi plant in Ontario. He acquired Tricopak Beverages, Cott's major competitor in Ontario, and Calgary-based Sun Mountain Beverages Ltd., a bottler of spring water and private-label soft drinks. Several other competitors folded under the pressure. Inadvertently, both Coca-Cola and Pepsi had a hand in Cott's initial success. When Cott bought the Pepsi plant, millions of dollars of equipment were left behind. When Coca-Cola exhausted its production capacity, it approached Cott about bottling. Pencer demanded and won a three-year, $6-million contract, an agreement Coke would come to regret.

Bottling upscale private-label cola and undercutting the national brands was seen by consumers and the investment community as a radical but brilliant idea. In September 1991, *Forbes* published a cover story, "The trend is not their friend," about the rise of private-label manufacturing. The success of Loblaw and Cott was prominently featured. "To beat pros like Coke or Pepsi at its own game is an amazing feat for Cott and an object lesson for those who believe that brand loyalty is guaranteed," wrote Gretchen Morgenson.

It did not take Pencer long to see that he could sell the Loblaw retail-brand methodology to other retailers — just as Don Watt had done with store design. In fact, Watt proved to be a valuable ally to Pencer in breaking into the U.S. market, introducing him to such U.S. retailers as Safeway, Finast, and Topco.

The Pencer-Watt connection was formalized when Watt sold Pencer an equity stake in The Watt Group. Watt had been shopping for a partner for a while. He had talked to John Thompson, a senior vice-president of finance at Loblaw, about setting up such a deal, but Dick

Currie had ultimately vetoed the proposal. Currie had no interest in getting into the design business. In 1990, Watt started talking to Pencer. "You've added $150 million to my family's net worth," Pencer told him, a reference to the benefits of Watt Group packaging. "Let's see if I can help you out." In January 1992, Cott acquired a 49% interest in The Watt Group for an undisclosed price and created a new division called Retail Brands. Jim White, formerly of Loblaw, was hired on contract to head product development. Within the industry, it was believed that Nichol had asked Pencer to hire White, who had been consulting to retailers in both Canada and the United States. Nichol was said to be concerned that someone with White's talent and knowledge be unavailable to competitors.

Retail Brands gave Pencer a marketing edge. Cott now could offer more than pop; it could provide retail clients with an intangible custom product development, package design, marketing, even store layout. Watt still governed over The Watt Group, which carried on its regular "total design" services. The following year, Cott upped its stake in The Watt Group to 72%; the remainder was held by Watt Group employees.

Pencer and Watt disliked the term "private label." "That's the old term for a lousy product," Pencer said. Their term for private label became retailer branded. Watt was named president of Retail Brands and was given a 25% interest. "Watty has worked for all the great retailers," Pencer explained. "And even though he had a great consulting practice, he never had the opportunity to make significant money for himself. He's just wasting time working for Kraft General Foods and Seagrams. Why not take his talent, combine it with our ability to produce at a lower price, and add rings of added value? Then we can do something that no one can do as a food manufacturer. We can help our customer to generate more gross margin. We're not just the soda supplier — we also design the store, solve packaging needs, create communications programs. These things get people to try the product. And once they've tried it, we have them hooked, because it's far better value. And if you give people more and better for less, it becomes more difficult for the national brands to handle what we're doing. We're not a soft drink company. We're a marketing company that helps retailers generate more profit." Platitude aside, Cott had developed a shrewd system. Cott Retail Brands did not charge directly for its services. These were available to retailers who bought Cott products. "We're trying to create a long-term relationship," Pencer said. "We think we're bonding ourselves with the retailer."

Pencer continued to hustle. Cott ceased to sell only cola and began selling a vision, a radical transformation in food manufacturing. He traveled three weeks out of four, often using the Cott Gulfstream II jet, which was leased to celebrities such as Bruce Springsteen when not in corporate use. Suddenly, Gerry Pencer was in demand again. The three telephones in his monster black Mercedes 600 SEL — a 1991 Christmas present to himself — rang constantly as he was ferried between appointments. He hired Nigel Argent, a discreet, slim Englishman, to act as his private security, driver, and houseman. Argent called him "Mr. P." Pencer referred to Argent as his majordomo. People close to Pencer began to worry about his health: the dawn-to-dusk appointments, the stress, the constant travel. His staff ordered in sushi lunches, in deference to his high blood-cholesterol. Pencer was much beloved at Cott. He was a genius, everyone said. Nothing could happen to him. Not when he had been given the keys to the universe. Again.

Steadily, Pencer's second empire grew, populated with Pencers. Gerry was loyal to family. Cott U.S.A. was registered in May 1991 and the company opened an office in Columbus, Georgia, to coordinate U.S. sales. In 1992, Cott purchased interests in Murphy's Potato Chips Inc., which produced Murphy's, Lay's, and private-label potato chips, and Menu Foods, the private-label pet food manufacturer. Both had strong ties to the President's Choice program. In fact, Joseph Murphy, who ran the Kitchener, Ontario-based snack food company, was related by marriage to Galen Weston; his wife, Josephine, was Hilary Weston's younger sister. Galen Weston and Joseph Murphy had known each other since Murphy was a boy. Murphy met Weston in 1960, shortly after Weston arrived in Dublin to take over the Power chain. Murphy was ten. Murphy's family was prominent in the country's food industry: his father was known as "the crisps king of Ireland." The Murphys played a role in introducing Galen to Hilary. A few years later Joe married Josephine. The young couple emigrated to Canada in 1972, after

Galen and Hilary. Murphy became a management trainee, working under Ziggy Wauro. Over the years, he worked in a variety of sales jobs, positions that made good use of his easy charm. In 1979, Joe Murphy founded Murphy's Potato Chips Inc. He took over production of Lay's and O'Grady's brands as well as a roster of private-label clients, including Loblaw. By the end of the 1980s Murphy's had sales of $25 million and over 250 employees, but the business was in trouble. The snack market is highly competitive, and dominated by the big players Kraft General Foods and Frito Lay Ltd. In 1991, Murphy found himself on the brink of bankruptcy. When Pencer was told by a Loblaw executive that Murphy's was foundering financially (and that Galen Weston had no interest in expanding into potato chips) he bought a 60% interest. Cola and junk food have a divine sort of symmetry. More to the point, snack food is a high-margin category.

Pencer started telling people he planned to make Cott the "General Foods" of retailer brands. Pop was only the beginning. "We have the opportunity to become the next great food company in the world," Pencer said. "We won't build it with bricks and mortar and goodwill and interest. We'll build it by using the infrastructure that exists and using excess capacity." Most bottling plants ran at only 60 to 65% capacity, based on two shifts, five days a week. Cott made use of the unused capacity. "It's just like Japan — seven days, twenty-four hours," Pencer explained. "It's part of the whole recycle, reuse sensibility." Employees began referring to Cott as a New Age company and spoke of empowerment, partnerships, new channels of distribution. The Revolution, they called it.

Much of this touch-feely lexicon was the influence of Heather Reisman, a former management consultant and long-time Pencer friend, who was appointed president of Cott Corp. in July 1992. Reisman, forty-four, is well-known and respected in Canadian business and political circles. Born in Montreal, she was trained as a social worker but gained a profile as the head of Paradigm Consultants, a company she set up to counsel business on coping with change. Although Reisman had never actually run a company, she assembled an impressive client list. Exuding competence, she is at once polished and sincere, articulate and expressive. She tends her image carefully and is known to send reporters notes after flattering stories. Both Reisman and her husband, Gerald Schwartz, are active in political circles. Schwartz was president of the federal Liberal party and its primary fund raiser. Reisman, the niece of Canada's free-trade negotiator Simon Reisman, who sat on the George Weston board, also has a high profile in the party and is active in policy decisions and fund raising. Her name frequently pops up as a prospect for political office.

Reisman met Pencer in the early 1980s, through Schwartz, a smooth, phenomenally successful man born in Winnipeg in 1941. After earning degrees in commerce and law from the University of Manitoba, he took his MBA from Harvard and went to work in Switzerland for Bernie Cornfeld, the playboy financier who counted actress Victoria Principal and Hollywood madam Heidi Fleiss among his former girl-friends. After Cornfeld's Overseas Investors Services collapsed in 1973 amid allegations of fraud, Schwartz landed a Wall Street position in mergers and acquisitions with Bear, Stearns & Co. There he met Jerome Kohlberg, the man who pioneered the "bootstrap deal," precursor of the leveraged buy-out. Among Schwartz's colleagues were the now-famous Henry Kravis and George Roberts, who would later join Kohlberg as principals of Kohlberg Kravis Roberts & Co., for a time one of Wall Street's major powerhouses.

Schwartz brought the leveraged buy-out to Canada. He had returned in 1977 to form CanWest Capital Corp. with communications mogul Izzie Asper. Six years later, Schwartz left Asper and started again, setting up Onex Corp.; it became the foremost leveraged buy-out firm in the country, a $2-billion company that made high-profile acquisitions, including the courier service Purolator, Sky Chef, and Burger King's U.S. distribution network. Between 1987 and 1991, Schwartz owned Beatrice Foods, the parent company of Colonial Cookies, where The Decadent was produced. Schwartz garnered attention, even awe, though critics often pointed to the millions Schwartz made at Onex while shareholders were not handsomely rewarded.

In the early 1980s, Pencer's Financial Trustco participated in several Onex deals. Pencer himself sat on the Onex board. In turn,

Schwartz sat on the board of Granite Street Inc., the company through which Pencer controlled Financial Trustco. Schwartz introduced Pencer to the people at Drexel Burnham. In the spring of 1985, Pencer asked Reisman to sit on Financial Trustco's board.

Reisman is a seasoned board-sitter. She was one of the first women to serve as governor of the Toronto Stock Exchange. She acted as consultant to the Federal Commission of Inquiry on Equality in Employment and was on the advisory board of the University of Toronto's business school. That some of her appointments were to boards of imperiled companies — Financial Trustco, the then-struggling auto parts manufacturer Magna International, and the oil company, Suncor Inc. — did nothing to tarnish her reputation. Reisman and Schwartz were steadfast friends to the Pencers throughout the Financial Trustco troubles. Years later, Reisman still talks about Financial Trustco in glowing terms. "It was visionary. It was an entrepreneur's bank. If it existed today, I believe it would be good for this country."

Reisman and Schwartz were a sanitized version of Donald and Ivana Trump, a Canadian power couple with a *Bonfire of the Vanities* lifestyle. Their house in Toronto's affluent Rosedale district was large and airy, filled with contemporary Canadian art. There was a wood-burning fireplace in the bathroom, a Nautilus-fitted exercise room, and a carwash in the underground garage. The couple could be spotted on Saturday morning jewelry shopping at Tiffany on Bloor Street. They were known for staging fund-raising events and hosting European-style salons, where experts were trotted out to discuss a range of topics.

Reisman was seen to add much-needed credibility to the Cott organization. She wanted to make Cott a "learning institution." She set up a relationship with Harvard to develop systems that clients could use for category management. She also sought to create partnership arrangements with the retailers Cott supplied. "Every time the customer pays something, he is reinforcing the brand," she says. "Why not pay the retailer to reinforce their own brand? The retailer is closer to the customer. He has better access to scanning data. It's our role to help them to enhance their brand. The employees become the salespeople." Later, Harvard Business School conducted a case study on Cott and cited it as being on "the cutting edge of change in the global food system."

In Gerry Pencer, Dave Nichol found a kindred spirit in the grandiosity department. The friendship did not gel instantly. At the outset of their relationship, Nichol tended to be dismissive toward Pencer, which hurt and bothered him. "He was a real jerk," Pencer recalls. After one particularly abusive telephone conversation with Nichol at the end of 1991, Pencer brooded for an entire day. He would stand up for himself, he decided, and made an appointment to see Nichol in Nichol's office. In his soft, conciliatory manner he told Nichol that if he didn't value him then he'd send in a salesman to handle the Cott business. "If we're going to work together, things are going to have to change," he said. Pencer appeared calm, but inside he was quaking, waiting for Nichol to blow up. To his surprise, Nichol was reasonable. He didn't know then that Nichol respected people who stood up for themselves and weren't afraid of him. From that day on, Nichol saw Pencer in a new light.

The success of Cott and the PC cola also abetted the relationship. Nichol and Pencer began socializing together. Nancy Pencer and Terri Nichol became friends. Pencer was fun, he could laugh at himself. He wasn't anything like the dry, narrowminded corporate executives Nichol had little time for. More important, the two men seemed to share a common goal. The death of the brands became their favorite topic of conversation. Nichol had never met anyone like Pencer before, anyone with Pencer's untrammeled vision and ambition. In Nichol, Pencer found an impressive ally who could be used to great marketing effect. Nichol offered Pencer instant legitimacy in the food business, something he sorely lacked. When he took his sales pitch on the road, to supermarket chains and financial analysts, Dave Nichol frequently accompanied him. Their argument was simple and compelling. "Retailers have been selling Coke and Pepsi at a loss for years because they had no choice," Pencer would say. "We've given them a choice. The bottom line is that there is little cola loyalty. Coke does better not because of flavor. Statistics show that 85% of cola drinkers switch between Coke and Pepsi because of price."

In theory, Cott's advantage as a lower-cost producer was clear-cut: because its overheads and marketing costs were lower than Coke's and Pepsi's, it could offer a lower price and yet maintain high margins. The infrastructure required to run Coca-Cola and Pepsi offered no flexibility, Pencer argued. "They don't have room to squeeze margins without losing money. Look at the numbers. Coke and Pepsi sell 7 billion cases a year in North America. A 10-cent reduction costs them $700,000. A $2 cut would cost $14 billion a year. The Coke/Pepsi system was also inefficient, Pencer preached. "By the time a cola company processes the order for delivering five cases to a Chinese restaurant — generating an invoice, picking up the order, putting it in accounts receivable — the cost of delivery is at least double the cost of the cola. Who pays for that? The consumer. The guy who's running the Chinese restaurant should be paying $20 a case. And the supermarket should be paying $5 a case. But it doesn't work that way. Loblaws pays $7, the Chinese restaurant pays $8. There's something wrong with that. Coke and Pepsi want to be everywhere. There is a cost to being everywhere." The argument seemed irrefutable.

Pencer's transformation from junk bond conglomerateur to junk food conglomerateur carried a certain irony. What had made the major manufacturers vulnerable to lower-priced corporate brands in the early 1990s stemmed in part from their strengths; with strong cash flow and brand equity, they were attractive leveraged buy-out candidates in the late 1980s. Given the dominance of national brands, it became easier to buy brands than to create or build them through intensive marketing. For a manufacturer who produced trusted household-name goods, acquisitors were ready to pay three to four times the value of a company's tangible assets.

Thus, in 1986, food giant Beatrice was taken private by Kohlberg Kravis Roberts for $6.2 billion. In 1988, RJR Nabisco, the tobacco, drink and food manufacturer — the producer of Ritz crackers, Del Monte products, Marlboro cigarettes and Chips Ahoy! — was the focus of a $25-billion fight between its own management and predators who wanted to buy the company. Again, Kohlberg Kravis Roberts won the company. Nabisco's European brands were later sold to the French food giant BSN for $2.5 billion. That same year, food and tobacco giant

Philip Morris bought Kraft for $12.9 billion, four times its tangible assets and 1.3 times sales. In 1990, Clorox paid two times sales to buy the household cleaner Pine-Sol and Combat, an insecticide. Grand Metropolitan, a U.K. food and drink titan, acquired Pillsbury (and its brand names Green Giant, Häagen-Dazs and Burger King) for $5.5 billion in 1988 — a 50% premium on the American firm's pre-bid value and several times the value of its tangible assets. Nestlé paid $4.5 billion, more than five times Rowntree's book value, to acquire the company that makes Kit Kat, After Eight, and Polo mints.

The takeovers, many financed by junk bonds, left many companies in disarray, carrying onerous debts. To cut costs, the quality of the products they produced was often diminished. Spending on research and marketing was also reduced. Thanks to Michael Milken's junk bonds, every time a shopper bought many national brand foods and beverages, she paid a premium for the leveraged buy-out-related debt. Pencer used this fact in his sales pitch. "RJR Nabisco was sold for three or four times sales," he argued. "Somebody should figure out how many cents in every package of Chips Ahoy! goes to interest, goodwill, and amortization. Let's say it's a buck a bag. Then there's the retailer's cut. So in the end, what's the consumer getting?"

The growth of Cott finally forced the cola giants to respond. Controlled or private-label soft drinks had been on supermarket shelves for years, but nobody took them seriously. Cott was rewriting the rules. In Canada, private-label share of a soft drink market worth over $1 billion jumped from 1% market share in 1987 to almost 20% in 1992. Cott, aggressively buying out smaller bottlers, controlled 90% of the Canadian private-label soft drink category. In the United States, small bottlers and limited control brands accounted for approximately 10% of the $48 billion market, up from less than 7% in 1988.

Coke's hammerlock on the market was slipping. In 1990, Coca-Cola Beverages controlled half the Canadian market, with Coke, Schweppes, Canada Dry, A&W Root Beer, Minute Maid Orange, and Sprite labels. By year end, its market share had declined nearly 2%. Then, in 1992, the unthinkable happened. For the first time ever, sales volumes of both Coke and Pepsi declined at the beginning of the peak summer selling season.

Cott was not the only problem. There was another force at work, even more worrisome to Coke and Pepsi than the private-label threat: North Americans seemed to be losing their taste for cola. Coke was sugary, non-nutritious, an accompaniment for greasy foods — none of which suited increasingly health-conscious consumers. Instead, a new category dubbed New Age beverages was gaining strength. These clear fruit drinks, flavored waters, and iced teas appealed to the consumer's need for clarity, for lightness. Of the 1,805 beverages that flooded the market in 1991, 480 were fruit and fruit-flavored drinks, iced teas, and bottled waters.

The confluence of these trends resulted in Coca-Cola Beverages reporting a $45-million loss in fiscal 1992, its first ever loss. That fall, the Canadian division underwent a management shuffle. President and CEO Neville Kirchmann was banished to Coca-Cola's South African office; William Casey, a veteran of the U.S. bottling system, replaced him. Casey believed that the private-label phenomenon was an aberration, a temporary condition caused by the recession. When economic conditions improved, he said, shoppers would return to the higher priced brands. His strategy, outlined at the May 1993 annual meeting, was to create an advertising campaign that would appeal to different market niches. He wanted to expand Coke's reach by making it more available in video and convenience stores, gas stations and vending machines. He acknowledged the Loblaw threat by noting that Coca-Cola was frequently "out of stock" on Saturday afternoons, peak shopping time; he said he would discuss it with Loblaw management.

Cott, basking in Coca-Cola's signs of duress, continued to grow. By 1993, Cott cola was outselling Coke in Canadian supermarkets. That year, Coke dropped to number three position in supermarket sales. According to U.S. trade magazine *Beverage Digest*, Pepsi was number one with 32.4%, private-label brands had 27.3%; Coca-Cola claimed 24.5%. Canada Dry, Schweppes (both of which are bottled by Coca-Cola Beverages in Canada), and other lesser-known brands had 11%.

Fighting back, Coca-Cola Beverages announced the closure of eight of its sixteen bottling plants, cut 560 jobs from its work force of 4,300, overhauled distribution, and centralized its warehousing system. Two weeks later, Pepsi-Cola Beverages announced a price cut. (Pepsi's

U.S. parent had even larger problems to contend with — a tampering scare, when syringes were found in cans, which turned out to be a hoax; and the Michael Jackson child-molestation scandal, which forced the termination of his Pepsi-sponsored "Dangerous" world tour.)

By 1993, Cott was the largest private-label pop manufacturer in North America, with agreements to supply retail brand soda to more than twenty-five chains. In addition to producing Wal-Mart's Sam's American Choice, a deal brokered through Loblaw, Cott produced house colas for a wide range of clients including A&P's Master Choice label in the United States and Canada; Safeway's Select program; First National Supermarkets Inc. in the northeastern United States; Chicago-based Topco Associates Inc; and the Life brand cola for Shoppers Drug Mart. In November 1992, it launched American Choice cola at Makro Club warehouse stores in South Africa, where Coke had monopolized the market for decades. Cott's gross sales grew astronomically, from $31 million in fiscal 1989 to $665.4 million in fiscal 1994, eliciting inevitable comparisons with Financial Trustco, which had shown similar stratospheric gains.

Cott's July 1993 annual meeting was a revival style love-in. Pencer took the stage and would not give it up. Other speakers, including Don Watt, were given only a few minutes in the spotlight, to their dismay. Bottlers from Columbus, Georgia, Cott's U.S. headquarters, offered testimonials. Pencer told the crowd that the company would sell 150 million cases in the following year, up from 63 million. Cott claimed it controlled 1% of the U.S. market. Forty-three U.S. retailers, he said, were now selling the product at 20,000 outlets; there had been four retailers the year before.

Cott's heady growth was reflected in its stock price. When Pencer walked into the LIM board room for the first time, the market capitalization of Cott stock on the Toronto Stock Exchange was $12 million. By 1994, it was over $3 billion. Owing to stock splits, a single share of Cott had multiplied twelve-fold since the fall of 1991. Adjusted for these splits, a Cott share traded around 31 cents in the spring of 1991. Two and a half years later, they were trading at just under $50. A $100 investment in Cott made in 1989 was worth close to $8,000 by 1994. Shares of Coke and Pepsi, meanwhile, were taking a beating, as Wall Street investors worried whether the soft-drink arch rivals would succumb to discount competition.

Cott stock made many people wealthy, most of all Cott executives. The primary beneficiary of success was the Pencer family. Between 1991 and 1993, the three Pencer brothers cashed out $78 million worth of Cott stock. Inevitably, among Cott's Bay Street detractors, the profit-taking raised concern about the real value of the company. Other hairline faults in Cott's façade began to appear. Cott's executive compensation was criticized as excessive. In 1992, Cott's five executive officers earned $1.2 million in salaries and another $1.4 million in cash bonuses under a senior management profit participation plan.

Questions about Cott's accounting methods also began to surface. Like most manufacturers, Cott paid retailers shelving fees, which it called contract costs. It was not clear, however, how large these fees were. And, the critics said, these costs were lumped in with packaging costs as assets. Listing items as assets that should have been listed as expenses would inflate reported assets and profits. And the higher the profits, the more people would like the stock.

As Cott grew, the importance of its business with Loblaw diminished. By late 1992, Loblaw made up just under 8% of Cott's sales, down from almost 60% two years earlier. More than 50% of the company's revenues, Pencer claimed, came from sales to the United States. Yet he continued to cultivate the association with Nichol. The two men flew to England in the spring of 1993 to make a pitch for President's Choice Cola at the Astra chain. Cott's contract at Kmart in Australia came through Loblaw's consultancy contract, as did a deal with Park 'N Shop in Hong Kong.

In time, the Pencer-Nichol relationship came to transcend the Weston-Nichol relationship. The Nichols and Pencers would join up for dinner and Sunday dim sum brunches. They traveled the world together, sharing a fondness for luxury, sun, first-rate food. In August 1992, they spent two weeks cruising the Sardinian coastline; Reisman and Schwartz joined them for a week. While Nancy and Terri swam, the others held seminars on the future of food distribution. At night they docked and went off to restaurants such as the famed Gallura, on the Mediterranean island of Olbia. From that trip came Nichol's Memories of Sardinia pasta sauce. For Christmas 1992, Pencer entertained Nichol, Doug Lunau, Robert Bras of Menu Foods and John Dunne, president of A&P, aboard his leased yacht, in the Caribbean. The Nichols also joined the Pencers on their twenty-fifth-wedding anniversary cruise in 1993.

Nichol accompanied Pencer on business trips as well, often traveling on Cott's corporate jet. He was a key speaker at the wedding of Pencer's daughter Stacey in August 1993. They went fishing for sailfish on Pencer's sixty-five-foot yacht, *Caught*, off the coast of Florida. "They're like brothers," says Robert Bras of Menu Foods. "They have a huge affection for one another." Nichol would refer to Pencer as Mr. Ponzu after Terri had mistakenly called him that after first meeting him. On the subject of Nichol, Pencer could be effusive. "Look, without him, Cott wouldn't be where it is," he said. "It isn't that he's done me any favors. But he has led the way, showing people that companies like Cott can do what it's done. He's a weakness of mine."

Pencer courted Nichol assiduously. "David demands a lot of attention," Heather Reisman said of Nichol. "He's found with Gerry someone who has true appreciation and respect for what he is doing. He's like Christopher Columbus; he's crossed the ocean and knows the world is round. He can't engage in dialogue with anyone who thinks it's square."

Pencer's influence played a direct role in Nichol's growing dissatisfaction at Loblaw. Appealing to Nichol's vanity and sense of infallibility, Pencer solidified Nichol's belief that he was being taken for granted by Loblaw management. Seducing Nichol with a vision of wealth and power, of global exposure, Pencer convinced him that he could take the President's Choice methodology outside of Loblaw, without Galen Weston and Dick Currie. All he needed was Gerry Pencer.

CHAPTER THIRTEEN

AN INCENDIARY BREW

W hen Dave Nichol returned from Australia in February 1992, one of the first messages waiting for him was from Bill Sharpe. "Who is this guy?" he asked his secretary, Anne Doremus. "Never heard of him." Doremus explained that the man wanted to discuss producing beer under the President's Choice label. Nichol was immediately skeptical. Both as a drink and as a topic of conversation, beer was the quintessence of dull as far as he was concerned. He saw it as base, the low-brow fuel of frat house parties. More relevantly, supermarkets in every province except Quebec were not allowed to sell beer; it was available only at provincially operated liquor stores and industry-run beer outlets. Still, Nichol was intrigued by the notion of extending his profile beyond the supermarket. So he told Doremus to set up an appointment. "Give the guy five minutes," he said.

A few weeks later, Nichol walked into the LIM conference room where Sharpe was waiting anxiously. "You know I can't sell beer in supermarkets," he said at once. Throw them off balance — that was Nichol's approach. But Sharpe, a genial man with a taste for Italian sports jackets and suede rubber-soled loafers, was not intimidated. He is a relentlessly positive soul who has taught himself the necessity of succeeding, whatever the odds.

He is also versed in the complexities of the Canadian beer industry. A high school dropout, Sharpe had worked at Canada Dry for years before joining Fort Brewing Co. (now Pacific Western Brewing Co.) in

Prince George, British Columbia. He got his first sampling of the mono-
lithic power of the beer establishment in 1981, when he attempted to
launch a lower-priced generic beer for Fort; he got quashed in a price
war ignited by Molson, Labatt, and Carling O'Keefe Canada Ltd.
Unable to beat them, he decided to join them, signing on at Carling
O'Keefe as a vice-president. When Molson acquired Carling O'Keefe in
1989, Sharpe became general manager of Santa Fe Beverage Co., a Molson division that distributed imported beer.

But Sharpe never saw himself as a company man. When Molson
started handing out voluntary severance and early retirement packages,
Sharpe took one in early 1992. His dream was to start his own brewery.
That he was fifty-six years old, that beer sales were on the decline, that
the industry was racked by closures and widespread layoffs — none of
this fazed him. For a year he had been pondering the potential of a
lower-priced, premium, private-label beer, inspired by President's
Choice. He watched Nichol on television. He felt instinctively that the
drinking public would welcome it. The timing, he convinced himself,
was perfect; long-standing interprovincial trade barriers would soon be
dismantled, opening up new markets in Quebec, Manitoba, and the
northeastern United States. His greatest fear was that someone would
beat him to Nichol.

In February 1992, Sharpe made an offer for an abandoned seven-
acre beer factory in Hamilton, Ontario. The building was owned by the
Netherlands-based Heineken Group, which had produced the Amstel
brand in Canada. The bid was accepted, conditional on financing. He
was given until March 11 to come up with $3.5 million.

Aware that Cott Beverages handled private-label soft drinks for
Loblaw, Sharpe called to ask how they had structured their arrangement. He got through to Don Watt, who spoke with him for more than
an hour. Watt thought the beer idea was interesting, but told him he'd
have to sell it to Nichol, which could prove tough. Now, in the LIM
board room, Sharpe was trying to do just that.

Bill Sharpe was persistent. In 1991, he told Nichol, 93 million
cases of twenty-four-packs of beer had been sold in Ontario; another 64
million had been sold in Quebec. The beer market in Ontario alone —

40% of the Canadian market — was worth more than $2 billion. Even if Loblaw captured a mere 1% of the market, he told Nichol, the profits would be considerable. No one had successfully produced a private-label beer in Canada. That meant they could count on widespread — and free — media coverage. Moreover, with the anticipated dismantling of trade barriers between Canada and the United States, the beer could be sold in northern American states.

"What you say is all very interesting," Nichol responded. "But the brewery is in Hamilton. That's a problem. I like to build on glamour. If your brewery were on the edge of Lake Louise in Alberta and had ice and glaciers behind it, well, maybe I'd consider it."

"Hamilton is a steel town in distress," Sharpe replied. "It would be perceived as a positive thing if you were to create jobs."

Nichol was unmoved. There was no mystique in being a good corporate citizen. Besides, he was listening to a pipe dream. Sharpe didn't even own the brewery yet. "You've twigged my curiosity," Nichol allowed. "But until you buy the brewery and get it up and running, you're wasting my time." Then, he walked out.

Characteristically, Sharpe remained optimistic. Nichol hadn't slammed the door in his face. In search of financing, Sharpe approached banks in the United States, investors in the Western provinces, and venture capital companies in Toronto. Ultimately, he found a sympathetic backer in Gerry Pencer's Cott Corporation, which was eager to expand its product roster. In return for a 70% equity interest, Cott secured the necessary financing for machinery and staff; Sharpe retained the remaining 30%.

Lakeport Brewing Co. was incorporated in March 1992. Sharpe spent the next few months producing Around Ontario and Laker beer, brands he had inherited with the brewery. His sales force was largely Molson and Labatt alumni, casualties of downsizing, who knew the big breweries' strategies and client lists. Sharpe also secured licencing agreements with U.S. brewers G. Heilman Brewing Co., to produce Lone Star, and with Pabst Brewing Co., to produce Pabst Blue Ribbon in Ontario. But that, he knew, would not be enough to keep the enterprise afloat.

In late August, in the board room of The Watt Group building, Sharpe and his brewmaster, Adam Foye, met again with Nichol, Pencer, and Fraser Latta, Cott's vice-chairman. Pencer had been working on Nichol, trying to persuade him of beer's potential. Nichol remained noncommittal.

Sharpe knew it would be a hard sell. Beer was an institutionalized business in Canada, nearly impossible to break into in a major way. The industry was closely regulated by both the federal and provincial governments. In Ontario, the government had held sway since 1927, the year prohibition was repealed with the Liquor Control Act. Ontario retained control of liquor sales and awarded the beer franchise to the Brewers Warehousing Co., a corporation privately owned by forty breweries. The product was heavily taxed; in 1993, 53% of the price of every bottle of beer sold in Ontario went to government coffers.

Over the ensuing decades, the beer market came to be monopolized by two breweries, Molson and Labatt. By 1992, the two controlled roughly 95% of the $9.6 billion national market; the balance went to microbreweries, small regional outfits that brewed no more than 75,000 hectoliters — less than 900,000 cases — a year. The majors competed with elaborate advertising campaigns that strove to differentiate products essentially identical in look, taste, and cost. In fact, but for the packaging, drinkers were scarcely able to tell one brand from another. As one industry adage put it, it was the marketing that people drank, not the beer.

Beer was one of the last bastions of brand loyalty. Both Molson and Labatt spent prodigious amounts of money to build brand equity, the fancy term for customer allegiance. Molson Companies Ltd., the parent of Molson Breweries, was the sixth largest advertiser in Canada. In 1992, the conglomerate spent $57.4 million on advertising, most of it to promote beer. The brewery, whose brands included Export, Canadian, Coors, Foster's, Miller, and Black Label, controlled approximately half the Canadian market. John Labatt Ltd., whose brands included Blue, 50, Budweiser, and John Labatt Classic, commanded 44% of the national market and spent an estimated $41 million a year on advertising, making it Canada's ninth largest advertiser. Those figures, of course, did not include the money spent sponsoring cultural events and sports franchises. Molson owned "Hockey Night in Canada," as well as the Montreal

Canadiens hockey team. Labatt had its own powerful sports properties: it owned The Sports Network and the Toronto Blue Jays.

Molson and Labatt are the Coca-Cola and Pepsi of malt and hops. When one launched a new product or marketing strategy, the other promptly responded with its own competitor. The two companies spent a lot of time in the courts, bickering about copyright infringements. But they were symbiotic adversaries. Both benefited from the tension and publicity generated by simultaneous product launches. Both profited by offering beer drinkers the illusion of choice. More cynically, their market dominance gave both companies the security of big profits.

For Dave Nichol, beer was a good way to test the currency of not only President's Choice but his own name outside the supermarket. Cott could sell the beer through its expanding accounts in the United States. And Lakeport could extend the label to produce President's Choice dealcoholized beer for Loblaw-owned supermarkets.

Even so, Nichol continued to nurse doubts. "Look," he told the assembled group in Watt's boardroom. "I'm not interested in putting any ordinary beer on the market. Tell me how beer is made, and tell me what you can do to make this beer different."

Brewmaster Foye then explained that beer is brewed from hops, yeast, water, and malt. The hop is a climbing perennial plant whose ripened cones impart a characteristic bitterness to beer. Malt is barley that has been soaked for days and dried in a kiln. So-called two-row malting barley is the best grade, Nichol was told, and the most expensive; because it contains more enzyme and starch, it yields a higher alcohol content after fermentation.

"What about the hops?" Nichol asked. "Where do they come from?"
"We use hops from Yakima, Washington," Sharpe replied.
"Is that unique?"
"No," said Sharpe. "Everyone else is using them."
"That doesn't interest me then," Nichol said.
"If you want the best," said Foye, "that would be Saaz hops from Czechoslovakia. They're in limited supply and impart a unique bitterness."
Eureka. Nichol had his hook. He turned to Sharpe. "I want those. Put that on the list. That's our first ingredient." Sharpe groaned inwardly.

Saaz hops cost ten times as much as the hops from Yakima.

"What else can you do for me that's different?" Nichol asked.

Sharpe cast about for ideas. "John Labatt ages its Classic in tanks longer," he said. "That mellows it out." Most beer was held in tanks for about two weeks, sometimes less. Classic was aged close to three weeks. The problem with longer aging was that it tied up tanks and cut capacity.

"I want it aged half that time again," Nichol said.

"What kind of water do you use?"

"We purchase it from the city," Sharpe said. "We run it through filters to adjust the pH levels."

Nichol sat back in his chair. There was no story in tap water — particularly tap water from the miasmal harbor of Canada's premier steel town.

"Everybody is talking about this Genuine Draft. Can you process this?"

Nichol was referring to cold-filtered, non-pasteurized draft beer that had been introduced by Molson and Labatt in Canada that summer. Instead of being heat-pasteurized to kill germs, the beer was triple-filtered in rooms set at a very chilly -1 degree Celsius. This stabilized the product while removing microorganisms that might cause secondary fermentation. Both Molson and Labatt in turn claimed that their beer was the only "genuine" cold-filtered draft. Molson accused Labatt of copying its package design. The publicity benefited both companies; in what was otherwise a declining market, cold-filtered draft was the only segment to record substantial growth in 1992.

"We don't have the equipment," Sharpe replied. To produce it, the brewery would have to be outfitted with stainless steel piping, a capital outlay of at least $1 million.

"That's what I want," Nichol insisted. "And I want it non-pasteurized with no preservatives." The heating process used in pasteurization was tough on juices and other foods because it could distort flavor. A lump formed in Sharpe's throat as he worked out the arithmetic. Most beer was made with artificial emulsifiers and preservatives to prolong shelf life. Lakeport was not equipped for non-pasteurized beer, which had to sit for four days before it went to microbiology. Inevitably, that slowed production.

"And I want it ready by the end of November," Nichol demanded. "So I can advertise it in the *Insider's Report*."

Sharpe and Foye drove back to Hamilton to start work. The first test batches were failures. Triple-filtered beer, they learned, had to be handled with kid gloves. Forty-five days later, in mid-October, Sharpe returned to Toronto with twenty-four beers in his car trunk. Nichol had no intention of tasting the beer, so a dozen beer drinkers from within the company were assembled. When Sharpe arrived, Nichol turned to the group. "Here's a guy who when I ask him to do something, he goes out and does it. Not like you people," he joked.

The beer was blind-tasted against Molson's Miller Genuine Draft and Labatt's Genuine Draft, the first samples, everyone agreed, lacked body. The second weren't creamy enough. Sharpe would make four more trial runs before Nichol's surrogate tasters were happy with the brew. He delivered the last batch to LIM at the end of October in the middle of a snowstorm, carrying the box through the parking lot at 7:30 in the morning. Paul Uys called him that afternoon. "Lock in that formula," Uys said. "It looks like we're in business."

Sharpe negotiated a five-year licensing agreement with Loblaw to brew the beer. Then he set about refitting the factory. The entire place had to be sterilized. Wiring and the existing filters were ripped out. An air purification system was installed and the floor was replaced. These renovations alone cost more than $400,000.

There are few secrets in the beer industry. Sharpe had heard that Labatt was planning to introduce a new format twelve-bottle carton in April 1993. A standard cardboard case with cardboard dividers cost 71 cents to produce. The new packaging cost 31 cents, a saving of 40 cents. Sharpe wanted to beat Labatt to market. Hearing that Labatt was testing a prototype in Halifax and distributing the cartons at five stores, he called Labatt and asked if he could look at the machine. He was granted permission. Little Lakeport was hardly a threat, after all.

He caught a late plane to Halifax and visited the beer stores to ask how they liked the carton. The next morning, he toured the factory, taking pictures of the machine in action. (Sharpe always carried a camera in his briefcase. "You never know when you'll be signing a contract with someone and they'll want to take a picture," he says sarcastically.) Sharpe called Mead, the Atlanta-based machine manufacturer, from the airplane. Mead then asked Labatt if another company could buy the machine. Again, Labatt said okay; it didn't need the machine immediately and it assumed the other company was a regional U.S. brewer. Sharpe had the packaging machine in place within the week.

Lakeport could not use the name President's Choice because Brights winery had a copyright on the word "President" for alcoholic drinks. They briefly toyed with the idea of calling the beer Dave Nichol's PC Premium Draft but settled on PC Premium Draft. Ownership of the PC copyright was ambiguous. Loblaw owned the trademark, but there was speculation that Pencer had managed to strike an agreement awarding Cott exclusive use of the PC logo on beverages. Patty Watt designed a dark brown carton with gold and red accents. She sprayed the artwork with water, so that little beads appeared to cling to the carton.

Sharpe drove to Toronto to meet Nichol again in mid-November. Sharpe had spent more than $1.2 million on the beer and not a drop had been produced. The factory was not yet operating. His staff was exhausted. Maintenance crews no longer wanted time and a half; they wanted to go home. "How are you going to accomplish this?" Nichol asked him. "What assurance do I have, in writing the *Insider's Report*, that you aren't going to embarrass me?"

Sharpe stood firm. "If it takes working around the clock, we'll deliver."

"What if the beer sells so fast it's out of stock?"

"If it does, I'll apologize," Sharpe told him. "But I'm sure that won't happen."

That same month, Lakeport applied to have the beer listed at Brewers' Retail Stores, as required by law. PC Draft was to be priced at $12.50 for a twelve-pack. This was the minimum price, dictated by the Ontario government. It was also nearly $2 a case lower than the $14.40 charged by Molson and Labatt for most of their twelve-pack brands, including cold-filtered draft. The big breweries had established a mutually advantageous détente in beer pricing to preserve profit margins. The regional micro-breweries usually sold their product at a premium and attracted a differ-ent clientele. Sharpe was threatening to disrupt this system. He wanted a new category — "value-priced" beer — introduced in stores. Brewers' Retail refused. Within a week, a confidential memorandum stating the name and price of the beer had been leaked to all breweries. An executive letter of apology was sent by Brewers' Retail to Sharpe, but he was not appeased. As he saw it, the bullying had begun.

Meanwhile, Nichol was gearing up the *Insider's Report* hype machinery. The Christmas 1992 edition waxed eloquent about Saaz hops. "Michael Jackson...no, not that Michael Jackson...rather the British one who is acknowledged to be the world's leading beer author-ity, says that the flowery tops of Saaz hops, which are grown only in Zatec, Bohemia (the beer-making capital of the world), produces the world's tastiest beer."

The central question was whether the PC image could be trans-planted from the retail food setting. Women constituted the majority of shoppers in the supermarket; the beer store was a very male domain. Would the macho beer drinker be embarrassed ordering Dave the home-maker's hero's discount beer?

That worry proved ill-founded. PC Premium Draft began produc-tion the first week of December, at a rate of 10,000 twelve packs a day. It hit the stores on December 12. There was no official press conference but, as predicted, it generated a lot of media coverage. Sharpe reveled in his role as the value-minded entrepreneur pitted against the industry's comfortable duopoly. When PC Premium Draft was launched, he wait-ed until eleven p.m. — when long-distance telephone rates were reduced — to fax a press release he had personally written to newspapers across the province. Sharpe and Nichol, it turned out, had tapped into a rich vein of pent-up consumer demand for cheaper beer. PC Premium Draft sold out the week it was released. The beer giants closely monitored the progress of Sharpe's chemistry experiment, however. That same month, Molson introduced a Valu-Pack of eighteen bottles for $18.80.

From Hawaii, Nichol called Sharpe for an update. Pencer checked in from California. The good news was that sales were strong. The bad news was production couldn't keep up with demand. Some stores were already out of stock.

"Now what are you going to do?" Nichol asked him.

"We'll try to get more into the stores."

"You said you'd apologize," Nichol reminded him. "You said you'd make it public. Otherwise, we're going to lose the momentum here."

Sharpe immediately called Jim White, who was consulting for Cott, to help him write the ad. Over the weekend, they took turns redrafting the text. On Monday, Sharpe went into LIM's art department to arrange the graphics. It was four days before Christmas and there was no photographer around, so they created a beer bottle on computer. Sharpe faxed it to the Liquor Control Board of Ontario for approval. By four o'clock, they had completed the ad, which was then sent to major newspapers across the province. On December 23, full-page displays ran in the *Toronto Star, Globe and Mail, Ottawa Citizen, London Free Press*, and *Hamilton Spectator*, each at a cost of $50,000.

The ad featured a photograph of Nichol and his French bulldog Georgie Girl, both in Santa Claus hats, framed by a wreath. The copy headline read: SORRY DAVE NICHOL!! WE LET YOU DOWN!! WE NEVER EXPECTED THE KIND OF DEMAND YOUR BEER HAS GENERATED!! The smaller print went on to explain that beer lovers in Ontario would have to wait a week for a fresh supply. It was a masterstroke. Nothing draws customers like a lineup.

To the alarm of Molson and Labatt, Lakeport grabbed almost 2% of the $3.6-billion Ontario beer market for domestic brands within six months. Even more distressing, Lakeport accomplished this feat by defying traditional beer marketing tenets. There were no commercials featuring pristine northern settings or fantasy party scenes overflowing with impossibly pretty people. There was no tie-in to a baseball team or rock concert. The brand instead became a hit on the strength of its price and perceived quality. And on the strength of Dave Nichol, Ontario's latest — and least likely — beer arbiter.

At one Toronto beer store, a worker offered his sanguine analysis: "It's Dave's beer and everybody trusts Dave. It's really kicking ass."

By January 1993, according to Sharpe, Lakeport was operating at a profit. It added more staff and by the spring was producing 36,000 twenty-four-bottle cases a day. Contracts were signed with A&P and IGA to produce de-alcoholized beer.

But the ultimate tribute to Lakeport's success was the petty retaliation by the big breweries. Molson launched the first salvo. On February 24, 1993, Sharpe received a letter from its lawyers in Ottawa. Molson claimed to hold an exclusive registered industrial patent to use water droplets on a carton. It requested that Lakeport recall its packaging for PC Premium Draft and Pabst Blue Ribbon, both of which featured water droplets. Molson wanted Lakeport to pay it a royalty on all beer that had been sold with that packaging. If the company failed to respond in two weeks, Molson would sue.

Sharpe countered with his own statement of claim. He wanted Molson's patent revoked. Water droplets were the only device the beverage industry had of portraying coldness, Sharpe insisted. But Molson was applying heat elsewhere as well, urging suppliers to stop making his cartons until the lawsuit was resolved. "They're just trying to tie me up," Sharpe said. "Trying to get me to spend money on lawyers."

As a precaution, Patty Watt withheld the droplets from the packaging of two new products, PC Lite, with 4% alcohol and PC Strong Draft, with 5.9% alcohol which were launched in the summer of 1993. At the same time, Molson and Labatt rushed to control the damage. Molson introduced its Carling brand in the Ontario market at the floor price established by PC; Labatt undercut it with Wildcat — $11.90 for twelve. Sharpe retaliated by lowering the price of Around Ontario to $11.60. He refused to involve the PC brand in a price war.

Although Sharpe relished his role as thorn in the flank of the beer establishment, not everything went his way. He wanted to sell his product in Quebec supermarkets, which were permitted to sell beer and wine. But the Brewers' Association of Quebec — like Brewers' Retail, controlled by Molson and Labatt — rejected Lakeport's beers on the grounds that it planned to use trucks and warehouses supplied by Cott Beverages. That would have violated regulations requiring breweries to have production facilities in the province in which they wanted to sell.

Interprovincial trade barriers were supposed to come down in the summer of 1992. But even at the end of 1993, the old rule — a clear threat to smaller producers — still prevailed.

Sharpe's plan to tap into Cott's U.S. distribution network was also put on hold when Washington slapped a $3-a-case duty on Ontario beer. The U.S. move was a countervailing action to the "environmental levy" of 10 cents per can that the Ontario government had slapped on imported U.S. beer.

Better than anyone, Sharpe understood that his success hinged on his contract with Loblaw. He had heard that officials from both Molson and Labatt had approached Galen Weston, making aggressive bids to take over production of the PC beer. Friends of the Weston family reported that some family members were unhappy that the venerable company was involved in such an unseemly product as beer. Dave Nichol's mother also voiced disapproval that her boy was involved in flogging alcoholic products. If one of the big breweries succeeded in usurping him at Loblaw, Sharpe conceded, "it would finish us." With competition out of the way, he reasoned, they'd raise prices again. It was only a matter of time. Galen Weston, he hoped desperately, would see through the breweries' clandestine plan.

Despite various roadblocks, Lakeport reached full production capacity in 1993 and by January 1994 claimed a substantial 3.8% of domestic beer sales in Ontario. For Nichol and Pencer, its success offered solid evidence that President's Choice — and more importantly, Dave Nichol — was more than capable of thriving in the universe beyond the supermarket.

CHAPTER FOURTEEN

DISSENT

In March 1992 an event occurred that would come to have a profound effect on life at Loblaw. Brian Davidson, the gargantuan human dynamo who ran the Intersave division, died suddenly of a stroke. The night before, he had been out with Dave Nichol and executives from Mitsubishi, eating sushi and talking deals. News of his death at the still-young age of fifty-nine rippled in shock waves throughout the Tower. True, Davidson had had a stroke ten years earlier and he was carrying 350 pounds on a five-foot-six frame. But everyone at Loblaw had assumed the recovery was complete. Davidson was always so robust. It was impossible to imagine the place without him.

Like the man himself, Davidson's funeral was large and emotional. A standing-room-only crowd of more than one thousand crammed into Benjamin's Funeral Home in north Toronto on a sunny morning. Mourners were consumed with sadness and the dislocation that follows sudden death. The congregation list underscored Davidson's stature within the company. Galen Weston flew back from Florida to be a pallbearer, joining a group that included Dick Currie, Dave Nichol, food broker Simon Zucker, Don Watt, and Ziggy Wauro, who had flown up from his home in Arizona. Davidson's children, Toby and Michael, offered heartfelt remembrances of their father. "Don't ever forget my dad," Toby said in tears. "Because I never will." Currie gave a eulogy that emphasized Davidson's qualities as an employee. "Brian was a 'doer,'" Currie said, a "hard worker who always delivered." Some more attentive members of the crowd noticed that his remarks sounded very similar to a keynote speech Currie had delivered a few years earlier, the night Davidson had been presented with the Scopus Award.

It was that night, in April 1988, that many saw as the acme of Davidson's career. The Scopus Award, given by the Canadian Friends of the Hebrew University, was presented to Davidson at a fund-raising dinner at Toronto's Royal York Hotel. Proceeds went toward the charity of Davidson's choice, the newly founded Brian Y. Davidson Research Centre in Agribusiness at the Hebrew University of Jerusalem. Davidson was an ardent supporter of Israel. As a young man, he had participated in the Habonim Zionist youth movement and had spent a year at Kibbutz Geva in the Valley of Jezreel. While at Loblaw, he introduced a wide range of Israeli products, including the highly successful No Name Passover Matzoh. Davidson was also active in other charitable causes. He created an industry coupon program called Cash for Kids, which raised more than $3 million for Variety Clubs in Canada and the United States.

The Royal York room was filled with heavyweights of Canadian business — Galen and Hilary Weston, George Cohon of McDonald's, Edward Bronfman, founder of the Edper conglomerate, Neville Kirchmann, then president of Coca-Cola Beverages, Currie, Nichol, other colleagues from Loblaw and the food manufacturing industry. Dr. Ray Goldberg, the Harvard Business School professor who coined the term "agribusiness" in 1959 to define the relationship between big industry and farming, praised Davidson for "contributing more to agribusiness than anyone alive." Like many hype-mongering Harvard faculty members, Goldberg may have overstated the case, but it was consistent with the effusive, laudatory tone of the evening. The two men had met at Harvard, where Davidson, at Dick Currie's suggestion each year attended an annual seminar on the food industry. Later, Goldberg supervised three case studies done by the Harvard Business School that examined the company as a model of innovative retailing. The Loblaw work led him to The Watt Group, which inspired a similar study.

But if the Scopus dinner was the public grand tribute to Davidson, the event that in his own mind had signaled his professional success was a back-yard party he hosted on August 23, 1986, to commemorate Dick

Currie's ten-year anniversary as president of Loblaw Companies. Nichol and Don Watt had planned the evening over the course of three months. Often, Davidson sat in on the Monday morning meetings, delighted to be part of the tribute. Here he was, a poor kid from Toronto's Jewish ghetto, hosting such a swell event.

Davidson had found his own corporate ascent within Loblaw improbable. Loblaw was the Big Time in his mind. He underestimated himself, though. Davidson offered something unique to the company. His backroom deal-making smarts had become a crucial, if inconspicuous, component of Loblaw's success. Loblaw legend had it that he earned the company somewhere in the area of $40 million buying and trading companies and setting up exclusive distribution deals. Davidson knew how to work the angles. He was often aided in this by the fact that the people across the bargaining table underestimated his savvy. Davidson, who could be loud and ebullient, didn't come across like a shark, even though he could be as ruthless. Next to him, most of the trim young WASP business school grads running around the Tower looked like greenhorns.

Even so, he was acutely aware of his lack of formal education. "Make this look like a report they would do at McKinsey," he would tell his secretary before he gave a presentation. His self-deprecating nature was summed up in a caricature that hung in his basement. In the drawing, Davidson was featured in a tight-fitting suit sitting astride a camel, a croquet mallet in hand. Beside him was Galen Weston seated on a pony, wearing his red and white polo colors. The caption read: "Ready to play, Galen?"

Currie's tenth anniversary party took place on one of those August evenings when summer's end hangs with an almost gravitational pull. A torrential downpour in the late afternoon stopped almost magically at 5:30, the precise time the event was scheduled to begin. For the guests, though, the real magic came in the form of the certificate for one share of Loblaw Companies inserted with each invitation. When Richard Currie was appointed president of Loblaw Companies on July 16, 1976, that share was worth $1.35. Ten years later, the stock's value had risen to $13.50, a one thousand percent appreciation.

The party's production values were brilliant, right down to the dancing on water. Clear plastic tents covered three levels of terraces descending into the ravine garden. Thousands of tiny white lights flickered like stars in the trees. Hundreds of pink azaleas were artfully arranged by Toronto florist Bruce Philpott. The steps descending into the garden were traced with neon green tubing. A Plexiglas shield that took days to install covered the illuminated swimming pool at the foot of the stone terraces, turning it into a magical dance floor. The bountiful, seafood-centric buffet prepared by David Wood Food Shop, Toronto's caterer of the moment, was designed to pay homage to Currie's Maritime heritage. Salmon flown in that day from both coasts flanked each end of a long table. In between were mounds of fresh clams, Malpeque oysters on the shell, scallop ceviche, New Brunswick lobster, and marinated fiddleheads.

Three hundred guests gathered from all over North America, giving the evening a "Dick Currie, This Is Your Life" feel. Currie's mother flew in from Moncton. His sisters, Anne and Elizabeth, were there, as were his three daughters, Jennifer, Bryn, and Elizabeth. Loblaw division presidents assembled from across the country. The guest list was peppered with names from the corporate establishment — publishing magnate Ken Thomson, Ray Wolfe, president of Loblaw rival Oshawa Group, and Terry O'Malley, president of Vickers & Benson, the advertising firm that had handled the Loblaw account in the mid-seventies.

The first thing guests saw upon entering the spacious foyer of Davidson's house was the photograph taken in 1972 of Currie and Nichol smiling at each other with the caption "...it's gonna be marvellous."

At the party's epicenter was Dick Currie, dressed in a lightweight gray suit, pale blue shirt and dark tie, chatting, a smile on his face. Dick Currie was no party animal, but that night he basked in the glory. The past year had been rough for him personally. He had separated from his wife, Beverly; she had lost interest in the role of corporate spouse and no longer wanted to endure his constant cross-country travel or his regular absence on weekends. In part, the party had been organized to cheer him up. But in greater part it was intended to pay homage to Currie's business acumen and the fact that he had served as an effective lieutenant to Galen Weston.

Silencing the crowd to toast Currie's management skill, Weston presented him with a certificate to have his portrait taken by the legendary photographer Yousuf Karsh. Nichol, in white dinner jacket, gave Currie a humidor filled with Davidoff cigars. That night, the politics that simmered beneath the surface at the Tower were left behind as they celebrated success. Currie responded to the toasts with a speech that drew from Lord Alfred Tennyson, Churchill and Elvis Presley. Then, Murray Alter and his orchestra played, the guests gliding across the Plexiglas-covered water.

A tribute to Loblaw's power and success, the evening also reflected the organization's hubris. The event cost more than a half dozen of Loblaw checkout clerks earned in a year. In *Behind Closed Doors*, a book that examined the Canadian tax system, journalist Linda McQuaig cited the Loblaw party as an example of how extravagant events could be written off as tax-deductible business expenses. But she grossly underestimated the extent of the extravagance. "With the catering, the orchestra, the serving staff, the liquor and the flowers, the party would easily cost $50,000," McQuaig wrote. "By reducing Loblaw's taxable income by that amount, this soirée would reduce the company's tax bill." This excerpt was faxed around Loblaw executive offices. "We all laughed when we read it," said Thelma Davidson, Brian's wife. "Fifty thousand wasn't even close. The food alone probably cost $50,000."

Dave Nichol cried when he heard of Davidson's death. He felt a kinship with Davidson that he did not share with anyone at the Tower. "We were partners in crime," Nichol said. "We both thrived on innovation." Nichol did not speak at Davidson's funeral, choosing instead to pay tribute in the June 1992 *Insider's Report*. That issue was uncharacteristically melancholy, containing two quasi-obituaries. Page one space was reserved for Nichol's beloved Georgie Girl, who had been put to sleep that April. Davidson's death was confined to page three, and pathetically commemorated with a special price on a contraption Davidson had patented — the Hot Diggity Dogger. The ingenious device toasted two hot dog buns and two wieners simultaneously. As a special, Nichol offered the Hot Diggity Dogger, plus coupons for President's Choice products worth $15, for $39.99. It was "a once-in-a-lifetime bargain to commemorate a unique lifetime," the item read.

In his tribute, Nichol revealed, if only partly, the conflict that pervaded his relationship with Davidson. Davidson may have lacked Nichol's marketing talent, but he was an original thinker, a ten-ideas-a-minute kind of guy. At Loblaw, where everyone took credit for every bold idea, but Nichol was given the public attribution for it, this could cause problems. "Brian had one habit that always annoyed me," Nichol wrote in his *Insider's Report.* "He took personal credit for everything I did. He told everyone that he thought up No Name, President's Choice and G.R.E.E.N. products — he even claimed the *Insider's Report* as his idea. I realize now that being exposed to Brian's fertile mind was the catalyst that sparked my creative juices over the past 20 years. I ONLY WISHED HE HAD LIVED LONG ENOUGH FOR ME TO TELL HIM SO."

It was telling also of the difficulty Nichol could have in expressing emotion or appreciation. Indeed, while Davidson was alive, Nichol never hesitated to establish that he stood higher than Davidson in the corporate pecking order. Once, at a meeting with the heads of Loblaw's U.S. supermarket division, Davidson started whispering loudly to Galen Weston in the audience as Nichol was delivering a speech about offshore products available through Loblaw. Nichol suspected Davidson was attempting to take credit for discovering the items. He stopped talking and yelled across the room: "Shut up, Brian."

Yet Nichol was always acutely aware that his power within the corporation was limited. Davidson, as the head of buying at Intersave, had more bottom line responsibility, even though Currie would come to decentralize Intersave's power, giving the divisions more say over what was ordered. Those who knew Davidson well regarded the *Insider's Report* tribute as an insult to his memory. "The Hot Diggity Dogger was a sore point of Brian's," said one old friend. "He thought it was the greatest invention, but it never sold as well as he had hoped. Being remembered for it wouldn't have made him happy at all."

But increasingly, happiness was a commodity in short supply at the Tower, a place where success was measured in terms of return on equity, sales per square foot, net margins, and bottom line profitability. There was no space for sentimentality.

People who failed to perform or conform were expendable, a phenomenon one former Loblaw employee called "the down elevator chute syndrome." David Stewart, who had replaced Nichol as the head of Loblaw Supermarkets, left the company. So did Ray Goodman, who created the Pierre system. So did Andy Wallace, who had headed up international buying at Intersave.

Both Weston and Loblaw, which accounted for close to 71% of Weston's business, were white male bastions, products of the old school, hierarchical style. In other words, it was a typical Canadian corporation. The place was overrun with upper level management. In one joke that circulated in the lower echelons, someone calls Loblaw to ask for the vice-president of prunes. "Would that be pitted or unpitted?" the receptionist asks.

Although the 1980s was a decade in which even seemingly invincible businesses lost their way, Weston companies soldiered along with varying degrees of success; Loblaw was at the forefront, the major success story. While Nichol worked on expanding the President's Choice — and by definition his own — universe, Dick Currie set about consolidating Loblaw's position within the Canadian industry. His final victory over former arch rival Dominion was celebrated in February 1987, when he completed a twenty-month negotiation with press baron Conrad Black, then chairman of Domgroup Ltd., a unit of Toronto-based Hollinger Inc., which owned Dominion Stores. Currie was seeking the vestiges of Dominion's faded empire. Most of it had been bought by Great Atlantic & Pacific Tea Co. Ltd. of Toronto in 1985, which had paid $115 million to acquire the Dominion name and ninety-three stores in prime Ontario locations. Currie bought from Domgroup fifty-eight Mr. Grocer franchise food stores for an estimated $35 to $40 million.

Currie's skill at the bargaining table was commemorated by *Wintery Marshes*, an impressionistic snowy landscape painted by Maurice Galbraith Cullen in 1896, which hung behind Plexiglas on the eighteenth floor. When Currie and Black completed the deal, Black suggested that Currie take the picture as a memento. Beside the picture was a letter from Currie to Loblaw staff, written in the language of a war memorial: "The painting hangs here in silent tribute to the thousands of people in Loblaw

Companies Limited who worked unceasingly during the many years Dominion Stores Limited was a major presence in the Canadian food distribution scene," it read in part. The painting represented the corporate equivalent of a scalp.

Under Currie's command, Loblaw added stores and diversified. It expanded in the American market; struck a better balance between its wholesaling and retailing operations; sold its underperforming U.S. wholesale business; strengthened investments in St. Louis and New Orleans; and opened Superstores — outlets larger than 60,000 square feet — in the Western provinces. The superstores concept had been heralded by retail analysts as the most important innovation in modern retailing. Between 1985 and 1988, Currie spent $850 million to enter the supercombo arena. The money was ill spent in Ontario, however, as supercombos failed to generate business and dragged down Loblaw's fiscal 1988 results. But this was seen as a glitch in an otherwise brilliant career. The following year, Currie was accorded the industry's highest honor, becoming the first non-American to hold the chair of the Washington-based Food Marketing Institute, the most powerful food distribution trade association in the world.

To motivate Loblaw upper management, Currie and Weston gave pep rallies each Christmas at Toronto's York Club, inviting the top 100 Loblaw executives and store managers. "Currie would stand up," recalls a former employee, "and single out a guy for special commendation, who had renegotiated debt at a half point lower than the going rate. It was criminal. All these guys would have been just busting their asses, and Dick singles out a financial wizard. It was all about making Galen richer. Whoever did that was rewarded." Yet Galen Weston never treated this wealth as though it was for his personal pleasure. Weston behaved as though the corporation was his only in trust for the next generation — his daughter, Alannah, and son, Galen Jr. Indeed, Galen Jr., who attended Harvard, was seen as the next logical successor, even though Alannah was also known for her cleverness. He had been groomed over summer holidays, as had his father, working at Loblaws stores.

The relationship between Currie and Nichol was complex. Sometimes, it resembled a sibling rivalry in which the pair competed for

Galen Weston's favor. Currie had the corporate clout; Nichol was closer to him personally. Yet there were times of solidarity. Nichol was best man at Currie's wedding to his second wife, Beth, in 1990. They spent a vacation together in Hawaii in January 1992. Occasionally, the men dined together with their wives. Nichol was cautious never to deride Currie publicly, although he had the habit of referring to him in a snidely deferential manner as "Mr. Currie."

Dick Currie believed in taking the high road in his business dealings, but at times his hostility toward Nichol percolated to the surface. Nichol was continually pushing the limit. Currie clamped down on Nichol's traveling expenses in the late 1980s. Nichol's proclivities for taking an entourage via helicopter to castles on Finnish fiords and ordering $250 bottles of wine with dinner did not go down well with Currie. Publicly, Currie declared that No Name — not President's Choice — was the real money maker for the company. "Turkeys are very dumb birds," Currie said, explaining the role of President's Choice within Loblaw. "In order to get them to eat, farmers put glass pellets into their regular food. The glass is shiny. It attracts them. So they come to eat. That's what President's Choice is to us: It brings shoppers into the store." Currie refused to regard Nichol as a strategic asset that offered the store a competitive advantage that ultimately translated into higher revenues. This was not traditional business school teaching. Business school taught that everyone is replaceable, and only the quantifiable is valuable.

What was more obvious was a slow de-emphasis on the President's Choice line. That would be Currie's retaliation. "In the absence of a clear vision," commented one ex-Loblaw employee, "raw, power politics substitute." In April 1991, Currie told Loblaw's annual general meeting that corporate strategy would shift away from President's Choice and back to No Name products. The biggest sales gains — in the order of 15% annually — were expected to be seen with No Name products, which were then worth close to $700 million in annual revenues. Currie did not expect President's Choice, worth $250 million, to show anywhere near the same rapid growth. He also admitted that the G.R.E.E.N. line had failed to meet expectations, delivering only $80 million in revenue in 1990, up from $60 million the year following its launch, but well below the $100 million that had been projected.

Currie told the crowd the company would emphasize higher volume, lower priced Club Pack formats — such as 24 rolls of G.R.E.E.N. toilet paper for $5.99 (the regular price for a four-roll pack was $1.99). This was a logical move. Shoppers, mindful of the morbid economy, were trading down when they shopped. Half of Loblaw's media budget was put toward promoting its 1,900 No Name items. Nichol was featured in commercials and Don Watt was hired to reformat packaging for the 500 most popular No Name products — scrapping the bold yellow and black format and adopting a more modern look, although the identifiable bright yellow backdrop remained.

Davidson's death marked a turning point for Nichol at Loblaw. In the years to come, insiders would comment that if Davidson were still there things wouldn't have turned out the way they did. "The organization liked to explain me away as a loose cannon," Nichol said. "Brian spent a lot of time running around after the loose cannon."

Davidson had acted as an intermediary and a buffer between Nichol and Currie, although his allegiance was to Currie, the man in power. "The pendulum only swings one way," Davidson liked to say. After his death, communication between the two men became increasingly strained. "Brian was Dick's eyes and ears," an associate said. "The fat man was the glue." Nichol, bonding with Gerry Pencer of Cott Corp., grumbled to friends that he was thinking of leaving. He didn't feel appreciated, he said. He didn't believe his salary was commensurate with the profits Loblaw International Merchants was delivering to the company. In 1992, he approached Galen Weston for a raise. He was then earning $450,000 in salary, plus bonuses. Weston responded by raising his salary to $710,000 and gave him an additional $274,564 as a bonus.

Davidson's death occurred right in the middle of the Nienkämper bailout, a seemingly trivial event that would have a profound effect on Nichol's future at Loblaw. Nichol first heard rumors that his friend, furniture designer and manufacturer Klaus Nienkämper was in financial trouble at the end of 1991. He was shocked; Nienkämper had been a visible success, an institution. Nichol occasionally joked that he would like to be reincarnated as the tall, suave, smooth-mannered German. "Nobody has more style than Klaus," he liked to say. Nienkämper over the years had become something of a Canadian design icon, which made him a rarity. Nienkämper catered primarily to the high-end corporate market, with sleek modular desk units, cabinetry, tables, chairs, and sofas, meticulously constructed from fine materials.

Nienkämper's life story read like Horatio Alger as told on the glossy pages of *Architectural Digest*. He was born in 1940 in Duisburg, Germany, and raised in the Rhineland area. His father was a stage technician in the theater; his mother ran an antique shop. As a young man, Nienkämper was a modernist. Antiques, to his thinking, were provincial, even oppressive. In what could be interpreted as an adolescent act of rebellion, he apprenticed at modern furniture Goliath Knoll International in Dusseldorf. Later, he went to work in Finland for Askos, another furniture company. At twenty-two, Nienkämper immigrated to Canada with his wife Beatrix — and less than $40 in his pocket. He found work with a small Toronto cabinet shop, where he drove the truck and did the payroll and other odd jobs. The Toronto that Nienkämper encountered in the 1960s was a stuffy and conservative place, more Queen Anne than Mies van der Rohe. Yet there were signs of change. Mies van der Rohe had designed Toronto's Toronto-Dominion Bank Centre, the city's first skyscrapers. The country was enjoying an outburst of nationalistic fervor at Expo 67, expressing a new-found confidence in Canadian design and manufacturing. Pierre Trudeau, a swinging bachelor, had been elected prime minister.

Nienkämper contemplated a move to the United States but recognized that Toronto had potential. "There was nothing here, so I decided to stay," he says. In 1968, he and Beatrix founded Nienkämper Furniture Inc. to import European furniture; they were its only employees. In 1973, the company became the Canadian licensee of Knoll International Inc. Later, Nienkämper designed and manufactured its own product line. As Toronto grew into a major financial center, so did Nienkämper's business. Toronto was a city of would-be financial players seeking a stage. Nienkämper provided the setting: bird's-eye maple and black leather conference tables, mahogany credenzas, cushy leather sofas, lots of glass and chrome. Nienkämper, the company, grew to employ 130 people. At its core was the glamorous Nienkämper family — Klaus, Beatrix, and their daughters, Ottilie and Rebecca, who worked in the showrooms until Ottilie married a furniture manufacturer and moved to North Carolina.

In the mid-1980s, just as Michael Milken was reaching the peak of his power, Beatrix opened Nienkämper Accessories, a boutique that provided rarefied leather goods such as $1,000 folding leather chairs and $600 leather throws lined with velveteen. There were also Tierno leather office supplies — $159 wastebaskets, $164 phone-book covers, $78 pencil cups.

Nienkämper built up a side business in contract work to Toronto's rich, people who could afford $10,000 sofas and appreciated leather imported from Switzerland and Germany, where cows were never exposed to barbed wire that might scratch their hides. When Hilary Weston went shopping for a fortieth birthday present for Prince Charles, she turned to Nienkämper, who created a leather polo bag and folding leather chair the Prince could use to watch the game from the sidelines. The polo bag was later added to the accessories collection with an $1,800 price tag.

The company did contract work for clients ranging from the prime minister's office to Air Canada's first-class lounge at Toronto's Pearson airport. In the mid-1980s, it began marketing in the United States, setting up showrooms in New York, Los Angeles, and Chicago. Prestigious commissions poured in: the executive offices of AT&T, Neiman Marcus department stores, the New York Stock Exchange. Nienkämper furniture was seen as the ideal complement to the Arthur Erickson-designed Canadian embassy in Washington, even though staid civil servants later replaced the white leather pieces with Queen Anne. When Nienkämper heard, he shook his head. "Why is it more important to please civil servants than to show the world that we are a country young at heart?" he asked.

The company appeared to be thriving. In 1989, Nienkämper reported earnings of $12 million. Nienkämper became a local hero — a Canadian manufacturer who had made it internationally. In retrospect, however, Nienkämper was a prototypical eighties business — high-end, high costs, trading in luxury based on the assumption that the boom would never end. Then it did. Recession came in through the back door. Interest rates were high, as was the Canadian dollar. Furniture was on the wrong side of the Canada-U.S. free trade deal.

Traits previously lauded as Nienkämper's strengths — demanding standards, attention to detail, unwillingness to compromise — suddenly became liabilities. What had been seen as expanded capacity suddenly became fat. Nienkämper's eclectic tastes, as reflected in his broad product line, were now viewed as signs of an unfocused businessman. By the end of 1991, Nienkämper's bank, the Royal, was skittish. A month later, in a move no one anticipated, the company was placed in receivership; if a buyer were not found, the bank would foreclose. Little did financial institutions care about Nienkämper's international reputation or his long list of design awards.

With his business in jeopardy, Nienkämper worked with the receiver Price Waterhouse to fulfill orders and review prospective buyers. Predictably, there was considerable interest in the company, given the status associated with the Nienkämper label. Yet none of the suitors proved a good fit. One large office-supply company wanted to affix the Nienkämper name to its plain filing cabinets and jack up the prices. Other prospective buyers planned to break up the company and sell its operations — two factories, upholstery operations, metal fabricator and woodworking facilities — individually. After studying the books, they recognized that the assets were not worth much without Klaus.

Nichol had known Nienkämper since the late 1970s, when he had ordered tobacco-brown leather sofas for his midtown apartment. Nienkämper had custom-built much of the furniture for Nichol's Clarendon Avenue house. If there were such a thing as President's Choice furniture, it would have been Nienkämper-created. The Nichols socialized from time to time with the Nienkämpers. They were even neighbors for a while, until Nienkämper moved his family to a farm in Mulmur Hills, south of Collingwood, Ontario, where he could raise Friesan carriage horses.

Nichol viewed Nienkämper's plight as a tragedy. There was so little taste in the world, he lamented, that seeing a tiny portion of it disappear was cause for despair. There were also more practical concerns. "Besides, where am I going to get my furniture reupholstered if Klaus goes out of business," he said, half in jest. Deciding to play Don Quixote,

Nichol organized a mission to bail out Nienkämper.

Ironically, the quest to save a Canadian design giant had been something Galen Weston had tried and failed to do a few years earlier. In 1988, Weston had joined Conrad Black, chairman of Hollinger, Peter Munk, chairman of American Barrick Resources Ltd., and Peter Bentley, chairman of Canfor Ltd., to bail out the celebrated but insolvent Canadian architect Arthur Erickson. The effort ultimately collapsed, and Erickson filed for bankruptcy a few years later.

Nichol called Gerry Pencer, who also banked with the Royal Bank. In late January 1992, before leaving for holidays in Australia and Hawaii, Nichol asked Pencer and Don Watt to invest their own money to save Nienkämper. After Nichol returned, in early March, Pencer organized a breakfast meeting at his house, with Watt, Nienkämper, and Nichol. "I left that meeting feeling so positive," Nienkämper says. "I felt they were empathetic to my interests and that the integrity of the company could be maintained." Neither Nichol nor Watt entertained serious thoughts about becoming furniture moguls. Rather, they liked what the investment symbolized: they were defenders of good taste. Pencer's motive was less grand. "I did it as a favor to Dave," he says.

Cott's Retail Brands and Nichol were to hold a majority interest, but they gave Nienkämper control of the day-to-day operations. There was no illusion that Nienkämper could be a profit center. They would underwrite the company until a more suitable buyer could be found. Geoff Belchetz, a director of Retail Brands, conducted the negotiations with the Royal over three weeks. "Our role was to preserve one of the icons of Canadian furniture design," Belchetz says. "Then, at the appropriate time, we'd find a better fit." On April 11, 1992, the deal was completed. Pencer and Watt each invested $200,000, Nichol less. People close to Nichol expressed surprise that Nichol would put up his own money. "I've never known Dave to pay for anything out of his own pocket," one says.

Belchetz worked closely with Nienkämper to redefine the company's strategy. Get back to basics, Belchetz recommended, which meant office furniture. They also sought ways to cut costs. That meant layoffs; the work force was pruned to fifty-five. They hired local designers. Furniture was built on a smaller scale, to fit more comfortably into down-sized office quarters. The Watt Group designed new promotion material. The following year, Nienkämper won contract work in Osaka and estab-lished relationships with dealers in London and Kuwait. In March 1993, Nienkämper started shopping for another buyer. After several false leads, he started talking to importer International Contract Furnishing in New York. Eleven months later, the company acquired control of Nienkämper.

The Nienkämper bailout was kept low-profile. Press coverage referred only to "unnamed investors." It is difficult, however, to keep Don Watt and Gerry Pencer quiet for long. Even Nichol talked openly about it. What happened then depends on who tells the story. According to Don Watt, Dick Currie frowned upon Nichol's involvement. Pencer's constant presence around LIM had become an irritant to Currie. The cola maker was brash and flamboyant, a Damon Runyon character. Not Currie's style at all. Currie, a territorial creature who thought in terms of turf, resented Pencer homing in on his. But Cott had become a fixture thanks to the agreement Davidson had signed with Pencer in 1991.

Currie was said to be upset with Watt for forging a relationship with Pencer through Retail Brands, even though Watt had approached Loblaw first with the idea. But it was thought within Loblaw that they had given Watt a platform to create a formidable business and Watt had turned around and shared his talent with a potential competitor. Currie had not expected that Watt would shop his business around after Loblaw had rejected his suggestion to enter into an equity partnership with The Watt Group. Retail Brands was teaching American supermarkets such as Wegman's, Finast, and National how to improve the quality of their own house brands. What was not clear was whether the Pencer-Watt venture would compete with Loblaw's efforts to put President's Choice in super-markets south of the border.

According to Watt's version of the story, Currie told Nichol to dis-engage from the Nienkämper rescue, and Nichol agreed. "David did it to preserve the peace," Watt said. Nichol denied that Currie had said one word to him about Nienkämper. "I'm paid to concentrate on creating and selling unique products," he said, "not to run a furniture business." Nichol would concede, however, that there was conflict between Currie and Watt. Nichol sold his stake to Retail Brands in November 1992. For Nichol's birthday the next February, the Nienkämpers gave him an elaborately wrapped box. Inside was an antique French iron firefighter's helmet with an inscribed message: "Thanks for putting the fire out, Dave." Little could the Nienkämpers have known that rescue had already sparked a more potent incendiary in Dave Nichol's life.

CHAPTER FIFTEEN

THE CHICAGO COOKIE CAPER

During the winter of 1992, Dave Nichol awoke every night to a black void, an empty space. His internal alarm went off at exactly 3:17 a.m., proof that his will was so systematically organized that it governed even his subconscious. The house was quiet; the dogs were in their pen downstairs, under The Dome. Cold air wafted through the open window. Lying on his featherbed, between flannelette sheets, under the eiderdown duvet, his mind raced at warp speed, the neurons colliding in free-form synaptic interchange.

The principal focus of his obsession was the U.S. invasion. Loblaw's U.S. invasion. His U.S. invasion. The one that would catapult President's Choice into the big leagues. It was step two of the master plan. He was close, very close, to the big payoff. His success, as it always had, would depend on timing. This was the critical moment; if he did not seize it, it would be gone forever. He gave himself a year, maybe eighteen months if his luck held, for the products to reach maximum impact in the United States. He knew that if he failed, he would never develop a serious business south of the border. The education, the work, the years of sleepless nights playing out alternative scenarios, would be for nothing.

Nichol had little time for statistics, unless they served his purposes, and suddenly they did. He liked to cite the numbers: in Canada, private labels accounted for 20% of sales in the food and beverage market, compared with 15% in 1986. At Loblaw-run stores, private-label accounted for close to half of the goods sold. In the United States, according to one study, the percentage of Americans buying national brands had dropped to 61% from 77% in 1975. In Europe, private-label goods had also been gaining a larger share of the market — more than 31% in England, more than 17% in Germany. Nichol played up these figures in speeches to U.S. audiences.

The phenomenon was increasingly chronicled in the press. *Fortune, Forbes,* the *Wall Street Journal,* the *New York Times*: all had explained how shoppers were shunning big national brands — American institutions such as RJR Nabisco, Procter & Gamble, Colgate-Palmolive — and choosing retailers' house labels. Economics had rendered generics fashionable. As *Food Business* pointed out, private labels helped retailers eliminate the middleman, cutting prices by up to one-third and returning gross profit margins as high as 30%, twice as attractive as those on many national brands. Always in these articles there was at least one paragraph of homage to him — Canadian Dave Nichol, originator of the species in North America.

The reason for disenchantment with the big national brands was not complicated. The big brands had become greedy. An eighteen-ounce box of Quakers Oats, for example, cost 73 cents (U.S.) in 1980. In 1991, that same box cost $1.73; its price had increased an average of 9% each year. Yet during that time, the wholesale price of oats had declined by one-third. The product price was 3,000% higher than the value of the raw material. Despite flat demand and falling commodity prices, manufacturers kept revenues growing by hiking prices. According to *Forbes,* H.J. Heinz's margins rose from 11.4% to 18.5% during the 1980s, Ralston Purina 9.4% to 15.7%, and the margins of frozen dessert treat mogul Sara Lee increased from 7.4% to 10.4%.

Shoppers were more vigilant about package contents. They had learned there were no significant differences in staples such as flour, salt, or baking soda, each of which was made up of a single, generic ingredient. Brands retaliated by spending less on advertising and more on rebate and coupon programs. This strategy, too, served only to erode brand loyalty, encouraging shoppers to switch brands solely on the basis of price. By November 1992, according to the *New York Times,* private-label cigarette sales were up 94.9% from the year earlier, disposable diapers had jumped 29.3%, and cold cereal was up 13.3%. It wasn't that brand names were becoming obsolete — a point often missed in these reports. Rather, a sub-species had emerged, store brands that by their price and quality gradually won the consumer's allegiance.

Filling shopping carts with alternatives to Oreo, Marlboro, Tide, and Coke had to do with much more than saving a few cents here, maybe a dollar there. Shifting shopping habits reflected a deeply rooted malaise. The comfort that had always been seen as the entitlement of the middle class, the hard-working people who traditionally defined American values, was disappearing. The American Dream of an ever-increasing standard of living was in peril. That message — "You're working harder and longer for less money than ten years ago" — had put Bill Clinton in the White House in 1992.

The class polarities that had developed over twenty years were everywhere in evidence. The income of the top 1% of the population had overtaken the combined income of the entire middle 20%. The poor were poorer, more numerous, and impossible to ignore. The subclass had surfaced, sleeping in subway stations, park shelters, atop the steam grates of city streets. They stood outside closed-down auto parts plant with signs that read, "Will work for food."

In a nation that had for so long seen itself as classless, a new vocabulary was required. "Carjacking" became a verb, as did "swarming" and "dissing." Violence became the language of frustration and despair. Blue-collar workers lost jobs to labourers in Mexico willing to work for a dollar a day, no time and a half. The middle class was angry, ready to lash back to preserve its quality of life. Suburbia was under siege. White picket fences were being replaced with industrial chain link. Household purchasing power declined, along with public services and real estate values. Schools had fewer teachers, libraries closed earlier, roads were bumpier. Medical and educational costs rose faster than income. The forty-year post-war boom was over, and everything that was thought to have made America great — General Motors, IBM, Sears, Roebuck — lay awash in a pool of red ink.

This was all good news for Dave Nichol. It meant that the average

North American shopper was seeking change as never before. If the government could not offer remedies, they would look elsewhere, to the place they were taught would offer salvation: the stores. In a society increasingly polarized between high and low — Neiman Marcus versus K mart, Lexus versus Subaru, Kobe beef versus Hamburger Helper — the retailer who could redefine distribution channels, eliminate middlemen, and control manufacturing to bring the Neiman Marcus knock-off to K mart would rule the marketplace. To the modern consumer, loyalty was the absence of something better, nothing more.

And Nichol had an ace up his tailored white French cuff. He had a system to put better quality food on the table at a lower price. All he had to do was figure out how to become the lifeline to the single mother of four, buying Kraft Dinner by the case, on special in Des Moines. Kraft Dinner claimed 45% of sales in its category, but lost many retailers 3 cents a box; Nichol's President's Choice Macaroni and Cheese Dinner netted a minimum 10% margin. And it was making money. Now, if he could establish distribution networks, he could share balsamic vinegar, Kobe frozen burgers, The Decadent Chocolate Chip Cookie, and Too Good To Be True! low-fat, high-fiber no-cholesterol microwave dinners with America — and offer solutions to the modern anxiety that looked to food as status, as entertainment, as consolation, as redemption.

Lying awake, he thought about last night's dinner. Fabulous. Terri had made osso bucco, meloni pasta in cream sauce, a bottle of his Memories of Napa cabernet. He made a mental note to tell Paul Uys at work tomorrow how Terri had combined President's Choice four-pepper sauce with President's Choice barbecue sauce — sheer inspiration. It should be a recipe in next summer's *Insider's Report*.

A metallic taste forms in the back of his throat. His inability to devise an airtight strategy had thrown him off balance. The anxiety had plagued him for two months. He had a crew of twenty-four working on the problem, but the commands came from him. Part of his anxiety, he knew, was his fear of change. This was a turning point. He was leaving the cocoon of Canadian supermarket retailing, the carefully constructed universe of his life. He had a major presentation in front of Jewel Tea supermarket executives in Chicago in two weeks. Two days later, he would be flying to England with Gerry Pencer to make a pitch to the Asda chain to carry PC soda pop. There was also that deal to distribute President's Choice in Hong Kong. He was getting ahead of himself. Conquering the world was step three, and he could only do that after he had completed step two.

He had a head start, of course. Wal-Mart, America's biggest retailer, was already a client. Nobody needed to know that some brash no-name Canadian was the mastermind behind Sam's American Choice program, named after the chain's founder Sam Walton. The Wal-Mart business would help him on the volume side so that he could take the very same cookies and other products down the road and sell them for less.

He had Don Watt to thank for Wal-Mart. For years, Watt had been Loblaw's unofficial ambassador for the President's Choice brand outside of Canada. Watt had introduced President's Choice to Jack Evans, president of Tom Thumb stores, in Dallas in 1986, where he was redesigning the stores. Similarly, Watt had recommended the line to Tom Nevers, president of the twenty-three-store D'Agostino's chain in Manhattan, which began stocking PC in 1989. Watt's greatest act of salesmanship, however, a cosmic coup in the world of retailing, was Wal-Mart.

In 1985, Sam Walton called Watt to ask him to design a couple of stores. Walton was chairman of Wal-Mart, then the third largest retailer in the United States, after Sears and K mart. With a net worth in the neighborhood of $10 billion, Walton was one of the richest men in the United States, although you'd never know it to look at him. In fact, Walton enjoyed playing the role of hillbilly billionaire, the Jed Clampett of retail, and could frequently be seen driving around tiny Bentonville, Arkansas, home to Wal-Mart headquarters, in a beat-up pickup truck.

Walton's life manifested the quintessential American success myth. He was born poor in 1918, and he built the Wal-Mart conglomerate from one store, Wal-Mart Discount City, which went into business in 1962 in Rogers, Arkansas. Walton gave shoppers exactly what they wanted: national brands at lower prices, clean stores, and friendly service. Adding stores slowly, he implemented state-of-the-art technology and efficient distribution channels that kept prices low. Along the way he championed a made-in-America ethic and set up scholarships to

American schools.

Wal-Mart grew like wildweed. During the 1980s, its compounded sales growth was 36% a year. By 1990, Wal-Mart had overtaken Sears as the country's largest retailer. In 1993, its 2,100 stores — often the size of football stadiums — reported sales of more than $55 billion. To the people who shopped and worked there, Wal-Mart was more than a store. It was the embodiment of middle-America values, linking patriotism with lower prices. Sam Walton became a populist folk hero, a cross between Jimmy Stewart, Billy Graham, P.T. Barnum, and Henry Ford. What Walton was selling was pride in America. He gave Americans jobs, set up scholarships, helped the vanishing middle class to make ends meet, championed products made by Americans for Americans. During store appearances, Walton liked to play evangelist, leading employees in cheers: "Give me a W. Give me an A." He encouraged employee participation. Harvard Business School called it empowerment. For Walton, it was just plain smart business. His autobiography, *Made in America: My Story*, stood for months on the *New York Times* best-seller list. It was a story of good old-fashioned Yankee ingenuity, the kind of tale Americans hungered to read during a decade when the Japanese were buying up Hollywood.

For all the homespun hype, Wal-Mart's success was the result of shrewd and tough business practices. Behind the soft-spoken, friendly front beat a piranha's heart. Wal-Mart used cheap non-unionized labor, which kept wages lower than unionized competition. The company was religiously cost-conscious. Employees called suppliers collect. Normal buyer-supplier mating rituals were verboten. No meals, no gifts, no football tickets. The store learned to use its buying power more forcefully than anyone else in America, securing volume deals that squeezed out the middleman. The company had a fast, responsive transportation system and advanced information linkups between stores, including video channels that kept managers up to date on market trends. Operating and selling expenses were maintained at 15% of sales, compared to 25% for Sears Roebuck & Co.

In the early 1980s, Walton was thinking about building hypermarkets. A consultant suggested he call Don Watt. Watt wanted the assignment desperately, but it presented a potential conflict with West-on interests in St. Louis. He needed the go-ahead from Loblaw president Dick Currie before he could say yes. In 1985, Watt invited Walton and David Glass, then Wal-Mart's president, to meet Currie and take a look at Canada's largest food retailer. Watt met them at Toronto airport in his Rolls-Royce Silver Shadow. Walton goaded Watt about the grand-ness of the car. He told him he had never ridden in a Rolls before. Just as they were leaving the airport, the engine began to smoke. "Is that the way this fancy car is supposed to run?" Walton teased Watt. They had to abandon the car and wait for a limousine to pick them up.

Watt, Glass, and Walton toured a Loblaws store. Walton and Glass liked what they saw. That night, Watt introduced them to Currie and Dave Nichol over dinner at Mövenpick, a restaurant in the business district. Currie and Glass hit it off immediately. Both were strategic thinkers, small-town boys with a mind for numbers. But the initial meet-ing between Nichol and Walton was prickly. Walton found Nichol overbearing. Nichol joked about Walton's "aw, shucks" demeanor. It didn't take long for Nichol to get on Walton's nerves. The more bois-terous Nichol grew, the quieter Walton became. "He was a bit too ram-bunctious for Walton's taste," Watt recalls.

Currie refused to waive the clause that prohibited Watt from work-ing for Loblaw's U.S. competitors. Watt went down to Wal-Mart's head office in Bentonville. "Gentlemen, I'm sorry," Watt said. "Without a com-mitment from Loblaw, I can't do it." Wal-Mart's lawyers suggested they keep up the pressure. Walton intervened. "I can't get too concerned about a person who won't go against his friends," he said. Watt did give Walton some free advice. He told him to abandon plans to build hypermarkets. They worked well in Europe, where distribution systems were less well-advanced, he explained, but in the U.S. expensive inventory would end up sitting on the books. He recommended that Wal-Mart concentrate on the superstore format, which at 125,000 square feet, was about half the size of the standard hypermarket. Walton paid no heed and built four Hyper-market USA stores, all of which lost money. In 1987, Walton called Watt again. "I should have listened to you in the first place," he said.

In 1987, Walton asked Watt to design what he called the Wal-Mart

"Store of the Future" in Palmdale, California. The store would stock more fresh produce than other Wal-Marts, but carry fewer products and keep lower inventories. Watt, with Loblaw's blessing, agreed. He worked on the project with Bill Fields, then Wal-Mart's executive vice-president of sales and merchandise, who had been with the company since the early 1970s, when there were only thirty-six stores. Watt also designed packaging for Wal-Mart's private-label line of pharmaceuticals and health and beauty products called Equate. Watt and Fields began talking about expanding the line. Fields was eager to increase the store's market share per square foot. To do this, he needed high-velocity items that would move quickly off the shelf. Food would do that, Watt said. "But don't go with Procter & Gamble or Heinz. Stock a national brand and develop a line of your own."

Initially, this idea didn't appeal to Wal-Mart's executives. Over time, they began to see the financial benefits. Watt gently pushed Fields to meet Dave Nichol. "You guys both think you were put on earth for the same reason," Watt told him. "To bring people good products at low prices." In 1989, Fields came to Toronto and sat through Dave Nichol's standard President's Choice slide show in the LIM board room. "It was too flashy for my taste," Fields remembers, "but it did have some meat in it." Fields was interested enough to schedule another meeting at a Ramada Inn in Chicago with Nichol, Watt, Doug Lunau, and Terry Couttie of Intersave, and Wal-Mart district managers.

The scene was Harvard Business School visits the set of "The Waltons." Among the items Nichol brought down to show off was a white terry-cloth bathrobe he had developed for Holt Renfrew, an upscale retailer owned by Galen Weston. When Galen Weston bought the clothing chain in 1986, he had asked Nichol and Watt to develop a private-label line of clothing, using the same approach as President's Choice — finding less expensive manufacturers and paying attention to detail. The line, called Classics, was launched in 1987. It included a fourteen-ounce bathrobe. In Chicago, the Wal-Mart people passed the robe silently around the table. Afterward, Nichol was discouraged. "We didn't do well with the robe," he said. "No one said anything." He would learn an understated approach was typical of the Wal-Mart culture. If they liked something, they never raved about it. Sam Walton was uncomfortable with hyperbole. Bragging wasn't his style. "If it's good, braggin' ain't right," he liked to say.

To some at Loblaw, particularly Brian Davidson, the prospect of hooking up with Wal-Mart was intoxicating. The volumes of product purchased would be staggering. Davidson started referring to it as The Big Deal. Currie was more cautious. "It talks like a good deal," he said. "Let's see whether it is a good deal." He suggested taking a cooperative approach. Loblaw International Merchants would develop products in consultation with Wal-Mart. Loblaw's Intersave division would source the products and receive a 3% commission. The Watt Group would design the packaging.

In 1990, after a year of correspondence and meetings, a three-year agreement was struck. The deal was sealed with a handshake. No written contract was signed until 1993. Wal-Mart's only rule was that products be made in the United States if possible. It took months to decide on a name for the line. The first choice was "Sam's," a logical choice, given that Walton was more popular than the president of the United States. Walton was uncomfortable with this, fearing that it might look like an ego statement. He suggested "Pride of America," but his colleagues complained that it sounded like coffee. They wrestled with over 150 names but always came back to "Sam's American Choice." Finally, at one of their regular Saturday 5:30 a.m. meetings, Walton agreed. "Just don't make my name too big," he instructed.

Watt spent almost nine months designing various package formats. The final version was patriotic red and blue on a white background with gold stars; "Sam's American Choice" ran down the side. Wal-Mart launched the line in November 1991 with cola and chocolate chip cookies, the two killer categories.

The chocolate chip cookie business was taken over by Weston-owned Interbake Foods, based in Elizabeth, New Jersey. Colonial, the Kitchener company that produced The Decadent chocolate chip cookie in Canada, supplied the recipe and sent bakers down to instruct Interbake how to achieve the correct flavor and finish. The rumor within the industry was that Weston paid Colonial $1 million in consulting fees. The cookie for Wal-Mart, however, was renamed "39% Chocolate

Chip Cookies." The Wal-Mart people wanted nothing to do with a cookie called Decadent. This was middle America; they would just as soon sell pornography in their stores.

Cott secured an agreement to produce cola for Wal-Mart's Sam's American Choice program. To comply with Wal-Mart's "Made in the U.S.A." policy, Cott purchased a small bottling plant in upstate New York, then set up a network of thirty bottlers in the United States to pack its product. Wal-Mart became Cott's largest customer.

Within the next two years, almost a hundred Sam's Choice products were created. In the spring of 1993, Loblaw helped Wal-Mart develop a lower-priced secondary line called Special American Value. Patty Watt designed the package. These items, said to match the leading national brand in quality included ketchup, dishwashing liquid, potato chips, and dog food. By January 1994, more than six hundred items had been developed for Wal-Mart's two lines.

Sam Walton died in April 1992. David Glass took over as chairman; Bill Fields assumed the president's position. Despite the orderly transition, a populist backlash against Wal-Mart developed. Mr. Sam had projected the image of the underdog, even though Wal-Mart was a retailing colossus that often put small-town merchants out of business. In December, a "Dateline" NBC television program alleged that the store's commitment to sell made-in-America products was fraudulent. It claimed Wal-Mart was importing increasing amounts of goods made outside the United States, exploited sweatshop child labor in Bangladesh to produce private-label clothes, had done business with a suspected garment-smuggling racket in China, and had sold foreign-made clothes on racks that said Made in the U.S.A. The stock lost ground when the report was broadcast. Wal-Mart denied the charges and the issue died down.

Inevitably, Wal-Mart's launch of a premium private-label line received wide media coverage. The *Wall Street Journal*, the *New York Times*, and *New York* magazine all followed the story. Never, though, was the connection between Loblaw and Wal-Mart or the President's Choice inspiration mentioned. What could a bunch of Canadians teach Wal-Mart about retailing? Certainly, Wal-Mart had little interest in advertising the fact. Ironically, the relationship reversed the standard

U.S.-Canadian stereotype. Usually, it was Canadians who were self-conscious and self-effacing. The sort of self-aggrandizing Nichol specialized in was normally considered an American trait, not Canadian. "Confidence is not one of Dave's problems," Fields says, in typical understatement. "But we don't care where people are from. They're the best in the world at what they do. They're visionaries, even though they probably think we're a bunch of hicks."

Don Watt also made the connection that led to a consultancy between Loblaw and Coles Myer Ltd., Australia's largest retailer. Coles Myer operates Coles supermarkets and Kmart stores (not to be confused with K mart U.S., which holds 20% of Coles Myer stock). Watt had designed stores for the company in the early 1980s.

In this case, the point man on the deal was Warren Tutton, LIM's former advertising manager who had left in 1989 to work with Watt. Tutton broke with Watt after a year, fed up with the organizational clogs caused by Watt's inability to delegate. Shortly after he resigned, Coles Myer approached Tutton about heading up advertising for Kmart. He moved to Melbourne in 1991. When the company discussed creating a private label for its Kmart stores, Tutton suggested they talk to Nichol. The deal was signed in August 1992. The name: Australia's Choice. Why tamper with success?

Like the Wal-Mart contract, Loblaw's arrangement with Coles Myer involved a royalty fee structure. That same autumn, Loblaw sent product developers Chris Grikscheit, his wife Christine Mullen, and Jean Palmier to Melbourne for several months to seek suppliers. (Leigh Gravenor, Terri Nichol's daughter, who had studied business at Harvard, also joined the group.) The product developers had a secondary mission — to look for potential President's Choice products from Down Under. Australia was hot style-wise, Nichol believed. He never missed an issue of Australian *Vogue*. Australia's Choice was launched in 139 stores in September 1993.

Every night, Nichol pondered his American challenge. The opening salvos were easy: a full frontal attack with The Decadent Chocolate

Chip Cookie and PC Cola. His McKinsey & Co. training still came in handy. He focused on the real issues. How would Nabisco and Coke respond? The national brands, he knew, would fight back, using intimidation tactics to keep his products off the shelves. Supermarketing was a brutal industry; people would sell their grandmothers for a fifth of a point, he liked to say. He needed a list. What are the ten best ways to attack? Then pare the list. Which of these ways would really work? The biggest obstacle was not owning the shelf. That stripped his control. Someone else was making the rules. How could he reverse that? Slowly, Dave Nichol drifted back into the hiatus of sleep.

The U.S. invasion began to take shape in December 1992 in the form of the great Chicago chocolate chip cookie crusade. The plan was to make The Decadent the number one-selling cookie in Chicago within twelve months. This, Nichol hoped, would generate enough publicity to launch a major assault in the $400-billion U.S. supermarket business. To anyone familiar with the machinations of market share measurement, such a crusade might have appeared unrealistic. The Decadent, sold only in Chicago at Jewel Supermarkets, was then ranked twenty-sixth in cookie sales in the greater Chicago area, according to A.C. Nielsen, the largest market research firm in North America. Chicago's top-selling chocolate chip cookie was RJR Nabisco's Chips Ahoy!

Nichol was not deterred by the Nielsen data. Market share numbers, he knew, were supple things that could be manipulated. Technically, it was possible to buy the number one position simply by giving the product away. Nichol had no intention of doing this. But he knew that carefully staged promotions, backed by store managers, could influence shoppers' choice and undermine Chips Ahoy! long enough to propel the cookie into number one spot.

The strategy sessions were reminiscent of the early days in the War Room. In January 1993, Nichol began mapping out a month-by-month time line in the LIM board room. It was one of those ideal "win-win" symmetries business likes so much. Jewel would use the popularity of The Decadent to lure shoppers into the store; LIM would use the results to spur interest in the line among other retailers. "Our job right now is to hammer the cookie," Nichol would begin the meetings. "I want to be the number one cookie. And I don't care what it costs me. Because then I can go on TV and go into the *Supermarket News* and buy a full page and say it's the number one cookie in Chicago and it's only available at Jewel. And would you like to have the number one cookie in your area?" He would promote the cookie into desirability. It was not unlike the Hollywood starmaker approach. Nichol would do for The Decadent what Columbia Pictures had done for Sharon Stone — create desirability. He would appeal to the consumer's most basic instinct: if everyone else buys it, I want it too.

Tom Stephens, a vice-president of LIM who coordinated the sale of President's Choice products in the United States, was charged with mapping out details of the cookie strategy with Daymon and Associates, the Chicago food broker that handled the PC account at Jewel. At five-foot-ten, with light brown hair, aviator-style glasses, and a frame that betrayed his fondness for good food and fine Burgundies, Stephens, then forty, resembled a shorter, rounder, lighter-haired Dave Nichol. He was a popular figure around LIM, known for his sense of humor and respected for his aggressiveness. Stephens had worked at LIM since May 1988. Like Uys, he had been recruited by Nichol from Woolworth's in Capetown, South Africa, where he had worked for twenty-two years. Stephens met Nichol in 1983 when Nichol was recruiting at the Marks & Spencer affiliate. They toured the stores and factories together. Nichol liked Stephens enough to offer him a job on the spot. Stephens turned him down. For the following five years, Nichol would call every few months and repeat his offer. Stephens finally relented.

When Stephens arrived at Loblaw, Nichol asked him to look around and see what he thought needed to be done. Stephens's response was tinged with the sort of bravado Nichol liked. "Dave," he said, "it's the U.S. or nothing." Until then, President's Choice products were available in the United States at Loblaw-owned National Supermarkets in St. Louis and New Orleans; at Peter J. Schmitt in upstate New York; and at the 54-store Tom Thumb chain in Dallas.

Stephens's knowledge of the U.S. market was slim. He had only visited the country once on a four-day trip to Los Angeles. His lack of exposure would prove advantageous, he discovered. "I found out Canadians tend to go into these meetings awed, like they didn't really belong," he said. "But here I was with this strange, funny accent. That tended to disarm everyone." Nevertheless, Stephens's first call, to Tom Thumb in Dallas, was a disaster. The reason for the meeting, he believed, was basic account maintenance and, if things went well, a possible expansion of the product line. But shortly after he was seated in the board room, he was told that the stores planned to stop selling President's Choice. Several reasons were put forth: there weren't enough products; management didn't like that the goods tended to be produced in Canada; and there was no U.S. warehousing, so trucking created supply and distribution problems.

Stephens returned to Canada in desperate need of a grand strategy. He papered his office walls with maps of the United States and drew rings with felt marker around major population centers. Within each ring, he made a list of supermarket chains to approach to carry the President's Choice line exclusively in that area. Stephens continued to experience setbacks. In 1989, he set up a relationship with Detroit's Great Scott chain; soon after, the stores filed for Chapter 11 bankruptcy. But then the path became smoother. Watt helped set up the deal with the D'Agostino's chain in Manhattan. Stephens signed a contract with the Harris-Teeter chain in the Carolinas. Brian Davidson, who had a house in Phoenix, cajoled him to get into that market as it was home to a large group of retired and vacationing Canadians. He struck a deal with Jean-Roc Vachon, president of Smitty's Supervalue. Vachon was a former president of Steinberg in Quebec and knew the line.

In November 1991, Stephens signed a deal with the 206-store Jewel chain in Chicago. He was negotiating with Jewel in the Dallas market when executives at Tom Thumb approached Loblaw about reinstating the President's Choice program. Dallas was then in the midst of a supermarket price war; Tom Thumb hoped the President's Choice line would give it an edge. The deal with Jewel in Dallas fell through, so Loblaw resumed its relationship with Tom Thumb. Every month, it seemed, there were new alliances — with Fred Myer stores in Portland, Oregon; with Star Market in Boston, Massachusetts; with Acme in

Philadelphia, Pennsylvania; with American Stores, including 415 Lucky outlets, in California.

Stephens built the U.S. division within LIM, which came to employ twenty-six people — fourteen in Buffalo, twelve in Toronto. With time, his pitch became more methodical. Stephens learned that American supermarket executives were interested in only a small percentage of the line — the Top 100, he called it. They wanted soft drinks, cookies, pet food, taco chips, and fruit juices — all familiar items with identifiable counterparts among the brand names. There was far less interest in unique, offbeat products, such as the Memories sauces or Lamburghini patties popular among Nichol devotees in Canada. "Without Dave reassuring people," Stephens says, "Memories of Bangkok is scary stuff."

Some President's Choice products had to be renamed for sale south of the border. Free and Clear cola became Very Clear. Tuxedo crackers became Top Hat since Tuxedo was similar to the name of another cracker in the market. Thick and Juicy Beefburgers were called Beef Patties, without the adjectives.

The strategy was to price President's Choice products below the national market leader. At Harris-Teeter, a three-ounce can of President's Choice Cat Food cost 25 cents, 11 cents less than the leading brand in the category. President's Choice offered retailers a higher profit margin than those available on the national brands. How much higher depended on the store's pricing structure. At Tom Thumb, for example, the margins on President's Choice were 7 to 10% higher. That way, chains could sell national brands below cost and recoup money lost with President's Choice.

There was also the problem of increasingly visible success. Many retailers, such as the Publix chain in Florida, which Stephens courted for years, figured they could create a President's Choice-style line on their own. Stephens knew in most cases this was a pipe dream. Few grocery chains had the resources of the multi-billion-dollar Weston conglomerate behind them. Yet President's Choice success inevitably inspired imitation. A&P introduced Master Choice; Topco Associates in Illinois developed a World Classics line; Shurfine-Central Corp., an Illinois cooperative that served 20,000 grocers and convenience stores, developed an upscale line using recipes from state and country fairs; and Safeway, assisted by Cott, launched its Safeway Select program.

Stephens discovered that selling President's Choice brand in the United States posed obstacles not faced in Canada. The fragmentation of the supermarket industry in the United States meant that President's Choice could never achieve in America the widespread penetration it enjoyed north of the border. In Canada, a handful of chains dominated the market; in the United States, there were scores of powerful regional chains.

But the most daunting challenge in the U.S. was the fact Loblaw did not control the shelf; that meant it was dependent on the store owner to support the program by offering the right price, in-store displays, and advertising. And few retailers had the time, resources, or inclination to sell the brand the way Nichol did in Canada. "I live in a non-Dave Nichol world," Stephens lamented.

Attempts to duplicate the *Insider's Report* for the U.S. market had mixed results. Jewel in Chicago produced an abbreviated version. National in St. Louis distributed its own *Report* for a time; when a new publicity-shy president was appointed, it was discontinued. This was a common response. Most supermarket executives were numbers men, lacking Nichol's unrelenting desire for public exposure. Chairman Nick D'Agostino of the eponymous Manhattan chain was not comfortable in ads. And in some markets, there were problems with the PC name. Who's choice were they talking about? The store president's? Or Bill Clinton's?

Maintaining momentum was another challenge. Stephens observed the emergence of a pattern: store owners greeted the line with enthusiasm, but eventually lost the impetus to keep products front and center.

Breaking through retailer resistance was a far easier task, Stephens learned, than dealing with the guerrilla tactics of national brand sales reps. "The War" was how Stephens refers to it. While national brand sales in U.S. supermarkets had declined only marginally to 81.8% in 1992 from 84.7% five years earlier, this was in the face of corporate restructurings and the imposition of everyday low pricing. The increasing presence of President's Choice, an upscale retailer brand, represented a dangerous trend. Soon after Acme, Fred Myer, and Smitty's began carrying the President's Choice label, Coca-Cola offered those chains price deals not seen in twenty years. At Lucky stores, Stephens claimed, Coke and Pepsi representatives rearranged the pop display to diminish the PC position. Other companies engaged in de facto sabotage. Shelf tags used for inventory control were defaced or ripped off, which interfered with reorders. There was also what Stephens called the "frying pan syndrome." National brand reps would place general merchandise such as frying pans or cheese graters in front of a President's Choice facing. This was a particularly dirty trick, because the loss of facing usually resulted in an immediate decline in sales. Eventually, Stephens realized that he had to fight back. He set up "a retail police force," which went into stores once a week to reorganize the shelf and report mischief to store managers.

Ironically, one of Stephens's major obstacles came from within. A cornerstone of his pitch to retailers was that President's Choice would be an exclusive within their region. The fact that Nichol was developing similar products for Wal-Mart, which sold at lower prices, did not technically breach the exclusivity agreement, but it clearly irked many grocery chains carrying the line. Although the presence of Sam's American Choice did not directly impinge on many of his supermarket chains, Stephens realized that it might in a few years. Stephens tried to distance himself from the line. He tried to diffuse the situation by telling retailers that the higher volumes resulting from the Wal-Mart deal lowered prices on all PC items. Yet it didn't take a genius to discern that The Decadent and Wal-Mart's 39% Chocolate Chip Cookie were essentially the same cookie, even though it cost less at Wal-Mart.

The cookie conundrum was particularly contentious. Cookies are a very serious business. Supermarkets in the United States sold an estimated $3.3 billion worth a year. One out of every five cookies sold in North America was a chocolate chip. Its importance as a symbol of traditional American values reached its crescendo during the 1992 presidential campaign, when Hillary Clinton and Barbara Bush engaged in a competitive bake-off; Hillary's winning recipe used rolled oats and made front-page news.

The Jewel chain was the logical setting from which to topple Chips Ahoy!'s supremacy. Jewel's brown and orange logo was a familiar icon in the Chicago area; the chain accounted for 40% of supermarket sales in the city. No other chain that carried the PC line in the United States dominated its market to such an extent. The Decadent was already the best-selling President's Choice product of the 160 items carried at Jewel in Chicago. As always, Nichol wasn't satisfied. The Chicago cookie crusade was coordinated between LIM, Daymon and Associates, and Jewel. Nichol would dominate meetings attended by Stephens, when he was in town, Scott Lindsay of Intersave, and Boris Polakow, director of corporate brands. Lindsay was an ambitious young man who, with his wire-rimmed glasses, conservative suits, and studious manner, appears older than his thirty-four years. Since joining Loblaw in 1986 from Nielsen Marketing Research, he had risen steadily to the position of vice-president of corporate brands within Intersave. Lindsay was always well-prepared; he also tended to be the first in meetings to tell Nichol that an idea was great. He had done well within Loblaw.

Polakow was there to offer advice on merchandising and display. Nichol could be so abusive toward Polakow on occasion that it was easy to lose sight of the extent to which he depended on him. Polakow was also Nichol's sidekick on the President's Choice infomercials, which were created in part to cultivate a following for the line in U.S. border towns. It had worked for Cher, Victoria Principal, Anthony Robbins, Dionne Warwick. Why not Dave? The first one-hour spots aired over three nights in November 1991 on cable, featuring still pictures with voice-overs. Nichol and Boris Polakow appeared like a vaudeville team in President's Choice sweatshirts. Nichol would needle Polakow about the pricing. "How much are we charging for this, Bo?" he would ask of one product. "$5.99?" "No, Dave," Polakow would respond woodenly. "We're charging $3.99." "$3.99?" Nichol would squeal. "That's an impossible price." And so it went on and on and on. The series, which cost $100,000, aired in upstate New York and southern Ontario. Sales in Ontario rose 50% in the following six weeks. Sales in 135 Ontario stores carrying the products reached $27 million, compared to $18 million in the same period in 1990. The infomercials became a regular event following the release of an *Insider's Report*.

To have A.C. Nielsen count The Decadent the number one cookie in Chicago, it was necessary to increase its shelf turnover at Jewel by eight times. There were several ways to achieve this goal. Most crucial was ensuring the support of Jewel store managers so that they would give the cookie prominent display. To do this, LIM arranged in-store contests with prizes for managers, assistant managers, and supervisors who sold the most cookies.

"That's a pretty comprehensive program you've put together," Nichol told a February 1993 meeting. "Is it going to work?"

"With the contest, with the pricing, I'd certainly bet yes," Lindsay replied.

Nichol was not satisfied. "What is the main thing that would do it?" he asked. This was how he approached every problem: isolate the most important challenge. He did not wait for an answer. "In my opinion, the strongest thing you can do are contests for store managers."

They debated giving away silk shirts and ties, covered with graphics of President's Choice cookie packages. But Nichol had other ideas. "Maybe a trip to Kitchener to see the [cookie] plant will do it," he joked. "Second prize will be two trips to Kitchener." Then, he was hit by another inspiration. "What about a year's supply of my beer? What about coupons I could give away that the beer stores would accept for free beer?" He was off on a beer riff. "Yeah, that's going to turn the store managers' cranks. We could give them a choice. They could have coupons for beer, or soft drinks or Memories of Champagne."

Nichol's eyes swept the room. "It's absolutely essential that by the end of this year The Decadent is the number one cookie in Chicago," he said. "Do you get that?"

"Right," Lindsay said. "You know what Nabisco salesmen are doing at Jewel? They're turning the package over so the French shows." Packaging law in Canada required that one side be printed in English, the other in French. Nichol hooted; he considered this a good sign, evidence that the guys at Nabisco were aggravated.

The meeting turned to pricing schedules, mapped out on a board beside him. Nichol paced back and forth. "On the first of May, I'd like to see them come back with a buy-one-get-one-free, and a two-packages-for-$4 for six weeks," he said. "In this period I want to go from a fourteen-ounce to a twelve-ounce pack so we can get EDLP of $1.99."

EDLP was grocery lingo for "everyday low price." It became a popular strategy in 1992 when the major manufacturers, realizing that they were getting squeezed on in-store specials, decided to institute one fixed price. Using the smaller format would enable LIM to lower the price to $1.99 and make it an easier sell.

Still, Nichol was not content. "What other ideas do we have?" he asked. Lindsay, who had been taking notes, spoke haltingly. "The only thing we thought of was the possibility of starting TV or radio [ads] in April or May. Not only do we need to sell more bags of cookies, we also need more customers to buy bags of cookies." Nichol quickly dismissed the suggestion. "I don't think at this stage we can move people into Jewel by talking about The Decadent," he said.

A larger concern was ensuring that bags sold in the two-for-one promotion would be recorded as two bags rather than one, by International Research Inc., the New York-based marketing firm that tracked sales for Jewel. "If they don't, I think we'll be in trouble," Nichol said. He pondered the plan for a moment. "The one thing that's missing is sampling. We should do this in July," he said, writing "sampling" on the board. In-store sampling was expensive, but essential to getting shoppers to try new products.

Lindsay cast about for something to say. "Does it pull any weight in Chicago to say it's Canada's best-selling cookie?"

"Absolutely not," Nichol replied. "They're already too sensitive about how many President's Choice products are made in Canada."

"What about going on TV with the results of a taste test against Chips Ahoy! in Chicago?" Lindsay suggested. "We can say of one hundred people we sampled, ninety-nine found The Decadent better. And you can only get it at Jewel."

Nichol liked this idea. "It also sets the stage for the number one cookie being something you talk about."

By the end of April, earlier than expected, A.C. Nielsen had declared The Decadent the best-selling cookie in Chicago. That performance was repeated in May, although in June, it fell to third, behind Chips Ahoy! and Oreo. In July, winners of the in-store contest were flown to Toronto to attend a Blue Jays baseball game.

That was all Nichol needed. In August, he went on television to announce that The Decadent was Chicago's number one cookie. Nielsen protested. It allowed clients to use tracking data in internal communications and within the trade but publishing or advertising was out of the question. Nielsen account manager Tracey Hodgen went to the Tower to visit Nichol. He backed down and the commercial was taken off the air. Again in September, The Decadent had catapulted to first place. In the year ended September 1993, sales of President's Choice cookies in the United States were $21.4 million, up 140% from the year earlier. In fact, while total sales in U.S. supermarkets rose 37% that year, the sales of PC products jumped 127%. Riding the popularity of The Decadent, President's Choice products were available in 1,200 stores in thirty-four American states in early 1994. "President's Choice," Brian Sharoff, president of the New York-based Private Label Manufacturers Association, told *Canadian Business* magazine "raises the standards by which every retailer who has a private-label program will have to judge the consequences of that program in terms of quality and price."

Inevitably, U.S. and offshore markets were of growing importance to President's Choice revenues. They constituted 10% of sales in 1992, 25% in 1993, and, according to Stephens, would reach 50% by 1994. It was all part of a longer-term plan to establish President's Choice as a world brand, sold on an exclusive basis.

Already, Stephens had cultivated contacts beyond the mainland United States. The line had been sold to The Market Place, a small, prestigious nine-store chain in Bermuda. Park 'N Shop Ltd., Hong Kong's second-largest chain, had test-marketed products. With five stores in mainland China and plans to open twelve more, Park 'N Shop represented access to the biggest consumer market in the world.

The more visible and successful President's Choice became outside Loblaw, the more frustrated and contained Nichol found himself within. Here he was pushing a once-nondescript grocery chain into the far corners of the globe, yet he was not reaping any of the benefits. He was still treated like a middle manager within the corporation, like a division head. Out in the world, his behavior could be imperious. He thought nothing of asking a bartender at a restaurant in a private Toronto club to drive his car around the block while he finished his meal, so he wouldn't get a parking ticket.

Then there was the lunch with Julia Child. Nichol met the high priestess of North American foodies at a small luncheon held by the *Toronto Star* newspaper in April 1992 to celebrate her eightieth birthday. A dozen people attended the event at the Four Seasons Hotel. Nichol sat to Child's left, a placement many people in the room cynically saw as linked to Loblaw's prominence as an advertiser in the *Star*'s food pages. True to form, Nichol couldn't resist talking about himself and President's Choice. Much to the astonishment of the people around him, he asked Child if she would be interested in endorsing The Decadent Chocolate Chip Cookie. "I don't do endorsements. I think they ruin your credibility," Child replied. Yet Child, known in the food community for her graciousness and hospitality, then suggested that Nichol come to visit her if he was ever in Boston. It is an invitation she offers freely. "It's not hard to get invited to Julia Child's house," sniffed one Toronto food writer. Nichol called her not long after when he and Terri were traveling to Boston to visit Terri's daughter Leigh at Harvard. The three had a simple breakfast of excellent coffee, strawberry jam and toast, which Child burned, in the kitchen of her Cambridge, Massachusetts, home. Nichol was clearly nervous in the presence of the grand lady. "It was the only time I've ever seen David scared," Leigh recalls.

That was the exception. His sisters talked about how he had changed. Joanne referred to him as David Nichol, a reference to his celebrity. Yet at work, his irrepressible will had hit an insurmountable wall. Dave Nichol shouldn't have to put up with this, he would say to himself. He was afraid of change, of leaving the cocoon, but the situation had become untenable. The choice was becoming less and less his to make.

CHAPTER SIXTEEN

THE PROMISED LAND

I t was inevitable that Dave Nichol would be seduced by the Napa Valley, that luxurious theme park devoted to North American high taste. By the 1990s, the northern Californian region had become a sylvan mecca for the food- and style-obsessed upper classes. Indeed, it was food, not wine, that drew Nichol there for the first time in 1981. The catalyst was an article by restaurant critic Gael Greene about the Great Chefs of France cooking school, operated by the Robert Mondavi Winery. She mentioned that a course had been taught by Jean Troisgros, from Nichol's favorite restaurant, Les Frères Troisgros. On learning that the next sessions were to be conducted by Jean's brother Pierre, Nichol and Terri signed up. The five-day course cost $1,500 per person, a sum that guaranteed exclusivity. The Nichols joined twenty-two others at the sprawling, yellow stucco Mission-style Mondavi winery. Each musician-serenaded meal revolved around a different theme, and much attention was given to table decor and presentation. The week culminated with a black-tie dinner. Nichol treasured the elegance, the detail, the exquisiteness of it all.

Wine was an elemental part of the package for Nichol, as was the presence of Napa patriarch Robert Mondavi. Nichol, having been raised in an abstemious household, did not start drinking wine until he embarked on his food tours of France in his early thirties. Early in his career as a would-be oenophile, he relied upon the big names. He often requested Corton-Charlemagne, an expensive full-bodied, golden liquid. But his first choice was a 1934 Musigny, which he tried after Jean Troisgros told him it was his favorite wine. Nichol also came to enjoy expensive white Burgundies, especially Ramonet's Montrachet and Chassagne. Among Californian labels, his tastes, predictably, ran to the more exclusive and expensive labels.

Wine had been produced in the Napa since 1841. Cesare Mondavi, Robert's father, had made bulk wine there after prohibition. But it was the son who turned the Valley into America's most prestigious wine region. He did it by breaking away from the family-owned wineries of Sunny St. Helena and Krug Winery and setting up his own vineyard in 1966. The younger Mondavi was the first winemaker in the Napa to employ marketing to cultivate an up-market image. He changed the pronunciation of his name back to the Italian Mon-*dah*-vi from the Anglicization Mon-*day*-vi his father had adopted. He had the gall to charge $2 for his Fumé Blanc. "If you charge a lot for it," he once said cynically, "it has to be good." Mondavi carefully fashioned himself after the European wine aristocrats and used cooking schools to subtly pair his wines with fine food.

Other vintners followed suit. Wineries were no longer places to crush fruit; they became statements of an owner's connoisseurship. New wineries mimicked Etruscan temples, Greek monasteries, and French chateaus and gained as much fame for their gardens, art galleries, jazz festivals, tastings, and cooking schools as for their Chardonnays. Over twenty-five years, the number of Napa wineries grew from fewer than a dozen to more than one hundred. Owning a vineyard conferred instant status. Heirs to the du Pont and Swanson fortunes, celebrities, a sprinkling of physicians, a smattering of corporate executives — all flocked to the Napa and neighboring Sonoma Valley. Corporatization soon followed, with multinational concerns such as Nestlé, Coca-Cola, and the liquor conglomerate Heublein buying stakes in vineyards. The Napa became chic. Fabulous restaurants popped up. A wine tour of the region became a fashionable holiday. Millions came every year, guidebooks in hand, much to the disdain of locals. Before its trendification, the Napa had been a poor, working-class region. After, it polarized along class lines, as evidenced by the mix of battered pickup trucks and stretch limos that clogged the Valley's Highway 29.

Inevitably, money dramatically altered the character of the neighborhood, which measured only twenty-five by three and a half miles.
The price of premium land climbed to $40,000 (U.S.) an acre. Concerned
about conservation, residents had the area designated an agricultural
preserve, with strict standards governing purchase and use.

In 1992 Nichol embarked on what he would come to call his "seminal" Napa trip. In March, he and Terri enrolled at another cooking
course at Mondavi, this one taught by Claude and Michel Troisgros, the
sons of Pierre. On his second morning there, he walked through French
doors onto his private veranda at the Auberge du Soleil resort in Ruther-
ford, to survey the bucolic scene. The valley was golden-green in the
sunlight, the temperature seventy degrees. He had just got off the phone
with Anne Doremus, who told him Toronto was in the grip of a monster storm. "If I'm so smart," he asked himself, "why am I slugging
through snow in Toronto when I could live in paradise?"

This epiphany posed some logistical problems. A year earlier,
Galen Weston had offered Nichol a parcel of land at Windsor, his 416-
acre ocean-front development in Vero Beach, Florida. Windsor was
being constructed independently of the real estate arm of George Weston, IPCF Properties Inc., an acronym for "If pigs could fly." By the summer of 1992, half the development of 320 lots was complete. Fittingly
located between Disneyland and West Palm Beach, Windsor was an
enclave of mansions nestled around a lush golf course and polo field. It
was a millionaire's country club, described in the promotional literature
as "upholding the traditional values of the community." Residents spent
a minimum of $185,000 (U.S.) for a lot and were obliged to build with-
in two years. Alternatively, they could buy a lot complete with a house
for less than $500,000. Windsor was governed by strictly enforced archi-
tectural and urban design codes. All the houses adhered to the traditional styles of the southern United States and colonial Anglo-
Caribbean. Colors, materials, forms — all were regulated. Only archi-
tects from a select list were permitted on the site. Nichol had contracted
an architect to work on preliminary drawings.

The Vero Beach project presented a major dilemma for Nichol.
He knew that Weston expected his support, but Windsor's style wasn't

to his taste. Furthermore, Nichol detested Florida. It had a low-style quotient. In Napa, the residents knew the difference between Pinot Noir and Pinot Gris. In Florida, they lined up for all-you-can-eat seafood buffets and washed it all down with diet cola.

Nichol's resistance also reflected his antipathy toward the old money likely to be drawn to Windsor. He was far more comfortable with the exuberance of the nouveau riche. "There is nobody who has less desire to be part of the Canadian establishment than I have," he would mutter. "I would rather spend my day with my gardener than with the president of the University of Toronto," he said. "I avoid it. I mean, the only time I go to the Royal Winter Fair in my little duck suit is when it's a command performance by Galen. I am very proud of my very humble beginnings. That is what North America is all about. That is the great curse that England has imposed upon this country. Because there are still jerks in Canada who think they are a better class of people than a station agent's son, for no other reason than that six generations of them have gone to Upper Canada College."

Nichol had to choose between disappointing Weston and satisfying his craving to live in the Napa and maybe even bottle his own wine. He couldn't afford to build in both places. Paralyzed, he decided to call his new friend Michael Steele. Nichol and Steele had bonded instantly after meeting in the first-class lounge of Toronto's Pearson airport in January of that year. Steele had been sitting with his wife, Laura, when Nichol and Terri came in. "Isn't that Dave Nichol?" whispered Laura, a fan of President's Choice products. "Who cares?" Steele responded. Having observed the exchange, Nichol later approached the couple. "You're less than impressed with my presence, aren't you?" he asked Steele. When the flight was delayed, the two couples struck up a conversation.

Nichol was impressed with Steele's background. He had studied structural engineering at the University of Waterloo, worked for Labatt, and spent ten years designing luxury resort interiors for the likes of Ritz-Carlton and Marriott in Hawaii, Bermuda, and Whistler, British Columbia. The Steeles were on their honeymoon — a trip to seven Asian countries, featuring some of Nichol's favorite luxury resorts in the Far East. Coincidentally, both couples were planning to stay in Hawaii at the Lodge at Koele and at Manele Bay Hotel on the private Hawaii island of Lanai, once owned by Dole Pineapple. After he perused the itinerary, Nichol turned to Laura. "You're one lucky woman."

An entrepreneur, Steele was ever on the lookout for new opportunities and had bought the patent for a system he dubbed the Terminator — an internal secondary condenser targeted companies that were heavy users of air conditioning and refrigeration systems. Most of these used chlorofluorocarbons, which ultimately depleted the ozone layer. The Terminator employed technology that reduced the volume of refrigerant by up to 25% and cut maintenance costs by about 15% annually. Nichol put Steele in touch with Dick Currie and advised his new friend to appeal to Currie's sense of one-upmanship — that Loblaw should be the first to use the Terminator. Loblaw soon became one of Steele's biggest clients; each of twenty stores bought one hundred Terminators. Loblaw executives, including Currie and Nichol, had Terminators installed in their homes.

Shortly after, Nichol asked Steele if he wanted to take a golfing holiday near Weston's Vero Beach development. There, he had Steele examine the architectural plans for his house. "This isn't for you," Steele told Nichol. "Unless you want a place that looks like something out of 'Gone with the Wind.'"

The comment strengthened Nichol's resolve to move to the Napa. He hired Van Moller, a real estate agent in the Valley. Moller began looking in the Stags Leap District, its most desirable section. Stags Leap had gained international renown during the Paris tastings of 1976, when California wines were surreptitiously entered into blind tastings with French vintages. The winner was a 1973 Cabernet Sauvignon from Stag's Leap Wine Cellars, a winery founded the previous year by Warren and Barbara Winiarski.

Moller located forty acres along the Silverado Trail, next to the Winiarskis' estate and overlooking the respected Chimney Rock Winery. The property was owned by Martin Blumberg, a vintner who ran the wine shop Groezingers in nearby Yountville. Blumberg had lived in the Valley since 1959 and had watched as hundreds of wealthy people arrived, all seeking exclusivity and a temperate climate. He referred to this influx as the "Falcon Crest syndrome" after a glossy TV soap opera set in the Napa. The clichéd joke in Napa was that all you needed to make a small fortune was to begin with a big one.

Even though only eight acres were plantable, Blumberg's property possessed some of the finest vineyards in the valley. Its elevation was hugely desirable, and it had to that point eluded the phylloxera blight that was decimating the region. The location also boasted residual snob appeal: the neighborhood was crammed with multimillionaires and billionaires. Mrs. Walt Disney ran the respected Silverado Vineyards across the road. Film producer Francis Ford Coppola operated the Niebaum-Coppola Estate Winery down the road. Romance writer Danielle Steele had a house nearby. You couldn't get much more Californian than that.

The Nichols visited the site in April and were immediately transfixed. It overlooked the valley, a green and gold quilt of cultivated earth. The landscape was addictive, always different, at once lush and austere, redolent of Arcadia, a luxurious paradise whose primitive beauty had been tamed by man to harness the pleasure of the grape. Eight hillside acres were planted with the classic Bordeaux blend of Cabernet Sauvignon, Cabernet Franc, Merlot, and Petit Verdot grapes. "When I walked through the site," Nichol said, "it felt like home." Nichol made one high bid for the property, an offer he figured Blumberg wouldn't turn down. There was no negotiation. Blumberg, conscious that the tone of the neighborhood be preserved, ran a check on Nichol. He passed. According to the deed, Nichol bought the property for just under $1 million (U.S.) cash in September 1992.

Nichol still had to resolve the Vero Beach issue. The tension gnawed at him. By his own admission, it nearly drove him into a nervous breakdown. Eventually, he announced his plans. Weston was disappointed in his old friend, but Nichol forged ahead, asking Steele to oversee the planning in the Napa. Nichol's original conceit was to copy Robert Mondavi, whose 9,000-square-foot house contained only one bedroom. Steele treated the development as if it were a luxury resort. The blueprints included an epic wine cellar, a movie theater, and more than 12,000 square feet on one level, with three bedrooms and a guesthouse. By Napa standards, where houses ran 25,000 square feet, this wasn't a major project. But it made The Dome seem like a minor renovation. "You could fit three Domes in the front entrance," Steele said. "This will be an *Architectural Digest* house," he reassured Nichol.

Steele estimated it would take two years and $3 million to build Nichol's retirement dream. Although only twenty-five building permits were given out annually in the Napa, Nichol was confident he could get one and set about trying to ingratiate himself into the community, which was notoriously hostile to newcomers. Despite the Napa's recent pedigree, winemaking in the region was governed by an old-boys' network. Nichol planned to build a tasting lab, either on site or in nearby St. Helena, that would develop products for retailers around the world. He and Terri designed the details for the house together. Their only major disagreement erupted over the style of the front door. Nichol wanted etched glass panels with back lighting, illuminating a vineyard tableau. Terri found the idea vulgar. They argued all the way back to nearby San Francisco. That night, on the way to dinner at Zuni Café, they noticed wooden doors with glass panel inserts. They decided that would work. Steele created a maquette of the finished house, with stone terraces, wood trim, and slate roof. The grounds included a lap pool with a cascading waterfall on one side. When Nichol saw the scale model, he dubbed it "Tuscany meets Kyoto," echoing a category of President's Choice sauces. This, after all, was the president's ultimate choice.

Nichol agreed to share the harvest with Blumberg and took an interest in Blumberg's 1990 and 1991 harvests, which where under contract to be produced at Monticello Cellars. Then he called Jim White. "I need help," he said. "I just bought the winery, and I've got stuff in wood. I need you to get out there tomorrow to blend it." White, eager to please, left for California the next day. White prided himself on his tasting prowess. The first time he had lunch at Noodles with Nichol, the men ordered wine by the glass. When it was served, White took one sip and said: "Dave, this isn't what we ordered." The waiter later confirmed White's analysis, with apologies.

Blending his own "reserve" vintage was a vanity rather than a profit project. Nichol had no aspirations to process wine on the property — that would cost millions. He would follow the private-label methodology and use someone else's capacity. White mixed sixty-five blends, and returned to Toronto with six bottles he believed would meet Nichol's taste specifications. By November 1992, a truckload of Memories of Napa was en route to Canada.

But back in Toronto, Nichol was becoming increasingly restless. He roamed the corridors of LIM. His staff noticed that he had lost vigor. In part, this was the result of the huge machine LIM had become. It was impossible for him to control everything. He busied himself with his next big project: the tenth anniversary *Insider's Report* and *The Dave Nichol Cookbook*. He had been courted for years by publishers to produce such a book, but had always turned them down, wanting to keep control. Now that his days at Loblaw were numbered, he realized it was time.

He could see that the name Dave Nichol had achieved almost a brand status of its own. Eager to test the concept beyond the supermarket, he turned his attention to President's Choice clothing. As always, the products were knock-offs. This time he borrowed from New York designer Nicole Miller, who had had great success selling silk clothing printed with brightly colored images of well-known consumer brands and logos. Designer Roger Edwards was hired to fashion a PC line of silk separates, including a short-sleeved shirt, dressing gown, boxer shorts, baseball cap, bomber jacket, bow tie, and cummerbund from black silk printed with garish graphics of President's Choice cookie packages.

Appropriately, the line was picked up by a Weston holding, the exclusive Holt Renfrew chain. Nichol went to the front lines to flog it. Two weeks before Christmas 1992, Nichol made a scheduled appearance in the men's department of Holt's flagship store in midtown Toronto, wearing a President's Choice shirt, black pants, and brown suede cowboy boots. Terri stood by his side — in leggings and a custom-order black suede jacket lined with the PC silk cookie motif.

The clothing deviated from his proven formula of providing a comparable product at a lower price. A baseball hat cost $45. A short-sleeved shirt was $195, a bomber jacket $300. Bow ties were $45, a bathrobe $245. Few bought, more gawked. "You are just wonderful," one middle-aged woman gushed. "I love all of your products." Nichol smiled and shook her hand, clearly uncomfortable. "Have you tried my new eggnog?" he asked. "Only 13% calories from fat."

A middle-aged couple approached him. "We live in Montreal but drive into Ontario to buy your products," the woman said shyly. "We were so disappointed when you didn't buy Steinberg."

"What do you like best?" Nichol quizzed them.

"The cookies, the café au lait, the sundried tomato purée, but not the one with black beans in it," she told him. He asked if they thought the products would sell in Quebec. Loblaw has no stores in the province. "Definitely," the couple answered in unison.

Gerry and Nancy Pencer arrived, Nigel Argent, Pencer's driver, in tow. Pencer whipped off his coat and tried on a bathrobe. "As my father would say, Ger, it's rich but not gaudy," Nichol laughed. Pencer held up a pair of large boxer shorts. "Do you think these would fit me?" he called out. He ended up buying three pairs of boxers and a bathrobe.

Over the two hours, Nichol found himself flagging. The night before, he and Terri had hosted the LIM Christmas party under The Dome. Nichol had fallen asleep. Staff had raided his wine cellar. He woke up annoyed. "After the first bottle, it's all plonk," he said. Now, at Holts, he was anxious, contemplative — a state induced, in part, by hangover.

He knew he was nearing a turning point. He was buoyed by the success of PC beer outside the supermarket, but at heart he did not care about beer. If it bombed, he said, it wouldn't really matter. His focus was on his goal for 1993: his assault on the U.S. market. Winners focused, losers sprayed; that's what grocery retailer Stew Leonard always said. Nichol feared he was becoming overexposed, that he was beginning to repeat himself. There was only so long you could flog cookies and salsa and barbecue sauce — even if you were Dave Nichol. He knew his identity had been constructed around food, yet he couldn't resist branching out beyond, to the President's Choice clothing, to a line of wines, maybe even his own television cooking show.

Extending his impimatur to wine was especially appealing. He and Jim White had earlier discussed selling relatively inexpensive wines to unsophisticated consumers who had come to trust Nichol's judgment in cookies and colas. That had planted the idea in his mind to edit the wines of the world for insecure yet eager wine neophytes.

It was not Nichol's first foray into the wine trade. In 1986, he had tangled with the provincially run Liquor Control Board of Ontario after the Christmas *Insider's Report* announced that wines from the Inniskillin Winery in Niagara-on-the-Lake, Ontario, could be ordered through Loblaws stores in Toronto, Ottawa, and London. The board reminded Loblaw executives that they were not licenced to sell wines. The offer was quickly retracted.

A few years later, Nichol teamed up with Donald Ziraldo, the gregarious president of Inniskillin, to develop wines for the President's Choice label. The two men arranged thirty tastings, but nothing appealed to Nichol. Napa had cachet and romance; Ontario was Ontario. And there was a further obstacle to President's Choice wine: another Niagara Falls winery, Brights, produced a sparkling wine called President and had the trademark on that name. Undeterred by these setbacks, or by his lack of experience in the wine business, Nichol called Eric Calladine, who operated California Wine Imports in Toronto. Calladine, who dealt in high-end wineries, had been importing wines for Nichol since Nichol called him up earlier that year for a Kistler Chardonnay he couldn't buy in Ontario. Nichol asked Calladine to start looking for a winery that could supply a private-label wine.

Meanwhile, Nichol was busy promoting his Memories of Napa Cabernet in Toronto restaurants. Even his fifty-third birthday celebration on February 9, 1993, was in part a marketing endeavor. That evening, he and Terri joined Don Watt, who was turning fifty-seven, to celebrate their joint birthdays at Centro, a fashionable Toronto restaurant. Among the guests were Don and Patty Watt, accompanied by their eighteen-year-old daughter, Sarah, Nichol's goddaughter; Gerry Pencer, this time solo — Nancy Pencer, was in hospital recovering from back surgery; and Jim and Carol White. White was under contract to Cott, developing new products for U.S. retailers. Carol White had been hired to edit *The Dave Nichol Cookbook*. The group was joined by Centro's owners, Franco and Barbara Prevedello.

The extravagant menu was standard fare to the food-obsessed group. The meal began with marinated salmon and oysters followed by a salad of seasonal bitter greens with sliced breast of partridge and foie gras from Quebec dressed with balsamic vinegar and grape seed oil. The next course was a tian of lobster in a carefully constructed ring of layers that included baby spinach, porcini mushrooms, ratatouille of seasonal vegetables, and fresh lobster finished with lobster butter sauce. This was followed by a wild mushroom risotto with hedgehog, porcini and black trumpet mushrooms, alongside a rack of lamb served with braised Savoy cabbage and grilled peppers. Dessert was a chocolate fudge brownie layered with raspberries, strawberries, and blackberries topped with sabayon flavored with Muscat.

The party began with several Chardonnays, which the diners critiqued while they sipped. The main course was accompanied by Nichol's own 1990 reserve. He had brought two magnums for Prevedello's approval. Centro needed another Californian Cabernet like a vineyard needs phylloxera. But Prevedello was a shrewd businessman and Nichol was a faithful and influential customer. The restaurateur judged the wine young, but well-blended, and decided to try it out in two or three restaurants.

Nichol also used a bizarre cross-promotion with Toronto's Sutton Place Kempinski Hotel to present his wine publicly. The hotel agreed to showcase an *Insider's Report* special menu for two weeks in April. The notion of going to a restaurant to eat food that could be purchased in the supermarket pushed the acceptance of President's Choice to its outer limit. Then again, the hotel was in financial trouble and willing to do almost anything for publicity.

In February, Jim White and Eric Calladine flew to California to seek candidates for Nichol's wine venture. They tasted forty reds and whites, most of them from the Napa. The challenge, as usual, was to find the quality they wanted from a winery that could supply the volumes they required at a price that assured certain margins. They returned with twenty candidates; Nichol rejected them all. Scouring the wine press, Calladine found a piece in *Wine Spectator* by wine critic Robert Parker listing "best buys" under $10. One was by R.H. Phillips, a well-known producer of wines in Yolo County, on the other side of the Napa, where land sold for $1,000 an acre. Nichol had great respect for Parker. His endorsement on the label would provide Nichol with a hook for his version of the wine. What would it matter if the novice wine buyer was oblivious to the specific vintage Parker had tasted? It was the same brand name, and that was what counted.

At the same time, Nichol was tasting potential Australian wines. In May, Calladine visited Nichol's back yard for a blind taste comparison. They used Bin 65, a popular wine produced by the Australian winery Lindeman, as the benchmark. The Phillips Chardonnay stood up well. Nichol was less pleased with the Cabernet, but recognized that negotiating for both the red and the white would offer him more clout at Phillips. Calladine returned to California to hammer out an agreement. Their goal was to have the wine in Ontario liquor stores by Christmas.

As Nichol extended his scope of endeavor beyond Loblaw, significant changes were underway within. In April 1993, Currie organized a massive shake-up of Intersave. John Thompson, a long-time Loblaw numbers man, was put in charge of the division. Nichol was busy traveling the continent with Pencer proselytizing about premium private label. It had become the story of the year. Loblaw's competitors, A&P and Oshawa Group, had introduced their own upscale corporate labels, not unlike President's Choice. A&P introduced the Master Choice line in the United States in 1988, and followed up with a Canadian launch in late 1989 with 136 SKUs (supermarket slang for store-counted units). Ladka Sweeney left Loblaw at the end of 1991 to head up product development. In June 1993, Oshawa Group launched Our Compliments line with cola, salsa, corn chips, a chocolate chip cookie — all of the big categories. In its product development, Oshawa Group followed the more traditional methology of focus groups and panels of tasters. Executives at both chains denied that President's Choice had been the model for their lines. In March 1993, Nichol gave the keynote address at the Private Label Manufacturing Conference in Miami. In May, he spoke in Chicago to a group of grocery retailers. "The expression private label should be expunged from the lexicon forever," he declared. He proposed changing it to "retailer-created and controlled brands," a phrase coined by Pencer and Watt. In June, he spoke at the New York brokerage Oppenheimer & Co. on the investment potential of the private-label revolution. Oppenheimer was a primary underwriter of Cott stock in the United States.

By this time, Cott's shares had become a favorite Wall Street tout as U.S. institutions bought large blocks of stock. Bay Street was far less enthusiastic. It hadn't forgotten Pencer's Financial Trustco fiasco. Indeed, as a stock play, Cott made Financial Trustco look like a lemonade stand. By the summer of 1993, Cott Corp. had close to 58 million shares outstanding, which at their then trading price gave the company a total market value, or capitalization, of $2.3 billion. Five years earlier, it had been $12 million. Revenues in 1992 reached $331 million; per share earnings were 25 cents.

Ironically, investors placed a higher value on Cott than on George Weston, which had a stock market value of $1.9 billion and much higher revenues of $11.6 billion, or of Loblaw Companies, which had a market capitalization of $1.7 billion on revenues of $9.2 billion. The market was clearly betting on Cott's growth potential. In light of Weston's results, this was hardly surprising. In 1992, Weston reported its lowest profits in more than a decade — $48 million on sales of $11.6 billion. Galen Weston stood before shareholders at the annual meeting and apologized for the company's lackluster performance.

Inevitably, Cott's rapid rise became the subject of Bay Street speculation. On occasion, the stock traded at 150 times its per-share earnings, a phenomenally high multiple given that a price-earning ratio of 20 was considered average. Cott's supporters scoffed at suggestions the stock was grossly overvalued, but experienced market players began waiting for gravity to exert itself. Cott became a target for short sellers, professional investors who bet that a stock's price will decline, rather than increase, in value. The short seller borrows shares of a company and promptly sells them. Then he waits for the price of the stock to fall, which allows him to repurchase the borrowed shares at the lower price and return them, pocketing the price difference. If a stock fails to drop in value, short sellers find themselves in what's known as a squeeze.

In the summer of 1993, a catalyst for short selling appeared in the person of small-time Toronto fund manager Larry Woods. Woods, who grew up in the tough east end of Hamilton, Ontario, had been a teacher, school principal, and government bureaucrat before turning to stock analysis. And he understood how things could go awry in the market. In

1991, he had been fined for insider trading of Petco, a small manufacturing company, of which he was a director. Later, his conviction was stiffened on appeal from a $50,000 fine to a ninety-day jail term, to be served on weekends.

Woods wrote several analyses of Cott. In the first, he frightened many investors and analysts by claiming to see similarities between Cott and Financial Trustco — the same meteoric revenue growth, the same stellar stock performance, even the same accounting team of auditors, Coopers & Lybrand in Toronto. Woods was particularly critical of Cott's accounting practices and maintained that Cott was inflating assets and downplaying expenses to paint a more positive picture of the company than it deserved. He also started looking at Dave Nichol's friendship with Gerry Pencer and asking whether there was anything about it that should make Cott investors nervous.

While the short sellers prayed for a reversal of Cott's fortunes that could give them a big payday, Nichol looked to Cott as his own ticket to wealth. Nichol was impressed that Pencer, a lowly supplier, was much wealthier than he was. Moreover, it seemed everyone associated with Pencer had already become stunningly rich. "I've made more money in this last year than Dave Nichol has made in his career," Don Watt boasted in 1993. That same year, reports filed with the Ontario Securities Commission revealed that insiders (those on the Cott board of directors, senior officers, or owners of more than 10% of the outstanding shares) had earned $115 million selling Cott shares. Gerry Pencer alone had sold $29.3 million in Cott stock since 1991. His brothers, Bill and Sam, had made $33.4 million and $17.4 million respectively. Heather Reisman had made $1.7 million, Don Watt $1.5 million. Even Jim White, Nichol's former right hand, had become a millionaire through Cott stock. Yet Dave Nichol was still on salary, taking orders from Dick Currie. As salaries go it was handsome — take-home pay of $710,000 and $294,913 in bonuses for a total package of $1,004,913. This did not include an undisclosed expense allowance covering first-class travel that ran into hundreds of thousands each year. Still, Nichol saw himself to be underappreciated and undercompensated. Nichol had been hurt by a remark Galen Weston had made in an interview with the

Toronto Star in early June. "Dave Nichol has launched more failed products than anyone I know," Weston said. "On the other hand, he has launched more products than anyone in the history of the world." That it was true didn't make it any less stinging to Nichol.

In late summer of 1993, he had it out again with Galen Weston. The unofficial break had been established with Nichol's decision to build in the Napa Valley in 1992. Then, in early 1993, Nichol discussed his plans to leave with John Thompson and Dick Currie. He and Weston hashed out his future again during their talk at Fort Belvedere, Weston's English estate, in July 1993. Even so, both Weston and Currie refused to believe that Nichol would leave the fold. Weston knew how much Nichol hated change and that, for all his bravado, he eschewed risk. This is reflected in a conversation which insiders claim was the final Nichol-Weston negotiation.

"Galen, I'm worth a lot more to you than you're paying me," Nichol said. It was an opinion Weston had heard before.

"You're right," Weston responded calmly. "You're worth $1.5 million annually plus expenses."

But Weston was grossly underestimating his friend's sense of self-worth. His number wasn't close to what Nichol wanted to hear. Nichol had told his inner circle his minimum value was $5 million a year.

Weston thought Nichol was grandstanding. "You'll never walk, Dave."

"You're wrong, Galen," Nichol responded.

"Dave, Dave, be reasonable," Weston said. "I'll give you $2 million a year."

"It's too late, Galen." Weston raised the amount to $3 million, but Nichol had stopped listening. He knew Weston couldn't possibly pay him more than he paid Dick Currie. "This is my last shot," Nichol told friends. "I could never afford my dreams as a salary man. They could never pay me enough."

Nichol claimed to feel relief at the prospect of leaving the Weston conglomerate. "I was never comfortable working for Galen," he said. "The two relationships were like oil and water. When we spent leisure time together, I had to be careful about what I said. I always was aware

I was talking to my boss." Nichol knew his actions had hurt Weston, who placed a high value on loyalty. He remembered the surprise fiftieth birthday party he and Hilary had thrown for Weston in November 1990. They had planned it secretly. Weston had arrived at Nichol's house in casual clothes, believing they were going out for dinner at a local seafood restaurant. "It's remarkable, you know," he said to Nichol, "that people who were friends at university could remain so close over the years."

Attempting to put a positive gloss on his defection, Nichol claimed that it might strengthen their relationship. "If it doesn't," he said, shrugging, "then there wasn't much of a relationship to begin with." He seemed to have forgotten that Weston's support had made him a grocery superstar, had given him the shelf space to display his creations, and had thrown $20 million a year into LIM to fund product development. Could Gerry Pencer promise that kind of financial backup?

By mutual agreement, it was decided that Nichol would stay on until after the tenth anniversary edition of the *Insider's Report* in November 1993. Then, he would quietly ease his way out of the company. By November, a rumor that Nichol might be leaving Loblaw had become hot industry gossip, in part because of growing speculation about his relationship with Gerry Pencer.

Galen Weston's attention at this time was focused on his life as Canada's most regal billionaire. There were his duties as president of the Royal Winter Fair to attend to. He also had to find the time to squire Princess Margaret around the Donna Karan boutique at Holt Renfrew while she was in Toronto to open the Fair. The month earlier, the Westons had attended the marriage of the princess's son, the Viscount Linley, in London. Then he had to pose with Hilary in evening wear for a photo spread accompanying an article about the Weston's Vero Beach project that was to run in the May issue of *Vanity Fair*. The usually publicity-shy Weston agreed to the story to drum up a bit of interest in Windsor. Sales were not as good as he had hoped.

Being a member of the working rich could have its drawbacks. While Weston had hired his managers wisely, there was always the risk that he was left outside the loop. "The problem with Galen," says one long-time associate, "was that he wanted to run the business responsibly but he also enjoyed having the Prince of Jaipur's ear."

On November 16, Bud Jorgensen, then a reporter with the *Globe and Mail*, called George Weston's legal counsel, John Stevenson of Smith Lyons in Toronto. He told Stevenson he was writing a story about Nichol leaving Loblaw to work at Cott. He repeated some of the rumors he had heard. Stevenson downplayed the rumors, explaining that Nichol was well-compensated and that there would be no reason to leave for money. Three days later, Jorgensen called back to say he was going to print the rumors, including one that Nichol had been compensated by Cott financially, while Cott was supplying products to Loblaw — an accusation Nichol and others at Loblaw (even his enemies) dismissed as ridiculous. "Dave Nichol has an impeccable sense of morality," said one Loblaw executive. "I could never see him doing anything remotely unethical," said another. "He is a man you can trust at his word."

Still, Galen Weston hated even the whiff of scandal. The situation reached its crescendo the day before the tenth anniversary *Insider's Report* was to be released. Weston called Nichol to tell him that they should preempt the *Globe* story by issuing a press release announcing his intended departure at year-end. Weston's office drafted the release, then sent it to Nichol. Anne Doremus typed it up in shock. It was the first indication she'd had that Nichol intended to leave.

The final release, unsigned, announced that Nichol would leave Loblaw at the end of 1993 to set up a personal consulting company with his wife Terri to create unique foods and related products for manufacturers and retailers. There was also mention of the wine venture based at his Napa Valley vineyard. He would continue to sit on the boards of Loblaw Companies and George Weston Limited, serve as a consultant to the President's Choice line, and act as spokesman for the brand.

The memo was seen as a compromise for both sides. Some Loblaw executives saw Nichol as being on probation — his behavior over the next few months would determine whether he stayed on the Weston board. Nichol told friends the move was without risk; if he failed, Loblaw would take him back. Yet this was not how Nichol wanted the news announced. He had lost control. The press release also detracted from the tenth anniversary *Insider's Report*. Nichol went home, exhausted. "I needed to lick my wounds," he said.

The next morning, he appeared at an east end Toronto store to sign *The Dave Nichol Cookbook* for adoring fans. The glossy, 335-page production contained almost two hundred recipes, all requiring President's Choice products as primary ingredients. It also exposed Nichol's completely consumer-referential life, with its lists of his favorite stores, favorite restaurants, even his favorite creature comforts (a great shower, a featherbed, The Dome, French bulldogs, Gravol, and Shahtoosh, an expensive fine cloth made from the neck hair of the ibex goat) for the diehard Dave Nichol groupies.

Loblaw shoppers eagerly lined up to pay $9.95 for what was in essence a promotional item. Loblaw had never intended to make money on it; the idea was to show people how to use President's Choice products. But when production costs began spiraling, as they usually did when Nichol was in charge, Loblaw turned to suppliers whose products were mentioned to subsidize its production.

At his in-store appearance, Nichol had been scheduled to stay for two hours, but lineups kept him there for four. He signed more than 1,000 books. Earlier, he had presented black, vinyl-bound versions of the cookbook to friends and associates. Gerry Pencer's copy was inscribed by Nichol with the words, "To Abraham Lincoln," a coded allusion to the fact that Nichol viewed Pencer as his emancipator from a life of slavery at Loblaw.

Most LIM employees were shocked to read news of Nichol's departure in the weekend newspapers. The following Monday, Nichol met with the staff of each department. He told them nothing would change, and that he would be in the office three days a week. The practical impossibility of maintaining alliances with both Loblaw and Cott was made evident later that week, when *USA Today* published an article on Watt, Nichol, and Pencer, calling the trio "big league, cross-border terrorists," leading the private-label revolution from the cheesy no-frills image of the 1970s. The story, prepared in August, noted that "Nichol — who is expected to leave Loblaw next month to set up his own private label consulting firm — Watt, and Pencer are setting up their assault on RJR Nabisco, Coca-Cola, and Anheuser-Busch." While acknowledging that the trio were still minor players in America's $26.4-billion private-label arena, it predicted that President's Choice and Cott "could be major U.S. powerhouses in food and beverages by decade's end." When senior Loblaw executives saw the piece, "they went ape," one official recalls.

Two weeks after the announcement that Nichol was leaving Loblaw, 146 liquor stores across Ontario began stocking Dave Nichol's Personal Selection wines. The Liquor Control Board of Ontario had purchased 7,000 cases of Chardonnay and 5,000 cases of the Cabernet, in expectation of strong sales. Space on LCBO shelves is tougher to obtain than shelf space in a supermarket. More than 95% of applications for new listings are rejected. In addition to chemical and taste standards, the LCBO wanted a sales strategy and some assurance that the wine would be promoted. If sales quotas are met, the wine keeps its listing.

Wine merchants don't pay outright for shelf space at the LCBO, as food manufacturers do in supermarkets. Instead, the money a supplier is willing to spend on marketing and promotion, combined with brand loyalty, ultimately dictates who gets listed and how a wine is displayed. Popular wines are given the best shelf positions and the greatest number of facings. "The Gallos of this world determine their shelf positions," comments an LCBO manager, a reference to Ernest & Julio Gallo, the largest winemaker in North America, with 1993 sales of $800 million.

Getting the wines in the stores for the busy holiday season had taken months of work on Calladine's part. Calladine, who had begun presentations to the board in July, won them over with promises of newspaper ads and back-lit transparencies featuring Nichol in the stores. He also purchased preferential displays at aisle ends and next to cash registers. Ironically, Nichol had to market himself in the wine store the way brand names sold themselves in the supermarket. Nichol and Calladine wanted to keep the price under $10, a psychological barrier in the wine market. More than half of wines sold by the LCBO were under $10. In the end, however, Nichol's Personal Selection wines were priced at $10.95. If the wine had been imported directly from R.J. Phillips, local wine importers estimated, it might have sold for about $8. The price of imported wines often rose more than 300% after taxes and margins are factored in. That meant a wine imported for less than $4 sells for $11 or more.

The LCBO nurtured great expectations for Nichol's wines. A management memo to store managers requested that the wine be given prominent display. That Nichol had elbowed his way into the Christmas buying season generated some grousing from other importers. Fielding the complaints, David Wilcox, vice-president of merchandising, said Nichol was a trusted name, which assured sales. Cardboard cutouts of Nichol and Georgie Girl in tuxedos, a champagne flute in his hand, were set up in the stores. Nichol, in three-dimensional form, also appeared at in-store tastings.

Nichol's game plan was to copy the formula used to market The Decadent cookie. If he could make his wine the best-selling Chardonnay in Ontario, Calladine could leverage that popularity elsewhere. He began decrying the brand tax on wine and liquor necessitated by the high marketing costs of brands like Absolut. He seemed to forget that without a distribution network, he too would be required to play the game. Still, he was confident that his success in food could be transferred to wine. "I don't just stand for food," he told a writer for *Winetidings*. "I stand for great value. I stand for quality. I stand for style."

But the wine business posed obstacles for Nichol that he had not faced in the food industry. For one, the gargantuan ego that made Nichol unique in the staid supermarket business did not differentiate him in the haughty world of wine. For another, he lacked control over production. Unlike processed foods, wine is a mercurial product, subject to the whims of Nature. Vintners are at the mercy of a host of variables, from sun to rain, from soil quality to pestilence. There was no such thing as a "bad year" for The Decadent Chocolate Chip Cookie or a poor harvest for PC Diet Cola. Most significantly, though, Nichol lacked access to the distribution channels in wine that gave him clout in the food industry.

However, a series of deals that mirrored Nichol's involvement in the wine trade was about to change that. In March 1992, a group of Toronto investors made an offer to buy the country's largest wine producer, T.G. Bright & Co. Ltd. of Niagara Falls, Ontario. The group was fronted by Leland Verner, a long-time Bay Street promoter who ran Hendron Financial Group, an outfit that specialized in management buy-outs. Brights, which produced popular though not critically acclaimed wines, had annual sales of $75 million. The company had been for sale since 1990. Verner, whose family had founded Jordan Wines, which had been sold to Brights in 1986, had previously engaged in unsuccessful buy-out talks with the company.

In April 1992, Verner joined members of Brights management acting independently of the winery and a group of unnamed investors, including the Ontario Teachers Pension Plan Board. This group incorporated a company known simply as 984478 Ontario Ltd. On December 3, 1992, the company changed its name to Wine Acquisition Inc. and soon after declared its desire for Brights. The company made a bid for 80% of Brights, paying $20 a share in February 1993. (The remainder was owned by Andrés Wines Ltd. [16.1%] and outside interests [3.9%].) A complicated takeover battle ensued. Control of the company was handed over in April 1993.

The offer of purchase revealed that the deal's banker was Gerry Schwartz, chairman of Onex Corp., long-time Pencer pal and business partner. According to the document, all Wine Acquisition's common shares were owned by Bacco Holdings Ltd., a wholly owned subsidiary of Vinexpra, which was wholly owned by Leland Verner. Financing for Vinexpra would be provided by Verner and other private investors. The majority of this financing was a loan from a private company controlled by Schwartz, who, under certain circumstances, could become the controlling shareholder of Vinexpra. The language of the purchase agreement reflected Cott's retailer-branded philosophy: "The Offeror intends to expand Brights business beyond its existing markets and plans to enter the private label segment and manufacture its products to be sold under retailer branded names."

In September 1992, Brights shareholders approved the takeover. In November Brights merged with Ontario wine producers Inniskillin & Cartier to form the largest wine company in Canada, with $130 million in annual sales. The combined strength allowed the companies to merge marketing efforts and to plan an assault on the United States. The pur-

THE EDIBLE MAN

chase also provided distribution through Inniskillin & Cartier's 131 Wine Rack company stores in Ontario, where wineries were permitted to operate their own stores.

Don Ziraldo, the president of Inniskillin & Cartier, was enthusiastic about the assistance his new partners could provide in selling to the U.S. market, which he called the "impenetrable free market. Now that I'm working with Schwartz and Pencer, it should be a lot easier," he says.

Gerry Pencer had what he termed "not a big interest" in Wine Acquisition Inc. through a small private investment company he ran with Schwartz. Ironically, years earlier, Coca-Cola had bought and then, after discovering wine profits pale next to those from cola, sold to Joseph E. Seagram & Co. two wine producers, Sterling Vineyards and Monterey Vineyard in the Salinas Valley. Wine didn't much interest Pencer. He didn't see it as a major profit center, and he preferred the taste of Cott cola. But he was willing to cater somewhat to Nichol's obsession, and the two men even joked about Pencer buying the famed Chimney Rock winery, located next to Nichol's land. Even so, Brights was rife with Cott-ites. Stephen Halperin, a Goodman & Goodman lawyer who sat on Cott's board and Pencer's brother-in-law, was named a Brights director in May 1993. (Halperin was one Cott director who made $1 million in Cott stock.) Jim White was hired to consult on marketing and product development.

At Loblaw, employees were instructed not to talk to the press about Nichol's departure. "We're a private company," explained Loblaw counsel John McCullough. When reminded that Weston was in fact a public company, McCullough corrected himself. "Well, most of the shares are owned by Weston," he said. Still, it was a telling remark, indicative of the closed shop that Loblaw and Weston had become.

In December, Nichol quietly stepped down from the Weston and Loblaw boards after his financial and legal advisers warned him of potential conflict of interests. It would be improper for him to sit on any Loblaw or Weston board if he were involved in business with Weston or Loblaw competitors. Nichol's consulting contract with Loblaw operated on a month-to-month basis. "That way, if either one of us changes our minds, it won't be difficult to get out of," he explained. The true measure of Nichol's reduced standing at Loblaw, however, was laid bare in a seemingly small gesture — one that anyone familiar with corporate life will recognize as the greatest indignity of all. They took away his parking spot.

CHAPTER SEVENTEEN

"THE DAVE NICHOL THING"

O n January 1, 1994, the de-Nicholizing of Loblaw began. First the name change. Loblaw International Merchants was renamed Loblaw Brands Ltd. No one informed Nichol; he learned about it when he called in to Anne Doremus one morning. Loblaw Brands merged the old LIM and Intersave buying arm into two new divisions headed by John Thompson. The Corporate Brands division, managed by Rob Chenaux, formerly of Intersave, was responsible for all aspects of product development, including quality assurance, package design, and product sourcing. It also took over development and sourcing of Sam's American Choice and Great Value labels for Wal-Mart. Chenaux had been one of the bright young men recruited by Nichol in the early seventies. He had come to Loblaw in 1975 from Nestlé's headquarters in Vevey, Switzerland. Intersave had also undergone a shakeup. Doug Lunau had left in October 1992 to run Beta Brands Ltd., a public company that specializes in manufacturing food for private-label clients. In early 1994, a prominent seafood buyer resigned, amid industry rumors that he had been accepting kickbacks.

The new International Division headed up by Tom Stephens would handle the sales of Loblaw corporate brands to retailers in the United States and offshore. Thompson sent a form letter to suppliers explaining that the changes were intended to "increase efficiency, simplify the organization and maintain effectiveness."

Loblaw Brands' management professed total commitment to continuing and expanding the President's Choice program, although there were mutterings that part of the Memories line, one of Nichol's fixations, would receive the heave-ho. It was believed both within the company and the industry the President's Choice brand had enough of a profile to thrive without Nichol's personal endorsement. Even so, Nichol's involvement — or the lack of it — was handled gingerly. No one knew exactly how much of President's Choice popularity or Loblaw traffic was attributable to shoppers' faith in Nichol. Paradoxically, much of Nichol's appeal to shoppers came from the false belief that he was above corporate interests, that he was motivated by good taste, not profit. In fact, some customers naïvely voiced irritation that *The Dave Nichol Cookbook* contained too many President's Choice items.

There was no illusion that Nichol could be replaced. It came down to personality. No one else was as abrasive in his quest to get things done or as obsessive about quality. Nichol's departure inspired an almost defiant attitude among staff. Paul Uys says he was motivated to improve the quality of products, to prove that the network could survive without Nichol. But others complain that without Nichol much of the energy had been sapped out of the place. "He may have been a bully," said one Loblaw employee. "But he pushed everyone to the limit and created a lot of enthusiasm." Loblaw Brands' management was acutely aware of the issue. "We have to be very sensitive about how we handle the Dave Nichol thing," one said. Nichol's role within the new structure was unclear to everyone, including himself.

Meanwhile, speculation continued over the nature of his financial relationship with Pencer, much of it fueled by the short sellers who by this time were in constant contact with the media. A *Globe and Mail* story in January examined Cott's practices in buying shelf space and setting up preferential arrangements with clients. Cash payments, essentially discounts paid in advance to retailers, were common in the supermarket business. Cott preferred to call these "prepaid contract costs" and list them as assets, rather than expenses, on its balance sheet. This was an unusual practice, though within general accounting guidelines.

According to the *Globe*, the wife and son of John Dunne, chief executive of Great Atlantic & Pacific Tea of Toronto, held sizable interests in Cott stock. Cott supplied A&P in Canada with products in its Master Choice line. Records revealed that Dunne's wife held shares worth $412,500; his son owned shares valued at $148,000. Rumors flew that A&P executives had been advised of the Dunnes' share ownership by Loblaw officials. As for Nichol, he repeatedly denied owning stock in Cott, either directly or indirectly, while employed at Loblaw. "If anybody can find out where this money is buried," he joked, "I'll share half of it with them."

The Cott short sellers were pushing for more disclosure. The number of shares held by short sellers on the over-the-counter Nasdaq exchange climbed from 1.86 million in October 1993 to over 8 million in June 1994. The pressure was on for Cott to fail. In October, the short sellers received a bad-news boost when a group of U.S. investors launched a class-action suit against Cott and senior officers, alleging that the share price had been artificially pumped up between July 19, 1993, and January 18, 1994. During that time, Cott shares had climbed in New York from $24 in July to $49.62 in October, before falling to $23.50.

Alleging that Cott insiders had benefited at the expense of public shareholders, the suit claimed that "in 1992 and 1993, Cott successfully completed several public offerings of stock, raising over $125 million [Canadian] in new capital from public investors, while Cott insiders pocketed over $100 million by selling Cott stock owned by them in the open market, some of which was obtained by them via the exercise of stock options at between 33 cents and 67 cents per share." Cott president Fraser Latta dismissed the suit as "utterly frivolous and without merit."

Undeterred, Pencer continued his quest to create "the General Foods of private label." He and Gerry Schwartz teamed up to buy Kik Corp., a privately held maker of bleach and fabric softener, two high-profit items. To maintain the momentum that saw Cott's sales grow from $31 million in 1989 to $502 million in fiscal 1994, the company had to expand beyond North America. In January 1994, Cott signed a five-year agreement with Cadbury Beverages Ltd., the European soft-drink arm of Britain's Cadbury Schweppes PLC, to produce Cott house brand beverages across continental Europe. Soon after, Cott paid $12 million for a 51% interest in Benjamin Shaw, the largest independent canning plant in the United Kingdom, with $80 million in annual sales. In February, Cott signed on with J. Sainsbury PLC, Britain's largest supermarket chain. Nichol had helped to broker the deal. Sainsbury had been selling private-label goods since its inception 125 years earlier. Ironically, Sainsbury was one of the stores that had inspired the No Name and President's Choice lines. It was the ultimate marketing challenge, a Zen riddle: selling to the client what the client already owned.

Pencer embarked on a well-orchestrated series of promotional meetings. Loblaw, worth 16% of Cott's fiscal 1993 sales of $331.6 million, remained a crucial element in Pencer's impassioned sales pitches. Some of Pencer's announcements of Cott's upcoming deals and contracts did not unfold as promised, feeding the short sellers' frenzy. Competitors outbid Cott on some contracts. Some publicized Cott rollouts did not materialize. Beer sales to the United States also proved more difficult than expected, due to competition and regulatory wrangles.

Within Loblaw, Pencer's success was a burr under the corporate saddle. Nobody cared particularly that Cott was the beneficiary of a significant pool of talent that had become marginalized at Loblaw, including Jim White, who was consulting on product development, and Ray Goodman and Peter Marshall, creators of Loblaw's Pierre system, who were in charge of new technologies for Cott. The real irritant was Cott's lock on the PC Cola business. In February 1994, Loblaw announced a three-year deal to give Coca-Cola more shelf space, thus reducing the space allocated to PC soft drinks. John Thompson explained that stores had been underperforming in the cola category, a comment apparently calculated to discredit Cott. Don Watt, for one, did not buy it. "Absolutely untrue," he said. "Before the President's Choice program, the category was losing 2% on margins. After, it had a 15% margin, one of the best in the business."

Although Loblaw's deal with Coke was given considerable media coverage, such deals were standard in the industry. Moreover, Loblaw's house brands were developed in part to hold the national brands ransom — in effect, to inspire them to offer more money for the shelf. But reading between the lines, the message was clear: Cott was out of favor at Loblaw. Once-bullish New York analysts put out sell recommendations on Cott stock.

Both Coke and Pepsi took practical steps to dismantle the private-label threat. Both cut their prices, and both provided retailers with improved margins and specials, so that their products sold regularly at or near Cott's prices. This strategy was intended to get the cost-conscious buyer of retailer brands to stock up on national brands. Gerry Pencer scoffed at the Loblaw-Coke arrangement. "It's the same deal they have every year," he said. "They just wanted to get Pepsi out of no-frills stores." Pencer shrugged off Loblaw's attitude toward Cott as jealousy over its stock market performance and huge capitalization. "Market cap envy," is how he dismissed it.

In March, NBC's evening news with Tom Brokaw featured a profile of Nichol, who was introduced as "the face behind President's Choice." Nichol used a segment from the report in a commercial for his Chocolate and Black Cherry Cola. In it, interviewer Keith Morrison tasted the cola and told Nichol nobody would ever drink it. Nichol, who had big plans for the cola, used the segment to say that Keith Morrison was wrong. He delighted in being contrary. Morrison, the host of the television program "Canada A.M." broadcast on the CTV television network, wasn't asked if the segment could be used in a Loblaw commercial, nor was he financially compensated for his appearance. He challenged Nichol and Loblaw on air to donate $10,000 to the Addiction Research Foundation in Toronto in lieu of salary. Nichol's office called him back to say they'd gladly donate $10,000 if CTV matched the donation, a solution they knew would bring the situation to a stalemate.

The U.S. network exposure could not have come at a better time. The day after the piece ran, Nichol's office was deluged by calls from U.S. retailers interested in learning more about the program. The episode underscored the symbiotic relationship that still existed between Loblaw and Nichol. On the street, people approached Nichol, asking him not to break his bond with Weston. "They don't want me to leave their lives, their family's lives," he said. The shopper's allegiance was borne out by sales of *The Dave Nichol Cookbook*. By June 1994, more than 200,000 had been sold, and there was demand for another 150,000. Plans were also made for a barbecue cookbook, to be released in 1995. On the cover,

Nichol wanted to use his favorite Kabuki warrior image, the one from the Memories of Kobe bottle. But Loblaw officials were more concerned about having Nichol's name on the cover, believing that Nichol would no longer be associated with the company when the book was published.

There were questions as well about Nichol's involvement in the Wal-Mart agreement. His services had originally been an essential part of the deal, which had been designed so that Loblaw could serve as a wholesaler when Wal-Mart came to Canada. Wal-Mart had announced plans to enter Canada in January 1994, by purchasing 120 Woolco Canada Ltd. stores and converting them into Wal-Marts. Canadian retailers expressed shock, although anyone who had been watching the American giant knew its arrival in Canada was inevitable. Share prices of several Canadian retailers dropped on the news, but Loblaw's private-label business did not appear threatened, although many suppliers were called into Loblaw Brands headquarters and told that they couldn't supply to Wal-Mart. Under its three-year contract with Loblaw, hammered out in 1993, Wal-Mart could not sell either the Sam's American Choice or Great American Value lines in Canada using Loblaw-created formulations.

The entry of the large-format warehouse stores presented serious competition for Loblaw. The retailing landscape was changing radically, and Loblaw, accustomed to dominating the scene, stood to suffer. The warehouse giants with their lower margins, posed a direct threat to supermarkets, because food accounted for almost 60% of their sales. The company had waged costly but unsuccessful legal battles to keep the Price Club-Costco Wholesale Group out of the Ontario market, attempts that had failed. Loblaw was accused by the Ontario Municipal Board of employing anti-competitive tactics and ordered it to pay $240,000 in costs. The company was estimated to have spent more than $3 million on the suit.

Meanwhile, Cott appeared to be defying the cynics. The company announced fiscal 1994 earnings of $35.4 million, on revenue of $665.4 million — up from $12.8 million on revenue of $331.6 million the year before. Its cola was sold to sixty chain stores, up from twenty-two the year before. In April, it launched Classic Cola at Sainsbury; the red and white packaging echoed the look of Coca-Cola, a resemblance that did not go unnoticed by Coke. The word "cola" was written in a script similar to that used by Coca-Cola. (Eventually, Cott was forced by Coke to modify the design.) The cola was sold at Sainsbury for 25 pence a can, 25% less than the price of Coca-Cola. Its success at Sainsbury led to talks between Cott and other major U.K. chains, Safeway and Tesco PLC. Elsewhere in Europe, it signed a contract with Pomodes SA, the French superstore group. It was already producing Continente Gold Cola for the Pomodes-controlled Spanish hypermarket group Centrol Comerciales Continente SA.

In the United States, Cott purchased two bottling plants in Missouri for $36 million, adding to the plants it owned in New York and California. Such acquisitions seemed at odds with Pencer's earlier assertion that Cott would build its business not with bricks and mortar but by exploiting the unused capacity of independent bottlers. The short sellers interpreted this purchase as evidence that independent bottlers in the United States were putting the squeeze on the company. Meanwhile, they were busy floating the rumor that Wal-Mart was pressuring Cott to lower prices, which would reduce its margin from 35 cents to 17 to 20 cents a case.

In late April, Nichol was asked to speak at an Empire Club lunch in Toronto at the Royal York Hotel. Galen Weston and Gerry Pencer both sat at the head table, at a discreet distance from each other. Weston and Pencer offered a study in contrasts — old and new money, the insider and the outsider, old and new styles of management. Weston was committed to growing the enterprise through conservative practice, sticking to core businesses of food processing and retailing. Cott was a meteor, growing at an exponential rate, a New Age company where employees were asked about personal goals. Pencer even brought in his psychiatrist, Dr. Danny Silver, to consult with staff.

Much to the audience's surprise, Nichol spoke not of food retailing, but about what was wrong with Canada. He lashed out at the Canadian establishment and at the country's complacency, which he dubbed the "English disease." He criticized people who belonged to institutions such as the York Club, a bastion of old money privilege. Weston, a member of the York Club, sat with a tight smile on his face.

With the veneer of civility increasingly stretched, the climate was ripe for rumor and innuendo. Both Cott and Loblaw engaged in school-yard style taunts of the other. Nichol claimed that Weston had hired a private investigator to check him out; allegedly, Weston feared that he might be confronted at Loblaw's next annual meeting by a short seller or reporter who had dug up damaging information on Nichol's rela-tionship with Pencer. (Galen Weston declined to confirm or deny Nichol's claim.) Nichol described his relationship with Weston as "strained." Weston, ever gracious, used the company's annual meeting to thank Nichol for his contribution over the years. Nichol was con-spicuously absent, although he sent Anne Doremus to see whether his name was mentioned; he was miffed that he received no mention in the company's 1993 annual report. Investor Pierre Panet-Raymond, one of the most ardent short sellers of Cott stock, used the occasion to ask Weston why news of Nichol's resignation from the Loblaw and Weston boards had not been disclosed in a more timely manner. The question seemed to upset Weston's characteristic elan. He denied that disclosure had been untimely and said Nichol's departure stemmed from the "financial straitjacket" he felt at Loblaw.

Pencer found time from his worldwide sales pitches to help estab-lish a chair in Nichol's name at the University of Toronto business school, an endeavor said to cost almost $2 million. A major contributor was Sam Ajmera, formerly of Dough Delight, who had resurfaced with his brother Shreyas at Synergy Foods Inc., which produced aromatic rice, fresh pasta, and meatless shelf-stable entrées. Pencer was also involved in endowing a chair in Don Watt's name at Watt's alma mater, the Ontario College of Art.

Through all this, Nichol continued to show up at Loblaw one or two days a week. There, he worked on the summer edition of *Insider's Report*, which contained line extensions of earlier President's Choice hits — a Decadent cookie dough ice cream, a Szechwan peanut sauce for the barbecue, a black cherry and chocolate cola, Key Lime Temptations cookies, and a lemon meringue pie. Among product developers there was a sense that the golden age had passed. The tasting process was giving way to departmental consensus, a premise Nichol had rejected.

There was also concern that quality would be sacrificed for cost; that fear was reinforced when the brix on President's Choice orange juice was altered. Brix is a scientific calculation that measures the soluble solids in a liquid. The higher the brix, the sweeter and more full-bodied the liquid. It is possible to alter brix by adding sugar, which changes the texture but lowers the cost of production. No one at Loblaw Brands could match Nichol's obsession with taste. "Was it all only a dream?" asked one staff member of the Nichol years.

In early June, Pencer told a few people Cott had signed an agreement to buy a 49% interest in Dave Nichol and Associates for $10 million. In return for the equity infusion, Nichol would consult and create products for Cott. Pencer was telling people privately that the first product Nichol would create for Cott would be Dave Nichol's Personal Selection beer. Pencer knew that both Molson and Labatt had visited Galen Weston, trying to take over the Lakeport contract to produce PC Premium Draft beer. Eventually, Pencer believed, Lakeport, which was 70% owned by Cott, would lose the business.

Nichol denied that any such deal had been signed. "The thing about Gerry," Nichol says, "is that he sees things before they happen. He says things are going to happen and then they do. That's the key to his success." The contradiction was a harbinger perhaps of conflict to come between the epic ego that was Gerry Pencer and the epic ego that was Dave Nichol.

On Cott's behalf, Nichol traveled to Japan and China in early June to meet officials at Japan's second largest retailer, Ito Yakodo, a Cott client that ran 5,300 7-Eleven stores. He also spoke to investment houses about the investment merit of Cott. Nichol had total faith in the company. "It's a moonshot," he says. "So there's bound to be inordinate interest and inordinate speculation."

Speculation certainly. Between June 1993 and June 1994, in the face of announcements of new contracts around the world, Cott's stock price declined from $49.63 to $22 (Cdn.) on the Toronto Stock Exchange and from $37 3/4 to $12 3/4 (U.S.) on the Nasdaq exchange. The short sellers had pocketed millions of dollars from the decline. Some of the volatility was attributable to a story in *Worth* magazine that painted Cott as a company with deep-rooted financial problems. There was also talk that Loblaw was trying to replace Cott as the supplier of its PC soft drinks.

On the subject of short sellers, Pencer shed his calm-as-Buddha exterior and began fighting back. He sued Michael Palmer, a stock analyst at Toronto's Equity Research Associates Inc., for $14 million for general, aggravated, and exemplary damages resulting from a Palmer memorandum that questioned Cott's health. Pencer also hired economists at Harvard and the University of Chicago to assess the short sellers' analysis of Cott's financial statements. They responded that the allegations about Cott's accounting were "unfair" and "unfounded." He fired off a letter to *Worth* demanding a rebuttal; none was forthcoming.

Pencer never deviated from his uber-salesman mode. At a meeting with North American analysts, Cott officials said the company was aiming at revenues of $2 billion by the year 2000. According to Pencer, Brights had offered Nichol a deal to consult. Pencer had bigger plans for Nichol, however. "It would be a great platform for Dave," he said of the Brights offer, "but really just a small opportunity when you look at the world picture."

Wine, in fact, was not panning out the way Nichol had hoped. By June 1994, the LCBO had ordered 14,500 cases of Dave Nichol's Personal Selection wines, but had sold fewer than 4,000 cases. Initially brisk, interest slowed after the novelty of Dave Nichol wine wore off. Certainly, wine was no match for the runaway success of PC Premium Draft beer. The explanation was all too obvious: the wine was too expensive for the mass market. Moreover, while Nichol's entry into the wine trade was perfectly in keeping with his epicurean tastes, he had no track record as an oenophile.

Thus it was not surprising that Memories of Napa Private Reserve wine from Nichol's own vineyard, with its $29 price tag, languished on the LCBO shelves. "People who buy Dave Nichol products don't tend to buy $30 wines," Nichol's business partner, Eric Calladine, concedes. The name, for one thing, was off the mark. Memories of Napa was produced in Napa. It wasn't a memory; it was the real thing. But when Nichol liked an idea, he couldn't let it go. In fact, he had dubbed his wine venture Georgie Girl International Ltd., much to the bemusement of his Napa neighbors.

Even Calladine admitted that the 1991 blend could have been better, given the soil that produced it. Nichol hired Joe Cafaro, one of the Valley's most respected winemakers, to blend the 1993 grapes. Calladine hoped that a new price under $20 would perk up sales. As ever, Nichol was irrepressible, refusing to believe that Memories of Napa might go the way of President's Choice silk boxer shorts. "I think we were victims of our own enthusiasm," Nichol said. "But I'm not going to give up."

The answer, Nichol believed, was to devote more time to marketing. Marketing, or creating sustainable differentiation, as he preferred to think of it, was always the solution. The drab black and white label on the Dave Nichol's Personal Selection was replaced with a more colorful one. He also cut his profit margin so that the product's price fell into the under-$10 category. Forging ahead, Calladine returned to the LCBO with proposals for four new Dave Nichol's Personal Selection wines — a Merlot and Cabernet Sauvignon from Chile, a Pinot Noir from California, and a Minervois from the Languedoc region in southwest France. All were priced under $10.

Nichol set up offices next to Cott Corp. on the eighth floor of a sleek, airy renovated terminal building overlooking Lake Ontario; Cott had moved into the premises in the spring of 1994. Renovated for Nichol's new venture was a 6,500-square-foot space, including a test kitchen that looked very much like the one on the ninth floor of Loblaw, though three times the size. Pencer had big plans to turn the place into a "retailer brand" center, a shrine to the concept that would draw retailers and manufacturers from around the world.

On June 30, the divorce was finalized. Nichol issued a press release announcing the end of his relationship with Loblaw through his lawyers. There was no mention of a link with Cott. He had asked to do a joint release with Loblaw but they refused. Cott stock rose $1.37 to $20 the next trading day. Loblaw stock dropped 25 cents. Currie, who was holidaying in Cape Cod, was relaxed and chatty in an interview with *Globe and Mail* reporter Marina Strauss about the break with Nichol. "For Loblaw Companies, the implication of Dave's leaving is neither negative nor positive. It's neutral," Currie said. He told her Nichol wouldn't be replaced. "We don't think the business demands a spokesman," he was quoted as saying. He then went on to imply that Nichol's public profile had been motivated purely by Nichol's vanity: "Dave needed it, but the business didn't need it." He denied rumors that Nichol had been pushed to leave and said that "we've never had any disagreements that I recall." At Loblaw, history was relative.

It was as if Nichol was being airbrushed out of Loblaw's corporate history. In July, there was a request for a reprint of 147,000 copies of *The Dave Nichol Cookbook* from store managers across the country, but Loblaw Brands executives chose not to go back to press. "We don't know what Dave will be doing next year," is how one official explained the decision. "He could be working for the competition." The stance reflected the general attitude toward Nichol. It didn't matter if the cookbook and the purchase of President's Choice products it would create could bring in over $1 million in sales. They didn't want the name Dave Nichol in the stores.

Nichol's secretaries Anne Doremus and Lena Mattei packed up his office the following week. Doremus joined him at Cott. Mattei lost her job. It was the end of an era. There was no more Dave Nichol's *Insider's Report*, no more Dave and Georgie Girl, no more risible infomercials with Bo, no more radio ads with his nasal, southern Ontario cadences extolling the latest product. At Loblaw Brands, handling the post-Nichol marketing was seen as "a challenge," a business euphemism for major problem. Predictably, they stressed the caliber of the "team" Nichol had assembled. But the public did not know or trust the team; it was Dave Nichol they knew and trusted.

The production values at Cott's annual meeting in mid-July were superb. Shareholders were trumpeted in with Handel and then viewed a glossy ten-minute video that presented the worldwide span of Cott's business, with testimonials from clients, shoppers, and analysts. Included was a segment from the BBC's Clive James "Sunday Live Clive" which showed the actress Carrie Fisher (a Coke expert, in her words) tasting both Coke and the Sainsbury cola blindfolded and confusing the two. Dave Nichol featured in the production, with segments from various interviews he had given.

Nichol sat in the front row, with his new close-cropped beard, a Sean Connery effect that made him look almost aristocratic. He had grown it on holiday, and Terri encouraged him to keep it. The beard was symbolic. "It's my AL beard," he joked, AL standing for "after Loblaw." The beard was anti-corporate, anti-Weston, a sign of rebellion. Just like Gerry.

Pencer proudly announced more Cott expansion, to Japan and Mexico. He also told the crowd that Cott and Dave Nichol would be forming a new company to develop products in one or two categories potentially as large as cola. Terms and details, he said, would be hammered out over the next few months. He did allow that Cott would purchase an interest and provide financing in the form of an interest-bearing loan.

Nichol had exchanged the security of George Weston for the extravagant promise of Cott, an organization that appeared to offer a custom-made landscape for the character he had become. Within Cott, management placed themselves in a grandiose framework, drawing upon the Bible for analogies to what they were doing. At a Cott management retreat in Palm Beach in December 1993, at which Nichol was present, Ray Goodman compared Nichol to Moses, spurning the golden idols of the past and delivering a new set of retailing commandments. The Walls of Jericho in this overblown analogy became "brand tax," the premium national brands charged to shoppers. Gerry Pencer was portrayed as Joshua, the figure who would topple this so-called "brand tax." Nichol shrugged off the speech as pure rhetoric. Pencer got a kick out of the analogy, however, and would refer to it from time to time with a slight amendment. He liked to say that he and Nichol together would topple the brand tax and profit from its demise.

Pencer did see the risks faced by Nichol, more clearly perhaps than Nichol himself. "Now the real challenges are beginning for Dave," Pencer says. "He's his own man, his own banker, his own personal agent. He's a revolutionary, and sometimes the revolutionary gets killed." Reverting to the Biblical allusion, he would amend the thought. "Of course, Moses didn't get killed," he added. There was something missing, of course.

Something that Nichol with his years of Sunday school training might have picked up. And that was, that although Moses wasn't killed, he also never made it into the Promised Land.

July brought more changes within George Weston Ltd. David Beatty, president of Weston Foods Ltd., which produced baked goods and candies, handed in his resignation amid speculation he had been pushed. The company's results were down, ironically, in the face of private-label competition. Although Weston Foods' U.S. division produced the 39% Chocolate Chip Cookie for Wal-Mart in the United States, it didn't have a hand in any of the successful President's Choice cookie line in Canada. It was as if Weston had created a commando team and then turned it on itself. A profound inconsistency in the organization was emerging. On one hand, there was President's Choice forging a new path in food manufacturing for Loblaw. On the other, the rest of Weston cleaved to an old style of business that President's Choice had been designed to decimate.

Beatty denied that the company's weak results had anything to do with his departure but admitted that the advent of private label had hurt Weston Foods, particularly in the bread business. "You're selling Wonder Bread at one price and then you're selling private label for either Oshawa Group or Loeb or Loblaw at a much lower price," he told the *Globe and Mail*.

Beatty, a straightshooter, had been Weston Food's president for nine years. He had watched Nichol and President's Choice expand up close, at times to his irritation. He took the private-label threat seriously, very seriously. He devoted spare time trying to quantify just how big the "so-called" brand tax Nichol was always going on about actually was. Putting a figure on this was tricky, but by his calculation, which looked at the decline in capitalization of advertising agencies that worked on big national brand accounts, it ran about $50 billion. Certainly the big brands were rethinking strategy. Not only had prices been slashed but in June Procter & Gamble began talking about selling its products via infomercials. Nichol's long-standing barb that the only way P&G could advertise its product would be on the "Crisco" channel, was strangely coming true.

Despite the growing acceptance of his crusade, Nichol's future was uncertain. Would he lead the private-label "revolution" to victory? Or would his life mirror that of the Duke of Windsor, estranged from the family that had given him his identity? The man who had fed the Canadian middle class for more than a decade was on a precipice, at a crossroads. He was no longer "a walking Loblaws logo."

He was also facing the paradox of fronting a revolution that had become mainstreamed. At Loblaw, premium private label had differentiated the chain; it had brought shoppers into the store. Once retailer brands were ubiquitous, retailers' competitive advantage could be kept only by offering something else. If everyone had a private-label cola, a salsa, tortilla chips, a premium chocolate chip cookie, what would draw shoppers to the store? The answer, according to Nichol, was him. Himself. Nichol would become that sustainable differentiation, marketing personified. "Cott has been so successful because they offer a unique product that people want and that in the past retailers have lost money on," Nichol says. "It's going to be my job to create other products that are just as attractive as cola." This is a considerable ambition. His victories at Loblaw had been won in the face of opposition. His creative energy stemmed in large part from his irrepressible will. *Paralyse resistance with persistence* was a motto that hung over his desk for many years.

Nichol knows that his work with Cott will likely pit him against Loblaw. On that subject, his voice conveys a bitterness. "I gave them a ten-, maybe fifteen-year lead in the private-label business," he says of his work at Loblaw. "I gave them 1,500 products. I gave them a worldwide reputation. If that changes, it won't be anyone's fault but their own."

He saw himself from a distance, as the boy from Blenheim in the Golden Horseshoe of Ontario who had singlehandedly taken on the food establishment, the big brands. That, he believes, puts him far ahead of where he was ten years ago, when he also faced a blank slate. Ironically, though, he has forfeited the competitive advantage that permitted his ascent to middle-class tastemaker: he no longer owns the shelf. Having helped retailers wrest control from manufacturers, Nichol — at the seeming apogee of his success — has abandoned a retailing colossus to hook up with a new-age manufacturer and marketing outfit.

Wally Olins of the British design company Wolff Olins has re-marked that "marketing is to the 1980s what sociology was to the 1960s." The difference of course is that sociologists could only dream of chang-ing the world. Marketing people actually did it. Dave Nichol actually did it. He understands that shopping is the opiate of the masses in the twen-tieth century. He offered salvation at the supermarket. He gave them lower prices. He gave them new products. He gave them taste. In return, he achieved celebrity, wealth, adulation. But somehow that wasn't enough. Nothing was ever enough. And, true to his packaged identity as the indefatigable consumer, he was ready, hungry, for the next.

ACKNOWLEDGMENTS

This book could not have been written without the assistance, shared knowledge, and recollections of hundreds of people. I thank them all.

Specifically, I am indebted to Terri Nichol for so graciously allowing me to intrude upon her life and to Anne Doremus for her kindness and assistance.

For sharing with me their memories, insights, and work, I thank, Don and Patty Watt, Jim and Carol White, Gladys Lowell, Joanne Ridley, Marilyn Oliver, Gerry Pencer, Galen Weston, Dick Currie, Thelma Davidson, Ziggy Wauro, Paul Uys, Larry Griffin, Russ Rudd, Patrick Carson, Scott Lindsay, Frances Litwin, Andy Wallace, Doug Lunau, Robin Periana, Dr. David Jenkins, Colin Isaacs, Robert Bras, Bill Sharpe, Lew Smith, Sam Ajmera, Fabio Miccachi, and Barbie Casselman. For their help in amassing the background information, I would like to thank David Beatty, Paul Break, Martin Blumberg, Joe Coloumbe, Bill Fields, Ray Goodman, Ray Goldberg, Harry Guest, John Lederer, Lena Mattei, Terry O'Malley, Richard Siklos, John Toma, Cynthia Wine, and Larry Woods. Credit should also be given to Bob Garner and Steve Buckley at A.C. Nielsen Research in Markham, Ontario, for providing market share data and statistics. Of course, any inaccuracies or errors committed in recounting this information are solely my responsibility.

A heartfelt appreciation to my publishers John Macfarlane, Jan

Walter, and Gary Ross, for their faith in this project throughout its tumultous passage. I am grateful also to my editor, Michael Posner, for his guidance and friendship; to Sara Borins, for her assistance and enthusiasm; and to Wendy Thomas and Liba Berry, for their careful reading of the manuscript and thoughtful suggestions.

I can find no words to adequately thank my family and friends for putting up with me for the past two years. My greatest debt, however, is to Beppi Crosariol for his unwavering support, endless enthusiasm, and wise counsel.

Finally, this book simply could not have been written without the generosity of Dave Nichol, who opened the door to me without condition and then, true to form, never flinched.

SELECTED BIBLIOGRAPHY

Aaker, David. A. *Managing Brand Equity*. New York: The Free Press, a division of Macmillan Inc., 1991.

Barr, Ann and Levy, Paul. *The Official Foodie Handbook*. New York: Timbre Books, Arbor House, 1984.

Barr, Nancy Verde. *They Called It Macaroni*. New York: Alfred A. Knopf, 1992.

Bartels, Robert. *The History of Marketing Thought*. Columbus, Ohio: Publishing Horizons Inc., 1988.

Bayley, Stephen. *Taste: The Secret Meaning of Things*. London: Faber and Faber, 1991.

Beck, Simone, Berthold, Louisette and Child, Julia. *Mastering the Art of French Cooking*. New York: Alfred A. Knopf, 1961.

Brillat-Savarin, Jean-Anthelme. *The Physiology of Taste*. Translation by M.F.K. Fisher. New York: The Heritage Press, 1949.

Brody, Jane. *Jane Brody's Nutrition Book*. New York: Bantam Books, 1987.

Burrough, Byran, and Hellyar, John. *Barbarians at the Gate*. New York: Harper & Row, Publishers Inc., 1990.

Business Week, September 8, 1975. "Galen Weston: Bringing Order to a Billion-Dollar Empire."

Campbell, Hannah. *Why Did They Name It?* New York: Fleet Publishing Corp., 1964.

Carson, Patrick, and Moulden, Julia. *Green Is Gold*. Toronto: Harper Collins Publishers Ltd., 1991.

Chisholm, Robert. *The Darlings: The Mystique of the Supermarket*. Toronto: McClelland and Stewart, 1970.

Conaway, James. *Napa*. New York: Avon Books, 1990.

Davies, Charles. *Bread Men*. Toronto: Key Porter Books Ltd., 1987.

Deveny, Kathleen. "More Shoppers Bypass Big Names and Steer Carts to Private Label," *Wall Street Journal*, September 29, 1993.

Dichter, Ernest. *Packaging: The Sixth Sense*. Cahners Publishing, 1975.

Donaldson, Gordon. "Dave Nichol's Brewhaha." *Business Journal*, March, 1993.

Elkington, John, Hailes, Julia, and Makower, Joel. *The Green Consumer*. New York: Penguin Books, 1988.

Fitzell, Phil. "A European-inspired 'Green Wave.'" *Private Label International*, June 1989.

Filler, Martin. "Weston Civilization." *Vanity Fair*, May, 1994.

Food Marketing Institute, Washington, D.C. *Trends: Consumers' Attitudes and The Supermarket. Annual Review* 1992/1993.

Fussell, Paul. *Class*. New York: Viking Press, 1983.

Gans, Herbert J. *Popular Culture and High Culture: An Analysis and Evaluation of Taste*. New York: Basic Books Inc., 1974.

Harris, Marvin. *Good to Eat: Riddles of Food and Culture*. New York: Simon and Schuster, 1985.

Harris, Marvin. *Food and Evolution*. Philadelphia: Temple University Press, 1987.

Hess, Karen, and Hess, John. *The Taste of America*. New York: Grossman, 1977.

Huey, John. "The World's Best Brand." *Fortune Magazine*, May 31, 1993.

Interbrand Group plc. *World's Greatest Brands*. London: John Wiley & Sons, Inc., 1992.

Kanner, Bernice. "Privates on Parade." *New York* Magazine, March 22, 1993.

Kates, Joanne. *The Taste of Things*. Toronto: Oxford University Press, 1987.

Lees, David. "How Green Were My Values." *Toronto Life*, October, 1990.

Loden, D. John. *Megabrands: How to Build Them, How to Beat Them*. Homewood, Illinois: Business One Irwin, 1992.

Mathews, Ryan. "Emperor of the North." *Grocery Marketing*, July 24, 1990.

Matthews, Glenna. *"Just a Housewife": The Rise and Fall of Domesticity in America*. New York: Oxford University Press, 1987.

Mathias, Philip. "Inside the Pencer Empire," *Financial Post*, September 8 and September 9, 1988.

McCracken, Grant. *Culture and Consumption*. Bloomington: Indiana University Press, 1988.

Messenger, Bob. "Store Brands Head Uptown." *Food Business*, January 19, 1990.

Morgenson, Gretchen. "Hell No–We Won't Pay." *Forbes*, September 16, 1991.

Morgenson, Gretchen. "Highflier Caught in Cash Crunch." *Worth*, June 1994.

Mukerji, Chandra. *From Graven Images: Patterns of Modern Materialism.* New York: Columbia University Press, 1983.

Nichol, Dave. *The Dave Nichol Cookbook.* Toronto: Loblaw Companies Limited, 1993.

Orlean, Susan. "All Mixed Up." *New Yorker*, June 22, 1992.

Pendergrast, Mark. *God, Country and Coca-Cola.* New York: Collier Books, 1993.

Philips, Kevin. *Boiling Point: Democrats, Republicans, and the Decline of Middle Class Prosperity.* New York: Random House, 1993.

Pollution Probe Foundation (in consultation with Warner Troyer and Glenys Moss). *The Canadian Green Consumer Guide.* Toronto: McClelland and Stewart Inc., 1989.

Roddick, Anita. *Body and Soul.* London: Ebury Press, 1991.

Root, Waverly L. *Food: An Authoritative and Visual History and Dictionary of the Foods of the World.* New York: Simon and Schuster, 1980.

Schremp, Gerry. *Kitchen Culture: Fifty Years of Food Fads.* New York: Pharos Books, 1991.

Sellers, Patricia. "Brands: It's Thrive or Die," *Fortune*, August 23, 1993.

Sokolov, Raymond. *Why We Eat What We Eat.* New York: Summit Books, 1991.

Stern, Jane, and Stern, Michael. *Square Meals.* New York: Alfred A. Knopf, 1985.

Stevenson, Mark. "Global Gourmet," *Canadian Business*, July 1993.

Tiger, Lionel. *The Pursuit of Pleasure.* Toronto: Little, Brown & Company (Canada) Limited, 1992.

Veblen, Thorstein. *The Theory of the Leisure Class.* New York: Macmillan, 1912.

Visser, Margaret. *Much Depends on Dinner.* Toronto: McClelland and Stewart Inc., 1991.

Walton, Sam. *Made in America: My Story.* New York: Bantam Books, 1993.

Wells, Jennifer. "Cheers!" *Report on Business Magazine*, March 1992.

Williams, Rosalind H. *Dream Worlds: Mass Consumption in Late Ninenteenth Century France.* Berkeley: University of California Press, 1982.

Waldman, Steven. "The Tyranny of Choice." *The New Republic*, January 27, 1992.

INDEX

This book was set into type by James Ireland Design Inc., Toronto Ontario.

The text is set in Sabon. Sabon was designed by Jan Tscichold and originally issued in 1964. Intended as a general-purpose book face, Sabon is based on the work of Claude Garamond and his pupil Jacques Sabon. It was issued in digitized form by Monotype and Adobe. This version is by Monotype. The heads, folios and captions are set in Cochin, a typeface that originated with the Peignot Foundary in Paris about 1915. It is based on the lettering of eighteenth century French copperplate engravers. In America, Monotype adapted it in 1917, followed by ATF in 1925. Today it is available in phototypesetting and as an Adobe face. The roman is distinctive but the italic even more so, being closer to formal handwriting or engraving than most italics.